Kickstart Modern Android Development with Jetpack and Kotlin

Enhance your applications by integrating Jetpack and applying modern app architectural concepts

Catalin Ghita

BIRMINGHAM—MUMBAI

Kickstart Modern Android Development with Jetpack and Kotlin

Group Product Manager: Rohit Rajkumar
Publishing Product Manager: Vaideeshwari Muralikrishnan
Senior Editor: Hayden Edwards
Content Development Editor: Abhishek Jadhav
Technical Editor: Simran Udasi
Copy Editor: Safis Editing
Project Coordinator: Rashika Ba
Proofreader: Safis Editing
Indexer: Rakha Nair
Production Designer: Shankar Kalbhor
Marketing Coordinator: Elizabeth Varghese and Teny Thomas

First published: May 2022

Production reference: 1200522

Published by Packt Publishing Ltd.
Livery Place
35 Livery Street
Birmingham
B3 2PB, UK.

ISBN 978-1-80181-107-1

www.packt.com

To my mother, Stefania Ghita, and my father, Nicolae, for their sacrifices made to support, encourage, and allow me to become what I am today – your affection and inspiration will always remain in my heart.

To my beloved wife, Ana, for being there for me mentally, spiritually, and emotionally – I'm surprised you haven't broken up with me after all the time I spent on this book.

To my great friend, Daniel Bälz, for constantly helping me review, arrange, and improve the contents of this book – your help should be engraved in stone.

To my devoted counselor, Thomas Künneth, for consistently providing insights and tips on technical writing and the concepts presented in the book.

Finally, to the awesome team at Packt, for making my dream of writing a book become reality.

– Catalin Ghita

Contributors

About the author

Catalin Ghita is a Udemy instructor and an Android engineer proficient in native Android development, while also being active in cross-platform development with React Native and Flutter. He has successfully built, deployed, and maintained huge scalable apps with millions of downloads and active users for industry giants. He is responsible for architecting applications into scalable, maintainable, and testable forms and shapes.

As the Android lead at Airtouch New Media, the owner of the Coding Troops blog, and a Udemy instructor, Catalin is an avid open source contributor and has written articles and taught courses reaching tens of thousands of students, thereby exposing and clarifying concepts and subtleties on hot topics in Android.

About the reviewer

Daniel Bälz is a keen Android developer who enjoys developing maintainable, high-quality apps with well-structured architecture. He works as a freelance developer and helps his customers in building and evolving their Android apps. His personal Android journey dates back to the Android 2.x days. Since then, he has worked on several large-scale apps with millions of installations. Daniel is active in the community by organizing the mobile development meetup in his hometown, Karlsruhe, as well as occasionally giving talks and writing articles.

Table of Contents

2

Handling UI State with Jetpack ViewModel

3

Displaying Data from REST APIs with Retrofit

4

Handling Async Operations with Coroutines

5

Adding Navigation in Compose With Jetpack Navigation

Part 2: A Guide to Clean Application Architecture with Jetpack Libraries

6

Adding Offline Capabilities with Jetpack Room

7

Introducing Presentation Patterns in Android

8

Getting Started with Clean Architecture in Android

9

Implementing Dependency Injection with Jetpack Hilt

10

Test Your App with UI and Unit Tests

Part 3: Diving into Other Jetpack Libraries

11

Creating Infinite Lists with Jetpack Paging and Kotlin Flow

12

Exploring the Jetpack Lifecycle Components

Preface

With Jetpack libraries, you can build and design high-quality, robust Android apps that have an improved architecture and work consistently across different versions and devices. This book will help you understand how Jetpack allows developers to follow best practices and architectural patterns when building Android apps while also eliminating boilerplate code.

Developers working with Android and Kotlin will be able to put their knowledge to work with this condensed practical guide to building apps with the most popular Jetpack libraries, including Jetpack Compose, ViewModel, Hilt, Room, Paging, Lifecycle, and Navigation. You'll gain an overview of relevant libraries and architectural patterns, including popular libraries in the Android ecosystem such as Retrofit, Coroutines, and Flow while building modern applications with real-world data.

By the end of this Android app development book, you'll have learned how to leverage Jetpack libraries and your knowledge of architectural concepts to build, design, and test robust Android applications for various use cases.

Who this book is for

This book is for junior and intermediate-level Android developers looking to level up their Android development skills to develop high-quality apps using Jetpack libraries and other cutting-edge technologies. Beginners with basic knowledge of Android development fundamentals will also find this book useful. Familiarity with Kotlin is assumed.

What this book covers

Chapter 1, Creating a Modern UI with Jetpack Compose, covers the new declarative way of building a UI on Android with the Jetpack Compose toolkit, while also starting to build an application from scratch with this new framework.

Chapter 2, Handling UI State with Jetpack ViewModel, explores the concept and usage of the ViewModel architecture component, as well as the concept of UI state in Compose apps and how the ViewModel can handle and cache such state.

Chapter 3, Displaying Data from REST APIs with Retrofit, covers what Retrofit is and how it can be used as a networking client for Android inside the project developed throughout the book.

Chapter 4, Handling Async Operations with Coroutines, covers the core concepts behind Kotlin coroutines. The chapter explores what a coroutine is, what suspend functions are, and other important components of coroutines.

Chapter 5, Adding Navigation in Compose with Jetpack Navigation, covers the basics of navigation between Compose-based screens with the help of the Jetpack Navigation library, while also exploring how to support deep links to your Compose UI.

Chapter 6, Adding Offline Capabilities with Jetpack Room, introduces Room as a solution for storing structured data and explores data persistence on Android as an architectural decision in building robust apps.

Chapter 7, Introducing Presentation Patterns in Android, explores architectural presentation patterns and why they are needed while also analyzing MVC, MVP, and MVVM.

Chapter 8, Getting Started with Clean Architecture in Android, explores how clean architecture translates into Android and how you can separate business logic by implementing Use Cases in the project developed throughout the book.

Chapter 9, Implementing Dependency Injection with Jetpack Hilt, explores what dependency injection is, why it's needed, and the advantages that it brings. This chapter also explores the basics of Dagger and introduces Jetpack Hilt.

Chapter 10, Test Your App with UI and Unit Tests, explores why tests are important and splits them into two main categories: UI and unit tests. In this chapter, you will learn how to test the Compose UI and application logic by creating unit tests.

Chapter 11, Creating Infinite Lists with Jetpack Paging and Kotlin Flow, explores the concept of pagination and explains how to integrate pagination on Android with the help of Jetpack Paging, while also using Kotlin Flow.

Chapter 12, Exploring the Jetpack Lifecycle Components, explores the inner workings of components that are part of Jetpack Lifecycle such as ViewModel and LiveData. In this chapter, you will also learn how to create your own lifecycle-aware component.

To get the most out of this book

You will need a version of Android Studio installed on your computer – the 2020.3.1 version or newer.

All code examples have been tested using Kotlin 1.6.10 and Android Studio 2020.3.1 on macOS and Windows.

Familiarity with Kotlin and the basics of Android is assumed.

Software/hardware covered in the book	Operating system requirements
Kotlin 1.6.10	Windows, macOS, or Linux
Android Studio 2020.3.1	Windows, macOS, or Linux

For part of *Chapter 3, Displaying Data from REST APIs with Retrofit*, it's expected that you have a Google account.

For part of *Chapter 6, Adding Offline Capabilities with Jetpack Room*, it's expected that you have minimal knowledge of SQL databases and queries.

If you are using the digital version of this book, we advise you to type the code yourself or access the code from the book's GitHub repository (a link is available in the next section). Doing so will help you avoid any potential errors related to the copying and pasting of code.

Download the example code files

You can download the example code files for this book from GitHub at `https://github.com/PacktPublishing/Kickstart-Modern-Android-Development-with-Jetpack-and-Kotlin`. If there's an update to the code, it will be updated in the GitHub repository.

We also have other code bundles from our rich catalog of books and videos available at `https://github.com/PacktPublishing/`. Check them out!

Download the color images

We also provide a PDF file that has color images of the screenshots and diagrams used in this book. You can download it here: `https://static.packt-cdn.com/downloads/9781801811071_ColorImages.pdf`.

Conventions used

There are a number of text conventions used throughout this book.

`Code in text`: Indicates code words in text, database table names, folder names, filenames, file extensions, pathnames, dummy URLs, user input, and Twitter handles. Here is an example: "`Text` is the Compose version of our old and beloved `TextView`."

A block of code is set as follows:

```
@Composable
fun FriendlyMessage(name: String) {
    Text(text = "Greetings $name!")
}
```

When we wish to draw your attention to a particular part of a code block meaning that a portion of code has been added or modified, the relevant lines or items are set in bold:

```
@Composable
fun ColoredBox() {
    Box(modifier = Modifier.size(120.dp))
}
```

Any command-line input or output is written as follows:

```
npm install component_name
```

Bold: Indicates a new term, an important word, or words that you see onscreen. For instance, words in menus or dialog boxes appear in **bold**. Here is an example: "In the **Phone and tablet** template section, select **Empty Compose Activity** and then choose **Next**."

> **Tips or Important Notes**
>
> Appear like this.

Get in touch

Feedback from our readers is always welcome.

General feedback: If you have questions about any aspect of this book, email us at `customercare@packtpub.com` and mention the book title in the subject of your message.

Errata: Although we have taken every care to ensure the accuracy of our content, mistakes do happen. If you have found a mistake in this book, we would be grateful if you would report this to us. Please visit `www.packtpub.com/support/errata` and fill in the form.

Piracy: If you come across any illegal copies of our works in any form on the internet, we would be grateful if you would provide us with the location address or website name. Please contact us at `copyright@packt.com` with a link to the material.

If you are interested in becoming an author: If there is a topic that you have expertise in and you are interested in either writing or contributing to a book, please visit `authors.packtpub.com`.

Share Your Thoughts

Once you've read *In-Memory Analytics with Apache Arrow*, we'd love to hear your thoughts! Scan the QR code below to go straight to the Amazon review page for this book and share your feedback.

`https://packt.link/r/1-801-07103-9`

Your review is important to us and the tech community and will help us make sure we're delivering excellent quality content.

Part 1: Exploring the Core Jetpack Suite and Other Libraries

In this part, we will build a modern and robust Android app with the help of Jetpack libraries such as Compose, ViewModel, and Navigation, as well as other popular libraries, including Coroutines and Retrofit.

This section comprises the following chapters:

- *Chapter 1, Creating a Modern UI with Jetpack Compose*
- *Chapter 2, Handling UI State with Jetpack ViewModel*
- *Chapter 3, Displaying Data from REST APIs with Retrofit*
- *Chapter 4, Handling Async Operations with Coroutines*
- *Chapter 5, Adding Navigation in Compose with Jetpack Navigation*

1
Creating a Modern UI with Jetpack Compose

Jetpack libraries enable you to build and design high-quality, robust Android apps that have a reliable architecture and work consistently across different versions and devices. At the same time, the Jetpack suite allows you to eliminate boilerplate code and ultimately focus on what matters – building the necessary features.

In this chapter, we will tackle one of the most popular Jetpack libraries for building **user interfaces (UIs)**, called **Compose**. Simply put, Jetpack Compose is a powerful modern toolkit that allows you to build a native UI in Android directly with Kotlin functions and APIs.

Compose accelerates and greatly simplifies UI development as it harnesses the power of declarative programming, combined with the ease of use of the Kotlin programming language. The new toolkit solely relies on Kotlin APIs when allowing you to construct UIs through declarative functions.

By the end of this chapter, you will know how building UIs on Android can be done with less code, powerful tools, intuitive APIs, and without the need for additional languages such as XML.

In the first section, *Understanding the core concepts of Compose*, we will explore the fundamental concepts behind Compose and understand how they are beneficial in helping us write better and cleaner UIs. We will see how UIs can be described with composable functions while also understanding how the new declarative way of building UIs on Android works. We will also explore how composition is favored over inheritance and how the data flow works in Compose. Finally, we will cover what recomposition is and see how essential it is to our declarative UI.

In the second section, *Exploring the building blocks of Compose UIs*, we will study the most important composable functions that Compose provides out of the box. Afterward, we will see how we can preview our Compose UI and how activities render it.

We will then put our knowledge to good use by creating our first Compose project about restaurants in the *Building a Compose-based screen* section. In the last section, entitled *Exploring lists with Compose*, we will learn how to correctly show more content in Compose with the help of lists.

To summarize, in this chapter, we're going to cover the following main topics:

- Understanding the core concepts of Compose
- Exploring the building blocks of Compose UIs
- Building a Compose-based screen
- Exploring lists with Compose

> **Note**
>
> As Compose is a dedicated native UI framework, we will only briefly cover the core concepts, common components, and usages of the toolkit without going into advanced topics.

Technical requirements

When building Compose-based Android projects, you usually require your day-to-day tools for Android development. However, to follow along smoothly, make sure you have the following:

- The Arctic Fox 2020.3.1 version of Android Studio. You can also use a newer Android Studio version or even Canary builds but note that the IDE interface and other generated code files might differ from the ones used throughout this book.

- The Kotlin 1.6.10 or newer plugin must be installed in Android Studio.
- Jetpack Compose 1.1.1 or greater. You should follow this chapter and use the projects with this version. You can explore newer versions if you wish, though API differences might arise.

You can find the GitHub repository containing the source code for this book here: `https://github.com/PacktPublishing/Kickstart-Modern-Android-Development-with-Jetpack-and-Kotlin/`.

To access the code presented in this chapter, navigate to the `Chapter_01` directory. The code snippets presented in the first two sections can be found in the `ExamplesActivity.kt` file, which is located in the root directory. The project coding solution for the Restaurants app, which we will develop in the last few sections of this chapter, can be found in the `chapter_1_restaurants_app` Android project directory.

Understanding the core concepts of Compose

Jetpack Compose dramatically changes the way we write UIs on Android. UIs are now developed with Kotlin, which enables a new declarative paradigm of writing layouts with widgets called **composables**.

In this section, we will understand what composable functions are and how they are used to write UIs. We will learn how the programming paradigm has shifted and how composition is now enforced, thereby increasing flexibility in the way we define UIs. We will also discuss the flow of data within UIs and what recomposition is while trying to understand the benefits that are brought by these new concepts.

To summarize, we will be covering the following topics:

- Describing UIs with composable functions
- The paradigm shift in creating UIs on Android
- Favoring composition over inheritance
- Unidirectional flow of data
- Recomposition

So, let's get started.

Describing UIs with composable functions

Compose allows you to build UIs by defining and calling **composable** functions. Composable functions are regular functions annotated with the `@Composable` annotation that represent widgets on the screen.

Compose works with the help of a Kotlin compiler plugin in the type checking and code generation phase of Kotlin. The Compose compiler plugin makes sure that you can create composables.

For example, a composable that displays a piece of text may look like this:

```
@Composable
fun FriendlyMessage(name: String) {
    Text(text = "Greetings $name!")
}
```

In the preceding code block, we've defined the `FriendlyMessage` composable function by annotating it with the `@Composable` annotation. Looking at the function definition and body, we can easily deduce that it displays a greeting message.

It's important to note that any function annotated with `@Composable` can be rendered on the screen as it will produce a piece of UI hierarchy that displays content. In their true sense, composable functions emit UI widgets based on their definition.

In our case, the previous function should display a greeting message by concatenating the `String` value it receives as a parameter with a predefined message. As the function relies on its input parameters to show different messages on every usage, it's correct to say that composable functions are functions of data (presented as **F(data)** in the following diagram) that are converted into pieces of UI or widgets:

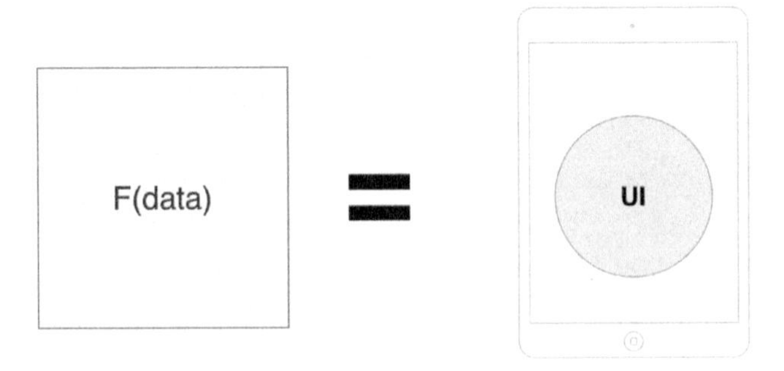

Figure 1.1 – In Compose, UI is a function of data

Later, in the *Unidirectional flow of data* subsection, we will understand why having functions to describe UI widgets is beneficial to our projects as it leads to a less bug-prone UI layer.

Getting back to our example, you might be wondering what the `Text` functional call represents. As with every other framework, Compose provides composable functions such as `Text` out of the box that we can use.

As its name suggests, the `Text` composable allows you to display some text on the screen. We will cover other composable functions provided by Compose in the *Exploring the building blocks of Compose UIs* section.

Until then, let's have another look at the previous code example and highlight the most important rules when it comes to defining a composable function:

- It should be a regular function marked with the `@Composable` annotation.
- Its UI output is defined by the data that's received through its input parameters. Composable functions should return `Unit` as they emit UI elements and do not return data as regular functions do. Most of the time, we omit defining the `Unit` return type or even returning `Unit` – as Kotlin marks it as redundant – just like in the previous example.
- It can contain other composable functions or regular Kotlin code. In the previous example, the `FriendlyMessage` composable function makes use of another composable, called `Text`, but it could also call regular Kotlin code (we will tackle that in the upcoming sections).
- It should be named as a noun or a noun preceded by a suggestive adjective (but never a verb). This way, composable functions envision widgets and not actions. Additionally, its name should respect the PascalCase naming convention, meaning that the first letter of each compound word in a variable is capitalized.
- It's recommended that the function is public and not defined within a class but directly within a Kotlin file. This way, Compose promotes the reuse of composable functions.

Now that we understand what a composable function is and how one is defined, let's move on and explore the paradigm shift that Compose brings to Android UI development.

The paradigm shift in creating UIs on Android

Compose brings a new approach to Android UI development and that is providing a declarative way of describing your UI. Before trying to understand how the declarative approach works, we will learn how the traditional View System relies on a different paradigm – the imperative one.

The imperative paradigm

When describing your UI with XML, you represent the view hierarchy as a tree of widgets that are commonly known as views. Views, in the context of the traditional View System, are all the components that inherit from the `android.view.View` class, from `TextView`, `Button`, or `ImageView` to `LinearLayout`, `RelativeLayout`, and so on.

Yet what's essential for the View System is the *imperative paradigm* that it relies on. Because your application must know how to react to user interactions and change the state of the UI accordingly, you can mutate the state of your views by referencing them through `findViewById` calls and then update their values through calls such as `setText()`, `setBackgroundResource()`, and so on.

Since views maintain their internal state and expose setters and getters, you must imperatively set new states for each component, as the following diagram suggests:

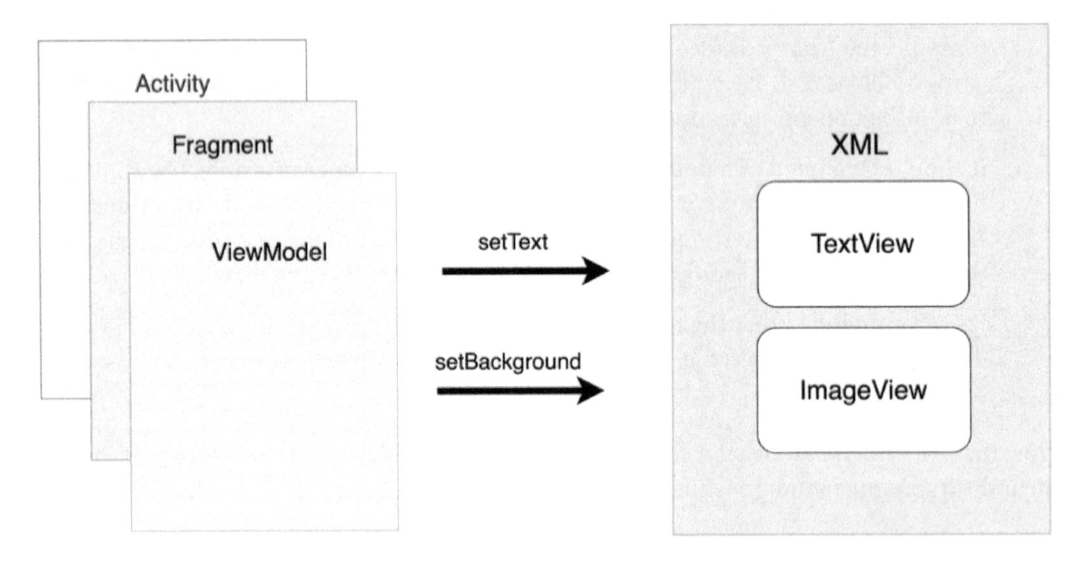

Figure 1.2 – The Android View System features in the imperative paradigm

Manually manipulating views' states increases the chance of bugs and errors in your UI. Because you end up treating multiple possible states and because chunks of data are displayed in several such states, it's relatively easy to mess up the outcome of your UI. Illegal states or conflicts between states can also arise relatively easily when your UI grows in complexity.

Moreover, since the layouts are defined in an additional component – that is, an XML file – the coupling between `Activity`, `Fragment`, or `ViewModel` and the XML-based UI increases. This means that changing something on the UI in the XML file will often lead to changes in `Activity`, `Fragment`, or `ViewModel` classes, which is where state handling happens. Not only that but cohesion is reduced because of language differences: one component is in Java/Kotlin, while the other one is in XML. This means that for the UI to function, it needs not only an `Activity` or `Fragment` but also XML.

The declarative paradigm

To address some of the issues within the standard View System, Compose relies on a modern declarative UI model, which drastically simplifies the process of building, updating, and maintaining UIs on Android.

If, in the traditional View System, the imperative paradigm described *how* the UI should change, in Compose, the declarative paradigm describes *what* the UI should render at a certain point in time.

Compose does that by defining the screen as a tree of composables. As in the following examples, each composable passes data to its nested composables, just like the `FriendlyMessage` composable passed a name to the `Text` composable in our code example from the previous section:

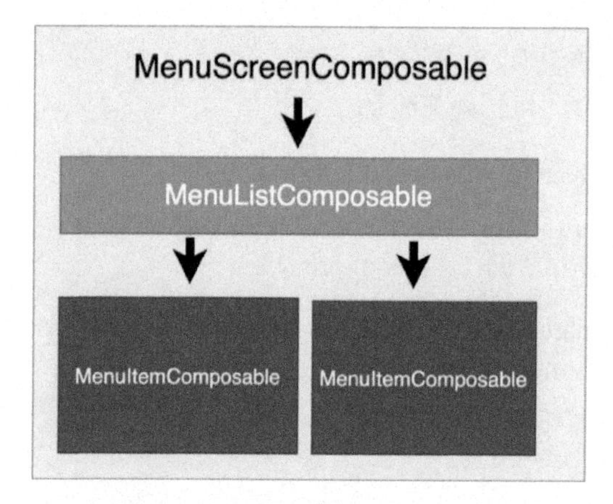

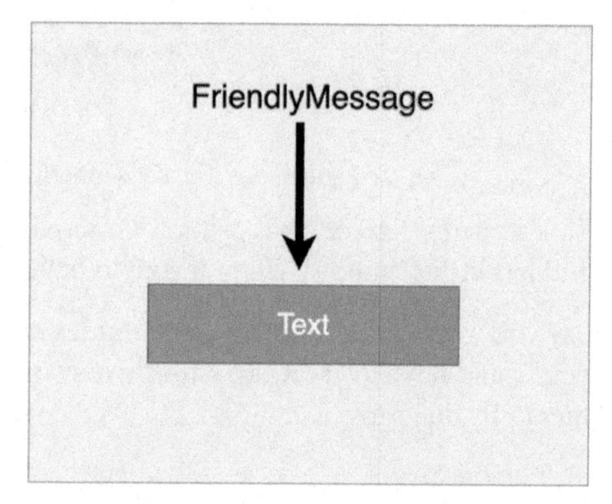

Figure 1.3 – Visualizing a tree of composable widgets and how data is passed downwards

When the input arguments change, Compose regenerates the entire widget tree from scratch. It applies the necessary changes and eliminates the need and the associated complexity of manually updating each widget.

This means that in Compose, composables are relatively stateless and because of that, they don't expose getter and setter methods. This allows the caller to react to interactions and handle the process of creating new states separately. It does that by calling the same composables but with different argument values. As we discussed in the *Describing UIs with composable functions* section, the UI in Compose is a function of data. From this, we can conclude that if new data is passed to composables, new UI states can be produced.

Lastly, compared to the View System, Compose only relies on Kotlin APIs, which means that UIs can now be defined with a single technology, in a single component, thereby increasing cohesion and reducing coupling.

Now, let's look at another shift in design brought by Compose and discuss how composition yields more flexible ways of defining UIs than inheritance does.

Favoring composition over inheritance

In the Android View System, every view inherits functionality from the parent `View` class. As the system relies solely on inheritance, the task of creating custom views can only be done through defining elaborate hierarchies.

Let's take the `Button` view as an example. It inherits functionality from `TextView`, which, in turn, inherits from `View`:

```
java.lang.Object
  ↳ android.view.View
      ↳ android.widget.TextView
          ↳ android.widget.Button
```

Figure 1.4 – The class inheritance hierarchy for the Button view

This strategy is great for reusing functionality, but inheritance becomes difficult to scale and has little flexibility when trying to have multiple variations of one view.

Say you want the `Button` view to render an image instead of text. In the View System, you would have to create an entirely new inheritance hierarchy, as shown in the following hierarchy diagram:

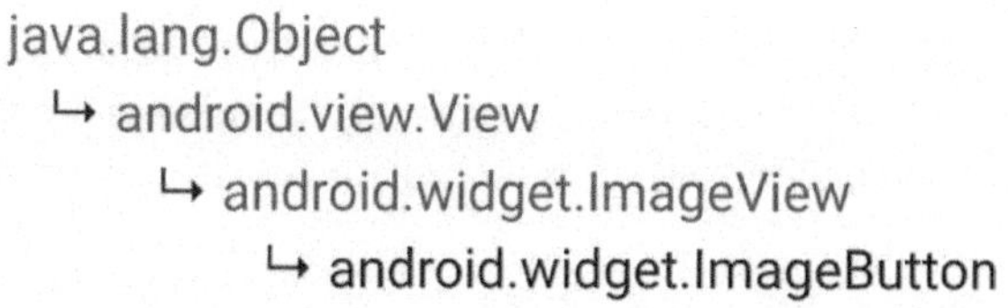

java.lang.Object
↳ android.view.View
↳ android.widget.ImageView
↳ android.widget.ImageButton

Figure 1.5 – The class inheritance hierarchy for the ImageButton view

But what if you need a button that accommodates both a `TextView` and an `ImageView`? This task would be extremely challenging, so it's easy to conclude that having separate inheritance hierarchies for each custom view is neither flexible nor scalable.

These examples are real, and they show the limitations of the View System. As we've previously seen, one of the biggest reasons for the lack of flexibility is the inheritance model of the View System.

To address this issue, *Compose favors composition over inheritance.* As shown in the following diagram, this means that Compose builds more complex UIs by using smaller pieces and not by inheriting functionality from one single parent:

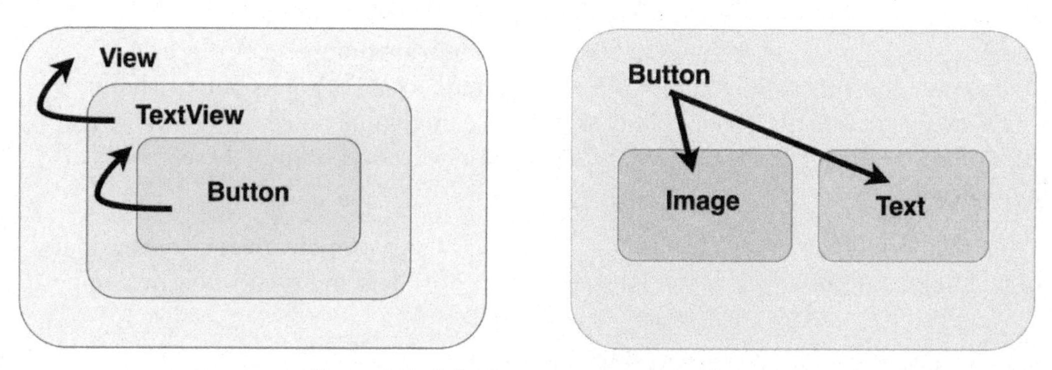

Figure 1.6 – Inheritance versus composition

Let's try to briefly explain our previous comparison between inheritance and composition:

- With inheritance, you are limited to inheriting your parent, just like `Button` inherits only from `TextView`.
- With composition, you can compose multiple other components, just like the `Button` composable contains both an `Image` composable and a `Text` composable, thereby giving you much more flexibility in building UIs.

Let's try to build a composable that features a button with an image and text. This was a huge challenge with inheritance, but Compose simplifies this by allowing you to compose an `Image` composable and a `Text` composable inside a `Button` composable:

```
@Composable
fun SuggestiveButton() {
    Button(onClick = { }) {
        Row() {
            Image(painter =
                      painterResource(R.drawable.drawable),
                  contentDescription = "")
            Text(text = "Press me")
        }
    }
}
```

Now, our `SuggestiveButton` composable contains both `Image` and `Text` composables. The beauty of this is that it could contain anything else. A `Button` composable can accept other composables that it renders as part of its button's body. Don't worry about this aspect or about that weird composable called `Row` for now. The *Exploring the building blocks of Compose UIs* section will cover both of these aspects in more detail.

What's important to remember from this example is that Compose gives us the flexibility of building a custom UI with ease. Next, let's cover how data and events flow in Compose.

Unidirectional flow of data

Knowing that each composable passes data down to its children composables, we can deduct that the internal state is no longer needed. This also translates into a unidirectional flow of data because composables only expect data as input and never care about their state:

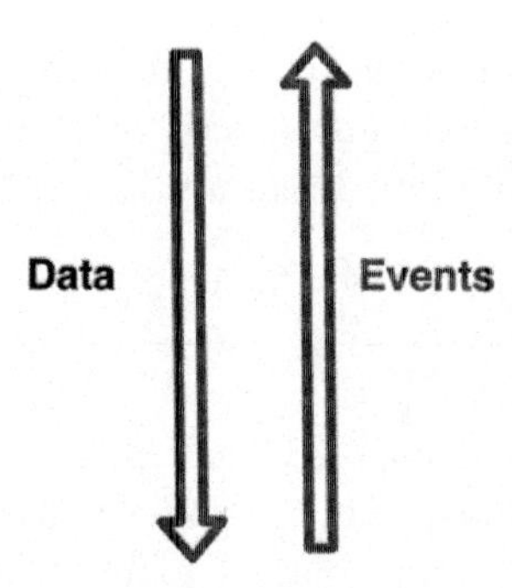

Figure 1.7 – Visualizing the unidirectional flow of data and events

Similarly, with data, each composable passes down callback functions to its children composables. Yet this time, the callback functions are caused by user interactions, and they create an upstream of callbacks that goes from each nested composable to its parent and so on. This means that not only the data is unidirectional but also events, just in opposite ways.

From this, it's clear that data and events travel only in one direction, and that's a good thing because only one source of truth – ideally, `ViewModel` – is in charge of handling them, resulting in fewer bugs and easier maintenance as the UI scales.

Let's consider a case with another composable provided by Jetpack Compose called `Button`. As its name suggests, it emits a button widget on the screen, and it exposes a callback function called `onClick` that notifies us whenever the user clicks the button.

In the following example, our `MailButton` composable receives data as an email identifier, `mailId`, and an event callback as a `mailPressedCallback` function:

```
@Composable
fun MailButton(
    mailId: Int,
    mailPressedCallback: (Int) -> Unit
) {
    Button(onClick = { mailPressedCallback(mailId) }) {
        Text(text = "Expand mail $mailId")
    }
}
```

While it consumes the data it receives via `mailId`, it also sets the `mailPressedCallback` function to be called every time its button is clicked, thereby sending the event back up to its parent. This way, data flows downwards and the callback flows upwards.

> **Note**
>
> It is ideal to construct your Compose UI in such a way that data provided by the `ViewModel` flows from parent composables to children composables and events flow from each composable back up to the `ViewModel`. If you're not familiar with the `ViewModel` component, don't worry as will cover it in the upcoming *Chapter 2, Handling UI State with Jetpack ViewModel.*

Recomposition

We have already covered how composable functions are defined by their input data and stated that whenever the data changes, composables are rebuilt as they render a new UI state corresponding to the newly received data.

The process of calling your composable functions again when inputs change is called **recomposition**. When inputs change, Compose automatically triggers the recomposition process for us and rebuilds the UI widget tree, redrawing the widgets emitted by the composables so that they display the newly received data.

Yet recomposing the entire UI hierarchy is computationally expensive, which is why Compose only calls the functions that have new input while skipping the ones whose input hasn't changed. Optimizing the process of rebuilding the composable tree is a complex job and is usually referred to as *intelligent recomposition.*

> **Note**
>
> In the traditional View System, we would manually call the setters and getters of views, but with Compose, it's enough to provide new arguments to our composables. This will allow Compose to initiate the recomposition process for parts of the UI so that the updated values are displayed.

Before jumping into an actual example of recomposition, let's have a quick look at the lifecycle of a composable function. Its lifecycle is defined by the composition lifecycle, as shown here:

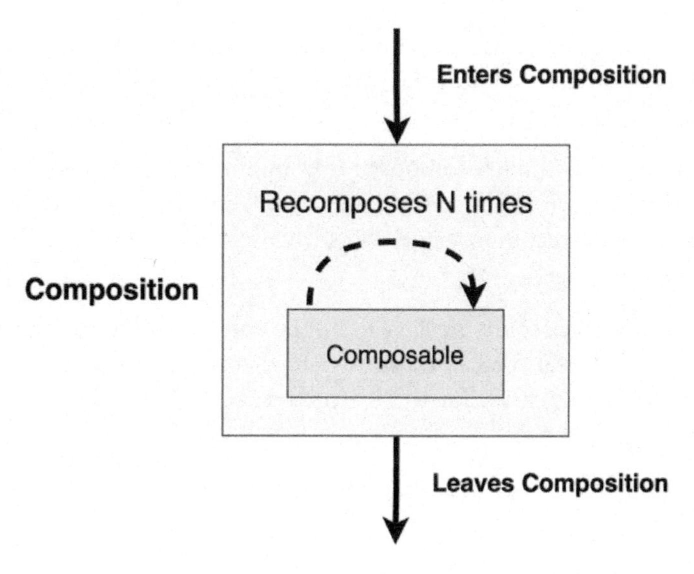

Figure 1.8 – The composition lifecycle of a composable function

This means that a composable first enters composition, and before leaving this process, it can recompose as many times as needed – that is, before it disappears from the screen, it can be recomposed and rebuilt many times, each time possibly displaying a different value.

Recomposition is often triggered by changes within `State` objects, so let's look at an example to explore how seamlessly this happens with little intervention from our side. Say you have a `TimerText` composable that expects a certain number of elapsed `seconds` that it displays in a `Text` composable. The timer starts from 0 and updates every 1 second (or 1,000 ms), displaying the number of seconds that have elapsed:

```
var seconds by mutableStateOf(0)
val stopWatchTimer = timer(period = 1000) { seconds++ }
    ...
@Composable
fun TimerText(seconds: Int) {
    Text(text = "Elapsed: $seconds")
}
```

In the *Defining and handling state with Compose* section of *Chapter 2, Handling UI State with Jetpack ViewModel*, we will define the state in Compose in more detail, but until then, let's think of `seconds` as a simple state object (instantiated with `mutableStateOf()`) that has an initial value of `0` and that its value changes over time, triggering a recomposition each time.

Every time `stopWatchTimer` increases the value of the `seconds` state object, Compose triggers a recomposition that rebuilds the widget tree and redraws the composables with new arguments.

In our case, `TimerText` will be recomposed or rebuilt because it receives different arguments – the first time, it will receive `0`, then `1`, `2`, and so on. This, in turn, triggers the `Text` composable to also recompose and that's why Compose redraws it on the screen to display the updated message.

Recomposition is a complex topic. As we will not be able to go into too much depth on it now, it's important to also cover more advanced concepts, as described in the documentation: `https://developer.android.com/jetpack/compose/mental-model#any-order`.

Now that we've covered what recomposition is and the core concepts behind Compose, it's time to have a better look at the composables that are used to build a Compose UI.

Exploring the building blocks of Compose UIs

We've only had a brief look at the `Text` and `Button` composables so far. That's why, in this section, we will not only understand how activities can render composables instead of XML and how we can preview them, but we will also have a better look at the most important and commonly used composable functions: from the ones we've seen, such as `Text` and `Button`, to new ones such as `TextField`, `Image`, `Row`, `Column`, and `Box`.

To summarize, this section will cover the following topics:

- Setting content and previewing composables
- Exploring core composables
- Customizing composables with modifiers
- Layouts in Compose

Let's jump in and understand how to render composable functions on the screen.

Setting content and previewing composables

We had a quick look at some composable functions, but we didn't quite touch on the aspect of making the application display Compose UIs.

Setting the composable content can easily be achieved and is encouraged to be done in your `Activity` class by simply replacing the traditional `setContentView(R.layout.XML)` call with `setContent()` and passing a composable function to it:

```
import androidx.activity.compose.setContent
class MainActivity : ComponentActivity() {
    override fun onCreate(savedInstanceState: Bundle?) {
        super.onCreate(savedInstanceState)
        setContent {
            Text("Hello world")
        }
    }
}
```

Because Compose no longer needs the `AppCompat` API for backward compatibility, we made our `MainActivity` inherit the base `ComponentActivity` class.

In the previous example, we called the `setContent` method in the `onCreate` callback of `MainActivity` and passed a `Text` composable function to it. If we run the app, we will see the `"Hello world"` message.

The `setContent` method is an extension function for `ComponentActivity` that composes the given composable into the given activity. It only accepts a `@Composable` function as a trailing lambda. The input composable function will become the root view of the activity and act as a container for your Compose hierarchy.

> **Note**
>
> You can add composable functions into fragments or activities that have an XML UI already defined with the help of the `ComposeView` class, but we will not go into too much detail as far as interoperability goes.

As XML provided us with a preview tool, a good question would be whether Compose also has one. Compose brings an even more powerful preview tool that allows us to skip running the application on the emulator or real devices every time we want to see how our UI evolves.

Previewing your composable is easy; just add the `@Preview` annotation to it:

```
@Preview(showBackground = true)
@Composable
fun FriendlyMessage() {
    Text(text = "Greetings!")
}
```

The IDE will automatically pick up that you want to preview this composable and show it on the right-hand side of the screen. Make sure that you *rebuild* your project and have the **Split** option enabled:

Figure 1.9 – Previewing composable functions in Android Studio

Optionally, you can specify for the preview to show a background for better visibility by passing the `showBackground` parameter with a value of `true`.

> **Note**
>
> Make sure that the composable function you are trying to preview has no input parameters. If it has, supply the default values for them so that the preview tools can work.

Yet this preview tool is much more powerful than this as it supports **Interactive mode**, which allows you to interact with the UI, and **Live Edit of literals**, which, if enabled, causes the preview to reload every time you change widths, heights, or others, just like a real UI would. You can see these two options in the following screenshot:

Figure 1.10 – Using the Preview feature in Compose

> **Note**
> To enable **Interactive mode** on Android Studio Arctic Fox, go to **File** | **Settings** | **Experimental** (Windows) or **Android Studio** | **Preferences** | **Experimental** (macOS).

Additionally, you can have multiple previews simultaneously if you annotate each function with the `@Preview` annotation. You can add names for each preview through the `name` parameter and even tell the preview tool which device it should display it on through the `device` argument:

```
@Preview(
    name = "Greeting preview",
    showSystemUi = true,
    device = Devices.PIXEL_2_XL
)
@Composable
fun FriendlyMessagePreview() { Text(text = "Greetings!") }
@Preview(
```

```
        showSystemUi = true,
        device = Devices.NEXUS_5)
@Composable
fun FriendlyMessagePreview2() { Text(text = "Goodbye!") }
```

Make sure that you also set `showSystemUi` to `true` to see the entire device.

> **Note**
>
> `@Preview` functions should have different names to avoid preview conflicts.

Now that we have learned how to set and preview Compose UI, it's time to explore new composables.

Exploring core composables

We've already had a quick look at some of the most basic composable functions: `Text`, `Button`, and `Image`. In this subsection, we will spend a bit more time exploring not only those composables but also new ones such as `TextField`.

Text

`Text` is the Compose version of our old and beloved `TextView`. `Text` is provided by Compose and achieves the most basic and yet important functionality in any application: the ability to display a piece of text. We've already used this composable in several examples:

```
Text(text = "Greetings $name!")
```

You might be wondering how we can customize it. Let's check out the source code or the documentation for `Text` to find the most basic and commonly used arguments for it:

- `text` is the only required argument. It expects a `String` and sets the output text.
- `color` specifies the color of the output text and expects a `Color` object.
- `fontSize` of type `TextUnit`, `fontStyle` of type `FontStyle`, `fontFamily` of type `FontFamily`, and `fontWeight` of type `FontWeight` all allow you to customize the look and appearance of your text.
- `textAlign` specifies the horizontal alignment of the text. It expects a `TextAlign` object.
- `maxLines` expects an `Int` value that sets the maximum number of lines in the output text.

- `style` expects a `TextStyle` object and allows you to define and reuse styles through themes.

Instead of going through all the arguments for `Text`, let's check out an example where we can customize the look of our `Text` composable function:

```
@Composable
fun MyAppText() {
    Text(
        text = stringResource(id = R.string.app_name),
        fontStyle = FontStyle.Italic,
        textAlign = TextAlign.Center,
        color = Color.Magenta,
        fontSize = 24.sp,
        fontWeight = FontWeight.ExtraBold)
}
```

Instead of passing some hardcoded text, we passed a string resource with the help of the built-in `stringResource` function and obtained the following result:

My first Compose project

Figure 1.11 – Exploring a customized Text composable

Now that we've learned how to display text with the `Text` composable, let's move on to buttons.

Button

Displaying text is essential in any application, yet having clickable buttons allows it to be interactive. We've used the `Button` composable (previously known in the View System as `Button` too) before and its main characteristic was the `onClick` callback function, which notified us when the user pressed the button.

While `Button` features plenty of customizing arguments, let's check out the most used parameters:

- `onClick` is a mandatory parameter and it expects a function that will be called whenever the user presses the button.
- `colors` expects a `ButtonColors` object that defines the content/background colors.

- `shape` expects a custom/Material theme `Shape` object that sets the shape of the button.
- `content` is a mandatory parameter that expects a composable function that displays the content inside this `Button`. We can add any composables here, including `Text`, `Image`, and more.

Let's try to build a `Button` function that makes use of these core arguments:

```
@Composable
fun ClickableButton() {
    Button(
        onClick = { /* callback */ },
        colors = ButtonDefaults.buttonColors(
            backgroundColor = Color.Blue,
            contentColor = Color.Red),
        shape = MaterialTheme.shapes.medium
    ) { Text("Press me") }
}
```

We've also passed a predefined `MaterialTheme` shape. Let's preview the resulting composable:

Figure 1.12 – Exploring a customized Button composable

With that, we've seen how easy it is to create a custom button with the `Button` composable. Next up, let's try to play around with another composable function – `TextField`.

TextField

Adding buttons is the first step toward having an interactive UI, but the most important element in this area is the `TextField` composable, previously known in the View System as `EditText`. Just like `EditText` did, the `TextField` composable allows the user to enter and modify text.

While `TextField` has many arguments, the most important ones that it features are as follows:

- `value` is a mandatory `String` argument as it's the displayed text. This value should change as we type inside it by holding it in a `State` object; more on that soon.
- `onValueChange` is a mandatory function that triggers every time the user inputs new characters or deletes existing ones.
- `label` expects a composable function that allows us to add a descriptive label.

Let's have a look at a simple usage of a `TextField` that also handles its own state:

```
@Composable
fun NameInput() {
    val textState = remember { mutableStateOf("") }
    TextField(
        value = textState.value,
        onValueChange = { newValue ->
            textState.value = newValue
        },
        label = { Text("Your name") })
}
```

It achieves this by defining a `MutableState` that holds the text displayed by `TextField`. This means that `textState` doesn't change across recompositions, so every time the UI updates because of other composables, `textState` should be retained. Moreover, we've wrapped the `MutableState` object in a `remember` block, which tells Compose that across recompositions, it should not revert the value to its initial value; that is, `""`.

To get or set the value of a `State` or `MutableState` object, our `NameInput` composable uses the `value` accessor. Because `TextField` accesses a `MutableState` object through the `value` accessor, Compose knows to retrigger a *recomposition* every time the `textState` value changes – in our case, in the `onValueChange` callback. By doing so, we ensure that as we input text in our `TextField`, the UI also updates with the new characters that have been added or removed from the keyboard.

Don't worry if these concepts about state in Compose don't make too much sense right now – we will cover how state is defined in Compose in more detail in *Chapter 2, Handling UI State with Jetpack ViewModel.*

> **Note:**
> Unlike `EditText`, `TextField` has no internal state. That's why we've created and handled it; otherwise, as we would type in, the UI would not update accordingly.

The resulting `NameInput` composable updates the UI correctly and looks like this:

Figure 1.13 – Exploring a TextField composable

Now that we've learned how to add input fields within a Compose-based app, it's time to explore one of the most common elements in any UI.

Image

Displaying graphical information in our application is essential and Compose provides us with a handy composable called `Image`, which is the composable version of the `ImageView` from the View System.

While `Image` features plenty of customizing arguments, let's check out the most used parameters:

- `painter` expects a `Painter` object. This argument is mandatory as it sets the image resource. Alternatively, you can use the overloaded version of `Image` to directly pass an `ImageBitmap` object to its `bitmap` parameter.
- `contentDescription` is a mandatory `String` that's used by accessibility services.
- `contentScale` expects a `ContentScale` object that specifies the scaling of the picture.

Let's add an `Image` composable that displays the application icon using `painterResource`:

```
@Composable
fun BeautifulImage() {
    Image(
        painter =
            painterResource(R.drawable.ic_launcher_foreground),
```

```
            contentDescription = "My app icon",
            contentScale = ContentScale.Fit
        )
}
```

Finally, let's preview the `BeautifulImage` function and then move on to the next section:

Figure 1.14 – Exploring the Image composable

We've also tried displaying images with Compose, yet you may still be wondering, how can we customize all these composable functions?

Customizing composables with modifiers

All the composables we've covered so far feature an argument that we haven't covered yet: `modifier`. This expects a `Modifier` object. In simple terms, *modifiers tell a composable how to display, arrange, or behave within its parent composable.* By passing a modifier, we can specify many configurations for a composable: from size, padding, or shape to background color or border.

Let's start with an example by using a `Box` composable and specifying a `size` modifier for it:

```
@Composable
fun ColoredBox() {
    Box(modifier = Modifier.size(120.dp))
}
```

We will cover the `Box` composable later but until then, you can think of it like a container that we will use to draw several shapes on the screen. What's important here is that we passed the `Modifier.size()` modifier, which sets the size of the box. It accepts a `dp` value that represents both the width and the height of the composable. You can also pass the width and height as parameters within the `size()` modifier or separately with the help of the `height()` and `width()` modifiers.

Specifying only one modifier for composables is usually not enough. That's why *modifiers can be chained*. Let's chain multiple modifiers by adding several other configurations to our `Box`:

```
@Composable
fun ColoredBox() {
    Box(modifier = Modifier
            .size(120.dp)
            .background(Color.Green)
            .padding(16.dp)
            .clip(RoundedCornerShape(size = 20.dp))
            .background(Color.Red))
}
```

As we mentioned previously, chaining modifiers is simple: start with an empty `Modifier` object and then chain new modifiers one after the other. We've chained several new modifiers, starting with `background`, then `padding`, `clip`, and finally another `background`. The modifiers, when combined, produce an output consisting of a green rectangle that contains a nested rounded corner rectangle that's red:

Figure 1.15 – Exploring chained modifiers

> **Note**
>
> The order of the modifiers in the chain matters because modifiers are applied from the outer layer to the inner layer. Each modifier modifies the composable and then prepares it for the upcoming modifier in the chain. Different modifier orders yield different results.

In the previous example, because modifiers are applied from the outermost layer to the innermost layer, the entire rectangular box is green because green is the first color modifier that's applied. Going inner, we applied a padding of 16 `dp`. Afterward, still going inner, the `RoundedCornerShape` modifier is applied. Finally, in the innermost layer, we applied another color modifier – this time, of the color red – and we got our final result.

Now that we've played around with the most common composables, it's time to start building actual layouts that make use of multiple composable functions.

Layouts in Compose

Often, building even a simple screen cannot be achieved by following the previous examples since most of them feature only one composable. For simple use cases, composable functions contain only one composable child.

To build more complex pieces of UI, layout components in Compose give you the option to add as many children composables as you need.

In this section, we will cover those composable functions that allow you to place children composables in a linear or overlayed fashion, such as the following:

- `Row` for arranging children composables in a horizontal fashion
- `Column` for arranging children composables vertically
- `Box` for arranging children composables on top of each other

Following these definitions, let's envision the layout composables with the following diagram:

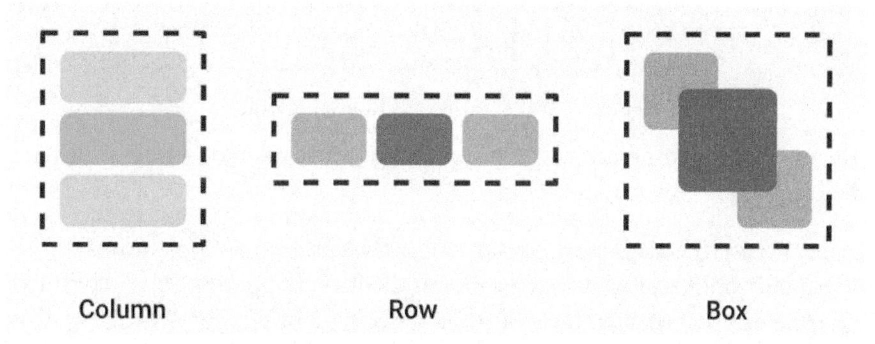

Figure 1.16 – Exploring Column, Row, and Box

It's clear now that arranging children composables in different ways can easily be achieved with `Column`, `Row`, and `Box`, so it's time to look at them in more detail.

Row

Displaying multiple widgets on the screen is achieved by using a `Row` composable that arranges its children composables horizontally, just like the old `LinearLayout` with horizontal orientation did:

```
@Composable
fun HorizontalNumbersList() {
    Row(
        horizontalArrangement = Arrangement.Start,
        verticalAlignment = Alignment.CenterVertically,
        modifier = Modifier.fillMaxWidth()
    ) {
        Text("1", fontSize = 36.sp)
        Text("2", fontSize = 36.sp)
        Text("3", fontSize = 36.sp)
        Text("4", fontSize = 36.sp)
    }
}
```

We've set `Row` to only take the available width and added several `Text` functions as children composables. We specified a `horizontalArrangement` of `Start` so that they start from the left of the parent but also made sure that they are centered vertically by passing a `CenterVertically` alignment for the `verticalAlignment` argument. The result is straightforward:

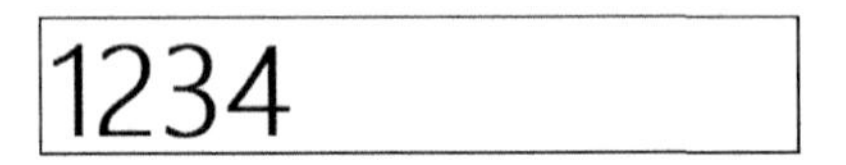

Figure 1.17 – Exploring the Row composable

Largely, the essential arguments for a `Row` composable are related to how children are arranged or aligned:

- `horizontalArrangement` defines how the children are positioned horizontally both relative to each other and within the parent `Row`. Apart from `Arragement.Start`, you can also pass `Center` or `End` or `SpaceBetween`, `SpaceEvenly`, or `SpaceAround`.
- `verticalAlignment` sets how the children are positioned vertically within the parent `Row`. Apart from `Alignment.CenterVertically`, you can pass `Top` or `Bottom`.

Now that we've arranged the children composables horizontally, let's try to arrange them vertically.

Column

Displaying a vertical list on the screen can be achieved by using a `Column` composable that arranges its children composables vertically, just like the old `LinearLayout` with vertical orientation did:

```
@Composable
fun NamesVerticalList() {
    Column(verticalArrangement = Arrangement.SpaceEvenly,
        horizontalAlignment = Alignment.CenterHorizontally,
        modifier = Modifier.fillMaxSize()
    ) {
        Text("John", fontSize = 36.sp)
        Text("Amanda", fontSize = 36.sp)
        Text("Mike", fontSize = 36.sp)
        Text("Alma", fontSize = 36.sp)
    }
}
```

We've set `Column` to take all the available space and added several `Text` functions as children composables. This time, we specified a `verticalArrangement` of `SpaceEvenly` so that children are spread out equally within the parent, but we also made sure they are centered horizontally by passing a `CenterHorizontally` alignment as `horizontalAlignment`:

Figure 1.18 – Exploring the Column composable

Similar to Row, the essential arguments for a Column are also related to how children are arranged or aligned. This time, though, the arrangement is vertical instead of horizontal, and the alignment is horizontal instead of vertical:

- verticalArrangement defines how the children are vertically positioned within the parent Column. The values are the same as the row's horizontalArrangement.
- horizontalAlignment defines how the children are aligned within the parent Column. Apart from Alignment.CenterHorizontally, you can pass Start or End.

> **Note**
> If you're feeling brave, this is a great time for you to explore different alignments and arrangements and see how the UI changes. Make sure that you preview your composable functions with the @Preview annotation.

Box

So far, we've learned how to arrange children horizontally and vertically, but what if we want to place them on top of each other? The Box composable comes to our rescue as it allows us to stack children composables. Box also allows us to position the children relatively to it.

Let's try to build our own **Floating Action Button** (**FAB**) with the help of Box. We will stack two composables inside Box:

- One green circle, which will be created with the help of Surface. The Surface composable allows you to easily define a material surface with a certain shape, background, or elevation.
- One plus sign (+) added as text inside the Text composable, which is aligned in the center of its parent Box.

This is what the code will look like:

```
@Composable
fun MyFloatingActionButton() {
    Box {
        Surface(
            modifier = Modifier.size(32.dp),
            color = Color.Green,
```

```
            shape = CircleShape,
            content = { })
        Text(text = "+",
            modifier = Modifier.align(Alignment.Center))
    }
}
```

The Surface composable is defined with a mandatory content parameter that accepts another composable as its inner content. We don't want to add a composable inside of it. Instead, we want to stack a Text composable on top of it, so we passed an empty function to the content parameter.

The result is similar to the FAB we are all used to:

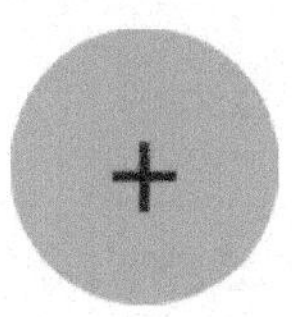

Figure 1.19 – Exploring the Box composable

To take advantage of Box, you must keep the following in mind:

- The order in which composables are added within Box defines the order in which they are painted and stacked on top of each other. If you switch the order of Surface and Text, the + icon will be painted beneath the green circle making it invisible.
- You can align the children composables relative to the Box parent by passing different values for each of the child's alignment modifiers. That's why, apart from Alignment.Center, you can also position children composables with CenterStart, CenterEnd, TopStart, TopCenter, TopEnd, BottomStart, BottomEnd, or BottomCenter.

Now that we covered the basics, it's time to roll up our sleeves and create our first Compose project!

Building a Compose-based screen

Let's say we want to build an application that showcases some restaurants. We will build the UI with Compose and go through the steps of creating a new Compose project. We will then build a list item for such a restaurant and finally display a dummy list of such items.

To summarize, in this section, we will build our first Compose-based application: a restaurant explorer app! To achieve that, we must display some restaurants, which we will do by covering the following topics:

- Creating your first Compose project
- Building a restaurant element layout
- Displaying a list of restaurants with Compose

Now that we have a clear path, let's get started.

Creating your first Compose project

To build a restaurant app, we have to create a new Compose-based project:

1. Open Android Studio and select the **New Project** option:

Figure 1.20 – Starting a new project with Android Studio

If you already have Android Studio open, go to **File**, then **New**, and finally **New Project**.

> **Note**
>
> Make sure that you have Android Studio version Arctic Fox 2020.3.1 or newer. If you're using a newer version though, some files might have differences in the generated code.

2. In the **Phone and tablet** template section, select **Empty Compose Activity** and then choose **Next**:

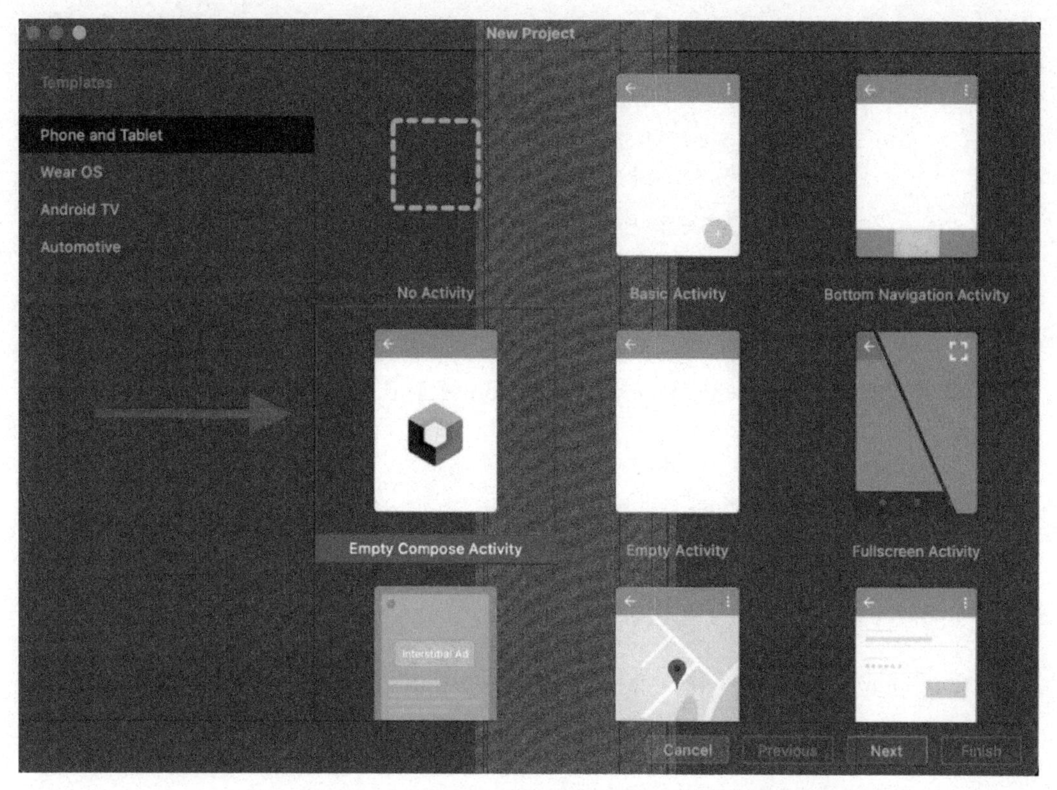

Figure 1.21 – Starting a new project with Android Studio

3. Next, enter some details about your application. In the **Name** field, enter `Restaurants app`. Leave **Kotlin** as-is for **Language** and set **Minimum SDK** to **API 21**. Then, click **Finish**.

> **Important note**
>
> The upcoming step is an essential configuration step. It makes sure that the project Android Studio has configured for you the same versions of dependencies (from Compose, to Kotlin and other dependencies) that we use throughout the book. By doing so, you will be able to follow the code snippets and inspect the code source without any API differences.

4. Inside the newly generated project, before inspecting the code, make sure that the generated project uses the versions of dependencies that are used throughout the book.

To do so, first go to the project-level `build.gradle` file and inside the `dependencies` block, make sure that the Kotlin version is set to `1.6.10`:

```
buildscript {
    [...]
    dependencies {
        classpath "com.android.tools.build:gradle:7.0.2"
        classpath "org.jetbrains.kotlin:kotlin-gradle-
            plugin:1.6.10"
      [...]
    }
}
```

Alternatively, if you're using a newer version of Android Studio, you might find the Kotlin version used in this project inside the `plugins` block, like so:

```
plugins {
    [...]
    id 'org.jetbrains.kotlin.android' version '1.6.10'
        apply false
}
```

If you haven't already, you might need to install the 1.6.10 plugin version of Kotlin in Android Studio. To do that, click on the **Tools** option of Android Studio on the **Kotlin** and on the **Configure Kotlin Plugin Updates** options. In the newly opened window, you can update your Kotlin version to `1.6.10`.

Still in the project-level `build.gradle` file, because Compose is tied to the Kotlin version used in our project, make sure that the Compose version is set to `1.1.1` inside the `ext { }` block:

```
buildscript {
    ext {
        compose_version = '1.1.1'
    }
    repositories {…}
    dependencies {…}
}
```

Then, move into the app-level `build.gradle` file. First check that the `composeOptions { }` block looks like this:

```
plugins { ... }

android {
    [...]
    buildFeatures { compose true }
    composeOptions {
        kotlinCompilerExtensionVersion compose_version
    }
    packagingOptions { ... }
}
```

In some versions of Android Studio, the `composeOptions { }` block would add an outdated `kotlinCompilerVersion '1.x.xx'` line that should be removed.

Finally, make sure that the `dependencies` block of the app-level `build.gradle` file includes the following versions for its dependencies:

```
dependencies {
    implementation 'androidx.core:core-ktx:1.7.0'
    implementation 'androidx.appcompat:appcompat:1.4.1'
    implementation 'com.google.android.material:
        material:1.5.0'
    implementation "androidx.compose.ui:ui:
        $compose_version"
    implementation "androidx.compose.material:
        material:$compose_version"
    implementation "androidx.compose.ui:ui-tooling-
        preview:$compose_version"
    implementation 'androidx.lifecycle:lifecycle-
        runtime-ktx:2.4.1'
    implementation 'androidx.activity:activity-
        compose:1.4.0'
    testImplementation 'junit:junit:4.+'
    androidTestImplementation
        'androidx.test.ext:junit:1.1.3'
```

```
        androidTestImplementation
            'androidx.test.espresso:espresso-core:3.4.0'
        androidTestImplementation "androidx.compose.ui:ui-
            test-junit4:$compose_version"
        debugImplementation "androidx.compose.ui:ui-
            tooling:$compose_version"
    }
```

If you had to make any changes, synchronize your project with its Gradle files by clicking on the **Sync your project with Gradle files** button in Android Studio or by pressing on the **File** menu option and then by selecting **Sync Project with Gradle Files**.

Now we're set. Let's return to the source code generated by Android Studio.

And here we are – our first Compose project has been set up! Let's check out the source code by navigating to the `MainActivity.kt` file. We can conclude that it consists of three main parts:

- The `MainActivity` class
- The `Greeting` composable function
- The `DefaultPreview` composable function

The `MainActivity` class is where content is passed to the `setContent` method in the `onCreate` callback. As we know by now, we need to call `setContent` to set up a Compose UI and pass composable functions as our UI:

```
setContent {
    RestaurantsAppTheme {
        Surface(color = MaterialTheme.colors.background) {
            Greeting("Android")
        }
    }
}
```

The IDE template has already implemented a `Greeting` composable that is wrapped into a `Surface` that uses the theme's background color. But what is that `RestaurantsAppTheme` function that was passed as the parent composable to the `setContent` method?

If you press *Ctrl* + *B* or *Command* + *B* on the function name, you will be taken to the `Theme.kt` file, which is where our theme is generated. `RestaurantsAppTheme` is a composable function that was auto-generated by the IDE as it holds the app's name:

```
@Composable
fun RestaurantsAppTheme(
    darkTheme: Boolean = isSystemInDarkTheme(),
    content: @Composable() -> Unit
) {
    ...
    MaterialTheme(
        colors = colors,
        typography = Typography,
        shapes = Shapes,
        content = content)
}
```

The app's theme is a wrapper over `MaterialTheme` and if we pass it to the `setContent` call, it allows us to reuse custom styles and color schemes defined within the app's theme. For it to take effect and reuse custom styles, we must pass our composables functions to the `content` parameter of our theme composable – in our case, in `MainActivity`, the `Greeting` composable wrapped in the `Surface` composable is passed to the `RestaurantsAppTheme` composable.

Let's go back inside the `MainActivity.kt` file to have a look at the other parts generated by Android studio. We can see that the `Greeting` composable displays text through `Text`, similar to our composable functions from the previous examples.

To preview the `Greeting` composable, the IDE also generated a preview composable for us called `DefaultPreview`, which allows us to preview the content that `MainActivity` displays; that is, `Greeting`. It also makes use of the theme composable to get the consistently themed UI.

Now that we've achieved a big milestone in that we've created a Compose-based application, it's time to start working on our Restaurants App!

Building a restaurant element layout

It's time to get our hands dirty and start building the layout for a restaurant within the app:

1. Create a new file by left-clicking the application package and selecting **New** and then **Kotlin Class/File**. Enter `RestaurantsScreen` for the name and select the type as **File**.
2. Inside this file, let's create a `RestaurantsScreen` composable function for our first Compose screen:

```
@Composable
fun RestaurantsScreen() {
    RestaurantItem()
}
```

3. Next, inside the `RestaurantsScreen.kt` file, let's define the `RestaurantItem` composable, which features a `Card` composable with elevation and padding:

```
@Composable
fun RestaurantItem() {
    Card(elevation = 4.dp,
         modifier = Modifier.padding(8.dp)
    ) {
        Row(verticalAlignment =
                Alignment.CenterVertically,
            modifier = Modifier.padding(8.dp)) {
            RestaurantIcon(
                Icons.Filled.Place,
                Modifier.weight(0.15f))
            RestaurantDetails(Modifier.weight(0.85f))
        }
    }
}
```

Make sure that every import you include is part of the `androidx.compose.*` package. If you're unsure what imports to include, check out the source code for the `RestaurantsScreen.kt` file at the following URL:

`https://github.com/PacktPublishing/Kickstart-Modern-Android-Development-with-Jetpack-and-Kotlin/blob/main/Chapter_01/chapter_1_restaurants_app/app/src/main/java/com/codingtroops/restaurantsapp/RestaurantsScreen.kt`

Getting back to the previous code snippet, we could say that the `Card` composable is similar to `Cardview` from the old View System as it allows us to beautify the UI piece that represents a restaurant with border or elevation.

In our case, `Card` contains a `Row` composable whose children composables are centered vertically and are surrounded by some padding. We used `Row` since we will show some details about the restaurant in a horizontal fashion: an icon and some text details.

We passed the `RestaurantIcon` and `RestaurantDetails` composables as children of the `Row` composable but these functions are not defined so we have compilation errors. For now, don't worry about the weight modifiers. Let's define the `RestaurantIcon` composable first!

4. Still inside the `RestaurantsScreen.kt` file, create another composable function entitled `RestaurantIcon` with the following code:

```
@Composable
private fun RestaurantIcon(icon: ImageVector, modifier:
Modifier) {
    Image(imageVector = icon,
          contentDescription = "Restaurant icon",
          modifier = modifier.padding(8.dp))
}
```

The `RestaurantIcon` composable sets an `ImageVector` icon to an `Image` composable – in our case, a predefined Material Theme icon called `Icons.Filled.Place`. It also sets a `contentDescription` value and adds padding on top of the modifier it receives.

However, the most interesting part is the fact that `RestaurantIcon` receives a `Modifier` as an argument from its parent `Row`. The argument it receives is `Modifier.weight(0.15f)`, which means that our `Row` assigns weights to each of its horizontally positioned children. The value – in this case, `0.15f` – means that this child `RestaurantIcon` will take 15% of the horizontal space from its parent `Row`.

5. Now, still inside the `RestaurantsScreen.kt` file, create a `RestaurantDetails` function that displays the restaurant's details:

```
@Composable
private fun RestaurantDetails(modifier: Modifier) {
    Column(modifier = modifier) {
        Text(text = "Alfredo's dishes",
             style = MaterialTheme.typography.h6)
        CompositionLocalProvider(
            LocalContentAlpha provides
                ContentAlpha.medium) {
            Text(text = "At Alfredo's … seafood dishes.",
                 style = MaterialTheme.typography.body2)
        }
    }
}
```

Similarly, `RestaurantDetails` receives a `Modifier.weight(0.85f)` modifier as an argument from `Row`, which will make it occupy the remaining 85% of the horizontal space.

The `RestaurantDetails` composable is a simple `Column` that arranges two `Text` composables vertically, with one being the title of the restaurant, and the other being its description.

But what's up with `CompositionLocalProvider`? To display the description that's faded out in contrast to the title, we applied a `LocalContentAlpha` of `ContentAlpha.medium`. This way, the child `Text` with the restaurant description will be faded or grayed out.

`CompositionLocalProvider` allows us to pass data down to the composable hierarchy. In this case, we want the child `Text` to be grayed out, so we passed a `LocalContentAlpha` object with a `ContentAlpha.medium` value using the infix `provides` method.

6. For a moment, go to `MainActivity.kt` and remove the `DefaultPreview` composable function as we will define our own a `@Preview` composable up next.

7. Go back inside the `RestaurantsScreen.kt` file, define a `@Preview` composable:

```
@Preview(showBackground = true)
@Composable
fun DefaultPreview() {
    RestaurantsAppTheme {
        RestaurantsScreen()
    }
}
```

   If you have chosen a different name for your app, you might need to update the previous snippet with the theme composable defined in the `Theme.kt` file.

8. Rebuild the project and let's inspect the `RestaurantsScreen()` composable by previewing the newly created `DefaultPreview` composable, which should display a restaurant item:

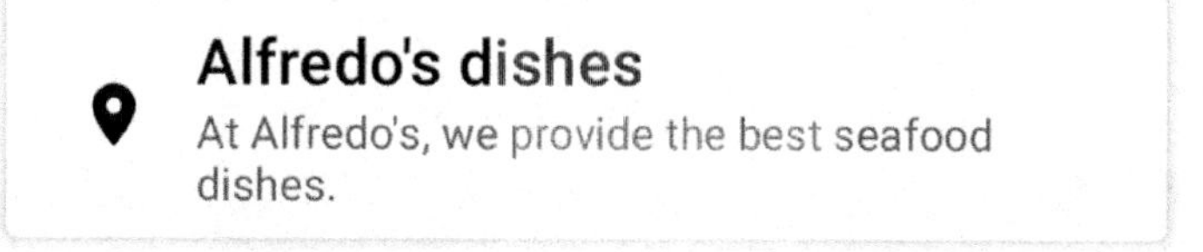

Figure 1.22 – Previewing a restaurant item

9. Finally, go back to `MainActivity.kt` and remove the `Greeting` composable. Also, remove the `Surface` and `Greeting` function calls in the `setContent` method and replace them with `RestaurantScreen`:

```
setContent {
    RestaurantsAppTheme {
        RestaurantsScreen()
    }
}
```

   By passing `RestaurantScreen` to our `MainActivity`'s `setContent` method, we ensure that the application will render the desired UI when built and run.

10. Optionally, you can now **Run** the app to see the restaurant directly on your device or emulator.

Now that we have built a layout for a restaurant, it's time to learn how to display more of them!

Displaying a list of restaurants with Compose

So far, we've displayed a restaurant item, so it's time to display an entire list of them:

1. First, create a new class in the root package, next to `MainActivity.kt`, called `Restaurant.kt`. Here, we will add a `data class` called `Restaurant` and add the fields that we expect a restaurant to have:

```
data class Restaurant(val id: Int,
                      val title: String,
                      val description: String)
```

2. In the same `Restaurant.kt` file, create a dummy list of `Restaurant` items, preferably at least 10 to fill up the entire screen:

```
data class Restaurant(val id: Int,
                      val title: String,
                      val description: String)

val dummyRestaurants = listOf(
    Restaurant(0, "Alfredo foods", "At Alfredo's …"),
    [...],
    Restaurant(13, "Mike and Ben's food pub", "")
)
```

You can find the pre-populated list in this book's GitHub repository, inside the `Restaurant.kt` file:

`https://github.com/PacktPublishing/Kickstart-Modern-Android-Development-with-Jetpack-and-Kotlin/blob/main/Chapter_01/chapter_1_restaurants_app/app/src/main/java/com/codingtroops/restaurantsapp/Restaurant.kt`.

3. Go back inside the `RestaurantsScreen.kt` file and update your `RestaurantItem` so that it receives a `Restaurant` object as an argument, while also passing the restaurant's `title` and `description` to the `RestaurantDetails` composable as parameters:

```
@Composable
fun RestaurantItem(item: Restaurant) {
    Card(...) {
        Row(...) {
            RestaurantIcon(...)
```

```
                RestaurantDetails(
                    item.title,
                    item.description,
                    Modifier.weight(0.85f)
                )
            }
        }
    }
```

4. We have passed the restaurant's `title` and `description` to the `RestaurantDetails` composable as parameters. Propagate these changes in the `RestaurantDetails` composable and pass the `title` into the first `Text` composable and the `description` into the second `Text` composable:

```
@Composable
fun RestaurantDetails(title: String, description: String,
modifier: Modifier){
    Column(modifier = modifier) {
        Text(text = title, ...)
        CompositionLocalProvider( … ) {
            Text(text = description, ...)
        }
    }
}
```

5. Go back to the `RestaurantsScreen` composable and update it to display a vertical list of `Restaurant` objects. We already know that we can use a `Column` to achieve this. Then, iterate over each restaurant in `dummyRestaurants` and bind it to a `RestaurantItem`:

```
@Composable
fun RestaurantsScreen() {
    Column {
        dummyRestaurants.forEach { restaurant ->
            RestaurantItem(restaurant)
        }
    }
}
```

This will create a beautiful vertical list that we can preview through our `DefaultPreview` composable.

6. Rebuild the project to see the updated preview generated by the `DefaultPreview` composable:

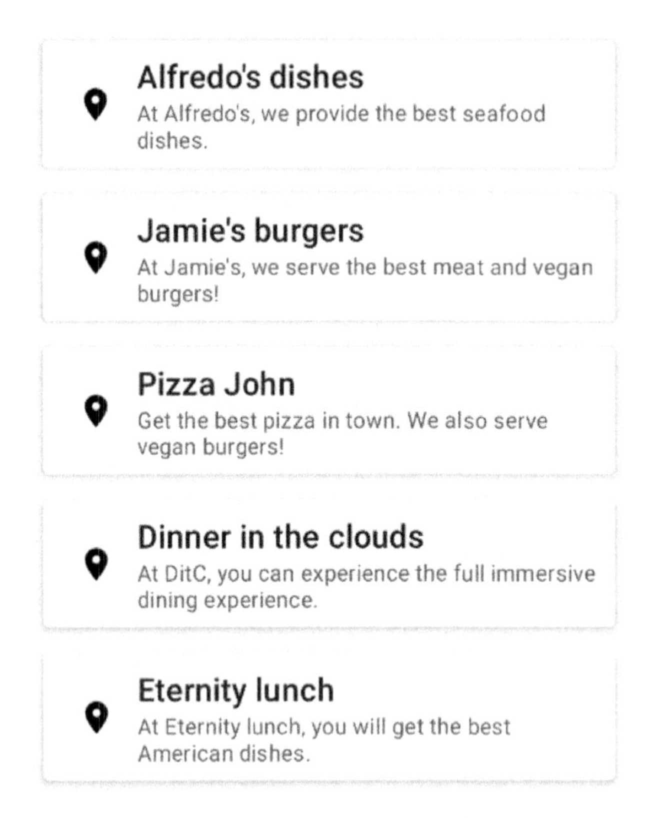

Figure 1.23 – Previewing RestaurantsScreen with the Column composable

Alternatively, you can **Run** the app to see the restaurants directly on your device or emulator.

We've finally created our first list with Compose! It looks very nice and beautiful, yet it has one huge issue – it doesn't scroll! We'll address this together in the next section.

Exploring lists with Compose

In the previous section, we built a Compose-based screen that features a list of restaurants. However, if you run the application or preview the screen in interactive mode, you will notice that the list doesn't scroll. This is a huge inconvenience that we will address in this section by adding scroll capabilities to our `Column` composable.

Next, we will specify why `Column` is suited for static content, whereas if the list is large and its size is dynamic or dictated by the server's response, we should use *lazy composables*. We will explore a variety of lazy composables and understand why they are better suited for large lists.

To summarize, this section will cover the following topics:

- Adding scrolling to the `Column` composable
- Introducing lazy composables
- Using `LazyColumn` to display restaurants

Let's start by adding scrolling capabilities to our `RestaurantsScreen` composable.

Adding scrolling to the Column composable

Our list of restaurants is long, and it can't scroll. This is a bad user experience, so let's fix it.

Let's make the `Column` scrollable by passing a `Modifier.verticalScroll` modifier that receives a `ScrollState`:

```
@Composable
fun RestaurantsScreen() {
    Column(Modifier.verticalScroll(rememberScrollState())) {
        ...
    }
}
```

We want the scrolling position to be retained across recompositions. That's why, by passing `rememberScrollState` to the `verticalScroll` modifier, we ensure that every time the UI recomposes, the scroll state is remembered and retained. The `rememberScrollState` persistence mechanism is similar to the `remember { }` block, which we used previously to retain the `TextField`'s state across recompositions.

Now, you can **Run** the app or preview it in **Interactive mode** and check out the scrolling effect.

However, we have one final issue with our `Column` that is related to how `Column` lays and composes its elements. Let's dive into that now and try to find a better alternative.

Introducing lazy composables

Let's take a short break from our restaurant app and try to think of a better way of handling large lists. Using `Row` or `Column` for displaying long lists of items, or maybe a list of unknown size, can prove detrimental to your UI and impact your app's performance. This happens because `Row` and `Column` render or lay all their children out, whether they are visible or not. They are good for displaying static content, yet passing a large list can cause your UI to become laggy or even unusable.

Two lazy composables called `LazyColumn` and `LazyRow` come to your rescue since they only compose or output those items that are currently visible on the screen, hence the term *lazy*. So, as you can see, they are somehow similar to the old `RecyclerView`.

As the only difference between `Row` and `Column` was the way children were laid out on the screen – horizontally or vertically – the same thing applies with `LazyRow` and `LazyColumn`. These lazy composables lay their children out horizontally or vertically and provide scrolling capabilities out of the box. As they only render the visible items, lazy composables are a much better fit for large lists.

Yet, lazy composables are different than the regular composables that we've used so far. That's mainly because instead of accepting `@Composable` content, they expose a **domain-specific language** (**DSL**) defined by a `LazyListScope` block:

```
@Composable
fun LazyColumn(
    ...
    content: LazyListScope.() -> Unit
) { … }
```

The `LazyListScope` DSL allows us to describe the *item* contents that we want to be displayed as part of the list. The most commonly used ones are `item()` and `items()`. Such example usage of `LazyColumn` that makes use of DSL is as follows:

```
LazyColumn {
    item() {
        Text(text = "Custom header item")
    }
    items(myLongList) { myItem ->
        MyComposable(myItem)
    }
```

```
    item(2) {
        Text(text = "Custom footer item")
    }
}
```

`item()` adds a single composable element to the list, while `items()` can receive not only a standalone list of content such as `myLongList` but also an `Int`, which will add the same item multiple times.

The code that we featured previously should render a vertical list that contains the following:

- A header `Text` composable
- A list of `MyComposable` composables that are the same size as `myLongList`
- Two `Text` footer composables

Returning from the DSL world, a noteworthy argument for the lazy composables is `contentPadding`, which allows you to define horizontal/vertical padding surrounding your list. This argument expects a `PaddingValues` object – we will use it soon; don't worry!

Now, we will soon receive the restaurants from a remote server, which means we don't know the size of the list, so it's time to implement such a lazy composable in our Restaurants application as well.

Using LazyColumn to display restaurants

We are currently using `Column` to display our `dummyRestaurants` list. We know why that's not the best practice, so to optimize our UI for dynamic content, we will replace it with `LazyColumn` so that we can continue displaying the restaurants vertically.

Go back to the `RestaurantsScreen.kt` file and, inside of the `RestaurantScreen` composable, replace the `Column` composable with `LazyColumn`:

```
@Composable
fun RestaurantsScreen() {
    LazyColumn(
        contentPadding = PaddingValues(
            vertical = 8.dp,
            horizontal = 8.dp)) {
```

```
            items(dummyRestaurants) { restaurant ->
                RestaurantItem(restaurant)
            }
        }
    }
```

We've used its DSL and specified the `items` properties that should populate our `LazyColumn` by passing the `dummyRestaurants` list. We obtained access to each item as a restaurant of type `Restaurant` and rendered it through a `RestaurantItem` composable.

We also added additional padding through the `contentPadding` argument to our `LazyColumn` by passing a `PaddingValues` object where we configured the vertical and horizontal padding.

You can now **Run** the app and check out the scrolling effect. In our case, the output is the same, yet if we were to test the app with a very long list of restaurants, we would have a much smoother scroll effect and a better UI experience with `LazyColumn` than with `Column`.

We've done it! We've built our first Compose-based app from scratch while exploring tons of composable functions. We've added a list that scrolls beautifully, and we can now be proud of the result!

Summary

In this chapter, we learned how to build modern UIs on Android directly in Kotlin by using the Jetpack Compose toolkit. You learned how, in Compose, everything is a composable function and how this new declarative way of defining UIs improves and makes the way we build UIs much easier and less prone to bugs.

We learned that Compose accelerates and greatly simplifies UI development with the help of concise Kotlin APIs and without the need for XML or other additional languages. We then covered the basic concepts behind Compose and the core components that allow you to build UIs.

Finally, we saw how easy it is to build UI with Compose by creating a Compose-based screen that displays a list of restaurants.

In *Chapter 2, Handling UI State with Jetpack ViewModel*, we will use the fundamentals we've learned in this chapter to revisit the concept of state in Compose and learn how it is represented, as well as how we can correctly manage it with the help of another Jetpack component: `ViewModel`.

First, we will understand what `ViewModel` is and why such a component is needed. Then, by continuing working on the Restaurants application that we started in this chapter, we will learn how to define and lift the UI's state in our own `ViewModel` class.

Further reading

Exploring a library with the magnitude of Compose is nearly impossible in a single chapter. That's why you should also explore other topics that are of great importance when building your UI with Compose:

- We've briefly mentioned how Compose works with the help of a Kotlin compiler plugin. To better how this compiler plugin helps us define composable functions, check out this great article written by the official Android developer team: `https://medium.com/androiddevelopers/under-the-hood-of-jetpack-compose-part-2-of-2-37b2c20c6cdd`.

  This article also covers the internals of Compose, so if you are curious about the execution model of Compose or what the compiler plugin does behind the scenes, make sure to check it out.
- Building UIs with Compose is simple, yet Compose is a very powerful framework that enables you to write highly reusable UIs. To take advantage of that, every Composable should receive a `Modifier` object that defines how it is arranged inside its caller parent. See what this means by checking out this great article, and then try to practice a bit: `https://chris.banes.dev/always-provide-a-modifier/`.
- Your layout should be adaptive and flexible for devices with different screen sizes or forms. You can learn more about this and try experimenting a bit by looking at the official documentation: `https://developer.android.com/jetpack/compose/layouts/adaptive`.

2
Handling UI State with Jetpack ViewModel

In this chapter, we will cover one of the most important libraries in Jetpack: **ViewModel**. In the first section, *Understanding the Jetpack ViewModel*, we will explore the concept and usages behind the `ViewModel` architecture component. We will see what it is, why we need it in our apps, and how we can implement one in our Restaurants app, which we started in the previous chapter.

In the next section, *Defining and handling state with Compose*, we will study how state is managed in Compose and exemplify usages of state inside our project. Afterward, in the *Hoisting state in Compose* section, we will understand what state hoisting is, why we need to achieve it, and then we will apply it to our app.

Finally, in the *Recovering from system-initiated process death* section, we will cover what a system-initiated process death is, how it occurs, and how essential it is for our applications to be able to recover from it by restoring the previous state details.

To summarize, in this chapter, we're going to cover the following main topics:

- Understanding the Jetpack ViewModel
- Defining and handling state with Compose
- Hoisting state in Compose
- Recovering from system-initiated process death

Before jumping in, let's set up the technical requirements for this chapter.

Technical requirements

When building Compose-based Android projects with Jetpack ViewModel, you usually require your day-to-day tools. However, to follow along smoothly, make sure you have the following:

- The Arctic Fox 2020.3.1 version of Android Studio. You can also use a newer Android Studio version or even Canary builds but note that IDE interface and other generated code files might differ from the ones used throughout this book.
- Kotlin 1.6.10 or newer plugin installed in Android Studio.
- The Restaurants app code from the previous chapter.

The starting point for this chapter is represented by the Restaurants app that we developed in the previous chapter. If you haven't followed the implementation side by side, access the starting point for this chapter by navigating to the `Chapter_01` directory of this book's GitHub repository and importing the Android project entitled `chapter_1_restaurants_app`.

To access the solution code for this chapter, navigate to the `Chapter_02` folder:

`https://github.com/PacktPublishing/Kickstart-Modern-Android-Development-with-Jetpack-and-Kotlin/tree/main/Chapter_02/chapter_2_restaurants_app`.

The project coding solution for the Restaurants app that we will develop throughout this chapter can be found in the `chapter_2_restaurants_app` Android project folder, which you can import.

Understanding the Jetpack ViewModel

While developing Android applications, you must have heard of the term **ViewModel**. If you haven't heard of it, then don't worry – this section aims to clearly illustrate what this component represents and why we need it in the first place.

To summarize, this section will cover the following topics:

- What is a ViewModel?
- Why do you need ViewModels?
- Introducing Android Jetpack ViewModel
- Implementing your first ViewModel

Let's start with the first question: what is this `ViewModel` that we keep hearing about in Android?

What is a ViewModel?

Initially, the `ViewModel` was designed to allow developers to persist UI state across configuration changes. In time, the `ViewModel` became a way to also recover from edge cases such as system-initiated process death.

However, often, Android apps require you to write code that is responsible for getting the data from the server, transforming it, caching it, and then displaying it. To delegate some work, developers made use of this separate component, which should model the UI (also called the **View**) – the *ViewModel*.

So, we can perceive a `ViewModel` class as a component that manages and caches the UI's state:

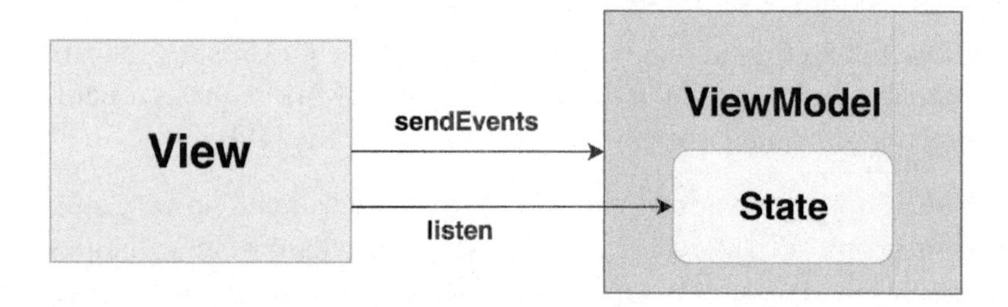

Figure 2.1 – ViewModel stores the state and receives interactions

As we can see, `ViewModel` not only handles the UI state and provides it to the UI but also receives user interaction events from `View` and updates the state accordingly.

In Android, the views are usually represented by **UI controllers** such as `Activity`, `Fragment`, or `Composable` since they are intended to display the UI data. These components are prone to being recreated when configuration changes occur, so `ViewModel` must find a way to cache and then restore the UI state – more on this in the next section, *Why do you need ViewModels?*.

> **Note**
>
> `ViewModel` oversees what data is sent back to the UI controllers and how the UI state reacts to user-generated events. That's why we can call `ViewModel` as a master of the UI controller – since it represents the authority that performs decision-making for UI-related events.

We can try to enumerate some core activities that a `ViewModel` should perform. `ViewModel` should be able to do the following:

- Hold, manage, and preserve the entire UI state.
- Request data or reload content from the server or other sources.
- Prepare data to be displayed by applying various transformations (such as map, sort, filter, and so on).
- Accept user interaction events and change the state based on those events.

Even though you now understand what a `ViewModel` is, you might be wondering, why do we need a separate class that holds the UI state or that prepares data to be displayed? Why can't we do that directly in the UI, in `Activity`, `Fragment`, or even inside the Composable? We'll address this question next.

Why do you need ViewModels?

Imagine that we put all the state-handling logic inside the UI classes. Following this approach, we may soon add other logic for handling network requests, caching, or any other implementation details – everything will be inside the UI layer.

Obviously, this is not a great approach. If we do that, we will end up with an `Activity`, `Fragment`, or `composable` function that has way too many responsibilities. In other words, our UI components will become bloated with so much code and so many responsibilities, thus making the entire project difficult to maintain, fix, or extend.

`ViewModel` is an architecture component that alleviates these potential issues. By adding `ViewModel` components to our projects, we are taking the first step toward a solid *architecture* since we can delegate the responsibilities of a UI controller to components such as `ViewModel`.

> **Note**
>
> `ViewModel` should not have a reference to a UI controller and should run independently of it. This reduces coupling between the UI layer and `ViewModel` and allows multiple UI components to reuse the same `ViewModel`.

Preventing multiple responsibilities in UI controllers is the cornerstone of a good system architecture since it promotes a very simple principle called **separation of concerns**. This principle states that every component/module within our app should have and handle one concern.

If, in our case, we add the entire application logic inside `Activity`, `Fragment`, or `composable`, these components will become huge pieces of code that violate the separation of concerns principle, simply because they know how to do everything: from displaying the UI to getting data and serving their UI states. To alleviate this, we can start implementing ViewModels.

Next, we'll see how ViewModels are designed in Android.

Introducing Android Jetpack ViewModel

Creating a `ViewModel` class to govern the UI state of a `View` is doable and straightforward. We can simply create a separate class and move the corresponding logic there.

However, as we mentioned previously, UI controllers have their own lifecycle: the `Activity` or `Fragment` objects have their own lifecycles, while composables have a composition cycle. That's why UI controllers are usually fragile and end up being recreated when different events occur, such as a configuration change or a process death. When this happens, any UI state information is lost.

Moreover, UI controllers usually need to make async calls (to obtain data from the server, for example) that have to be managed correctly. This means that when the system destroys UI controllers (such as by calling `onDestroy()` on an `Activity`), you need to manually interrupt or cancel any pending or ongoing work. Otherwise, your application can leak memory since your UI controller's memory reference cannot be freed up by the system. This is because it's still trying to finish some asynchronous work.

To preserve the UI state and to manage async work easier, our `ViewModel` class should be able to get around these *downsides*. But how?

Jetpack ViewModel comes to the rescue! Because the Android `ViewModel` is lifecycle aware, this means that it knows how to outlive events such as configuration changes, which are triggered by the user.

It does that by having a *lifecycle scope* tied to the lifecycle of its UI controller. Let's see how the lifecycle of an `Activity` and a `composable` are defined as opposed to the one of `ViewModel`:

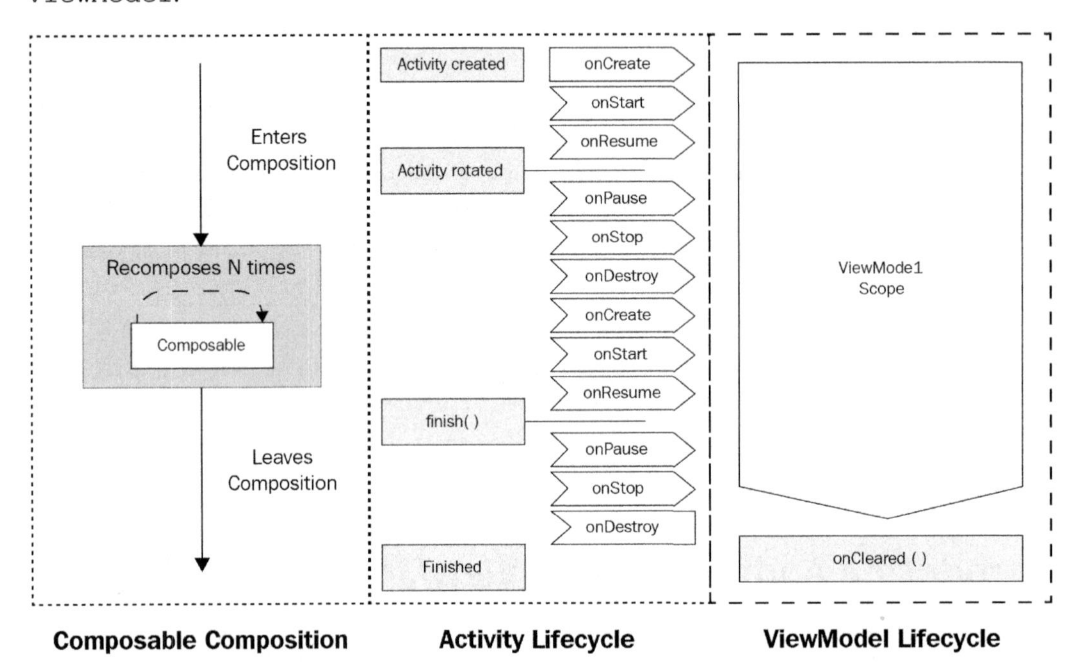

Figure 2.2 – The ViewModel's lifecycle in comparison to UI controller's lifecycle

> **Important note**
>
> When the `ViewModel` is used in Compose, it lives by default for as long as the parent `Fragment` or `Activity` does. For the `ViewModel` to live as long as a top-level composable (or screen composable) function does, as shown in the previous diagram, the composable must be used in conjunction with a navigation library. More granular composables can have smaller lifetimes. Don't worry, we will cover the aspect of scoping the lifetime of a ViewModel to the lifetime of a screen composable in *Chapter 5, Adding Navigation in Compose with Jetpack Navigation.*

When the UI is recreated or recomposed because of such events, the `ViewModel`'s lifecycle awareness allows it to outlive those events and avoid being destroyed, thus allowing the state to be preserved. When the entire lifecycle is finalized, the `ViewModel`'s `onCleared()` method is called to allow you to easily clean up any pending async work.

Yet one question arises: how can the Jetpack ViewModel do that?

By design, the `ViewModel` classes outlive specific instantiations of `LifecycleOwners`. In our case, UI controllers are `LifecycleOwners` since they have a designated lifecycle, and they can be `Activity` or `Fragment` objects.

To understand how `ViewModel` components are scoped to a specific `Lifecycle`, let's have a look at a traditional way of getting a reference to a `ViewModel` instance:

```
val vm = ViewModelProvider(this)[MyViewModel::class.java]
```

To obtain an instance of `MyViewModel`, we pass a `ViewModelStoreOwner` to the `ViewModelProvider` constructor. We used to get our `ViewModel` like this in `Activity` or `Fragment` classes, so this is a reference to the current `ViewModelStoreOwner`.

To control the lifetime of the instance of our `MyViewModel`, `ViewModelProvider` needs an instance of `ViewModelStoreOwner` because when it creates an instance of `MyViewModel`, it will link the lifetime of this instance to the lifetime of `ViewModelStoreOwner` – that is, of our `Activity`.

The `Activity` or `Fragment` components are `LifecycleOwners` with a lifecycle, meaning that every time you get a reference to your `ViewModel`, the object you receive is scoped to the `LifecycleOwner`'s lifecycle. This means that your `ViewModel` remains alive in memory until the `LifecycleOwner`'s lifecycle is finished.

> **Note**
>
> We will explain the inner workings of `ViewModel` components and how they are scoped to the lifecycle of a `LifecycleOwner` in more detail in *Chapter 12, Exploring the Jetpack Lifecycle Components.*

In Compose, the `ViewModel` objects are instantiated differently by using a special inline function called `viewModel()`, which abstracts all the boilerplate code that was needed previously.

> **Note**
>
> Optionally, if you need to pass parameters whose values are decided at runtime to your `ViewModel`, you can create and pass a `ViewModelFactory` instance to the `viewModel()` constructor. `ViewModelFactory` is a special class that allows you to control the way your `ViewModel` is instantiated.

Now that we have provided an overview of how the Android `ViewModel` works, let's create one!

Implementing your first ViewModel

It's time to create a `ViewModel` inside the Restaurants application that we created in the previous chapter. To do this, follow these steps:

1. First, create a new file by left-clicking the application package, selecting **New**, and then selecting **Kotlin Class/File**. Enter `RestaurantsViewModel` as the name and select **File** as the type. Inside the newly created file, add the following code:

```
import androidx.lifecycle.ViewModel

class RestaurantsViewModel(): ViewModel() {
    fun getRestaurants() = dummyRestaurants
}
```

   Our `RestaurantsViewModel` inherits from the `ViewModel` class (previously referenced as the Jetpack ViewModel) that's defined in `androidx.lifecycle.ViewModel`, so it becomes lifecycle aware of the components that instantiate it.

   Moreover, we've added the `getRestaurants()` method to our `ViewModel`, allowing it to be the provider of our `dummyRestaurants` list – a first and shy step toward giving it responsibility for governing the UI state.

   Next, it's time to prepare to instantiate our `RestaurantsViewModel`. In Compose, we can't use the previous syntax for instantiating `ViewModel` objects, so we will use a special and dedicated syntax instead.

2. To gain access to this special syntax, go to the `build.gradle` file in the app module and inside the `dependencies` block, add the ViewModel-Compose dependency:

```
dependencies {
        [...]
    debugImplementation "androidx.compose.ui:ui-
        tooling:$compose_version"
    implementation "androidx.lifecycle:lifecycle-
        viewmodel-compose:2.4.1"
}
```

   After updating the `build.gradle` file, make sure to sync your project with its Gradle files. You can do that by clicking on the **File** menu option and then by selecting **Sync Project with Gradle Files**.

3. Going back to the `RestaurantsScreen` file, we want to instantiate our `RestaurantsViewModel` inside our `RestaurantsScreen` composable function. We can do this using the `viewModel()` inline function syntax and specifying the type of `ViewModel` that we expect; that is, `RestaurantsViewModel`:

```
@Composable
fun RestaurantsScreen() {
    val viewModel: RestaurantsViewModel = viewModel()
    LazyColumn( ... ) {
        items(viewModel.getRestaurants()) { restaurant->
            RestaurantItem(restaurant)
        }
    }
}
```

Behind the scenes, the `viewModel()` function gets the default `ViewModelStoreOwner` for our `RestaurantsScreen()` composable. Since we haven't implemented a navigation library, the default `ViewModelStoreOwner` will be the calling parent of our composable – the `MainActivity` component. This means that for now, even though our `RestaurantsViewModel` has been instantiated inside a composable, it will live for as long as our `MainActivity` does.

In other words, our `RestaurantsViewModel` is scoped to the lifecycle of our `MainActivity`, thereby outliving our `RestaurantsScreens` composable, or any other composable we would pass to the `setContent()` method call from within `MainActivity`.

To make sure that our `ViewModel` lives for as long as the composable function that needs it does, we will implement a navigation library in *Chapter 5, Adding Navigation in Compose with Jetpack Navigation.*

We also made sure that we now get the restaurants to be displayed from our `RestaurantsViewModel` by calling `getRestaurants()` on the `viewModel` variable.

> **Note**
>
> From this point on, on certain older Compose versions, the Compose Preview functionality might not work as expected anymore. As the `RestaurantsScreen` composable now depends on a `RestaurantsViewModel` object, Compose can fail to infer the data that is passed to the previewed composable, thereby not being able to show us the content. That's why directly referencing a `ViewModel` inside your screen composable isn't a good practice. We will fix this in *Chapter 8, Getting Started with Clean Architecture in Android*. Alternatively, to see any changes in your code, you can just run the application on your emulator or physical device.

Getting back to our Restaurants app, we have successfully added a `ViewModel`, yet our `RestaurantsViewModel` doesn't handle any state for our UI. It only sends a hardcoded list of restaurants, which has no state. We envisioned that its purpose is to govern the state of the UI, so let's take a break from `ViewModel` and work on understanding state.

Defining and handling state with Compose

State and events are essential to any application since their existence implies that the UI can change over time as you interact with it.

In this section, we will cover the concept of state and events and then integrate them into our Restaurants app.

To summarize, this section will cover the following topics:

- Understanding state and events
- Adding state to our Restaurants app

Let's start by exploring the basic concepts of state and events in Android applications.

Understanding state and events

State represents a possible form of the UI at a certain point in time. This form can change or mutate. When the user interacts with the UI, an event is created that triggers a change in the state of the UI. So, an **event** is represented by different interactions that are initiated by the user that target the app and that consequently cause its state to update.

In simple terms, state changes over time because of events. The UI, on the other hand, should observe the changes within the state so that it can update accordingly:

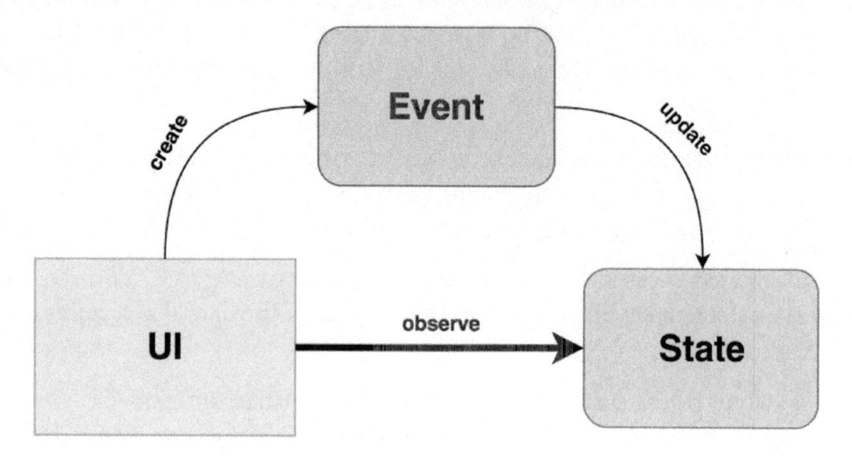

Figure 2.3 – UI update flow

In Compose, composable functions are, by default, stateless. That's why, when we tried to use a `TextField` composable in the previous chapter, it didn't present anything to the UI that we typed in with the keyboard. This happened because the composable had no state defined and it didn't get recomposed with the new values that had to be displayed!

This is why, in Compose, it's our job to define state objects for our composables. With the help of *state* objects, we make sure that recomposition is triggered every time a state object's value is changed.

To make such a `TextField` display the text that we are typing in, remember that we added a `textState` variable. Our `TextField` needed such a state object that holds a `String` value. This value represents the text that's written by us, which can change as we keep on typing:

```
@Composable
fun NameInput() {
    val textState: MutableState<String> =
        remember { mutableStateOf("") }
    TextField(...)
}
```

Let's have a closer look at how we defined a state object for our `TextField`:

- First, we created a variable to hold our state object and made sure that its value can change over time by making it `MutableState`. We did that by defining a `textState` variable that is of type `MutableState`, which, in turn, holds data of type `String`.

  At its core, `textState` is a `androidx.compose.runtime.State` object, yet since we want to be able to change its value over time, we directly used a `MutableState` that implements `State`.

- We instantiated `textState` with the `mutableStateOf("")` constructor to create a state object and passed an initial value of the data that it holds: an empty string.

  We also wrapped the `mutableStateOf("")` constructor inside a `remember { }` block. The **remember** block allows the state value to be preserved across recompositions. Every time the UI is recomposed because other composables received new data or maybe because of an animation, this state value will be the same because of the `remember` block.

Now that we've covered how state objects are defined, some questions remain: how can we alter the state to retrigger recomposition and how can we make sure our `TextField` accesses the updated values from our `textState`? Let's add these missing pieces:

```
@Composable
fun NameInput() {
    val textState = remember { mutableStateOf("") }
    TextField(
            value = textState.value,
            onValueChange = { newValue ->
                textState.value = newValue
            },
            label = { Text("Your name") })
}
```

Let's have a closer look at how we wired everything up inside `TextField`:

- For `TextField` to always have access to the latest value of the `textState` state object, we obtained the current state value with the `.value` accessor using `textState.value`. Then, we passed it to the `TextField`'s `value` parameter to display it.
- To change the state value, we made use of the `onValueChange` callback, which can be portrayed as an *event*. Inside this callback, we updated the `textState` state value by using the same `.value` accessor and set the new value that was received, called `newValue`. Since we updated a `State` object, the UI should recompose and our `TextField` should render the new input value from the keyboard. This will repeat for as long as we keep on writing.

Now that we have got the hang of defining and altering state in Compose, it's time to add such state functionality to our Restaurants app.

Adding state to our Restaurants app

Let's imagine that the user can scroll through the list of restaurants and then tap a particular one, thereby marking it as a favorite. For this to be more suggestive, we will add a heart icon for each restaurant. To do this, follow these steps:

1. Inside the `RestaurantsScreen.kt` file, add another composable inside `RestaurantItem` called `FavoriteIcon`. Then, pass a weight of `0.15f` to make it occupy 15% of the parent `Row`:

```
@Composable
fun RestaurantItem(item: Restaurant) {
    Card(...) {
        Row(...) {
            RestaurantIcon(..., Modifier.weight(0.15f))
            RestaurantDetails(..., Modifier.weight(0.7f))
            FavoriteIcon(Modifier.weight(0.15f))
        }
    }
}
```

   We have also made sure to decrease the weight of `RestaurantDetails` from 85% to 70%.

2. Still inside the `RestaurantsScreen.kt` file, define the missing `FavoriteIcon` composable, which receives an `imageVector` as a predefined icon with `Icons.Filled.FavoriteBorder`. Also, make it receive a `Modifier` object with `8.dp` of padding:

```
@Composable
private fun FavoriteIcon(modifier: Modifier) {
    Image(
        imageVector = Icons.Filled.FavoriteBorder,
        contentDescription = "Favorite restaurant icon",
        modifier = modifier.padding(8.dp))
}
```

3. If we try to refresh the preview or run the app, we can see several `RestaurantItem` composables similar to the following:

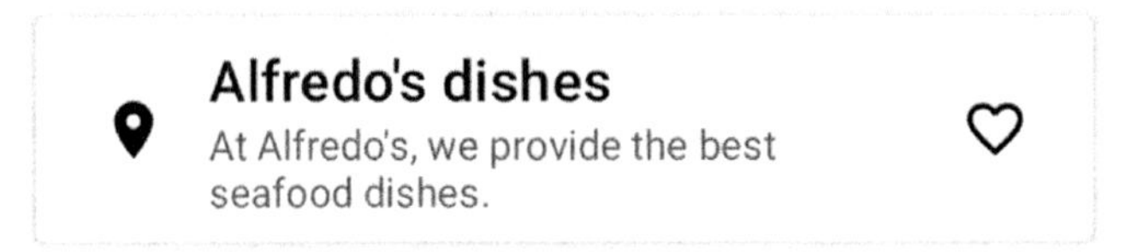

Figure 2.4 – The RestaurantItem composable with a favorite icon

Our `RestaurantItem` composable now has a favorite icon. However, when we click it, nothing happens. Clicking it should change the heart icon into a filled one, marking the restaurant as a favorite. To fix this, we must add a state that allows us to hold the favorite status of a restaurant.

4. Add state to the `FavoriteIcon` composable by adding the following code:

```
@Composable
private fun FavoriteIcon(modifier: Modifier) {
    val favoriteState = remember {
        mutableStateOf(false) }
    val icon = if (favoriteState.value)
        Icons.Filled.Favorite
    else
        Icons.Filled.FavoriteBorder
```

```
        Image(
            imageVector = icon,
            contentDescription = "Favorite restaurant icon",
            modifier = modifier
                .padding(8.dp)
                .clickable { favoriteState.value =
                        !favoriteState.value
                }
        )
    }
```

To hold the state of being a favorite or not and to trigger a change in this state value, we've done the following:

1. We added a `favoriteState` variable that holds a `MutableState` of type `Boolean` with an initial value of `false`. As usual, we wrap the `mutableStateOf` constructor inside a `remember` block to preserve the state's value across recompositions.
2. We defined an `icon` variable that can hold a value of `Icons.Filled.Favorite`, which means that the restaurant is your favorite, or a value of `Icons.Filled.FavoriteBorder`, which means that the restaurant is not your favorite.
3. We passed the value of `icon` value to the `imageVector` parameter of our `Image` composable.
4. We added a `clickable` modifier that's chained after the `padding` one. In this callback, we made sure to update `favoriteState` with the `.value` accessor by obtaining it and writing the previously negated value.

> **Note**
>
> When defining state objects in Compose, you can replace the assignment (=) operator with property delegation, which can be achieved with the `by` operator: `val favoriteState by remember { ... }`. By doing this, you will not need to use the `.value` accessor anymore as it is delegated.

When we're running or live previewing the application, we can see that upon clicking the empty heart icon of each restaurant, it becomes filled, marking the restaurant as a favorite:

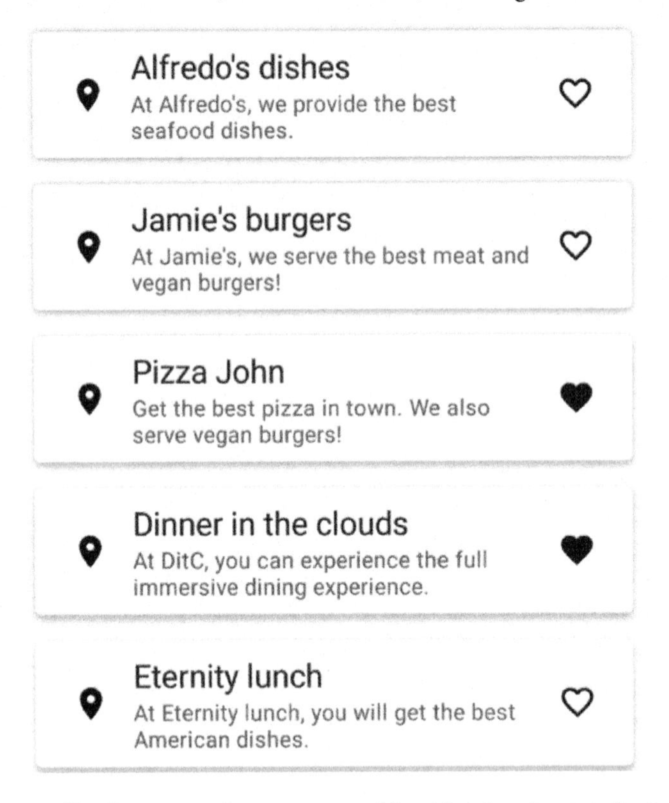

Figure 2.5 – The RestaurantsScreen composable with a favorite state for its items

Most of the time, keeping state and state handling logic inside composable functions is not recommended. Let's explore why this is not the best practice and how we can improve the way we manage state with the help of state hoisting.

Hoisting state in Compose

Composable functions are usually categorized in terms of state handling in two main categories:

- **Stateful**, which allows the composable to hold and manage its state. Stateful composables are those functions where the caller (or parent composable) doesn't need to manage the state. They model basic UI interactions such as animations or expanding content, and they are usually okay to be stateful and hold a `State` object.

- **Stateless**, which allows the composable to delegate the state management and to forward event callbacks to its parent composable. Composables that not only impact the UI as their state changes but are also of interest to the presentation or business logic are usually ok to be stateless. This way, the `ViewModel` component can be the only source of truth for their state to control and manage UI changes but also to avoid illegal states.

In our case, state changes when a restaurant is marked as a favorite or not. Since we want to control this interaction at the presentation level in the `ViewModel` class to keep track of which restaurants have been favorited, we need to move the state up from the `FavoriteIcon` composable.

The pattern of moving state up from a composable to its caller composable is called **state hoisting**. To achieve this, we must replace the `State` object with two parameters:

- One `value` parameter for the data that defines the current state
- A callback function that is triggered as an event when a new value is emitted

By receiving data as input and forwarding events to the parent composable, we make sure that our Compose UI obeys the previously introduced concept of the unidirectional flow of state and events. This concept defines how state values and events should only flow in one direction: the events upwards and the state downwards, and with state hoisting, we enforce just that.

The benefits of state hoisting are as follows:

- **Single source of truth for the state**: The state of our Compose UI can have a single source of truth: the parent composable or, even better, `ViewModel`. Composables can be decoupled from their state to avoid illegal states in your UI.
- **Reusability**: Since composables only render the data that's received as input, it's much easier to reuse them within other composables as you can simply pass different values.
- **Encapsulation limitation**: Only stateful composables can change their state internally. This means that you can limit the number of composables that handle their state, which could lead to illegal UI states.

Now that we've briefly covered what state hoisting is and why it is beneficial, it's time to hoist the state within our Restaurants application:

1. First, lift the state from the `FavoriteIcon` composable by removing the existing `favoriteState` and `icon` variables along with their instantiation logic from the top of the body of the function. At the same time, update the `FavoriteIcon` composable to accept an `icon` parameter for receiving input data and also an `onClick` event callback for forwarding upwards events:

```
@Composable
private fun FavoriteIcon(icon: ImageVector,
                         modifier: Modifier,
                         onClick: () -> Unit) {
    Image(
        imageVector = icon,
        contentDescription = "Favorite restaurant icon",
        modifier = [...]
            .clickable { onClick() })
}
```

   Additionally, we passed `icon` to the `imageVector` parameter of the `Image` composable and triggered the `onClick` callback function whenever the `clickable` event is triggered. By applying these changes, we lifted the state up and transformed `FavoriteIcon` from a stateful composable into a stateless one.

2. Now, move the `favoriteState` variable in the `RestaurantItem` parent composable of `FavoriteIcon`. The `RestaurantItem` composable provides the state to `FavoriteIcon` and is also in charge of updating its state over time:

```
@Composable
fun RestaurantItem(item: Restaurant) {
    val favoriteState = remember {
        mutableStateOf(false) }
    val icon = if (favoriteState.value)
        Icons.Filled.Favorite
    else
        Icons.Filled.FavoriteBorder
```

```
        Card(...) {
            Row(...) {
                [...]
                FavoriteIcon(icon, Modifier.weight(0.15f)) {
                    favoriteState.value =
                        !favoriteState.value
                }
            }
        }
    }
```

The corresponding `icon` for each state is now passed to `FavoriteIcon`. Additionally, `RestaurantItem` is now listening for `onClick` events in the trailing lambda block, where it mutates the `favoriteState` object, triggering recomposition upon every click.

Yet, looking at `FavoriteIcon` and `RestaurantIcon`, we can see many similarities. Both are stateless composables that receive an `ImageVector` as a parameter. Since they are stateless and perform similar functions, let's reuse one of them and delete the other.

3. Inside `RestaurantIcon`, add a similar `onClick` function parameter (just like `FavoriteIcon` has) and bind it to the `clickable` modifier's callback:

```
@Composable
private fun RestaurantIcon(icon: ImageVector, modifier:
Modifier, onClick: () -> Unit = { }) {
    Image([...],
        modifier = modifier
            .padding(8.dp)
            .clickable { onClick() }
    )
}
```

Since we don't want to execute anything on click events for the restaurant profile icon, we provided a default empty function (`{ }`) value to the `onClick` parameter.

Once you've done this, you can delete the `FavoriteIcon` composable since we won't need it anymore.

4. Inside the `RestaurantItem` composable, replace `FavoriteIcon` with `RestaurantIcon`:

```
@Composable
fun RestaurantItem(item: Restaurant) {
    val favoriteState = ...
    Card(...) {
        Row(...) {
            RestaurantIcon(…)
            RestaurantDetails(...)
            RestaurantIcon(icon, Modifier.weight(0.15f)) {
                favoriteState.value = !favoriteState.value
            }
        }
    }
}
```

You have now hoisted the state from `RestaurantIcon` to the `RestaurantItem` composable.

Let's keep on hoisting the state even further uphill, into the `RestaurantsScreen` composable. However, we cannot keep individual `State` objects for each `RestaurantItem` inside this composable, so we will have to change the `State` object to hold a list of `Restaurant` objects, each having a separate `isFavorite` value.

5. Inside the `Restaurant.kt` file, add another property for `Restaurant` called `isFavorite`. It should have a default value of `false` since, by default, restaurants are not marked as favorites when the application starts:

```
data class Restaurant(val id: Int,
                      val title: String,
                      val description: String,
                      var isFavorite: Boolean = false)
val dummyRestaurants = listOf(…)
```

6. Going back inside the `RestaurantsScreen.kt` file, hoist the state up again, this time from `RestaurantItem`, by adding an `onClick` function parameter that's triggered inside the `RestaurantIcon`'s callback function parameter. We won't add a new argument for the input data since we already have the `item` argument of type `Restaurant`, and you can also safely remove the `favoriteState` variable since we won't be needing it anymore:

```
@Composable
fun RestaurantItem(item: Restaurant,
                   onClick: (id: Int) -> Unit) {
    val icon = if (item.isFavorite)
        Icons.Filled.Favorite
    else
        Icons.Filled.FavoriteBorder
    Card(...) {
        Row(...) {
            ...
            RestaurantIcon(...)
            RestaurantDetails(...)
            RestaurantIcon(...) {
                onClick(item.id)
            }
        }
    }
}
```

This time, the `item` parameter will be our `Restaurant` object. `Restaurant` now holds an `isFavorite: Boolean` property that states whether the restaurant is favorited or not. That's why we set the correct value for the `icon` variable based on the item's field by checking the `item.isFavorite` value.

Now, `RestaurantItem` is a stateless composable, so it's time to add a `State` object to its parent.

7. Inside `RestaurantsScreen`, add a `state` variable that will hold our list of restaurants. Its type will be `MutableState<List<Restaurant>>` and we will set the restaurants from `viewModel` as it initial value, finally passing the state's `value` to the `items` constructor of `LazyColumn`:

```
@Composable
fun RestaurantsScreen() {
   val viewModel: RestaurantsViewModel = viewModel()
   val state: MutableState<List<Restaurant>> =
      remember {
         mutableStateOf(viewModel.getRestaurants())
      }
   LazyColumn(...) {
    items(state.value) { restaurant ->
       RestaurantItem(restaurant) { id ->
          val restaurants = state.value.toMutableList()
          val itemIndex =
             restaurants.indexOfFirst { it.id == id }
          val item = restaurants[itemIndex]
          restaurants[itemIndex] =
             item.copy(isFavorite = !item.isFavorite)
          state.value = restaurants
        }
     }
   }
}
```

Inside `RestaurantItem`'s `onClick` trailing lambda block, we must toggle the favorite status of the corresponding restaurant and update the state. Because of this, we did the following:

1. We obtained the current list of restaurants by calling `state.value` and converting it into a mutable list so that we could replace the item whose `isFavorite` field's value should be updated.
2. We obtained the index of the item whose `isFavorite` field should be updated via the `indexOfFirst` function, where we matched the `id` property of the `Restaurant` objects.

3. Having found `itemIndex`, we obtained the `item` object of type `Restaurant` and applied the `copy()` constructor, where we negated the `isFavorite` field. The resulting value replaced the existing `item` at `itemIndex`.
4. Finally, we passed the updated `restaurants` list back to the `state` object with the `.value` accessor.

> **Note**
> For Compose to observe changes within a list of objects of type `T` called `List<T>,` where `T` is a data class, you must update the memory reference of the updated item. You can do that by calling the `copy()` constructor of `T` so that when the updated list is passed back to your `State` object, Compose triggers a recomposition. Alternatively, you can use `mutableStateListOf<Restaurant>()` to have easier recomposition events triggered.

If we try to run the app, we should notice that the functionality is the same, yet the state was hoisted and that we can now reuse composables such as `RestaurantItem` or `RestaurantIcon` much easier.

But what happens if we toggle a couple of restaurants that are favorites and then rotate the device, thereby changing the screen orientation?

Even though we used the `remember` block to preserve the state across recompositions, our selections were lost, and all the restaurants are marked as not favorites again. This is because the `MainActivity` host of our `RestaurantsScreen` composable has been recreated, so any state was also lost when the configuration change occurred.

To fix this, we can do the following:

- Replace the `remember` block with `rememberSaveable`. This will allow the state to be automatically saved across configuration changes of the host `Activity`.
- Hoist the state to `ViewModel`. We know that `RestaurantsViewModel` is not scoped to the lifecycle of our `RestaurantsScreen` yet since no navigation library was used, so this means it's scoped to `MainActivity`, which allows it to survive configuration changes.

You can try replacing the `remember` block with `rememberSaveable` and then rotate the screen to see that the state is now preserved across configuration changes. However, we want to take the high road and make sure `ViewModel` is the only source of truth for our state. Let's get started:

1. To lift the state to `ViewModel`, we must move the `State` object from the `RestaurantsScreen` composable to the `RestaurantsViewModel` and we must also create a new method called `toggleFavorite` that will allow the `RestaurantsViewModel` to mutate the value of the `state` variable every time we try to toggle the favorite status of a restaurant:

```
class RestaurantsViewModel() : ViewModel() {
    val state = mutableStateOf(dummyRestaurants)

     fun toggleFavorite(id: Int) {
         val restaurants = state.value.toMutableList()
         val itemIndex =
             restaurants.indexOfFirst { it.id == id }
         val item = restaurants[itemIndex]
         restaurants[itemIndex] =
             item.copy(isFavorite = !item.isFavorite)
         state.value = restaurants
     }
}
```

The new method called `toggleFavorite` accepts the `id` property of the targeted restaurant. Inside this method, we moved the code from the `RestaurantItem`'s `onClick` trailing lambda block, where we toggle the favorite status of the corresponding item and update its state.

By this time, you can safely remove the `getRestaurants()` method from the `RestaurantsViewModel` class since we won't be needing it anymore.

> **Note**
>
> The `State` object that's contained within the `ViewModel` should not be publicly available for other classes to modify it, since we want it to be encapsulated and allow only the `ViewModel` to update it. We will fix this in *Chapter 7, Introducing Presentation Patterns in Android*.

2. Inside the `RestaurantsScreen` composable, remove the `state` variable and pass the restaurants from `RestaurantsViewModel` by accessing the value of its state through the `.value` accessor with `viewModel.state.value`:

```
fun RestaurantsScreen() {
    val viewModel: RestaurantsViewModel = viewModel()
    LazyColumn(...) {
        items(viewModel.state.value) { restaurant ->
            RestaurantItem(restaurant) { id ->
                viewModel.toggleFavorite(id)
            }
        }
    }
}
```

We also removed the old code from the `RestaurantItem`'s `onClick` trailing lambda block and replaced it with a call to our `ViewModel`'s `toggleFavorite` method.

If you run the application, the UI should perform as expected, so you should be able to toggle any restaurants as favorite and your selections should be saved upon events like orientation change.

The only difference is that now, `RestaurantsViewModel` is the only source of truth for the state of `RestaurantsScreen` and we no longer need to hold or save the UI state inside the composables themselves.

We now know how to hoist the state up into the `ViewModel`. Now, let's cover a very important scenario in the world of Android that's related to process death.

Recovering from system-initiated process death

We've already learned how, whenever a configuration change occurs, our `Activity` is recreated, which can cause our UI to lose its state. To bypass this issue and to preserve the UI's state, we ended up implementing a `ViewModel` component and hoisted the UI state there.

But what would happen in the case of a system-initiated process death?

A **system-initiated process death** happens when the user places our application in the background and decides to use other apps for a while – in the meantime, though, the system decides to kill our app's process to free up system resources, which initiates process death.

Let's try to simulate such an event and see what happens:

1. Start the Restaurants app using the IDE's **Run** button and mark some restaurants as favorites:

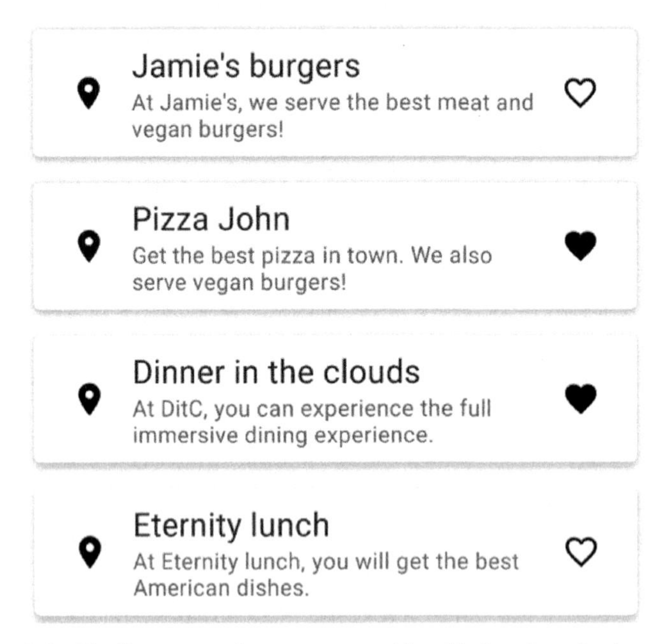

Figure 2.6 – The RestaurantsScreen composable with favorite selections made

2. Place the app in the background by pressing the **Home** button on the device/emulator.

3. In Android Studio, select the **Logcat** window and then press the red square button on the left-hand side to terminate the application:

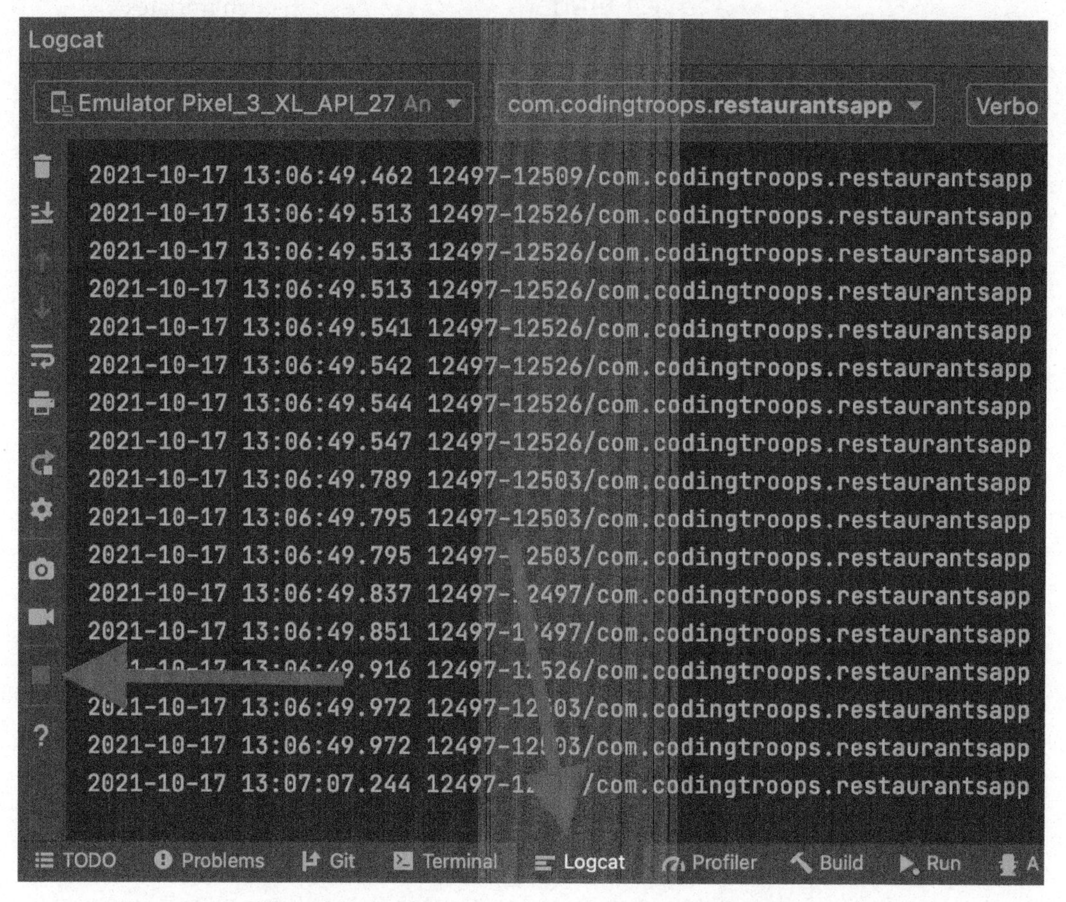

Figure 2.7 – Killing the process in Logcat to simulate system-initiated process death

4. Relaunch the application from the application drawer:

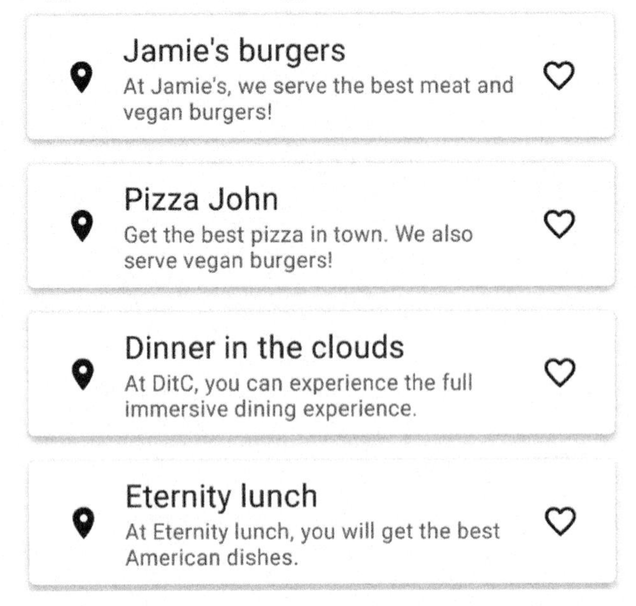

Figure 2.8 – The RestaurantsScreen composable with favorite selections lost

We have now simulated a situation where the system would kill our process. When we return to the app, we can see that our selections are now gone and that the restaurants that were favorited are now in their default states.

To restore state upon system-initiated process death, we used to use the **Saved State module**, which allowed us to save state-related details in the `onSaveInstanceState()` callback of our activity.

Similarly, every `ViewModel` that uses the default `ViewModelFactory` (like we did with the `viewModel()` inline syntax previously) can access a `SavedStateHandle` object through its constructor. If you use a custom `ViewModelFactory`, make sure that it extends `AbstractSavedStateViewModelFactory`.

The `SavedStateHandle` object is a key-value map that allows you to save and then restore objects that are crucial to your state. This map survives the event of process death when this event is initiated by the system, which allows you to retrieve and restore your saved objects.

> **Note**
>
> When we're saving state-related data, it's crucial to save lightweight objects that define the state and not the entire data that is described on the screen. For large data, we should use local persistence.

Let's try to do this in our application by saving a list of `id` values of the restaurants that were toggled as favorites in `SavedStateHandle`. Saving the `id` values is better than saving the entire list of restaurants since a list of `Int` values is lightweight. And since we can always get the restaurant list back at runtime, the only thing that's missing is to remember which of them were favorited.

> **Note**
>
> Usually, `SavedStateHandle` is used for saving transient data like sorting or filtering selections performed by the user, or other selections that you need to restore upon system-initiated process death. In our case though, favorited restaurants should be restored not only upon system-initiated process death but also upon a simple application restart. That's why we will save these selections as part of the domain data of the app inside a local database later in *Chapter 6, Adding Offline Capabilities with Jetpack Room.*

Let's use a `SavedStateHandle` object to recover from system-initiated process death:

1. Add the `SavedStateHandle` parameter to your `RestaurantsViewModel`:

```
class RestaurantsViewModel(
    private val stateHandle: SavedStateHandle) :
        ViewModel() {
    ...
}
```

2. Call a `storeSelection` method whenever we toggle the favorite status of a restaurant inside the `toggleFavorite` method and pass the respective restaurant:

```
class RestaurantsViewModel(…) {
    fun toggleFavorite(id: Int) {
        …
        restaurants[itemIndex] = item.copy(isFavorite =
            !item.isFavorite)
        storeSelection(restaurants[itemIndex])
        state.value = restaurants
    }
    ...
}
```

This code won't compile though because we haven't yet defined the `storeSelection` method. Let's do that up next.

3. Inside `RestaurantsViewModel`, create a new `storeSelection` method that receives a `Restaurant` object whose `isFavorite` property has just been altered, and saves that selection inside the `SavedStateHandle` object provided by the `RestaurantsViewModel` class:

```
private fun storeSelection(item: Restaurant) {
    val savedToggled = stateHandle
        .get<List<Int>?>(FAVORITES)
        .orEmpty().toMutableList()
    if (item.isFavorite) savedToggled.add(item.id)
    else savedToggled.remove(item.id)
    stateHandle[FAVORITES] = savedToggled
}
companion object {
   const val FAVORITES = "favorites"
}
```

This new method will try to save the `id` value of a restaurant in our `stateHandle` object every time we toggle its favorite status. It does this as follows:

I. It obtains a list containing the IDs of the previously favorited restaurants from `stateHandle` by accessing the `FAVORITES` key inside the map. It stores the result in a `savedToggle` mutable list. If no restaurants were favorited, the list will be empty.

II. If this restaurant was marked as favorite, it adds the ID of the restaurant to the `savedToggle` list. Otherwise, it removes it.

III. Saves the updated list of favorited restaurants with the `FAVORITES` key inside the `stateHandle` map.

We have also added a `companion object` construct to the `RestaurantsViewModel` class as a static extension object. We used this `companion object` to define a constant value for the key used to save the restaurant's selection inside our `stateHandle` map.

Now, we've made sure to cache the selections of favorite restaurants before process death, so our next step is to find a way to restore these selections after the app recovers from a system-initiated process death event.

4. Call a `restoreSelections()` extension method on the `dummyRestaurants` list that we are passing as an initial value to our `state` object. This call should restore the UI selections:

```
class RestaurantsViewModel(
    private val stateHandle: SavedStateHandle):
        ViewModel() {
    val state = mutableStateOf(
      dummyRestaurants.restoreSelections()
    )
     ...
}
```

   This code won't compile though because we haven't yet defined the `restoreSelections` method. Let's do that up next.

5. Inside `RestaurantsViewModel`, define the `restoreSelections` extension function that will allow us to retrieve the restaurants that were favorited upon process death:

```
private fun List<Restaurant>.restoreSelections():
        List<Restaurant> {
    stateHandle.get<List<Int>?>(FAVORITES)?.let {
            selectedIds ->
        val restaurantsMap = this.associateBy { it.id }
        selectedIds.forEach { id ->
            restaurantsMap[id]?.isFavorite = true
        }
        return restaurantsMap.values.toList()
    }
    return this
}
```

This extension function will allow us to mark those restaurants that were marked by the user previously as favorites upon system-initiated process death. The `restoreSelections` extension function achieves that in the following way:

I. First, by obtaining the list with the unique identifiers of the previously favorited restaurants from `stateHandle` by accessing the `FAVORITES` key inside the map. If the list is not `null`, this means that a process death occurred, and it references the list as `selectedIds`; otherwise, it will return the list without any modifications.

II. Then, by creating a map from the input list of restaurants with the key being the `id` value of the restaurant and the value the `Restaurant` object itself.

III. By iterating over the unique identifiers of the favorited restaurants and for each of them, by trying to access the respective restaurant from our new list and sets its `isFavorite` value to `true`.

IV. By returning the modified restaurants list from `restaurantMap`. This list should now contain the restored `isFavorite` values from before the death process occurred.

6. Finally, build the app and then repeat *steps 1*, *2*, *3*, and *4* from when we simulated a system-initiated process death.

   The application should now correctly display the UI state with the previously favorited restaurants from before the system-initiated process death.

With that, we've made sure that our application not only stores the UI state at the `ViewModel` level but that it also can recover from extraordinary events, such as system-initiated process death.

Summary

In this chapter, we learned what a `ViewModel` class is, we explored the concepts that define it, and we learned how to instantiate one. We tackled why a `ViewModel` is useful as a single source of truth for the UI's *state*: to avoid illegal and undesired states.

For that to make sense, we explored how a UI is defined by its state and how to define such a state in Compose. We then understood what *state hoisting* is and how to separate widgets between *stateless* and *stateful* composables.

Finally, we put all these new concepts into practice by defining state in our Restaurants app, hoisting it, and then lifting it even higher into the newly created `ViewModel`.

Finally, we learned how system-initiated process death occurs and how to allow the app to recover by restoring the previous state with the help of `SavedStateHandle`.

In the next chapter, we will add real data to our Restaurants app by connecting it to our database using Retrofit.

Further reading

Working with ViewModels and handling state changes in Compose represent two essential topics for reliable projects. Let's see what other subjects revolve around them.

Exploring ViewModel with runtime-provided arguments

In most cases, you can declare and provide dependencies to your `ViewModel` inside the constructor, at compile time. In some cases, though, you might need to initialize a `ViewModel` instance with a parameter that's only known at runtime.

For example, when we're adding a composable screen that displays the details of a restaurant, instead of sending the ID of the target restaurant from the composable to `ViewModel` through a function call, we can provide it directly to the `ViewModel` constructor through **ViewModelFactory**.

To explore the process of building a `ViewModelFactory`, check out the following Codelab: `https://developer.android.com/codelabs/kotlin-android-training-view-model#7`.

Exploring ViewModel for Kotlin Multiplatform projects

While this chapter covered the Jetpack ViewModel for Compose in pure Android apps, if you're aiming to build cross-platform projects using **Kotlin Multiplatform** (**KMP**) or **Kotlin Multiplatform Mobile** (**KMM**), the Jetpack ViewModel might not be your best option.

When we're building cross-platform projects, we should try to avoid platform-specific dependencies. The Jetpack ViewModel is suited for Android and therefore is an Android dependency, so we might need to build or define a ViewModel.

To learn more about KMM and platform-agnostic ViewModels, check out the following GitHub example: `https://github.com/dbaroncelli/D-KMP-sample`.

Understanding how to minimize the number of recompositions

In this chapter, we learned how to trigger recompositions by using `State` objects. While in Compose, recompositions happen often, we haven't had a chance to optimize the performance of our Compose-based screens.

We can reduce the number of recompositions by ensuring that the input of the composables is deeply stable. To learn more about how to achieve this, go to `https://developer.android.com/jetpack/compose/lifecycle?hl=bn-IN&skip_cache=true#skipping`.

3

Displaying Data from REST APIs with Retrofit

In this chapter, we'll be taking a break from the Jetpack libraries and focusing on adding real data within our Restaurants application by using a very popular networking library on Android called **Retrofit**.

Retrofit is an HTTP client library that lets you create an HTTP client declaratively and abstracts most of the underlying complexity associated with handling network requests and responses. This library allows us to connect to a real web API and retrieve real data within our app.

In the *Understanding how apps communicate with remote servers* section, we will focus on exploring how mobile applications retrieve and send data to remote web APIs. In the *Creating and populating your database with Firebase* section, we will create a database for our Restaurants application with the help of Firebase and fill it with JSON content.

In the *Exploring Retrofit as an HTTP networking client for Android* section, we will learn what Retrofit is, and how it can help us create network requests within our Restaurants app.

Lastly, in the *Improving the way our app handles network requests* section, we will tackle some common issues that occur when Android applications create async work to retrieve data from web APIs. We will identify those issues and fix them.

To summarize, in this chapter, we're going to cover the following main topics:

- Understanding how apps communicate with remote servers
- Creating and populating your database with Firebase
- Exploring Retrofit as an HTTP networking client for Android
- Improving the way our app handles network requests

Before jumping in, let's set up the technical requirements for this chapter.

Technical requirements

Building Compose-based Android projects with Retrofit usually requires just your day-to-day tools. However, to follow along smoothly, make sure you have the following:

- The Arctic Fox 2020.3.1 version of Android Studio. You can also use a newer Android Studio version or even Canary builds but note that IDE interface and other generated code files might differ from the ones used throughout this book.
- Kotlin 1.6.10 or newer installed in Android Studio.
- The Restaurants app code from the previous chapter.
- A Google account to create a Firebase project.

The starting point for this chapter is the Restaurants application that we developed in the previous chapter. If you haven't followed the coding steps from the previous chapter, access the starting point for this chapter by navigating to the `Chapter_02` directory of this book's GitHub repository and importing the Android project entitled `chapter_2_restaurants_app`.

To access the solution code for this chapter, navigate to the `Chapter_03` directory:

`https://github.com/PacktPublishing/Kickstart-Modern-Android-Development-with-Jetpack-and-Kotlin/tree/main/Chapter_03`.

Understanding how apps communicate with remote servers

Modern applications need to show real content that can change over time and need to avoid hardcoding data, as we did in the previous chapters. Let's briefly cover how they do that.

Most network-connected apps use the HTTP protocol to send or receive data in the format of JSON from REST web services through a REST API.

That's a lot of words we've just thrown at you, so let's break them down:

- **Hypertext Transfer Protocol** (**HTTP**) is a protocol for asynchronously fetching various resources from web servers. In our case, the resources are the data that our application needs to display.
- **JavaScript Object Notation** (**JSON**) is the data format of the content that's transferred in HTTP requests. It's structured, lightweight, and human-readable as it consists of key-value pairs that are easy to parse and commonly used as a suitable format for data exchange between apps and web servers. In our app, we will receive the data from the web server in such JSON format.
- **REST web services** are those sources that contain the requested data and that conform to the **representational state transfer** (**REST**) architecture. REST means that the web server uses the HTTP protocol to communicate resources and that its resources are manipulated with the common HTTP methods: `GET`, `PUT`, `POST`, `DELETE`, and so on.
- A **REST API** is an **application programming interface** (**API**) that conforms to the constraints of the REST architecture and allows you to interact with REST web services. The REST API is the contract and the entry point that's used by apps to obtain or send data to and from the backend.

Let's try to visualize the relationship between these entities:

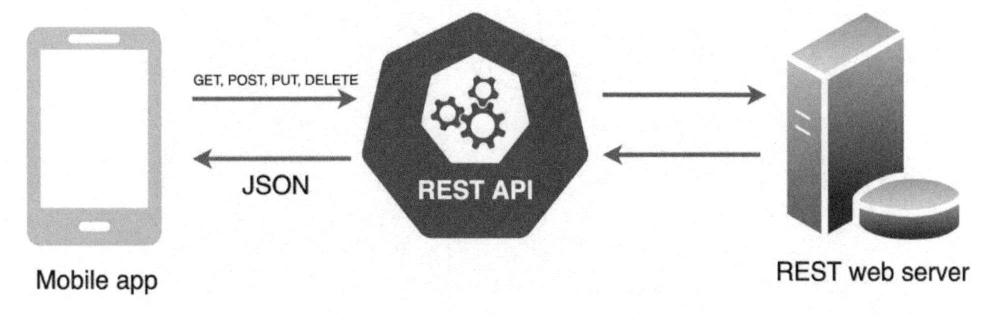

Figure 3.1 – Overview of HTTP communication between apps and web servers

We want to implement something similar for our Restaurants application. For this to work, we will need a REST server. For the sake of simplicity, we will use the Firebase Realtime Database and create a database.

Creating and populating your database with Firebase

So far, we've only used hardcoded data as the source of content for our Restaurants app. Since almost every real application uses dynamic data that comes from a backend server through a REST API, it's time to step up our game and create a database that simulates such a remote API.

We can do this for free with the help of Firebase. Firebase is backed by Google and represents a **Backend-as-a-Service** (**BaaS**), which allows us to build a database very easily. We will use the Realtime Database service from Firebase without using the Firebase Android SDK. Even though such a database is not a proper REST web service, we can use its database URL as a REST endpoint and pretend that that is our REST interface, therefore simulating a real backend.

> **Note**
> As we mentioned in the *Technical requirements* section, make sure that you have an existing Google account or that you create one beforehand.

Let's start creating a database:

1. Navigate to the Firebase console and log into your Google account by going to `https://console.firebase.google.com/`.
2. Create a new Firebase project:

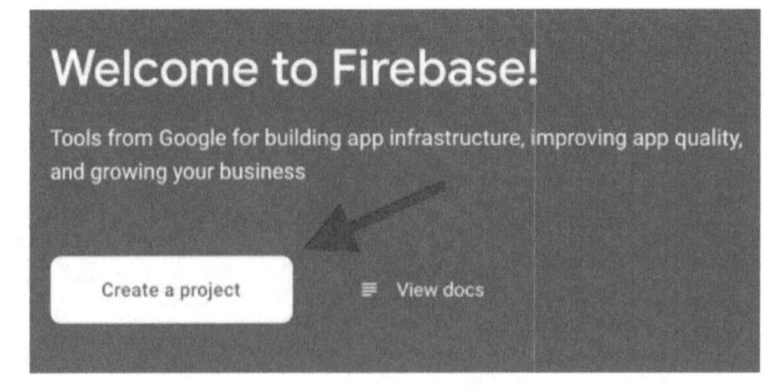

Figure 3.2 – Creating a new Firebase project

3. Input the name of your project (it should be about restaurants!) and press **Continue**.
4. Optionally, in the next dialog, you can opt out from Google Analytics since we won't be using the Firebase SDK. Press **Continue** again. At this point, the project should be created.
5. From the left menu, expand the **Build** tab, search for **Realtime Database**, and then select it:

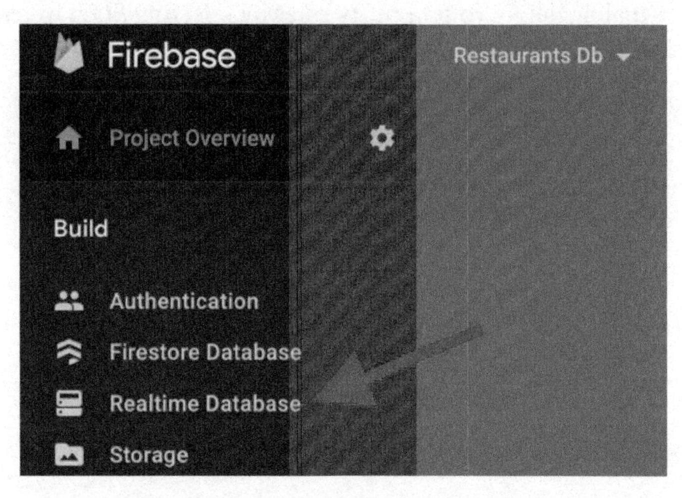

Figure 3.3 – Accessing Realtime Database

6. On the newly displayed page, create a new database by clicking **Create Database**.
7. In the **Set up database** dialog, select a location for your database and then click **Next**:

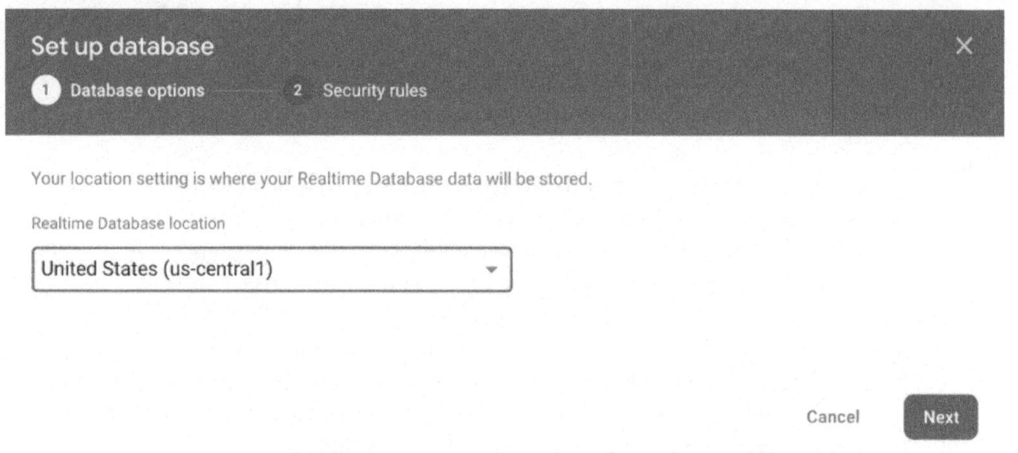

Figure 3.4 – Setting up a Realtime Database

> **Note**
>
> If later on any network calls to your Firebase Database fail for no apparent reason, you might find yourself in a Firebase restricted location – as I am writing this chapter, because of the current situation caused by the eastern war, all internet providers from Romania are restricted and any network calls to Firebase Database are failing. If this happens to you, try selecting a different location for your Realtime Database instance.

8. In the same dialog, define your security rules by selecting **Start in test mode** and then clicking **Enable**.

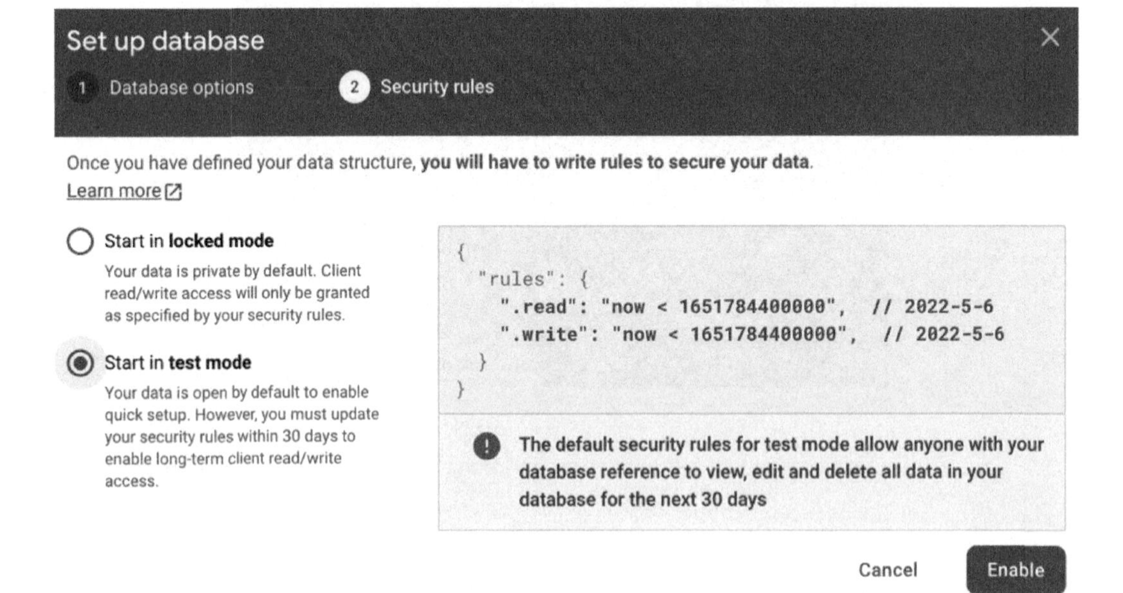

Figure 3.5 – Setting up the security rules of your database

> **Important Note**
>
> The default security rules for test mode allow anyone to view or modify the content within your database for the next 30 days since creation. After these 30 days, if you want to keep using the database in test mode, you will need to update the security rules by changing the timestamp values for the `".read"` and the `".write"` fields with greater timestamp values. To skip this, we will just set the `".read"` and the `".write"` fields to `true` in the next steps. However, Firebase might still restrict your access if you leave the database open for access without any rules indefinitely – that's why I recommend you visit the Firebase console and check the security rules for your database often to make sure that access was not revoked.

At this point, you should be redirected to your database's main page in the **Data** tab:

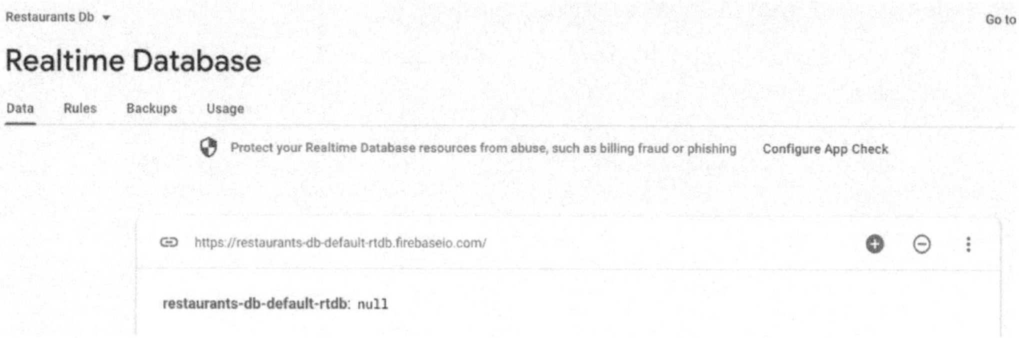

Figure 3.6 – Observing the Realtime Database main page

You will now notice your URL for this database: `https://restaurants-db-default-rtdb.firebaseio.com/`.

Your URL should be similar but may differ, depending on the name you have chosen for your database.

Note that the database seems to be empty; we only have an empty root node being called after our database: `restaurants-db-default-rtdb`. It's time to add data to our database.

9. Access the solution code for this chapter by navigating to the `Chapter_03` directory of this book's GitHub repository. Then, select the `restaurants.json` file. You can also access it by following this link: `https://github.com/PacktPublishing/Kickstart-Modern-Android-Development-with-Jetpack-and-Kotlin/blob/main/Chapter_03/restaurants.json`.

   From here, download the `restaurants.json` file as we will need it shortly. To do that, press on the **Raw** button provided by the Github website and then right click the document that has been opened and download the JSON file by selecting **Saves As**.

10. Go back to the Firebase console, press on the three-dots menu to the right of the database URL, and select **Import JSON**:

Figure 3.7 – Importing JSON content into Realtime Database

Make sure that you select the `restaurants.json` file that you've previously downloaded from the book's GitHub repository.

11. Wait for the page to refresh and check out the content that is populated in the database:

Figure 3.8 – Observing the content's structure in our database

Here, we can see that our database contains a list of **restaurants**. Each restaurant has attributes that are similar to the ones in our `Restaurant` class: an ID, title, and description. The restaurants in our database also contain other fields that we will not need right now, so let's ignore them.

> **Note**
>
> If you compare the structure of the content in our database with the one from the JSON file we've uploaded, we can see that it is very similar: we have a `restaurants` node that contains an array of objects, each containing consistent key-value pairs. The only exception is the presence of the indexes (0, 1, 2, and so on) for each restaurant, which were automatically created by Firebase. We should ignore these as they won't affect us.

Now, even though we set the security rules to **Test Mode** previously, let's revisit them.

12. Move away from the **Data** tab and select the **Rules** tab. Here, to make sure that we can always read data from this database, change the `".read"` key's value to `"true"`:

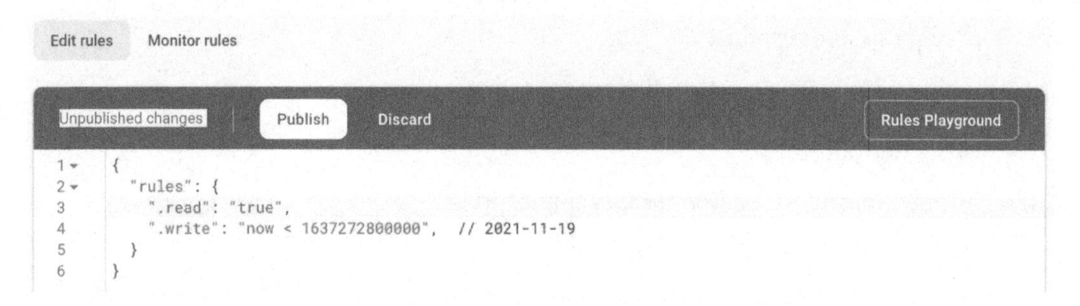

Figure 3.9 – Updating security rules in Realtime Database

13. Press **Publish** to save the changes.

> **Note**
>
> The security rules that we've set should not be used in a production application. We are hardcoding our security rules to `true` since we are testing and not publishing anything to production.

Now, we can access the database URL as a simple REST endpoint, simulating a real REST server that we can connect to. To experiment, copy the URL of your newly created database, append `restaurants.json`, and paste it into your browser.

Accessing this URL should return the JSON response of our restaurants, whose structure we will cover shortly. Until then, we need to instruct our application to create HTTP requests to obtain that data from our newly created database. So, let's do that next.

Exploring Retrofit as an HTTP networking client for Android

For the application to obtain data from our database, we need to implement an HTTP client that will send network requests to the REST API of the database.

Instead of working with the HTTP library provided by default by Android, we will use the **Retrofit** HTTP client library, which lets you create an HTTP client that is very easy to work with.

If you plan to develop an HTTP client that interfaces with a REST API, you will have to take care of a lot of things – from making connections, retrying failed requests, or caching to response parsing and error handling. Retrofit saves you development time and potential headaches as it abstracts most of the underlying complexity associated with handling network requests and responses.

In this section, we will cover the following topics:

- Using Retrofit
- Adding Retrofit to the Restaurants application
- Mapping JSON to model classes
- Executing GET requests to the Firebase REST API

Let's start with some basics about Retrofit!

Using Retrofit

Retrofit makes networking simple in Android apps. It allows us to consume web services easily, create network requests, and receive responses while reducing the boilerplate code that's usually associated with their implementation.

> **Note**
>
> Retrofit also allows you to easily add custom headers and request types, file uploads, mocking responses, and more.

To execute network requests with Retrofit, we need the following three components:

- An interface that defines the HTTP operations that need to be performed. Such an interface can specify request types such as `GET`, `PUT`, `POST`, `DELETE`, and so on.
- A `Retrofit.Builder` instance that creates a concrete implementation of the interface we defined previously. The Builder API allows us to define networking parameters such as the HTTP client type, the URL endpoint for the HTTP operations, the converter to deserialize the JSON responses, and so on.
- Model classes that allow Retrofit to know how to map the deserialized JSON objects to regular data classes.

Enough with the theory – let's try to implement Retrofit and use the components we introduced previously in our Restaurants application.

Adding Retrofit to the Restaurants application

We want to connect our Restaurants application to the newly created Firebase database and send HTTP network requests to it. More specifically, when the Restaurants application is launched and the `RestaurantsScreen` composable is composed, we want to get the list of restaurants at runtime and not depend on hardcoded content within the app.

Let's do that with the help of Retrofit:

1. Inside the `build.gradle` file in the app module, add the dependency for Retrofit inside the `dependencies` block:

```
implementation "com.squareup.retrofit2:retrofit:2.9.0"
```

2. After updating the `build.gradle` file, make sure to sync your project with its Gradle files. You can do that by clicking on the **File** menu option and then by selecting **Sync Project with Gradle Files**.
3. Create an interface that defines the HTTP operations that are executed between our app and the database. Do so by clicking on the application package, selecting **New**, and then selecting **Kotlin Class/File**. Enter `RestaurantsApiService` as the name and select **Interface** as the type. Inside the newly created file, add the following code:

```
import retrofit2.Call
import retrofit2.http.GET

interface RestaurantsApiService {
    @GET("restaurants.json")
    fun getRestaurants(): Call<Any>
}
```

Let's break down the code we've just added into meaningful actions:

- Retrofit turns your HTTP API into a simple Java/Kotlin interface, so we've created a `RestaurantsApiService` interface that defines the HTTP actions we need.
- We've defined a `getRestaurants` method inside the interface that returns a `Call` object with an undefined response type marked by Kotlin's `Any type`. Each `Call` from `RestaurantsApiService` can make a synchronous or asynchronous HTTP request to the remote web server.

- We've annotated the `getRestaurants` method with the `@GET` annotation, thereby telling Retrofit that this method should execute a `GET` HTTP action to obtain data from our web server. Inside the `@GET` annotation, we passed the endpoint's path, which represents the `restaurants` node within our Firebase database. This means that when we execute this request, the `restaurants.json` endpoint will be appended to the base URL of the HTTP client.

> **Note**
>
> We mentioned that we can use our Firebase Realtime Database URL as a REST API. To access a specific node, such as the `restaurants` node of our database, we also appended the `.json` format to make sure that the Firebase database will behave like a REST API and return a JSON response.

Later on, after we instantiate a Retrofit builder, the library will know how to turn our `getRestaurants` method into a proper HTTP call.

But before that, you have probably noticed that the `getRestaurants` HTTP request from our interface has its response type defined as `Any`. We expect to receive the JSON content of our restaurants mapped to data classes that we can use in our code. So, let's work on that next.

Mapping JSON to model classes

Retrofit lets you automatically serialize request bodies and deserialize response bodies. In our case, we're interested in deserializing the response body, from JSON into Java/Kotlin objects.

To deserialize the JSON response, we will instruct Retrofit to use the GSON deserialization library, but until then, let's have a look at the JSON response that our database returns. Remember that we imported a JSON file called `restaurants.json` when we populated the Firebase database.

Let's open that file with any text editor and observe its structure:

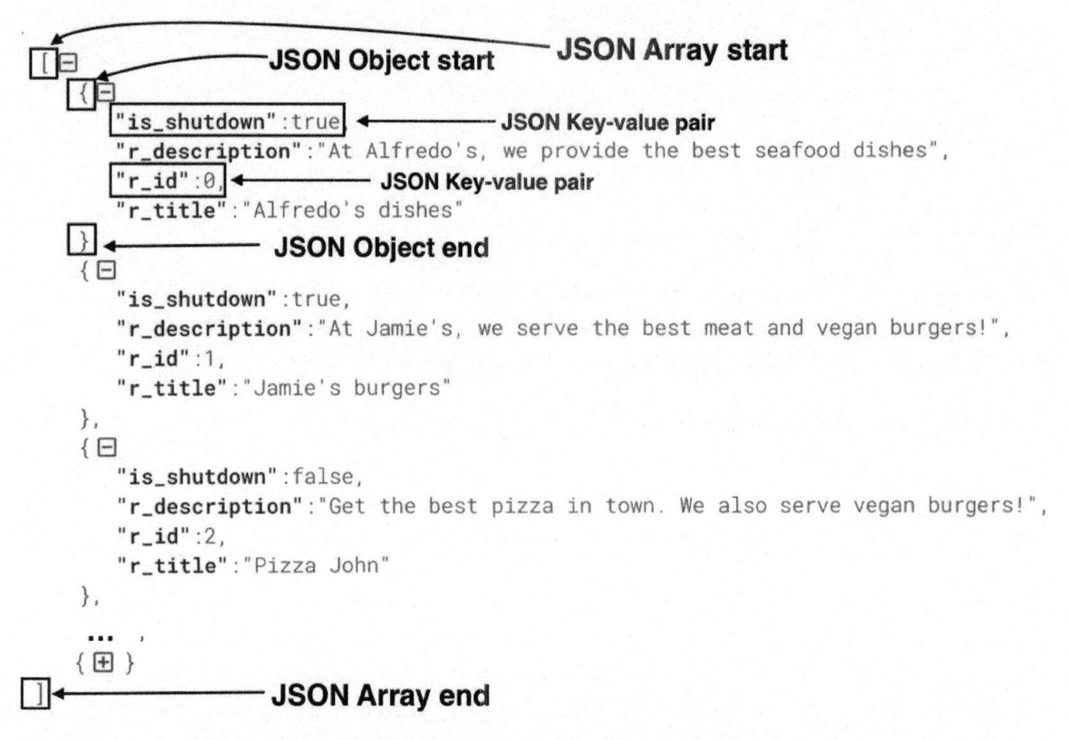

Figure 3.10 – The JSON structure of the Firebase database's content

We can observe the following elements in the JSON response structure:

- It contains an array of JSON objects marked by the `[` and `]` identifiers.
- The contents of the JSON array's element are marked by the { and } identifiers and they enclose the JSON object structure of a restaurant.
- The restaurant JSON object contains four key-value pairs, separated by the `,` separator.

The response from our database will be of type `List<?>` since the response holds an array of JSON objects. The main question that remains is, what data type should our application expect inside that list?

To answer that, we must inspect the structure of the restaurant JSON object a bit closer:

```
{⊟
    "is_shutdown":false,
    "r_description":"Get the best pizza in town. We also serve vegan burgers!",
    "r_id":2,
    "r_title":"Pizza John"
},
```

Figure 3.11 – The structure of the restaurant JSON object

Here, we can see that the JSON restaurant has four key-value pairs that refer to the `id`, `title`, `description`, and `shutdown` statuses of the corresponding restaurant. This structure is similar to our `Restaurant.kt` data class within the project:

```
data class Restaurant(val id: Int,
                      val title: String,
                      val description: String,
                      var isFavorite: Boolean = false)
```

Our `Restaurant` also contains the `id`, `title`, and `description` fields. We are not interested in the `shutdown` status for now, so it's tempting to use the `Restaurant` class as the model for our response, thus making our `getRestaurants()` method in `RestaurantsApiService` return `List<Restaurant>` as the response of the request.

The issue with this approach is that we need to tell Retrofit to match the `r_id` key's value with our `id` field. The same goes for `r_title`, which should be matched with the `title` field and so on. We can approach this in two ways:

- Rename the `Restaurant` data class fields so that they match the response keys: `r_id`, `r_title`, and so on. In this case, the deserialization will automatically match our fields with the fields from the JSON objects since the JSON keys are identical to the fields' names.
- Annotate the `Restaurant` data class fields with special serialization matchers that tell Retrofit which keys should be matched with each field. This won't change the variable names.

The first approach is bad because our `Restaurant` data class would end up with fields that contain underscore naming dictated by the server. It would also not comply with Kotlin's CamelCase guideline for defining field variables anymore.

Let's choose the second approach, where we specify the serialization keys ourselves. To do that, we will tell Retrofit to deserialize the JSON with the GSON deserialization library, which is a powerful framework for converting JSON strings into Java/Kotlin objects and vice versa:

1. First, we need to add the GSON library dependency to mark our fields with custom serialization keys. Inside the `build.gradle` file in the app module, add the dependency for GSON inside the `dependencies` block:

```
implementation "com.google.code.gson:gson:2.8.6"
```

2. After updating the `build.gradle` file, make sure to sync your project with its Gradle files. You can do that by clicking on the **File** menu option and then by selecting **Sync Project with Gradle Files**.
3. Inside `Restaurant.kt`, add the `@SerializedName` annotation for each field and specify the corresponding serialization keys from the JSON structure:

```
import com.google.gson.annotations.SerializedName

data class Restaurant(
    @SerializedName("r_id")
    val id: Int,
    @SerializedName("r_title")
    val title: String,
    @SerializedName("r_description")
    val description: String,
    var isFavorite: Boolean = false)
```

By doing so, we've made sure that Retrofit will correctly match each of the JSON key's values with our corresponding field inside the `Restaurant` data class while also matching the data type:

- The `r_id` key matches the `id` field. The `r_id` key has a whole number as its value in the JSON structure, so we stored this key's value in the `id: Int` field.
- The `r_title` key matches the `title` field. The `r_title` key has text as its value marked with the `"` and `"` identifiers, so we stored this key's value in the `title: String` field.
- The `r_description` key matches the `description` field. The `r_description` key has text as its value marked with the `"` and `"` identifiers, so we stored this key's value in the `description: String` field.

> **Note**
>
> For now, we are using the Restaurant data model both as the API response model and as the domain model that's used throughout the application. Architecturally, this practice is not recommended, and we will cover why this is the case and fix it in *Chapter 8, Getting Started with Clean Architecture in Android.*

4. Update the `getRestaurants()` method inside `RestaurantsApiService` so that it returns a `Call` object from the server with the type parameter that matches the response that is expected. In our case, that would be `List<Restaurant>`:

```
interface RestaurantsApiService {
    @GET("restaurants.json")
    fun getRestaurants(): Call<List<Restaurant>>
}
```

With that, our Retrofit API interface has been defined to receive the content of the Restaurants database from our Firebase database. The only step left is to configure a Retrofit builder instance and execute the request.

Executing GET requests to the Firebase REST API

Let's configure the last component that's needed to perform requests with Retrofit – the `Retrofit.builder` object:

1. First, we need to add the GSON Converter library dependency for Retrofit so that Retrofit deserializes the JSON response while following the GSON serialization annotations we added previously. Inside the `build.gradle` file in the app module, add the dependency for the Retrofit GSON converter inside the `dependencies` block:

```
implementation "com.squareup.retrofit2:converter-
    gson:2.9.0"
```

2. After updating the `build.gradle` file, make sure to sync your project with its Gradle files. You can do that by clicking on the **File** menu option and then by selecting **Sync Project with Gradle Files**.

3. Inside `RestaurantsViewModel`, add a `restInterface` variable of type `RestaurantsApiService` and create an `init` block where we will instantiate the `Retrofit.builder` object:

```
class RestaurantsViewModel(…) : ViewModel() {
    private var restInterface: RestaurantsApiService
    val state = mutableStateOf(
        dummyRestaurants.restoreSelections()
    )
    init {
        val retrofit: Retrofit = Retrofit.Builder()
            .addConverterFactory(
                GsonConverterFactory.create()
            )
            .baseUrl(
                "https://restaurants-db-default
                        -rtdb.firebaseio.com/"
            )
            .build()
        restInterface = retrofit.create(
            RestaurantsApiService::class.java
        )
    }
    […]
}
```

We've added all the necessary pieces for our networking client. Let's break this code down:

- First, we've defined a `restInterface` variable of type `RestaurantsApiService` that we will call upon to execute the desired network requests. At this point, the `restInterface` variable holds no value.
- We've added an `init` block to instantiate the Retrofit builder object. As the primary constructor can't contain any code, we are placing the initialization code in an initializer block prefixed with the `init` keyword.

- We've instantiated a `retrofit: Retrofit` variable with the `Retrofit.Builder` accessor and specified the following:
  - A `GsonConverterFactory` to explicitly tell Retrofit that we want the JSON to be deserialized with the GSON converter, following the `@Serialized` annotations we specified in the `Restaurant` data class.
  - A `baseUrl` for all the requests that are to be executed – in your case, replace this URL with the URL of your Firebase database.
- Finally, we called `.create()` on the previously obtained `Retrofit` object and passed our interface with the desired requests: `RestaurantsApiService`. Behind the scenes, Retrofit creates a concrete implementation of our interface that will handle all the networking logic, without us having to worry about it. We store this instance from Retrofit inside our `restInterface` variable.

Now, we can execute requests – in our case, the request to get the list of restaurants.

4. Inside `RestaurantsViewModel`, add the `getRestaurants` method:

```
fun getRestaurants() {
    restInterface.getRestaurants().execute().body()
        ?.let { restaurants ->
            state.value = restaurants.restoreSelections()
        }
}
```

We've added all the necessary steps for our networking request to be executed. Let's break this code down:

I. We've obtained a `Call` object called `Call<List<Restaurant>>` from our Retrofit `restInterface` variable by calling the `getRestaurants()` interface method. The `Call` object represents the invocation of a Retrofit method that sends network requests and receives a response. The type parameter of the `Call` object matches the response type; that is, `<List<Restaurant>>`.

II. On the previously obtained `Call` object, we called `execute()`. The `execute()` method is the most simple approach to starting a network request with Retrofit as it runs the request synchronously on the main thread (the UI thread) and blocks it until the response arrives. No network request should block the UI thread yet, though we will fix this soon.

III. The `execute()` method returns a Retrofit `Response` object that allows us to see if the response was successful and obtain the resulting body.

IV. The body() accessor returns a nullable list of type List<Restaurant>>?. We apply the Kotlin let extension function and name the list restaurants.

V. We pass the resulting restaurants list to our state object after restoring the selections in case of system-initiated process death, similar to what we did for the initial state value.

With that, we've instructed our ViewModel on how to obtain the list of restaurants from the database and to pass this result to our screen's state. One issue that we will have to address later is that we are not catching any errors that may be thrown by Retrofit if the request fails. Until then, let's focus on updating the state with the new result.

5. Inside RestaurantsViewModel, we need to update the state's initial value so that it contains an empty list. This is because, when the screen is first displayed, we no longer have restaurants to render – we will get them later in the network request. Update the initial value of the state object by removing dummyList and placing an emptyList() instead:

```
val state = mutableStateOf(emptyList<Restaurant>())
```

6. Inside the Restaurant.kt file, remove the dummyRestaurants list since we will be obtaining the restaurants at runtime through the previously defined request.

7. We want to trigger the network request to obtain the restaurants from the server. Inside RestaurantsScreen.kt, update the RestaurantsScreen composable function so that it calls the getRestaurants() method of viewModel, which will trigger the network request to obtain the restaurants from the server:

```
@Composable
fun RestaurantsScreen() {
    val viewModel: RestaurantsViewModel = viewModel()
    viewModel.getRestaurants()
    LazyColumn( … ) { … }
}
```

By calling viewModel.getRestaurants(), we are trying to load the list of restaurants when the RestaurantsScreen composable is composed for the first time. This practice is not recommended and we will see in the following steps why that is and how we can fix it.

8. Add internet permission inside the `AndroidManifest.xml` file:

```
<manifest xmlns:android="..."
    package="com.codingtroops.restaurantsapp">

    <uses-permission
android:name="android.permission.INTERNET" />
      <application> ... </application>
</manifest>
```

9. Run the application by clicking the **Run** button.

   Unfortunately, the application will most likely crash. If we check **Logcat**, we will notice an exception stack similar to the following:

```
2021-10-27 10:38:47.918 23484-23484/com.codingtroops.restaurantsapp E/AndroidRuntime: FATAL EXCEPTION: main
    Process: com.codingtroops.restaurantsapp, PID: 23484
    android.os.NetworkOnMainThreadException
```

Figure 3.12 – Crash stack trace for executing a network request on the main thread

   The exception that's been thrown here is a `NetworkOnMainThreadException` and it's clear what's wrong with our code: we are executing a network request on the Main thread.

   This has happened because with the Android Honeycomb SDK, *executing network requests on the Main thread is forbidden* because the UI of the application will freeze until the response from the server arrives, making the app unusable in that timeframe. In other words, we can't and shouldn't use the `.execute()` method of a Retrofit `Call` object because the request will run synchronously on the Main thread.

   Instead, we can use an alternative that not only will execute the requests asynchronously and on a separate thread, but also allow us to handle any errors that are thrown by Retrofit.

10. In the `getRestaurants()` method of `ViewModel`, replace the `.execute()` call with `.enqueue()`:

```
fun getRestaurants() {
    restInterface.getRestaurants().enqueue(
     object : Callback<List<Restaurant>> {
         override fun onResponse(
             call: Call<List<Restaurant>>,
             response: Response<List<Restaurant>>
```

```
            ) {
                response.body()?.let { restaurants ->
                    state.value =
                        restaurants.restoreSelections()
                }
            }

            override fun onFailure(
                call: Call<List<Restaurant>>, t: Throwable
            ) {
                t.printStackTrace()
            }
        })
}
```

When adding the missing imports for the `Call`, `Callback` and `Response` classes, make sure that you're adding the Retrofit2 imports that start off like this: `import retrofit2.*`.

Getting back to the code that we've added, let's look at it in more detail:

- On the `Call` object that we obtained from our `restInterface.getRestaurants()` method, we called the `.enqueue()` function. The `enqueue()` call is a better alternative to `.execute()` since it runs the network request asynchronously on a separate thread, so it will no longer run on the UI thread and it won't block the UI.
- The `.enqueue()` function receives a `Callback` object as an argument that allows us to listen for success or failure callbacks. The `Callback` object's type parameter defines the expected `Response` object. Since we expect a response of type `<List<Restaurant>>`, the returned `Callback` type is defined as `Callback<List<Restaurant>>`.
- We've implemented the required `object : Callback<List<Restaurant>>` and implemented its two callbacks:
  - `onResponse()`, which is the success callback that's invoked when the network request succeeds. It provides us with the initial `Call` object, but more importantly the `Response` object; that is, `Response<List<Restaurant>>`. Inside this callback, we get the body from the response and update the value of the `state` variable, just like we did with `execute()`.

- `onFailure()`, which is the failure callback. It's invoked when a network exception occurs while talking to the server or when an unexpected exception occurs while creating the request or processing the response. This callback provides us with the initial `Call` object and the `Throwable` exception that was intercepted and whose stack trace we print.

Now, you can run the application. It shouldn't crash anymore since calling `enqueue()` allowed the request to run on a separate thread so that we could safely wait for the response without blocking the UI.

> **Note**
>
> As a good practice, make sure that when you're making requests with Retrofit, you always call the `enqueue()` function and not `execute()`. You want your users to not experience crashes and to be able to interact with the app while they're waiting for the network response.

Yet even with this addition, there are still two concerning issues with our code. Were you able to notice them? Let's try to identify them.

Improving the way our app handles network requests

Our application now successfully obtains data from the server dynamically, at runtime. Unfortunately, we have made two major mistakes in our code, and both are related to how the app handles the requests. Let's identify them:

- First, we are not canceling our network request as a cleanup measure. If our UI component that is bound to `RestaurantsViewModel` – in our case, `MainActivity` – is destroyed before the response from the server can arrive (for example, if the user navigates to another activity), we could potentially create a memory leak. This is because our `RestaurantsViewModel` would still be tied to the `Callback<List<Restaurant>>` object, which waits for the server's response. Due to this, the garbage collector won't free up the memory associated with both of their instances.
- Secondly, we are not triggering the network request from a controlled environment. The `viewModel.getRestaurants()` method is called inside the `RestaurantsScreen()` composable function without any special considerations. This means that every time the UI is recomposed, the composable will ask `ViewModel` to execute network requests, resulting in possible multiple and redundant requests.

Let's focus on the first issue for now.

Canceling network requests as a cleanup measure

The main problem in our `RestaurantsViewModel` is that we are enqueueing a `Call` object and we're waiting for the response through the `Callback` object, but we are never canceling that enqueued `Call`. We should cancel it when the host `Activity` or `ViewModel` is cleared to prevent memory leaks. Let's do that here:

1. Inside `RestaurantsViewModel`, define a class variable of type `Call` with the `List<Restaurant>>` type parameter. Call this variable `restaurantsCall` as we will use it to hold a reference to our enqueued `Call` object:

```
class RestaurantsViewModel(…): ViewModel() {
    private var restInterface: RestaurantsApiService
    val state = […]
    private lateinit var restaurantsCall:
        Call<List<Restaurant>>

    init {…}
   […]
}
```

   We've marked `restaurantsCall` as a `lateinit` variable to instantiate it later when we perform the network request.

2. Inside the `getRestaurants()` method of `RestaurantsViewModel`, assign the `Call` object that you obtained from the `restInterface.getRestaurants()` method call to the `restaurantsCall` member variable and call `enqueue()` on it:

```
fun getRestaurants() {
    restaurantsCall = restInterface.getRestaurants()
    restaurantsCall.enqueue(object :
 Callback<List<Restaurant>> {…})
}
```

3. Inside `RestaurantsViewModel`, override the `onCleared()` method and call the `cancel()` method of the `restaurantCall` object:

```
override fun onCleared() {
    super.onCleared()
```

```
        restaurantsCall.cancel()
    }
```

The `onCleared()` callback method is provided by the Jetpack `ViewModel` and is called just before `ViewModel` is destroyed as a consequence of the attached activity/fragment or composable being destroyed or removed from the composition.

This callback represents the perfect opportunity for us to cancel any ongoing work – or in our case, to cancel the pending `Call` object that's enqueued in the `restaurantCall` object. This way, we prevent leaking memory and therefore fix the first issue in our code.

Now, it's time to focus on the second issue, where the `RestaurantsScreen()` composable calls the `viewModel.getRestaurants()` method without any special considerations.

Triggering network requests from a controlled environment

The `viewModel.getRestaurants()` method is called because we want to apply a **side effect** in our UI. A side effect is a change that's made to the state of the application that usually happens outside the scope of a composable function. In our case, the side effect is that we need to start loading the restaurants for the first time when the user enters the screen.

As a rule of thumb, composables should be side-effect free, but in our application, we need to know when to trigger the network request, and what better place than the moment when our UI is initially composed?

The problem with the existing approach of simply calling a method on `ViewModel` from the composable layer is that the Compose UI can be recomposed many times on the screen. For example, when an animation is rendered, the Compose UI is recomposed many times to execute the animation's keyframes. On every recomposition of the UI, our composable calls the `getRestaurants()` method on `RestaurantsViewModel`, which, in turn, executes network requests to obtain the restaurants from the server, which could result in multiple and redundant requests.

To prevent this issue from happening, Compose has the right tool for us to handle side-effects efficiently: the **Effects** API.

An *effect* is a composable function that, instead of emitting UI elements, causes side effects that run when a composition process completes. Such composables are based on the Kotlin Coroutine API, which allows you to run async work in their bodies. However, we will disregard coroutines for now as we will cover them in *Chapter 4, Handling Async Operations with Coroutines*.

In Compose, there are many types of effect composables that we can use but we will not go too deep into that. In our case, though, a suitable effect could be the `LaunchedEffect` composable since it allows us to run a task only once when it first enters composition.

The signature of `LaunchedEffect` is simple – it contains a `key1` parameter and a `block` parameter where we can execute our code. For now, we should ignore the Coroutine terminology and just think of the `block` function parameter as a block of code that can be executed asynchronously:

```
329    @Composable
330    @NonRestartableComposable
331    @OptIn(InternalComposeApi::class)
332    fun LaunchedEffect(
333        key1: Any?,
334        block: suspend CoroutineScope.() → Unit
335    ) {...}
```

Figure 3.13 – The signature of the LaunchedEffect composable

When `LaunchedEffect` enters the composition process, it runs the `block` parameter function, which is passed as an argument. The execution of the block will be canceled if `LaunchedEffect` leaves the composition. If `LaunchedEffect` is recomposed with different keys that have been passed to the `key1` parameter, the existing execution of the block of code will be canceled and a new iteration of execution will be launched.

Now that we know how `LaunchedEffect` works, we can agree that it seems a viable solution for our issue, at least for now: we want to make sure that the call to `ViewModel` is only executed once on the initial composition, so `LaunchedEffect` seems to suffice our needs.

Let's add a `LaunchedEffect` to prevent our UI from asking for restaurants from `ViewModel` repeatedly on every recomposition:

1. Inside the `RestaurantsScreen` composable, wrap the `viewModel.getRestaurants()` call in a `LaunchedEffect` composable:

```
@Composable
fun RestaurantsScreen() {
    val viewModel: RestaurantsViewModel = viewModel()
    LaunchedEffect(key1 = "request_restaurants") {
        viewModel.getRestaurants()
    }
    LazyColumn(...) { ... }
}
```

To implement the `LaunchedEffect` composable, we did the following:

- We passed a `String` hardcoded value of `"request_restaurants"` to the `key1` parameter. We passed a hardcoded value to the `key1` argument because we want the block of code passed inside the `LaunchedEffect` composable to not execute on every recomposition. We could have passed any constant to `key1`, yet what's important here is that the value shouldn't change over time.
- We passed our code that calls the `getRestaurants()` method on our `ViewModel` inside the `block` parameter of the effect. Since the `block` parameter is the last parameter of the `LaunchedEffect` composable and is a function, we used the trailing lambda syntax.

2. Run the application. Now, the code inside `LaunchedEffect` should only be executed once.

Yet even with this addition, our code still has an issue. If you try rotating the emulator or device you're testing with, you will trigger a configuration change and another network will be executed. But we mentioned previously that `LaunchedEffect` will only execute the `viewModel.getRestaurants()` call once, so why is this happening?

`LaunchedEffect` works fine – the issue lies in the activity being destroyed on configuration change. If the activity is destroyed, the UI will be composed again from scratch, and for all it knows, `LaunchedEffect` will run the code inside the `block` parameter for the first time.

Can you think of a better alternative to get around the issue of the activity being destroyed due to configuration changes?

An alternative would be to use the `ViewModel` component because it survives configuration changes. If we trigger the request only once in `RestaurantsViewModel`, we no longer care if a configuration change occurs – the request will not be executed again. Follow these steps:

1. Inside `RestaurantsViewModel`, locate the `init` block and inside it, call `getRestaurants()`:

```
init {
    val retrofit: Retrofit = Retrofit.Builder().[...].
build()
    restInterface = retrofit.create(
        RestaurantsApiService::class.java
    )
```

```
        getRestaurants()
    }
```

The `init` block is called once when an instance of `ViewModel` is created, so placing our network request here is a safer bet than at the UI level in any composable. Make sure you've placed the `getRestaurants()` call after the instantiation of the `restInterface` variable since the `getRestaurants()` method depends on that variable being ready to work.

2. Still inside `RestaurantsViewModel`, navigate to the `getRestaurants()` method and mark it as `private`:

```
private fun getRestaurants() {
    ...
}
```

We no longer need to expose this method publicly to the UI since it's now only called inside `ViewModel`.

3. Inside the `RestaurantsScreen` composable, remove the `LaunchedEffect` composable function with all the code inside it since we no longer need it.
4. Run the application. The network request should not be executed again when a configuration change is made since the `RestaurantsViewModel` instance is preserved and the code inside its `init` block is not executed again.

We've taken quite a few steps to make sure that our application handles network requests correctly, and this was a great first step toward creating a modern application.

Summary

In this chapter, we learned how mobile apps communicate with remote web APIs using HTTP connections and REST APIs. Then, we created a database for our Restaurants application with the help of Firebase and populated it with content.

After that, we explored what Retrofit is and how it abstracts the complexity associated with handling network requests and responses within HTTP connections between apps and web APIs.

Then, we executed a network request with Retrofit in our Restaurants application and learned how the JSON content that is sent by the server can be parsed or deserialized by our Retrofit networking client. We also learned how to correctly wait for network responses and how to notify the application when responses arrive.

Finally, we solved some common issues that occur when our applications communicate with web APIs asynchronously to retrieve data, especially in the context of Compose.

In the next chapter, we'll explore a very efficient tool in Android for async work that comes bundled with Kotlin: coroutines!

Further reading

With the help of custom annotations inside the Retrofit interface, this library hides most of the complexity associated with handling network requests. We've seen that with simple `GET` requests in our `RestaurantsApiService` interface when we annotated our request with the `@GET` annotation:

```
interface RestaurantsApiService {
    @GET("restaurants.json")
    fun getRestaurants(): Call<List<Restaurant>>
}
```

Yet apart from plain `GET` operations, such Retrofit interfaces can also handle other request types, such as `PUT`, `POST`, and `DELETE`.

For example, if you need to define a request that passes some data to the server that is likely to be stored, you can use a `POST` request by adding the `@POST` annotation to your desired method:

```
@POST("user/edit")
fun updateUser(@Field("first_name") firstName: String):
    Call<User>
```

To understand how to use Retrofit for such cases, or more advanced ones, check out the official documentation: `https://square.github.io/retrofit/`.

4
Handling Async Operations with Coroutines

In this chapter, we're focusing on another library that, although is not in the Jetpack library suite, is essential for writing solid applications: **Kotlin coroutines**.

Coroutines represent a more convenient way of handling async work and concurrency jobs on Android.

In this chapter, we will study how we can replace callbacks with coroutines in our Restaurants application. In the first section, *Introducing Kotlin coroutines*, we will gain a better understanding of what coroutines are, how they work, and why we need them in our apps.

In the next section, *Exploring the basic elements of coroutines*, we will explore the core elements of coroutines, and we will understand how to use them to handle asynchronous work more concisely.

Finally, in the *Using coroutines for async work* section, we will implement coroutines in our Restaurants application and let them handle the network requests. Additionally, we will add error handling and integrate some of the best practices when working with coroutines in Android apps.

To summarize, in this chapter, we're going to cover the following main topics:

- Introducing Kotlin coroutines
- Exploring the basic elements of coroutines
- Using coroutines for async work

Before jumping in, let's set up the technical requirements for this chapter.

Technical requirements

Building Compose-based Android projects with coroutines usually requires your day-to-day tools. However, to follow along with this chapter smoothly, make sure you have the following:

- The Arctic Fox 2020.3.1 version of Android Studio. You can also use a newer Android Studio version or even Canary builds but note that IDE interface and other generated code files might differ from the ones used throughout this book.
- Kotlin 1.6.10, or a newer plugin, installed in Android Studio
- The Restaurants app code from the previous chapter.

The starting point for this chapter is represented by the Restaurants application developed in the previous chapter. If you haven't followed the implementation from the previous chapter, access the starting point for this chapter by navigating to the `Chapter_03` directory of the repository and importing the Android project entitled `chapter_3_restaurants_app`.

To access the solution code for this chapter, navigate to the `Chapter_04` directory:

`https://github.com/PacktPublishing/Kickstart-Modern-Android-Development-with-Jetpack-and-Kotlin/tree/main/Chapter_04/chapter_4_restaurants_app`.

Introducing Kotlin coroutines

Coroutines are part of the Kotlin API. They introduce a new and easier way of handling async work and concurrency jobs.

Often, with Android, we need to run or execute different tasks behind the scenes. In the meantime, we don't want to block the main thread of the application and get an unresponsive UI.

To mitigate this issue, coroutines allow you to execute async work much easier while providing main-thread safety for your Android apps. You can use the Coroutines API by launching one **coroutine**, or more, depending on your needs.

In this section, we will cover three essential questions about the Coroutines API that derive from what we stated earlier:

- What is a coroutine?
- What are the features and advantages of coroutines?
- How do coroutines work?

Let's jump in!

What is a coroutine?

A coroutine is a concurrency design pattern for async work. A *coroutine represents an instance of suspendable computation.*

In other words, coroutines are sequences or blocks of code that represent a computational task that can be suspended. We call them **suspendable** because coroutines can be suspended and resumed mid-execution, which makes them efficient for concurrent tasks.

When comparing coroutines with threads, we can say the following:

- A coroutine is a lightweight version of a thread but not a thread. Coroutines are light because creating coroutines doesn't allocate new threads – typically, coroutines use predefined thread pools.
- Like threads, coroutines can run in parallel, wait for each other, and communicate.
- Unlike threads, coroutines are very cheap: we can create thousands of them and pay very few penalties in terms of performance.

Next, let's understand the purpose behind coroutines a bit better.

The features and advantages of coroutines

By now, we know that on Android, coroutines can help us to move long-running async work from the main thread into a separate thread. Essentially, coroutines have two primary possible usages:

- For handling async work
- For handling multithreading

In this chapter, we will only cover how to correctly handle async work with coroutines in Android apps.

However, before we try to understand how to do that with coroutines, let's explore the advantages that coroutines bring over other alternatives that we've used in the past: `AsyncTask` classes, callbacks, and reactive frameworks. A coroutine is described as the following:

- **Lightweight**: We can launch many coroutines on a single thread. Coroutines support execution suspension on the thread as opposed to blocking it, resulting in less memory overhead. Additionally, a coroutine is not always bound to a specific thread – it might start its execution on one thread and yield the result on a different one.
- **Easily cancelable**: When canceling the parent coroutine, any children coroutines that were launched within the same scope will be canceled. If you have launched multiple coroutines that run operations concurrently, cancelation is straightforward and applies to the entire affected coroutine hierarchy; therefore, this eliminates any potential memory leaks.
- **Easily integrated with Jetpack libraries**: By providing a suite of extensions. For example, coroutines provide custom scopes for many common Android components such as `Activity`, `Fragment`, `ViewModel`, and more. This means that you can launch coroutines safely from these components, as they will be canceled automatically when different lifecycle events occur, so you don't have to worry about memory leaks.

> **Note**
>
> We have mentioned the word *scope* several times, and I promise that we will explain it later. Until then, you can think of the coroutine scope as an entity that controls the lifetime of launched coroutines.

Now we have an idea of the features of coroutines. Yet, to better understand their purpose, first, we need to understand why we should offload async work from the main thread to a separate worker thread.

How do coroutines work?

In Android runtime, the main thread is responsible for two things:

- Drawing the UI of the application on the screen
- Updating the UI upon user interactions

Simplistically viewed, the main thread calls a drawing method on the screen canvas. This method might be familiar to you as the `onDraw()` method, and we can assume that for your device to render UI at 60 frames per second, the Android Runtime will call this method roughly every 16 milliseconds.

If, for some reason, we execute heavy async work on the main thread, the application might freeze or stutter. This happens because the main thread was busy serving our async work; therefore, it missed several `onDraw()` calls that could have updated the UI and prevented the freezing effect.

Let's say that we need to make a network request to our server. This operation might take time because we must wait for a response, which depends on the web API's speed and the user's connectivity. Let's imagine that such a method is named `getNetworkResponse()` and we are calling it from the main thread:

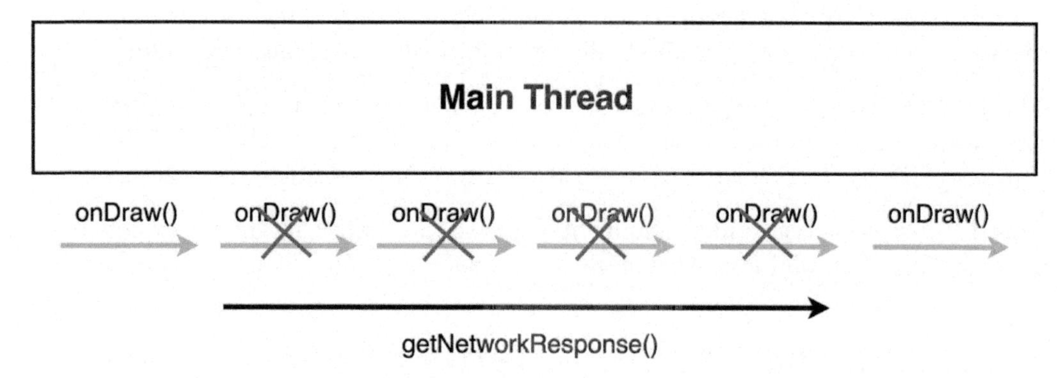

Figure 4.1 – Blocking the main thread with async work

From the time it launched the network request, the main thread kept waiting for a response and couldn't do anything in the meantime. We can see that several `onDraw()` calls were missed because the main thread was busy executing our `getNetworkResponse()` method call and waiting for a result.

To mitigate this issue, we've used many mechanisms in the past. Yet, coroutines are much easier to use and work perfectly with the Android ecosystem. So, it's time to see how they can enable us to execute async work:

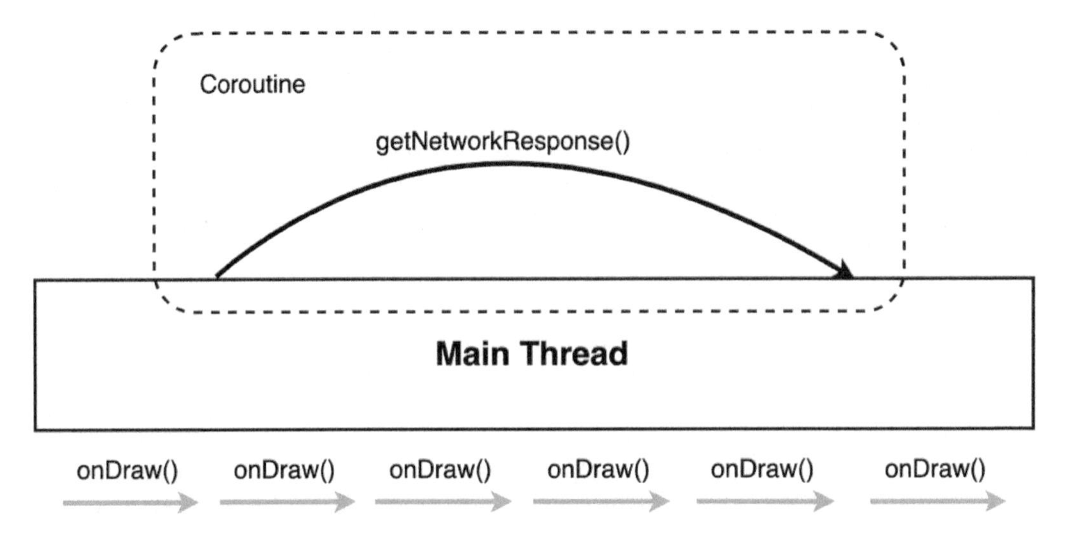

Figure 4.2 – Executing async work on a different thread by using a coroutine

With coroutines, we can offload any nasty blocking calls – such as the `getNetworkResponse()` method call – from the main thread onto a coroutine.

The coroutine works on a separate thread and is in charge of executing the network request and waiting for the response. This way, the main thread is not blocked, and no `onDraw()` calls are missed; therefore, we avoid getting any freezing screen effects.

Now that we have a basic understanding of how coroutines work, it's time to explore the components that coroutines are based on.

Exploring the basic elements of coroutines

A very simplistic approach for getting async work done with coroutines could be expressed as follows: first, define the suspended functions and then create coroutines that execute the suspended functions.

Yet, we're not only unsure what suspending functions look like, but we also don't know how to allow coroutines to perform asynchronous work for us.

Let's take things, step by step, and start with the two essential actions that we need to execute async work with coroutines:

- Creating suspending functions
- Launching coroutines

All of these terms make little sense now, so let's address this, starting with suspending functions!

Creating suspending functions

The first thing that we need in order to work with coroutines is to define a suspending function where the blocking task resides.

A **suspending** function is a special function that can be paused (suspended) and resumed at some later point in time. This allows us to execute long-running jobs while the function is suspended and, finally, resume it when the work is complete.

Our regular function calls within our code are mostly executed synchronously on the main thread. Essentially, suspending functions allow us to execute jobs asynchronously in the background without blocking the thread where those functions are called from.

Let's say that we need to save some details about a user to a local database. This operation takes time, so we need to display an animation until it finishes:

```
fun saveDetails(user: User) {
    startAnimation()
    database.storeUser(user)
    stopAnimation()
}
```

If this operation is called on the main thread, the animation will freeze for a few hundreds of milliseconds while the user's details are saved.

Take a closer look at the code presented earlier and ask yourself the following: *which method call should be suspendable?*

Since the `storeUser()` method takes a while to finish, we want this method to be a suspending function because this function should be paused until the user's details are saved and then resumed when the job is done. This ensures that we do not block the main thread or freeze the animation.

Yet, how can we make the `storeUser()` method a suspending function?

A suspending function is a regular function that is marked with the `suspend` keyword:

```
suspend fun storeUser(user: User) {
    // blocking action
}
```

We know that the `storeUser()` method saves details to a database, which takes a good while. So, in order to prevent this job from blocking the UI, we've marked the method with an additional `suspend` keyword.

However, if we mark a method with the `suspend` keyword, trying to call it in our code results in a compilation error:

```
fun saveDetails(user: User) {
    startAnimation()
    database.storeUser(user)
    stopAnimation()
}
```

Suspend function 'storeUser' should be called only from a coroutine or another suspend function

Figure 4.3 – Calling suspending functions from regular functions results in a compilation error

Suspending functions can only be called from inside a coroutine or from inside another suspending function. Instead of calling our `storeUser()` suspending method from a regular method, let's create a coroutine and call it from there.

Launching coroutines

To execute a suspend function, first, we need to create and launch a coroutine. To do that, we need to call a coroutine builder on a coroutine scope:

```
fun saveDetails(user: User) {
    GlobalScope.launch(Dispatchers.IO) {
        startAnimation()
        database.storeUser(user)
        stopAnimation()
    }
}
```

We have just launched our first coroutine and called our suspending function inside it! Let's break down what just happened:

- We've used a `GlobalScope` coroutine scope, which manages the coroutines that are launched within it.
- In the coroutine scope, we called the `launch()` coroutine builder to create a coroutine.
- Then, we passed the `Dispatchers.IO` dispatcher to the coroutine builder. In this case, we want to save the user details inside the database on a thread reserved for I/O operations.
- Inside the block that the `launch()` coroutine builder has provided us with, we call our `storeUser()` suspending function.

Now we have successfully moved our blocking work away from the main thread to a worker thread. Therefore, we have made sure that the UI will not be blocked, and the animation will run smoothly.

However, now that we have implemented suspending work in our `saveDetails()` method, you might be wondering what the order of function calls within this method will be.

To better understand how the regular synchronous world blends with the suspending world, let's add some logs to our previous code snippet:

```
fun saveDetails(user: User) {
    Log.d("TAG", "Preparing to launch coroutine")
    GlobalScope.launch(Dispatchers.IO) {
        startAnimation()
        Log.d("TAG", "Starting to do async work")
        database.storeUser(user)
        Log.d("TAG", "Finished async work")
        stopAnimation()
    }
    Log.d("TAG", "Continuing program execution")
}
```

Remember, the only suspending function in this block of code that will take some time to compute is `database.storeUser()`. Now, let's imagine that we have run the preceding piece of code.

> **Exercise**
>
> Before checking the following output, try to think about the order of the logs yourself. What do you expect the order of function calls to be?

Let's see the output:

```
2021-11-09 17:49:45.931 D/TAG: Preparing to launch coroutine
2021-11-09 17:49:45.947 D/TAG: Continuing program execution
2021-11-09 17:49:45.964 D/TAG: Starting to do async work
2021-11-09 17:49:48.971 D/TAG: Finished async work
```

Figure 4.4 – The output order of regular and suspending functions

The order of the function calls is a bit out of order, but it is definitely correct. Let's see what happened:

1. First, the log function with the `Preparing to launch coroutine` message was called. This method call was done on the main (UI) thread.
2. Even though up next, we launched the coroutine, we can see that the second log function called was the last one in our code: `Continuing program execution`.

   This is because the coroutine is a bridge to the suspending world, so every function call from the coroutine will be run on a different thread from the main thread. More precisely, the operation of switching from the main thread to `Dispatchers.IO` will take some time. This means that all of these methods inside the coroutine will be executed after the method call outside of the coroutine.
3. The next log function call is with the `Starting to do async work` message. This method is called inside the coroutine on a thread reserved for I/O operations. This log marks the start of execution for all suspending work.
4. Finally, after all of the blocking work from the `database.storeUser()` suspending function has been finished, the last log function call with the `Finished async work` message is called. This log marks the end of the coroutine execution.

Now that we've understood how the regular world blends with the suspended world in terms of function calls, there are still many terms and concepts that have been thrown at you. Mainly, you might be wondering the following:

- What is a coroutine scope?
- What's a coroutine dispatcher?
- What's a coroutine builder?

Let's clarify these concepts, starting with coroutine scopes.

Coroutine scopes

Essentially, coroutines run in **coroutine scopes**. To start a coroutine, first, you need a coroutine scope because it tracks all of the coroutines launched inside it and has the ability to cancel them. This way, you can control how long the coroutines should live and when they should be canceled.

A coroutine scope contains a `CoroutineContext` object, which defines the context in which the coroutine runs. In the previous example, we used a predefined scope, `GlobalScope`, but you can also define a custom scope by constructing a `CoroutineContext` object and passing it to a `CoroutineScope()` function, as follows:

```
val job = Job()
val myScope = CoroutineScope(context = job + Dispatchers.IO)
```

The `CoroutineScope()` function expects a `CoroutineContext` object passed to its `context` parameter and knows how to build one out of the box. It does this by receiving elements with a special `plus` operator and then constructing the context behind the scenes.

Most of the time, the two most important elements to construct a `CoroutineContext` object are the ones that we just passed:

- A `Job` object: This represents a cancelable component that controls the lifecycle of a coroutine launched in a specific scope. When a job is canceled, the job will cancel the coroutine it manages. For example, if we have defined a `job` object and a custom `myScope` object inside an `Activity` class, a good place to cancel the coroutine would be in the `onDestroy()` callback by calling the `cancel()` method on the `job` object:

  ```
  override fun onDestroy() {
      super.onDestroy()
      job.cancel()
  }
  ```

  By doing this, we've ensured that our async work done within our coroutine, which uses the `myScope` scope, will stop when the activity has been destroyed and will not cause any memory leaks.

- A `Dispatcher` object: Marking a method as suspended provides no details about the thread pool it should run on. So, by passing a `Dispatcher` object to the `CoroutineScope` constructor, we can make sure that all suspended functions called in the coroutine that use this scope will default to the specified `Dispatcher` object. In our example, all coroutines launched in `myScope` will run their work, by default, in the `Dispatchers.IO` thread pool and will not block the UI.

Note that the `CoroutineContext` object can also contain an exception handler object, which we will define later on.

Apart from the custom scopes that you can define, as we did earlier, you can use predefined coroutine scopes that are bound to a certain lifecycle component. In such cases, you will no longer need to define a scope with a job or to manually cancel the coroutine scope:

- `GlobalScope`: This allows the coroutines to live as long as the application is alive. In the previous example, we used this scope for simplicity, but `GlobalScope` should be avoided since the work launched within this coroutine scope is only canceled when the application has been destroyed. Using this scope in a component that has a narrower lifecycle than the application – such as an `Activity` component, might allow the coroutine to outlive that component's lifecycle and produce memory leaks.
- `lifecycleScope`: This scopes coroutines to the lifecycle of a `LifecycleOwner` instance such as an `Activity` component or a `Fragment` component. We can use the `lifecycleScope` scope defined in the Jetpack KTX extensions package:

```
class UserFragment : Fragment() {
    ...
    fun saveDetails(user: User) {
        lifecycleScope.launch(Dispatchers.IO) {
            startAnimation()
            database.storeUser(user)
            stopAnimation()
        }
    }
}
```

  By launching coroutines within this context, we ensure that if the `Fragment` component gets destroyed, the coroutine scope will automatically be canceled; therefore, this will also cancel our coroutine.

- `viewModelScope`: To scope our coroutines to live as long as the `ViewModel` component does, we can use the predefined `viewModelScope` scope:

```
class UserViewModel: ViewModel() {
    fun saveDetails(user: User) {
        // do some work
        viewModelScope.launch(Dispatchers.IO) {
            database.storeUser(user)
        }
        // do some other work
    }
}
```

  By launching coroutines within this context, we ensure that if the `ViewModel` component gets cleared, the coroutine scope will cancel its work – in other words, it will automatically cancel our coroutine.

- `rememberCoroutineScope`: To scope a coroutine to the composition cycle of a composable function, we can use the predefined `rememberCoroutineScope` scope:

```
@Composable
fun UserComposable() {
    val scope = rememberCoroutineScope()
    LaunchedEffect(key1 = "save_user") {
        scope.launch(Dispatchers.IO) {
            viewModel.saveUser()
        }
    }
}
```

  Therefore, a coroutine's lifecycle is bound to the composition cycle of `UserComposable`. This means that when `UserComposable` leaves the composition, the scope will be automatically canceled, thereby preventing the coroutine from outliving the composition lifecycle of its parent composable.

  Since we want the coroutine to be launched only once upon composition and not at every recomposition, we wrapped the coroutine with a `LaunchedEffect` composable.

Now that we covered what coroutine scopes are and how they allow us to control the lifetime of coroutines, it's time to better understand what dispatchers are.

Dispatchers

A **CoroutineDispatcher** object allows us to configure what thread pool our work should be executed on. The point of coroutines is to help us move blocking work away from the main thread. So, somehow, we need to instruct the coroutines what threads to use for the work that we pass to them.

To do that, we need to configure the `CoroutineContext` object of the coroutines to set a specific dispatcher. In fact, when we covered coroutine scopes, we've explained how `CoroutineContext` is defined by a job and a dispatcher.

When creating custom scopes, we can specify the default dispatcher right when we instantiate the scope, just as we did previously:

```
val myScope = CoroutineScope(context = job + Dispatchers.IO)
```

In this case, the default dispatcher of `myScope` is `Dispatchers.IO`. This means that whatever suspending work we pass to the coroutines that are launched with `myScope`, the work will be moved to a special thread pool for I/O background work.

In the case of predefined coroutine scopes, such as with `lifecycleScope`, `viewModelScope`, or `rememberCoroutineScope`, we can specify the desired default dispatcher when starting our coroutine:

```
scope.launch(Dispatchers.IO) {
    viewModel.saveUser()
}
```

We start coroutines with coroutine builders such as `launch` or `async`, which we will cover in the next section. Until then, we need to understand that when launching a coroutine, we can also modify the `CoroutineContext` object of the coroutine by specifying a `CoroutineDispatcher` object.

Now we've used `Dispatchers.IO` as a dispatcher throughout our examples. But are there any other dispatchers that are of use to us?

`Dispatchers.IO` is a dispatcher offered by the Coroutines API, but in addition to this, coroutines offer other dispatchers too. Let's list the most notable dispatchers as follows:

- `Dispatchers.Main`: This dispatches work to the main thread on Android. It is ideal for light work (which doesn't block the UI) or actual UI function calls and interactions.

- `Dispatchers.IO`: This dispatches blocking work to a background thread pool that specializes in handling disk-heavy or network-heavy operations. This dispatcher should be specified for suspending work on local databases or executing network requests.
- `Dispatchers.Default`: This dispatches blocking work to a background thread pool that specializes in CPU-intensive tasks, such as sorting long lists, parsing JSON, and more.

In the previous examples, we set a specific dispatcher of `Dispatchers.IO` for the `CoroutineContext` object of the coroutines launched, ensuring that suspended work will be dispatched by this specific dispatcher.

But we've made a critical mistake! Let's take a look at the code again:

```
class UserFragment : Fragment() {
    ...
    fun saveDetails(user: User) {
        lifecycleScope.launch(Dispatchers.IO) {
            startAnimation()
            database.storeUser(user)
            stopAnimation()
        }
    }
}
```

The main issue with this code is that the `startAnimation()` and `stopAnimation()` functions are probably not even suspending functions, as they interact with the UI.

We wanted to run our `database.storeUser()` blocking work on a background thread, so we specified the `Dispatchers.IO` dispatcher to the `CoroutineContext` object. But this means that all the rest of the code in the coroutine block (that is, the `startAnimation()` and `stopAnimation()` function calls) will be dispatched to a thread pool intended for background work instead of being dispatched to the main thread.

To have more fine-grained control regarding what threads our functions are being dispatched to, coroutines allow us to control the dispatcher by using the `withContext` block, which creates a block of code that can run on a different dispatcher.

Since `startAnimation()` and `stopAnimation()` have to work on the main thread, let's refactor our example.

Let's launch our coroutine with the default dispatcher of `Dispatchers.Main`, and then wrap our work, which has to be run on a background thread (the `database.storeUser(user)` suspending function), with a `withContext` block:

```
fun saveDetails(user: User) {
    lifecycleScope.launch(Dispatchers.Main) {
        startAnimation()
        withContext(Dispatchers.IO) {
            database.storeUser(user)
        }
        stopAnimation()
    }
}
```

The `withContext` function allows us to define a more granular `CoroutineContext` object for the block that it exposes. In our case, we had to pass the `Dispatchers.IO` dispatcher to make sure our blocking work with the database will run on the background thread instead of being dispatched to the main thread.

In other words, our coroutine will have all its work dispatched to the `Dispatchers.Main` dispatcher, unless you define another more granular context that has its own `CoroutineDispatcher` set.

Now we've covered how to use dispatchers and how to ensure more granular control over how our work is dispatched to different threads. However, we haven't covered what the `launch { }` block means. Let's do that next.

Coroutine builders

Coroutine builders (such as `launch`) are extension functions on `CoroutineScope` and allow us to create and start coroutines. Essentially, they are a bridge between the normal synchronous world with regular functions and the suspending world with suspending functions.

Since we can't call suspending functions inside regular functions, a coroutine builder method executed on the `CoroutineScope` object creates a scoped coroutine that provides us with a block of code where we can call our suspending functions. Without scopes, we cannot create coroutines – which is good since this practice helps to prevent memory leaks.

We can use three builder functions to create coroutines:

- `launch`: This starts a coroutine that runs concurrently with the rest of the code. Coroutines started with `launch` won't return the result to the caller – instead, all of the suspending functions will run sequentially inside the block that `launch` exposes. It's our job to get the result from the suspending functions and then interact with that result:

```
fun getUser() {
    lifecycleScope.launch(Dispatchers.IO) {
        val user = database.getUser()
        // show details to UI
    }
}
```

  Most of the time, if you don't need concurrent work, `launch` is the go-to option for starting coroutines since it allows you to run your suspending work inside the block of code provided and doesn't care about anything else.

  If no dispatcher is specified in the coroutine builder, the dispatcher that is going to be used is the dispatcher provided by default by the `CoroutineScope` used to start the coroutine. In our case, if we wouldn't have specified a dispatcher, our coroutine launched with the `launch` coroutine builder will have used the `Dispatchers.Main` dispatcher defined by default by `lifecycleScope`.

  Apart from `lifecycleScope`, `viewModelScope` also provides the same predefined dispatcher of `Dispatchers.Main`. `GlobalScope` on the other hand, defaults to `Dispatchers.Default` if no dispatcher was provided to the coroutine builder.

- `async`: This starts a new coroutine, and it allows you to return the result as a `Deferred<T>` object, where `T` is your expected data type. The deferred object is a promise that your result, `T`, will be returned in the future. To start the coroutine and get a result, you need to call the suspending function, `await`, which blocks the calling thread:

```
lifecycleScope.launch(Dispatchers.IO) {
    val deferredAudio: Deferred<Audio> =
        async { convertTextToSpeech(title) }
    val titleAudio = deferredAudio.await()
    playSound(titleAudio)
}
```

We can't use `async` in a normal function as it has to call the `await` suspending function to get the result. To fix that, first, we've created a parent coroutine with `launch` and started the child coroutine with `async` inside it. This means the child coroutine that was started with `async` inherits its `CoroutineContext` object from the parent coroutine that was started with `launch`.

With `async`, we can get the results of the concurrent work in one place. Where the `async` coroutine builder shines (and where it's recommended to be used) is in tasks with parallel execution where results are required.

Let's say that we need to simultaneously convert two pieces of text into speech and then play both results at the same time:

```
lifecycleScope.launch(Dispatchers.IO) {
    val deferredTitleAudio: Deferred<Audio> =
        async { convertTextToSpeech(title) }
    val deferredSubtitleAudio: Deferred<Audio> =
        async { convertTextToSpeech(subtitle) }
    playSounds(
        deferredTitleAudio.await(),
        deferredSubtitleAudio.await()
    )
}
```

In this particular example, both the resulting `deferredTitleAudio` and `deferredSubtitleAudio` tasks will run in parallel.

Since our Restaurants application hasn't featured concurrent work until now, we won't go any deeper in terms of concurrency topics.

- `runBlocking`: This starts a coroutine that blocks the current thread on which it is invoked until the coroutine has been completed. This builder should be avoided for async work within our app since creating threads and blocking them is less efficient. However, this coroutine builder can be used for unit tests.

Now that we have covered the basics of coroutines, it's high time we implement coroutines in our Restaurants application!

Using coroutines for async work

The first thing that we have to do is identify the async/heavy work that we have done in our Restaurants application.

Without looking at the code, we know that our app retrieves a list of restaurants from the server. It does that by initiating a network request with Retrofit and then waits for a response. This action qualifies as an async job because we don't want to block the main (UI) thread while the app waits for the network response to arrive.

If we check out the `RestaurantsViewModel` class, we can identify that the `getRestaurants()` method is the one place in our application where heavy blocking work is happening:

```
private fun getRestaurants() {
    restaurantsCall = restInterface.getRestaurants()
    restaurantsCall.enqueue(object : Callback
        <List<Restaurant>> {
            override fun onResponse(...) {
                response.body()?.let { restaurants -> ... }
            }

            override fun onFailure(...) {
                t.printStackTrace()
            }
        })
}
```

When we implemented the network request, we used Retrofit's `enqueue()` method to which we passed a `Callback` object where we could wait for the result without blocking the main thread.

To simplify the way we handle this async operation of getting the restaurants from the server, we will implement coroutines. This will allow us to ditch callbacks and make our code more concise.

In this section, we will cover two main steps:

- Implementing coroutines instead of callbacks
- Improving the way our app works with coroutines

Let's get started!

Implementing coroutines instead of callbacks

To handle async work with coroutines, we need to do the following:

- Define our async work in a suspending function.
- Next, create a coroutine and call the suspending function inside it to obtain the result asynchronously.

Enough with the theory, it's time to code! Perform the following steps:

1. Inside the `RestaurantsApiService` interface, add the `suspend` keyword to the `getRestaurants()` method and replace the `Call<List<Restaurant>>` return type of the method with `List<Restaurant>`:

```
interface RestaurantsApiService {
    @GET("restaurants.json")
    suspend fun getRestaurants(): List<Restaurant>
}
```

   Retrofit supports coroutines out of the box for network requests. This means that we can mark any method in our Retrofit interface with the `suspend` keyword; therefore, we can transform the network requests to suspending work that isn't blocking the main thread of the application.

   Because of this, the `Call<T>` return type is redundant. We no longer need Retrofit to return a `Call` object on which we would normally enqueue a `Callback` object to listen for the response – all of this will be handled by the Coroutines API.

2. Since we will no longer receive a `Call` object from Retrofit, we will also not need the `Callback` object in our `RestaurantsViewModel` class. Clean up the `RestaurantsViewModel` component:

   - Remove the `restaurantsCall: Call<List<Restaurant>` member variable.
   - Remove the `restaurantsCall.cancel()` method call inside the `onCleared()` callback.
   - Remove the entire body of the `getRestaurants()` method.

3. Inside the `getRestaurants()` method, call the `restInterface.getRestaurants()` suspending function and store the result in a `restaurants` variable:

```
private fun getRestaurants() {
    val restaurants = restInterface.getRestaurants()
}
```

The IDE will throw an error telling us that we cannot call the `restInterface.getRestaurants()` suspending function from the regular `getRestaurants()` function within the `ViewModel` component.

To fix this, we must create a coroutine, launch it, and call the suspending function there.

4. Before creating a coroutine, we need to create a `CoroutineScope` object. Inside the `ViewModel` component, define a member variable of type `Job` and another of type `CoroutineScope`, just as we learned earlier:

```
class RestaurantsViewModel(…): ViewModel() {
    private var restInterface: RestaurantsApiService
    val state = mutableStateOf(…)
    val job = Job()
    private val scope = CoroutineScope(job +
        Dispatchers.IO)
    ...
}
```

The `job` variable is the handle that will allow us to cancel the coroutine scope, while the `scope` variable will ensure we keep track of the coroutines that are going be to be launched with it.

Since the network request is a heavy blocking operation, we want its suspending work to be executed on the `IO` thread pool to avoid blocking the main thread, so we specified the `Dispatchers.IO` dispatcher for our `scope` object.

5. Inside the `onCleared()` callback method, call the `cancel()` method in the newly created job variable:

```
override fun onCleared() {
    super.onCleared()
    job.cancel()
}
```

By calling `cancel()` on our `job` variable, we ensure that if the `RestaurantsViewModel` component is destroyed (for example, in scenarios where the user navigates to a different screen) the coroutine `scope` object will be canceled through its `job` object reference. Effectively, this will cancel any suspending work and prevent the coroutine from causing a memory leak.

6. Inside the `getRestaurants()` method in our `ViewModel` component, create a coroutine by calling `launch` on the previously defined `scope` object, and inside that body exposed by the coroutine add the existing code where we obtain the restaurants:

```
private fun getRestaurants() {
    scope.launch {
        val restaurants = restInterface.getRestaurants()
    }
}
```

Success! We have launched a coroutine that executes our suspending work of obtaining the restaurants from the server.

7. Next, add the initial code to update our `State` object with the newly received restaurants so that the Compose UI displays them:

```
scope.launch {
    val restaurants = restInterface.getRestaurants()
    state.value = restaurants.restoreSelections()
}
```

However, this approach is flawed. Can you point out why?

Well, we are updating the UI on an incorrect thread. Our `scope` is defined to run the coroutine on a thread from the `Dispatchers.IO` thread pool, but updating the UI should happen on the Main thread.

8. Inside the `getRestaurants()` method, wrap the line of code where the Compose `State` object is updated with a `withContext` block that specifies the `Dispatchers.Main` dispatcher:

```
scope.launch {
    val restaurants = restInterface.getRestaurants()
    withContext(Dispatchers.Main) {
        state.value = restaurants.restoreSelections()
    }
}
```

   By doing this, we ensure that while heavy work is being done on the background threads, the UI is updated from the main thread.

   We have now successfully implemented coroutines in our app. We have defined a scope and created a coroutine where we executed our suspending work: a network request.

9. You can now **Run** the application and notice that on the outside, the behavior of the app hasn't changed. However, behind the scenes, our async work was done with the help of coroutines in a more elegant manner than before.

Even so, there are a few things that could be improved. Let's tackle those next.

Improving the way our app works with coroutines

Our app uses a coroutine to move heavy work from the main thread to specialized threads.

However, if we think about our particular implementation, we can find some ways to improve our coroutine-related code:

- Use predefined scopes as opposed to custom scopes.
- Add error handling.
- Make sure that every `suspend` function is safe to be called on any `Dispatcher` object.

Let's start with the fun one: replacing our custom scope with a predefined one!

Using predefined scopes as opposed to custom scopes

In our current implementation, we've defined a custom `CoroutineScope` object that will make sure that its coroutines will live as long as the `RestaurantsViewModel` instance. To achieve this, we pass a `Job` object to our `CoroutineScope` builder and cancel it when the `ViewModel` component is destroyed: on the `onCleared()` callback method.

Now, remember that coroutines are well integrated with the Jetpack libraries, and when we define scopes, we also talk about predefined scopes such as `lifecycleScope`, `viewModelScope`, and more. These scopes make sure that their coroutines live as long as the component they are bound to, for example, `lifecycleScope` is bound to a `Fragment` or `Activity` component.

> **Note**
>
> Whenever you are launching a coroutine inside components such as `Activity`, `Fragment`, `ViewModel`, or even composable functions, remember that instead of creating and managing your own `CoroutineScope` object, you can use the predefined ones that take care of canceling coroutines automatically. By using predefined scopes, you can better avoid memory leaks as any suspending work is cancelled when needed.

In our scenario, we can simplify our code and replace our custom `CoroutineScope` object with the `viewModelScope` one. Behind the scenes, this predefined scope will take care of canceling all of the coroutines launched with it when its parent `ViewModel` instance has been cleared or destroyed.

Let's do that now:

1. Inside the `getRestaurants()` method of the `RestaurantsViewModel` class, replace `scope` with `viewModelScope`:

```
private fun getRestaurants() {
    viewModelScope.launch {
        val restaurants = …
        …
    }
}
```

2. Since we will no longer use our `scope` object, we need to make sure that our coroutine will run the suspending work in the background, just as it did with the previous scope. Pass a `Dispatchers.IO` dispatcher to the `launch` method:

```
viewModelScope.launch(Dispatchers.IO) {
    val restaurants = restInterface.getRestaurants()
    withContext(Dispatchers.Main) {
        state.value = restaurants.restoreSelections()
    }
}
```

   Usually, the `launch` coroutine builder inherits `CoroutineContext` from its parent coroutine. In our particular case though, if no dispatcher is specified, coroutines launched with `viewModelScope` will default to using `Dispatchers.Main`.

   However, we want our network request to be executed on a background thread from the specialized I/O thread pool, so we passed an initial `CoroutineContext` object with a `Dispatchers.IO` dispatcher to our `launch` call.

3. Remove the `onCleared()` callback method entirely from the `ViewModel` class. We will no longer need to cancel our coroutine `scope` from a `job` object because `viewModelScope` takes care of that for us.
4. Remove the `job` and `scope` member variables from the `RestaurantsViewModel` class.
5. You can now **Run** the application and again notice that on the outside, the behavior of the app hasn't changed. Our code now works the same but is greatly simplified because we used a predefined scope instead of handling everything by ourselves.

Next, we must re-add error handling to our project. However, this time, we will do it in the context of coroutines.

Adding error handling

In the previous implementation with callbacks, we received an error callback from Retrofit. However, with coroutines, it appears that since our suspending function returns `List<Restaurant>>`, there is no room for error.

Indeed, we are not handling any error that could be thrown. For example, if you try to launch the application without internet right now, Retrofit will throw a `Throwable` object, which, in turn, will crash our app with a similar error as follows:

```
E/AndroidRuntime: FATAL EXCEPTION: DefaultDispatcher-worker-1
```

To handle errors, we can simply wrap suspending function calls in a `try catch` block:

```
viewModelScope.launch(Dispatchers.IO) {
    try {
        val restaurants = restInterface.getRestaurants()
        // show restaurants
    } catch (e: Exception) {
        e.printStackTrace()
    }
}
```

The preceding approach is fine, but the code becomes less concise because of another level of nesting. Additionally, to better support a single point of error handling, coroutines allow you to pass a `CoroutineExceptionHandler` object to the context of your `CoroutineScope` object:

```
Creates a CoroutineExceptionHandler instance.
Params: handler - a function which handles exception thrown by a coroutine
@Suppress( ...names: "FunctionName")
public inline fun CoroutineExceptionHandler(crossinline handler: (CoroutineContext, Throwable) → Unit): CoroutineExceptionHandler =
    object : AbstractCoroutineContextElement(CoroutineExceptionHandler), CoroutineExceptionHandler {
        override fun handleException(context: CoroutineContext, exception: Throwable) =
            handler.invoke(context, exception)
    }
```

Figure 4.5 – The signature of CoroutineExceptionHandler

The `CoroutineExceptionHandler` object allows us to handle errors thrown by any coroutine launched within a `CoroutineScope` object, no matter how nested it might be. This handler gives us access to a function that exposes the `CoroutineContext` object and the `Throwable` object thrown in this particular context.

Let's add such a handler to the `RestaurantsViewModel` class. Perform the following steps:

1. Define an `errorHandler` member variable of type `CoroutineExceptionHandler` and print the stack trace of the `exception: Throwable` parameter:

```
class RestaurantsViewModel() : ViewModel() {
    ...
    private val errorHandler =
        CoroutineExceptionHandler { _, exception ->
            exception.printStackTrace()
    }
    ...
}
```

   We're not interested in the first parameter of type `CoroutineContext`, so we named it with an underscore, _.

2. Inside the `getRestaurants()` method, pass the `errorHandler` variable to the `launch` block using the + operator:

```
private fun getRestaurants() {
      viewModelScope.launch(Dispatchers.IO +
                              errorHandler) {
            ...
      }
}
```

   By passing our `errorHandler` variable to the `launch` method, we make sure that the `CoroutineContext` object of this coroutine sets this `CoroutineExceptionHandler`, which will allow us to handle errors inside our handler.

3. Try running the app again without the internet.

   Now the app shouldn't crash because the `errorHandler` variable will catch the `Throwable` object thrown by Retrofit and allow us to print its stack trace.

> **Note**
>
> As an improvement, try to find a way of notifying the UI that an error has occurred, thereby informing the user of what just happened.

We are now handling errors with coroutines, so it's time to move to the last point of improvement – handling the switch of dispatchers correctly.

Making sure that every suspending function is safe to be called on any dispatcher

When defining suspending functions, a good practice is to make sure that every suspending function can be called on any `Dispatcher` object. This way, the caller (in our case, the coroutine) doesn't have to worry about what thread will be needed to execute the suspending function.

Let's analyze our code with the coroutine:

```
private fun getRestaurants() {
    viewModelScope.launch(Dispatchers.IO + errorHandler) {
        val restaurants = restInterface.getRestaurants()
        withContext(Dispatchers.Main) {
            state.value = restaurants.restoreSelections()
        }
    }
}
```

The `getRestaurants()` method of the `restInterface: RestaurantsApiService` interface is a suspending function. This function should always be run on `Dispatchers.IO` since it executes a heavy I/O operation, that is, the network request.

However, this would mean that whenever we have to call `restInterface.getRestaurants()`, we either have to call this suspending function from a coroutine that has a scope of `Dispatchers.IO` – just as we did previously – or always wrap it in a `withContext(Dispatchers.IO)` block inside the caller coroutine.

Both of these alternatives don't scale well. Imagine that you have to call `restInterface.getRestaurants()` 10 times in the `RestaurantsViewModel` class. You would always have to be careful with setting the dispatcher when calling this function.

Let's address this by creating a separate method where we can specify the correct dispatcher for our suspending function:

1. Inside the `RestaurantsViewModel` class, create a separate suspending method, called `getRemoteRestaurants()`, and wrap the `restInterface.getRestaurants()` call there with a `withContext()` block:

   ```
   private suspend fun getRemoteRestaurants():
   List<Restaurant> {
       return withContext(Dispatchers.IO) {
           restInterface.getRestaurants()
       }
   }
   ```

   To the `withContext` method, we've passed the corresponding dispatcher for this suspending function: `Dispatchers.IO`.

   This means that whenever this suspending function is called (from a coroutine or another suspending function), the dispatcher will be switched to `Dispatchers.IO` for the `restInterface.getRestaurants()` call's execution.

   By doing so, we make sure that whoever is calling `getRemoteRestaurants()` will not have to care about the correct thread dispatcher for the content of this method.

2. In the `getRestaurants()` method of the `ViewModel` component, replace the `restInterface.getRestaurants()` method call with `getRemoteRestaurants()`:

   ```
   private fun getRestaurants() {
       viewModelScope.launch(Dispatchers.IO + errorHandler)
       {
           val restaurants = getRemoteRestaurants()
           withContext(Dispatchers.Main) {
               state.value = restaurants.restoreSelections()
           }
       }
   }
   ```

3. Since the content of the `getRemoteRestaurants()` method will be called on its appropriate dispatcher, we no longer have to pass `Dispatchers.IO` to the launch block. Remove the `Dispatchers.IO` dispatcher from the coroutine `launch` block:

```
private fun getRestaurants() {
    viewModelScope.launch(errorHandler) {
        val restaurants = getRemoteRestaurants()
        withContext(Dispatchers.Main) {
            state.value = restaurants.
                restoreSelections()
        }
    }
}
```

   By default, the launch block will inherit the `CoroutineContext` (and so its defined `Dispatcher` object) from its parent coroutine. In our case, there is no parent coroutine, so the `launch` block will launch a coroutine on the `Dispatchers.Main` thread which was predefined by the `viewModelScope` custom scope.

4. Since the coroutine will now run on the `Dispatchers.Main` thread, we can remove the redundant `withContext(Dispatchers.Main)` block from within the `getRestaurants()` method. The `getRestaurants()` method should now look like this:

```
private fun getRestaurants() {
    viewModelScope.launch(errorHandler) {
        val restaurants = getRemoteRestaurants()
        state.value = restaurants.restoreSelections()
    }
}
```

Now, the `getRestaurants()` method where we launched the coroutine is much easier to read and understand. Our suspending function call, for instance, `getRemoteRestaurants()`, is called inside this coroutine on the `Dispatchers.Main` dispatcher. However, at the same time, our suspending function has its own `withContext()` block with its corresponding `Dispatcher` object set:

```
private suspend fun getRemoteRestaurants()
        : List<Restaurant> {
    return withContext(Dispatchers.IO) {
        restInterface.getRestaurants()
    }
}
```

This practice allows us to call suspending functions from coroutines with any given `Dispatcher` object, simply because the suspending functions have their own `CoroutineContext` object set with their appropriate `Dispatcher` objects.

At runtime, even though the coroutines are launched on their initial `Dispatcher` object, when our suspending functions are called, the `Dispatcher` object is briefly overridden for every suspending function that is internally wrapped with a `withContext` block.

> **Note**
>
> For Retrofit interface calls such as `restInterface.getRestaurants()`, we can skip wrapping them in `withContext()` blocks because Retrofit already does this behind the scenes and sets the `Dispatchers.IO` dispatcher for all suspending methods from within its interface.

Finally, the application should behave the same. However, in terms of good practices, we made sure that the correct `Dispatcher` object is set for every suspending function out of the box, and without us having to manually set it in every coroutine.

Now that we improved the way dispatchers are set within our suspending function and coroutine, it's time to wrap this chapter up.

Summary

In this chapter, we learned how coroutines allow us to write async code in a much clearer and more concise way.

We understood what coroutines are, how they work, and why they are needed in the first place. We unveiled the core elements of coroutines: from `suspend` functions to `CoroutineScope` objects, to `CoroutineContext` objects and `Dispatcher` objects.

Then, we replaced the callbacks with coroutines in our Restaurants application and noticed how the code is much easier to understand and less nested. Additionally, we learned how to perform error handling with coroutines and integrated some of the best practices when working with coroutines.

In the next chapter, we will add another Compose-based screen to our Restaurants application and learn how to navigate between screens in Compose with yet another Jetpack library.

Further reading

While canceling coroutines might seem simple with the help of the associated `Job` objects, it's important to note that any cancelation must be cooperative. More specifically, when coroutines perform suspending work based on conditional statements, you must ensure the coroutine is cooperative with respect to canceling.

You can read about this topic, in more detail, in the official documentation: `https://kotlinlang.org/docs/cancellation-and-timeouts.html#cancellation-is-cooperative`.

5
Adding Navigation in Compose With Jetpack Navigation

In this chapter, we'll focus on a core Jetpack library, the Navigation component. This library is essential to us since it allows us to easily navigate between application screens.

So far, we have only created a screen in our Restaurants application, where we displayed a list of diners. It's time to step up the game and add another screen to our application!

In the first section, *Introducing the Jetpack Navigation component*, we will explore the basic concepts and elements of the Navigation component. In the second section, *Creating a new Compose-based screen*, we will create a new screen to display the details of a specific restaurant and realize that we don't know how to navigate to it.

In the third section, *Implementing navigation with Jetpack Navigation*, we will add the Navigation component to the Restaurants application and use it to navigate to the second screen. Finally, in the *Adding support for deep links* section, we will create a deep link to our newly created screen and make sure that our application knows how to handle it.

To summarize, in this chapter we're going to cover the following main topics:

- Introducing the Jetpack Navigation component
- Creating a new Compose-based screen
- Implementing navigation with Jetpack Navigation
- Adding support for deep links

Before jumping in, let's set up the technical requirements for this chapter.

Technical requirements

Building Compose-based Android projects with Jetpack Navigation usually requires your day-to-day tools. However, to follow along smoothly, make sure you have the following:

- The Arctic Fox 2020.3.1 version of Android Studio. You can also use a newer Android Studio version or even Canary builds, but note that the IDE interface and other generated code files might differ from the ones used throughout this book.
- Kotlin 1.6.10 or newer plugin installed in Android Studio
- The Restaurants app code from the previous chapter

The starting point for this chapter is represented by the Restaurants application developed in *Chapter 4, Handling Async Operations with Coroutines*. If you haven't followed the implementation from the previous chapter, access the starting point for this chapter by navigating to the `Chapter_04` directory of the repository and importing the Android project named `chapter_4_restaurants_app`.

To access the solution code for this chapter, navigate to the `Chapter_05` directory: `https://github.com/PacktPublishing/Kickstart-Modern-Android-Development-with-Jetpack-and-Kotlin/tree/main/Chapter_05/chapter_5_restaurants_app`.

Introducing the Jetpack Navigation component

The **Navigation** component is Jetpack's solution to navigation within Android apps. This library allows you to easily implement navigation between the screens of your application.

To promote a predictable user experience and consistent manner of handling app flows, the Navigation component adheres to a set of principles. The two most important principles are as follows:

- The application has a fixed start **destination** (screen) – this allows the application behavior to be predictable because the app will always present this destination first, no matter where it is being launched from.

  In our Restaurants application, we plan to set the start destination as our existing screen with the list of restaurants (represented by the `RestaurantsScreen()` composable function). In other words, this is the first screen that the user will always see when launching the app from the Android launcher screen.

- The navigation state is defined as a stack of destinations, often called the **back stack**. When the app is initially started, the stack will contain the app's start destination – let's call this *Screen A*. If you navigate from *Screen A* to *Screen B*, *B* will be added on top of the stack. This applies when navigating to *Screen C* too. To better understand how the back stack works, let's try to illustrate it in such a scenario:

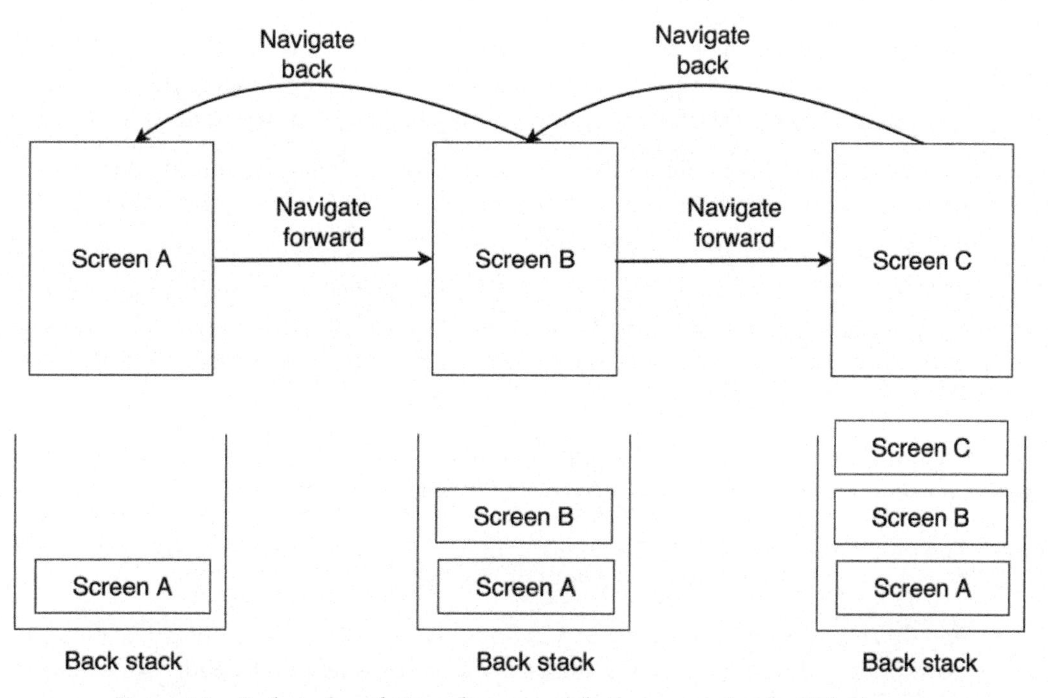

Figure 5.1 – Back stack evolution of screens while the user navigates within the app

At the top of the back stack, you will always have the current screen the user is at right now. When navigating back to the previous screen, the top of the back stack is popped, just as we did in *Figure 5.1*, where navigating from *Screen C* to *Screen B* resulted in the pop of *Screen C* from the back stack.

All these operations are always done at the top of the stack, while the back of the stack will always contain the fixed start destination – in our case, *Screen A*.

The Navigation component takes care of handling the back stack operations behind the scenes for us.

> **Note**
>
> Initially, the Navigation component specialized in offering navigation mainly between `Fragment` components. Today, the library also supports Compose and the navigation between composable functions.

Apart from following clear principles when it comes to UI navigation, the Navigation component has three main constituent elements:

- **Navigation graph**: The core source of information related to navigation within your app. In the navigation graph, you define all the destinations as well as the possible paths that the user can take throughout the app to achieve different tasks.
- **NavHost**: A container composable function that will display the composable destinations. As the user navigates between different destinations, the content of the navigation host is swapped and recomposed.
- **NavController**: A stateful object that handles the navigation between composable screens and is, therefore, in charge of propagating updates inside the destinations back stack. The navigation controller sets the correct destinations to `NavHost` as the user starts navigating between screens.

Now, when you implement the Navigation component in your Compose-based Android app, you will gain a lot of benefits. The following lists some examples:

- You don't need to handle the complexity of navigation between composable functions. The library does that out of the box for you.
- You don't need to handle *Up* or *Back* actions on your own. If you press the system's **Back** button, the library will automatically pop the current destination from the back stack and send the user to the previous destination.

- You benefit from scoped `ViewModel` components to a specific Navigation graph or destination. This means that the `ViewModel` instance used by a composable destination will live for as long as the composable screen does.
- You don't need to implement deep links from scratch. Deep links allow you to directly navigate to a specific destination within the app without having to traverse the entire path of screens that get you there. We will see how they work in the *Adding support for deep links* section of this chapter.

Now that we have a basic overview of the elements and advantages of using Jetpack Navigation, it's time to create a new screen so we can implement navigation in our Restaurants application.

Creating a new Compose-based screen

Real-world applications are required to display a lot of content, so one screen probably won't suffice. So far, our Restaurants application features a simple screen where all the restaurants that we receive from our remote database are displayed.

Let's practice all the skills we've learned so far by creating a new screen that will display the details of a particular restaurant. The plan is that when users press on a particular restaurant from the list inside our `RestaurantsScreen()` composable screen, we should take them to a new details screen for that particular restaurant.

Yet to perform navigation between two screens, we need first to build the second screen. Unlike with the first composable screen, it's time to change our tactic and build it from top to bottom. Let's build this second feature first by defining the network request, then executing it inside its own `ViewModel`, and finally creating the composable UI that will consume the data, as follows:

- Defining the HTTP request for the contents of a restaurant
- Getting the contents of a specific restaurant
- Building the restaurant details screen

Let's start!

Defining the HTTP request for the contents of a restaurant

We need to know how to obtain the data for our new restaurant details screen. Instead of relying on the previously retrieved data (the list of restaurants), we want to make every screen in our application as independent as possible. This way, we design our application to easily support deep links and we better defend ourselves from events such as a system-initiated process death.

That's why we will build this new screen so that it gets its own content. In other words, in the new screen, we will get the details for a particular restaurant from the same database where we've obtained the list of restaurants. But how will we do that?

Remember that the restaurants within our Firebase database have a unique `Integer` identifier field called `r_id`, as shown in the following screenshot:

Figure 5.2 – Identifying the unique identifier field for restaurants in Firebase

We can use this field to get the details of one specific restaurant. And since `r_id` is mapped to the `id: Int` field of the `Restaurant` object, this means that when the user presses on a restaurant in our `RestaurantsScreen` composable, we can forward the `id` value to the second screen.

In the second screen, we will execute an API request to our Firebase REST API and pass the value of the unique ID of the restaurant within our app that corresponds to the `r_id` identifier of the restaurant inside the remote database.

The Firebase REST API has us covered for such cases. If we want to get the details of one element from the restaurants JSON content, we must append two query parameters to the same URL used to retrieve the entire restaurants list:

- `orderBy=r_id` to instruct Firebase to filter the elements by their `r_id` field.
- `equalTo=2` to let Firebase know the value of the `r_id` field of the restaurant element that we're looking for – in this case `2`.

To practice, place in your browser address bar the Firebase URL that you've used to get the restaurants until now and append the previous two query parameters as follows:

```
https://restaurants-db-default-rtdb.firebaseio.com/restaurants.
json?orderBy="r_id"&equalTo=2
```

If you access your link, the response will, unfortunately, look like this:

```
{ "error" : "Index not defined, add \".indexOn\": \"r_id\", for
path \"/restaurants\", to the rules" }
```

Firebase needs some additional configuration so that we can get the details of only one element within the list, so let's do that now:

1. Navigate to your Firebase console and log into your Google account by accessing this link: `https://console.firebase.google.com/`.
2. From the list of Firebase projects, select the one you've previously created to store the restaurants.
3. In the left menu, expand the **Build** tab, search for **Realtime Database**, and then select it.
4. Move away from the preselected **Data** tab and select the **Rules** tab.
5. We need to allow Firebase to index the restaurants based on their `r_id` field, so update the write `rules` as follows:

```
{
    "rules": {
        ".read": "true",
        ".write": "true",
        "restaurants": {
```

```
                ".indexOn": ["r_id"]
            }
        }
    }
```

By doing so, we've instructed Firebase that the JSON array content located at the `restaurants` node can be indexed and accessed individually.

6. Now, try to access the URL with the details for the restaurant with the `id` field value of `2` again:

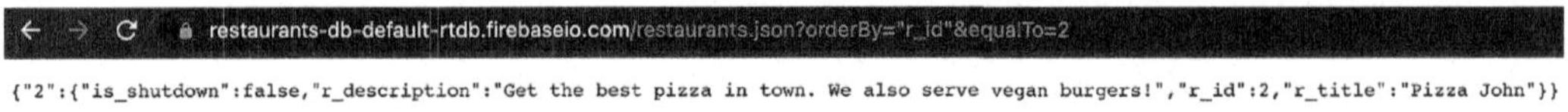

restaurants-db-default-rtdb.firebaseio.com/restaurants.json?orderBy="r_id"&equalTo=2

{"2":{"is_shutdown":false,"r_description":"Get the best pizza in town. We also serve vegan burgers!","r_id":2,"r_title":"Pizza John"}}

Figure 5.3 – Obtaining the response from Firebase for one restaurant JSON object

> **Note:**
> To see the structure of the JSON response in a more readable manner in your browser, you can add the `&print=pretty` query parameter at the end of the request URL.

Success! We've obtained the details of the restaurant with the `r_id` field's value of `2`.

Now, let's implement this request in our app:

1. First, inside the `RestaurantsApiService` interface, define a `suspend` function called `getRestaurant()`, which will serve as another `@GET` HTTP method that will get the details of one restaurant:

```
interface RestaurantsApiService {
    [...]
    @GET("restaurants.json?orderBy=\"r_id\"")
    suspend fun getRestaurant(
      @Query("equalTo") id: Int): Unit
}
```

Let's break down the code we've just added to our second HTTP method:

- The HTTP call defined by this method is an async job that takes some time to finish, so we've marked the method as a suspending function by adding the `suspend` keyword.
- Inside the `@GET` annotation, we specified not only that we want to access the `restaurants.json` JSON content, but this time we also hardcoded the `orderBy` query parameter and specified the `r_id` value so that we filter the elements by the value of their `r_id` key.
- This method receives one essential parameter – `id: Int` that represents the unique ID of the restaurant corresponding to the `r_id` field in the database. To tell Retrofit that this method parameter is a query parameter in the required HTTP call, we've annotated it with the `@Query` annotation and passed the `"equalTo"` value.

Yet our HTTP call defined by our `getRestaurant()` method is missing something crucial: the response type. We've set `Unit` as the response type, but we need to receive a proper response object. To see what to expect, let's have a closer look at the response we received earlier on inside our browser:

```
1 {
2     "2": {
3         "is_shutdown": false,
4         "r_description": "Get the best pizza in town. We also serve vegan burgers!",
5         "r_id": 2,
6         "r_title": "Pizza John"
7     }
8 }
```

Figure 5.4 – The JSON response structure of the restaurant object

If we look at these fields, `is_shutdown`, `r_description`, `r_id`, and `r_title`, we can easily identify the response JSON object as the same JSON object that we receive in the existing HTTP request that gets all the restaurants.

And since we've mapped such a JSON object in the past to our `Restaurant` data class using the `@Serialized` annotations, we could very well say our new `getRestaurant()` HTTP call will receive a simple `Restaurant` object as a response.

We wouldn't be far from the truth, yet this response wouldn't be fully correct.

If we look closer at the previous JSON response, we notice that the restaurant JSON object is a value object that corresponds to a `String` key with the value of `2`:

```
1 {
2     "2": {
3         "is_shutdown": false,
4         "r_description": "Get the best pizza in town. We also serve vegan burgers!",
5         "r_id": 2,
6         "r_title": "Pizza John"
7     }
8 }
```

Figure 5.5 –Identifying the key field for the restaurant object

This key corresponds to an internal index generated by Firebase that represents the order number in which the corresponding restaurant was added to the database. This response structure isn't typical for most REST API responses, yet Firebase has this quirk of wrapping your JSON object in a key that is unknown at compile time.

2. To get around this, inside the `RestaurantsApiService` interface, update the `getRestaurant()` method to return a `Map` object with an unknown `String` key and a `Restaurant` data type as the value:

```
interface RestaurantsApiService {
    ...

    @GET("restaurants.json?orderBy=\"r_id\"")
    suspend fun getRestaurant(@Query("equalTo") id: Int)
        : Map<String, Restaurant>
}
```

Great work! We have our app ready to execute a second network request that obtains the details about a specific restaurant, so it's time to call this request.

Getting the contents of a specific restaurant

Now that we know how to obtain the details about a specific restaurant, it's time to execute our newly defined network request.

Our existing `RestaurantsScreen` composable delegates the responsibility of requesting the list of restaurants that must be displayed to a `ViewModel` class, so let's create another `ViewModel` so that our second screen can do the same:

1. Create a new file by left-clicking the application package, selecting **New**, and then **Kotlin Class/File**. Enter `RestaurantDetailsViewModel` as the name and select **File** as the type. Inside the newly created file, add the following code:

```
class RestaurantDetailsViewModel(): ViewModel() {
    private var restInterface: RestaurantsApiService
    init {
        val retrofit: Retrofit = Retrofit.Builder()
            .addConverterFactory(GsonConverterFactory
                .create())
            .baseUrl("your-firebase-base-url")
            .build()
        restInterface = retrofit.create(
            RestaurantsApiService::class.java)
    }
}
```

   In the preceding snippet, we've created a `ViewModel` class where we instantiated a Retrofit client of type `RestaurantsApiService`, just like we did in the `RestaurantsViewModel` class.

   The block of code that initializes a Retrofit client is indeed duplicated in both our `ViewModel` classes, but don't worry because you will be able to fix this during *Chapter 9, Implementing Dependency Injection with Jetpack Hilt.*

> **Note**
>
> Remember to pass your Firebase database URL to the `baseUrl()` method. This URL should be identical to the one used in the `RestaurantsViewModel` class and should correspond to your Firebase Realtime Database project.

2. Inside the newly created `ViewModel`, create a `getRemoteRestaurant()` method that receives an `id` parameter and takes care of executing the network request to get the details of a specific restaurant:

```
class RestaurantDetailsViewModel() : ViewModel() {
    private var restInterface: RestaurantsApiService
     init { [...] }
    private suspend fun getRemoteRestaurant(id: Int):
            Restaurant {
        return withContext(Dispatchers.IO) {
            val responseMap = restInterface
                .getRestaurant(id)
            return@withContext responseMap.values.first()
        }
    }
}
```

Let's break down what happens inside the `getRemoteRestaurant()` method:

- It receives an `id` parameter corresponding to the restaurant whose details we need and returns the specific `Restaurant` object.
- It is marked by the `suspend` keyword since the job of executing a network request is a suspending work that shouldn't block the main thread.
- It is wrapped in a `withContext()` block that specifies the `Dispatchers.IO` dispatcher since the suspending work should be run on the specialized IO thread.
- It executes the network request to obtain the details of a restaurant by calling the `getRestaurant()` suspending function on `restInterface` while passing `id` of the specific restaurant.
- Finally, it obtains `Map<String, Restaurant>` from the REST API. To unwrap this and obtain the restaurant, we call the `values()` function of `Map` and get the first `Restaurant` object with the `.first()` extension function.

> **Note:**
>
> The `first()` extension function is called on the `Collection<Restaurant>` object returned by the `values()` function of `Map`. With this extension function, we are obtaining the first element, that is, the `Restaurant` object we're interested in. However, the `first()` extension function can throw a `NoSuchElementException` if for some reason we query for a non-existent restaurant. In production, you should cover this case as well by catching such an exception.

3. Since `RestaurantDetailsViewModel` will hold the state of the restaurant details screen, add a `MutableState` object that will hold a `Restaurant` object and initialize it with a `null` value until we finish executing the network request that retrieves it:

```
class RestaurantDetailsViewModel(): ViewModel() {
    private var restInterface: RestaurantsApiService
    val state = mutableStateOf<Restaurant?>(null)
     [...]
}
```

4. Inside the `init` block of `RestaurantDetailsViewModel`, below the instantiation of the Retrofit client, launch a coroutine with the help of the `viewModelScope` builder:

```
init {
    [...]
    restInterface = retrofit.create(...)
    viewModelScope.launch {
        val restaurant = getRemoteRestaurant(2)
        state.value = restaurant
    }
}
```

We needed to launch a coroutine because the job of getting a `Restaurant` object from our remote Firebase API would have blocked the main thread. We've used the built-in `viewModelScope` coroutine builder to make sure that the launched coroutine will live as long as the `RestaurantDetailsViewModel` instance does. Inside the coroutine, we did the following:

1. We first called the suspending `getRemoteRestaurants()` function and passed a hardcoded value of `2` as the `id` of the restaurant. At this time, `RestaurantsViewModel` has no idea what's the `id` of the restaurant that it's looking for – we will fix this soon when we perform the navigation.
2. We stored the obtained `Restaurant` inside the `restaurant` variable and passed it to the `state` variable of the `RestaurantDetailsViewModel` class so that the UI will be recomposed with the freshly received restaurant content.

We've executed the network request to obtain the details about a restaurant and prepared the state so that a Compose-based screen can display its contents. Let's build the new screen up next.

Building the restaurant details screen

We need to create a new composable screen that will display the details about a specific restaurant:

1. Create a new file inside the application package called `RestaurantDetailsScreen` and create the `RestaurantDetailsScreen` composable:

```
@Composable
fun RestaurantDetailsScreen() {
    val viewModel: RestaurantDetailsViewModel =
        viewModel()
    val item = viewModel.state.value
    if (item != null) {
        // composables
    }
}
```

Inside of it, we've instantiated its corresponding `ViewModel` and accessed the `State` object, just like we previously did in the `RestaurantsScreen` composable. The `State` object holds the `Restaurant` object, which we're storing inside the `item` variable. If `item` is not `null`, we will display the details about the restaurant by passing a composable hierarchy.

2. Since we plan to reuse some composable functions from the first screen, head back inside the `RestaurantsScreen.kt` file and mark the `RestaurantIcon` and `RestaurantDetails` composables as public for use by removing their `private` keywords.

3. Add a new parameter to the `RestaurantDetails` composable called `horizontalAlignment` and pass it to the column's `horizontalAlignment` parameter:

```
@Composable
fun RestaurantDetails(
    … ,
    modifier: Modifier,
    horizontalAlignment: Alignment.Horizontal
                                = Alignment.Start
) {
    Column(
        modifier = modifier,
        horizontalAlignment = horizontalAlignment
    ) { ... }
}
```

By doing so, we can control how the `Column` children are horizontally aligned so we can change this behavior in the new screen. Since we want `Column` to position its children horizontally to the left by default (so that its effect in the `RestaurantsScreen` composable won't differ), we passed `Alignment.Start` as the default value.

4. Inside the `RestaurantDetailsScreen` composable, add a `Column` instance that contains `RestaurantIcon`, `RestaurantDetails`, and `Text` composables, all positioned vertically and centered horizontally:

```
@Composable
fun RestaurantDetailsScreen() {
    val viewModel: RestaurantDetailsViewModel =
        viewModel()
    val item = viewModel.state.value
    if (item != null) {
        Column(
            horizontalAlignment =
                Alignment.CenterHorizontally,
            modifier =
                Modifier.fillMaxSize().padding(16.dp)
        ) {
            RestaurantIcon(
                Icons.Filled.Place,
                Modifier.padding(
                    top = 32.dp,
                    bottom = 32.dp
                )
            )
            RestaurantDetails(
                item.title,
                item.description,
                Modifier.padding(bottom = 32.dp),
                Alignment.CenterHorizontally)
            Text("More info coming soon!")
        }
    }
}
```

To prove how simple it is to reuse composables, we've passed the same `RestaurantIcon` and `RestaurantDetails` composables used in the first screen to our `Column`. We've configured them with different `Modifier` objects and additionally passed `Alignment.centerHorizontally` to the `RestaurantDetails` composable's new alignment parameter added previously.

5. To test that everything works fine, and our new screen renders the details of the hardcoded restaurant with an `id` value of `2`, navigate back to `MainActivity` and inside the `setContent` method, replace the `RestaurantsScreen` composable with `RestaurantDetailsScreen`:

```
setContent {
    RestaurantsAppTheme {
        //RestaurantsScreen()
        RestaurantDetailsScreen()
    }
}
```

6. Run the application and we get the following screenshot:

6:32
Pizza John
Get the best pizza in town. We also serve vegan burgers!
More info coming soon!

Figure 5.6 – Displaying the RestaurantDetailsScreen() composable

Awesome! We have now created our second screen, the restaurant details screen. We can now start thinking about the navigation between our two screens.

Implementing navigation with Jetpack Navigation

Navigation within apps represents those interactions that allow the user to navigate back and forth between several screens.

In our Restaurants application, we now have two screens, and we want to navigate from the first one to the second one. In the first screen, we display a list of restaurants and when the users press on one restaurant item from the list, we want to take them to the second screen, the details screen:

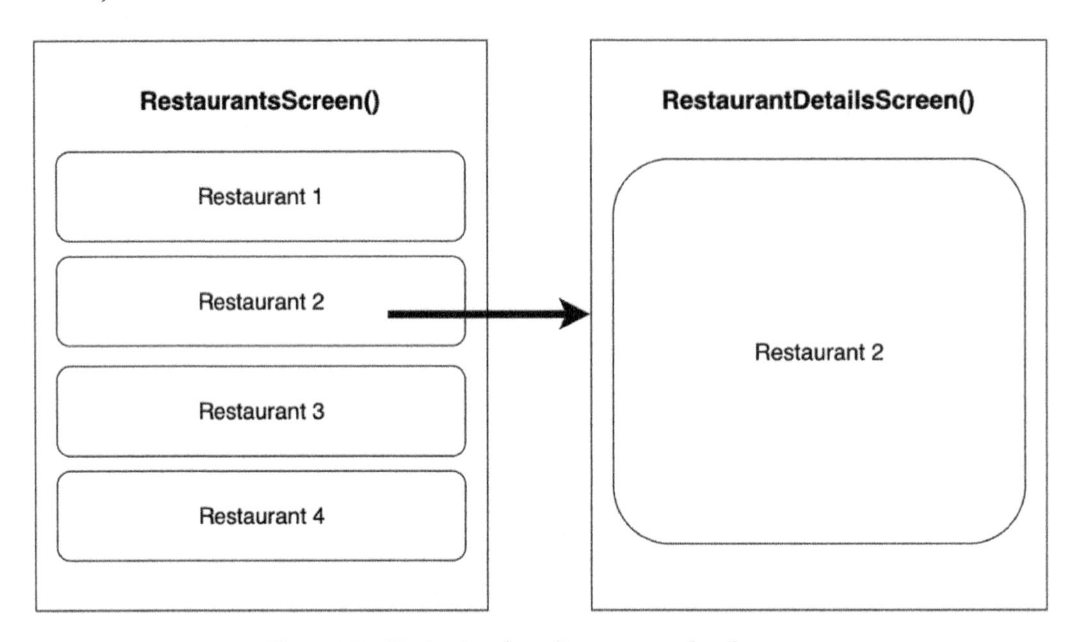

Figure 5.7 – Navigation from list screen to details screen

Basically, we want to perform a simple navigation action from the `RestaurantsScreen` composable to the `RestaurantDetailsScreen` composable. To achieve a simple navigation action, we need to implement a navigation library that will not only allow us to transition from the first screen to the second screen but should also allow us to return to the previous screen with the press of the **Back** button.

As we already know, the Jetpack Navigation component comes to our rescue as it will help us implement such a behavior! Let's start with the following steps:

1. Inside the `build.gradle` file in the app module, add the dependency for the Navigation component with Compose inside the dependencies block:

```
implementation "androidx.navigation:navigation-
compose:2.4.2"
```

After updating the `build.gradle` file, make sure to sync your project with its Gradle files. You can do that by pressing on the **File** menu option and then by selecting **Sync Project with Gradle Files**.

2. Inside the `MainActivity` class, create a new empty composable function called `RestaurantsApp()`:

```
@Composable
private fun RestaurantsApp() {
}
```

   This composable function will act as the parent composable function of our Restaurants application. Here, all the screens of the app will be defined.

3. Inside the `onCreate()` method, replace the `RestaurantsDetailsScreen()` composable that is passed to the `setContent` method with the `RestaurantsApp()` composable:

```
setContent {
    RestaurantsAppTheme {
        RestaurantsApp()
    }
}
```

4. Inside the `RestaurantsApp()` composable function, instantiate `NavController` via the `rememberNavController()` method:

```
@Composable
private fun RestaurantsApp() {
    val navController = rememberNavController()
}
```

   The `NavController` object handles the navigation between composable screens – it operates on the back stack of composable destinations. This means that across recompositions, it must keep the current state of the navigation stack. For that to happen, it must be a stateful object – that's why we used the `rememberNavController` syntax, which is similar to the `remember` block we've been using when defining `State` objects.

5. Next up, we need to create a `NavHost` container composable that will display the composable destinations. Every time a navigation action between composables is done, the content within `NavHost` is recomposed automatically.

   Add a `NavHost` composable and pass both, the `NavController` instance created previously and an empty `String` to the `startDestination` parameter:

```
import androidx.navigation.compose.NavHost
[...]
```

```
@Composable
private fun RestaurantsApp() {
    val navController = rememberNavController()
    NavHost(navController, startDestination = "") {
    }
}
```

Among other parameters, `NavHost` specifies three mandatory parameters:

- A `navController: NavHostController` object that is associated with a single `NavHost` composable. `NavHost` links `NavController` with a navigation graph that defines the possible destinations of the application. In our case, we've passed the `navController` variable to this parameter.
- A `startDestination: String` object that defines the entry-point **route** of the navigation graph. The route is `String`, which defines the path to a specific destination (composable screen). Every destination should have a unique route. In our case, since we haven't defined any routes, we've passed an empty `String` to `startDestination`.
- The `builder: NavGraphBuilder.() -> Unit` trailing lambda parameter, which uses the lambda syntax from the Navigation Kotlin DSL (just like `LazyColumn` or `LazyRow` did with their own DSL) to construct a navigation graph. In here, we should define routes and set corresponding composables, yet so far we've set an empty body { } function to the trailing lambda parameter.

6. To build the navigation graph, we must make use of the `builder` parameter and instead of passing only an empty function, inside of it, we need to start adding routes that specify composable destinations.

   To do that, make use of the DSL function called `composable()` where you can provide a route string to the `route` parameter and a composable function corresponding to the desired destination to the trailing lambda `content` parameter:

```
@Composable
private fun RestaurantsApp() {
    val navController = rememberNavController()
    NavHost(
        navController,
        startDestination = "restaurants"
```

```
        ) {
            composable(route = "restaurants") {
                RestaurantsScreen()
            }
        }
    }
```

Through the `composable()` DSL function, we've created a route with the value of `"restaurants"` that navigates to the `RestaurantsScreen()` composable.

Additionally, we've passed the same route to the `startDestination` parameter of `NavHost`, thereby making our `RestaurantsScreen()` composable the unique entry point of our application.

7. By calling the `composable()` DSL function again inside the navigation graph builder, add another route that points to the `RestaurantDetailsScreen()` destination and that derives from the `"restaurants"` route by appending the `{restaurant_id}` argument placeholder:

```
    NavHost(navController, startDestination = "...") {
        composable(route = "restaurants") { … }
        composable(route = "restaurants/{restaurant_id}") {
            RestaurantDetailsScreen()
        }
    }
```

We want to navigate from the `"restaurants"` route to this new route that points to the `RestaurantDetailsSreen()` composable, so the `{restaurant_id}` placeholder will take the `id` value of the restaurant to which we are trying to navigate.

In practice, this route branches off the `"restaurants"` route, and while being structured similarly to a URL (because of the `"/"` element that delimitates a new path), we can say that this route can have multiple values, depending on `id` of the restaurant we're looking to navigate to. For example, this route can have values at runtime such as `"restaurants/0"` or `"restaurants/2"`.

8. Inside the navigation graph, we've defined the routes and their corresponding destinations, but we haven't really performed the actual navigation between the two screens. To do that, we first need to have a trigger or callback that notifies us when the user pressed on a restaurant item within the restaurant list, so we can navigate to the restaurant details screen.

Inside the `RestaurantsScreen.kt` file, modify the `RestaurantItem` composable to expose an `onItemClick` callback function that provides us with `id` of the restaurant that is clicked, and also call it when the entire restaurant's `Card` is pressed on:

```
@Composable
fun RestaurantItem(item: Restaurant,
                   onClick: (id: Int) -> Unit,
                   onItemClick: (id: Int) -> Unit) {
    val icon = …
    Card(elevation = 4.dp,
         modifier = Modifier
            .padding(8.dp)
            .clickable { onItemClick(item.id) }) { … }
}
```

9. To prevent confusion, refactor the `RestaurantItem` composable by renaming the old `onClick` parameter to a more suggestive name, such as `onFavoriteClick`:

```
@Composable
fun RestaurantItem(item: Restaurant,
                   onFavoriteClick: (id: Int) -> Unit,
                   onItemClick: (id: Int) -> Unit) {
    val icon = …
    Card(…) {
        Row(…) {
            …
            RestaurantIcon(icon, Modifier.weight(0.15f))
            {
                onFavoriteClick(item.id)
            }
        }
    }
}
```

10. Inside the `RestaurantsScreen()` composable, add a similar `onItemClick` callback function as a parameter, and call it when the `onItemClick` callback comes from the `RestaurantItem` composable:

```
@Composable
fun RestaurantsScreen(onItemClick: (id: Int) -> Unit = {
}) {
    val viewModel: RestaurantsViewModel = viewModel()
    LazyColumn(...) {
        items(viewModel.state.value) { restaurant ->
            RestaurantItem(
                restaurant,
                onFavoriteClick =
                  { id -> viewModel.toggleFavorite(id) },
                onItemClick = { id -> onItemClick(id) })
        }
    }
}
```

Additionally, we've changed the `onClick` parameter name of the `RestaurantItem` composable call to match its signature of `onFavoriteClick`.

What we are essentially doing is propagating events through callbacks from child composables to parent composables.

11. Inside `NavHost`, update the `RestaurantsScreen()` composable destination to listen for navigation callbacks and then, inside the callback, trigger the navigation between composables by calling the `navigate()` method, which expects `route` as a parameter:

```
@Composable
private fun RestaurantsApp() {
    val navController = rememberNavController()
    NavHost(navController, startDestination = "...") {
        composable(route = "restaurants") {
            RestaurantsScreen { id ->
                navController.navigate("restaurants/$id")
            }
        }
        composable(
```

```
                route = "restaurants/{restaurant_id}"
            ) {
                RestaurantDetailsScreen()
            }
        }
    }
```

Inside the new trailing lambda function of `RestaurantsScreen`, we now receive the `id` value of the restaurant we need to navigate to. To trigger the navigation, we called the `navigate()` method, and to its `route` parameter, we passed the `"restaurants/$id"` string to match the route of our other composable destination, `RestaurantDetailsScreen()`.

12. Try running the application and verify the following.

When the app is launched, the `RestaurantsScreen()` composable is composed and displayed. In other words, you are at the `"restaurants"` route because we've set this route as `startDestination` for our navigation graph. On the navigation back stack, this destination will be added:

Figure 5.8 – Back stack with the start destination

When pressing on one of the restaurants on the list, navigation is triggered and you arrive at the `RestaurantDetailsScreen()` composable destination. On top of the navigation back stack this destination will be added:

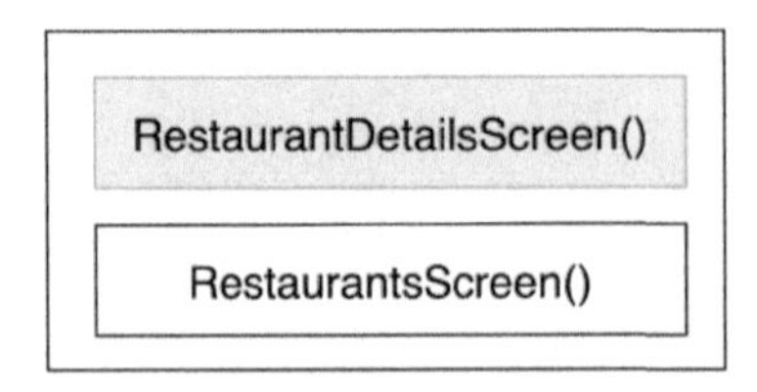

Figure 5.9 – Back stack after navigating to another destination

When pressing the system's **Back** button while being at the `RestaurantDetailsScreen()` destination, you are sent back to the existing destination in the back stack, `RestaurantsScreen()`. This means that on the back stack, the top destination is popped, and only the root destination remains:

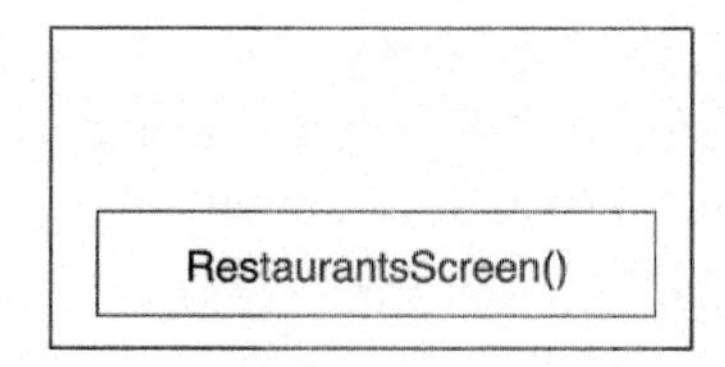

Figure 5.10 – Back stack after returning to start destination

The navigation works, but if you noticed, it always points to the same restaurant. This happens because of two reasons:

- While we defined the `{restaurant_id}` placeholder argument in the route that points to `RestaurantDetailsScreen()`, we didn't define this argument inside the DSL `composable()` function as a navigation argument, so the Navigation component has no idea how to send it to the route's composable destination.
- Inside `RestaurantDetailsViewModel`, we've hardcoded the id of the restaurant to the value of `2`.

We want the user to see details about the restaurant that is pressed on, so let's fix these issues and pass the ID of the restaurant dynamically.

13. For the `RestaurantDetailsScreen()` destination, apart from `route`, add the `arguments` parameter that expects a list of `NamedNavArgument` objects, and pass such an argument using the `navArgument` function:

```
NavHost(navController, startDestination = "..."){
    composable(route = "restaurants") { … }
    composable(
        route = "restaurants/{restaurant_id}",
        arguments =
            listOf(navArgument("restaurant_id") {
                type = NavType.IntType
            })
    ) { RestaurantDetailsScreen() }
}
```

This argument specifies the same `"restaurant_id"` key that we've added as a place holder within `route` and allows the Navigation library to expose this argument to the destination composable. Additionally, the `navArgument` function exposes `NavArgumentBuilder`, where we specified the type of the argument to be `IntType`.

To obtain the argument's value inside the `RestaurantDetailsScreen()` destination, the `composable()` DSL function exposes a `NavBackStackEntry` object that allows us to get the value as follows:

```
composable(...) { navStackEntry ->
    val id =
        navStackEntry.arguments?.getInt("restaurant_id")
    RestaurantDetailsScreen()
}
```

Yet our `RestaurantDetailsScreen()` destination doesn't expect the `id` of a restaurant, but `RestaurantDetailsViewModel` does, so we will not perform the previous changes where we access `navStackEntry`; instead, we will do something similar in the `ViewModel` soon enough.

14. Behind the scenes, the Navigation component saves the navigation arguments stored in `NavStackEntry` into `SavedStateHandle`, which our VM exposes. This means that we can take advantage of that, and instead of obtaining the ID of the restaurant inside the `RestaurantDetailsScreen()` composable, we can directly obtain it in `RestaurantDetailsViewModel`.

    First, add the `SavedStateHandle` parameter to the `RestaurantDetailsViewModel` constructor, just like we did within `RestaurantsViewModel`:

```
class RestaurantDetailsViewModel(
    private val stateHandle: SavedStateHandle
) : ViewModel() {
    [...]
    init { [...] }
    private suspend fun getRemoteRestaurant(id: Int) {
        [...]
    }
}
```

15. Inside of the `init { }` block of `ViewModel`, below the instantiation of the Retrofit client, store the ID of the restaurant inside a new `id` variable while obtaining it dynamically from the `SavedStateHandle` object, and then pass it to the `getRemoteRestaurant()` method call:

```
class RestaurantDetailsViewModel(private val stateHandle:
SavedStateHandle): ViewModel() {
```

```
    ...
    init {
        val retrofit: Retrofit = Retrofit[...].build()
        restInterface = [...]
        val id = stateHandle.get<Int>("restaurant_id")
            ?: 0
        viewModelScope.launch {
            val restaurant = getRemoteRestaurant(id)
            state.value = restaurant
        }
    }
    ...
}
```

We've instructed `navArgument` that the argument is of type `Int`, so we've obtained it as an `Int` value from `stateHandle` and passed the same `"restaurant_id"` key that we've used to define `navArgument`.

This approach will protect us from system-initiated process death scenarios as well. The user could navigate to the `RestaurantDetailsScreen()` destination of a restaurant with an `id` value of `2`, and then minimize the app for a while. In the meantime, the system could decide to kill the process of the app to free up memory, so when the user resumes the app, the system would restore it and provide us with a `SavedStateHandle` object that contains the ID of the restaurant with the value of `2`.

In conclusion, the app would know to obtain the details of the restaurant the user initially navigated to, so the application behaves correctly for this edge case.

16. Run the app again and verify that this time when pressing on one restaurant item in the `RestaurantsScreen()` start destination, the details about this restaurant are displayed in the second destination, `RestaurantDetailsScreen()`.

> **Note**
>
> We used the Navigation component with destinations that are composable functions. Inside these composables, we instantiate `ViewModel` objects. Since these composables are in a back stack of destinations, their `ViewModel` objects become scoped to the lifetime of the composables. In other words, with the addition of the Navigation component, the `ViewModel` objects have the same lifetime as the composable screen that they are attached to.

Perfect! Now our Restaurants app has two screens that you can navigate between whenever the user presses on a restaurant from within our list. It's time to explore another type of navigation event.

Adding support for deep links

Deep links allow you to redirect users to specific parts of your application without having them go through all the intermediary screens. This technique is especially useful for marketing campaigns because it can boost user engagement while also providing a good user experience.

Deep links are usually incorporated within URI schemes or custom schemes. This allows you to configure anything from an image advertisement, text advertisement, or even a QR code that when clicked or scanned redirects you to a specific page of the app. If your app is configured to know how to handle such schemes, the user will be able to open that particular link with your application.

For example, say that for our Restaurants application, we start a marketing campaign where we include some advertisements on the internet that showcase some special restaurants. We configure the advertisements to be clickable and to redirect to the following link, which contains the ID of the advertised restaurant, such as 2: `https://www.restaurantsapp.details.com/2`.

This URI will not work when loaded into a browser application (because there is no such website), yet we can configure our app to know how to interpret it as a deep link.

When a user is browsing a search engine and presses on a campaign advertisement for one of our restaurants, the app should know how to handle these actions and should allow the user to be redirected to our application:

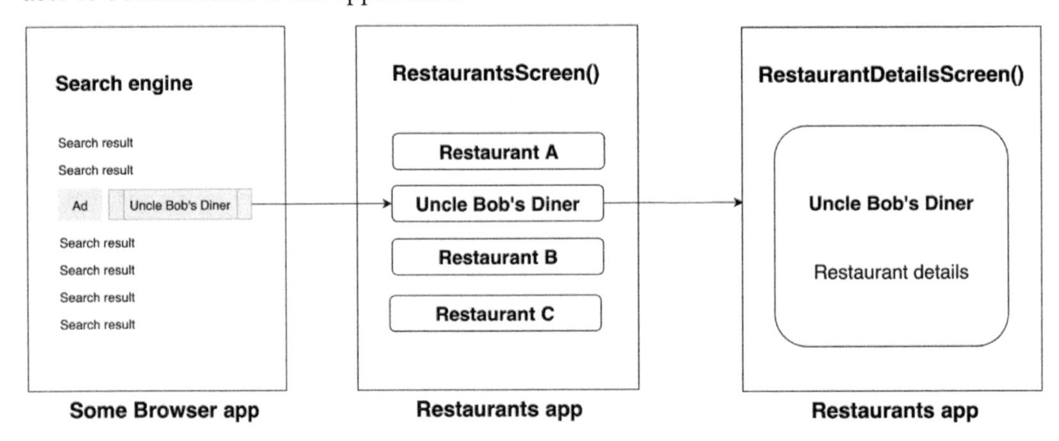

Figure 5.11 – Inefficient redirect to our Restaurants app

Our application has as the start destination the `RestaurantsScreen()` composable, so the user should manually find the restaurant that was initially presented on the advertisement, and press on it to navigate to the `RestaurantDetailsScreen()` destination.

This is obviously a bad practice because we don't want the user to perform manual navigations within our app to get to the advertised restaurant. Imagine if other apps required the user to navigate not through one or two screens as per our application, but more screens – this would result in a bad user experience and the campaign would be ineffective.

Deep links, however, allow you to automatically redirect the user to your desired destination:

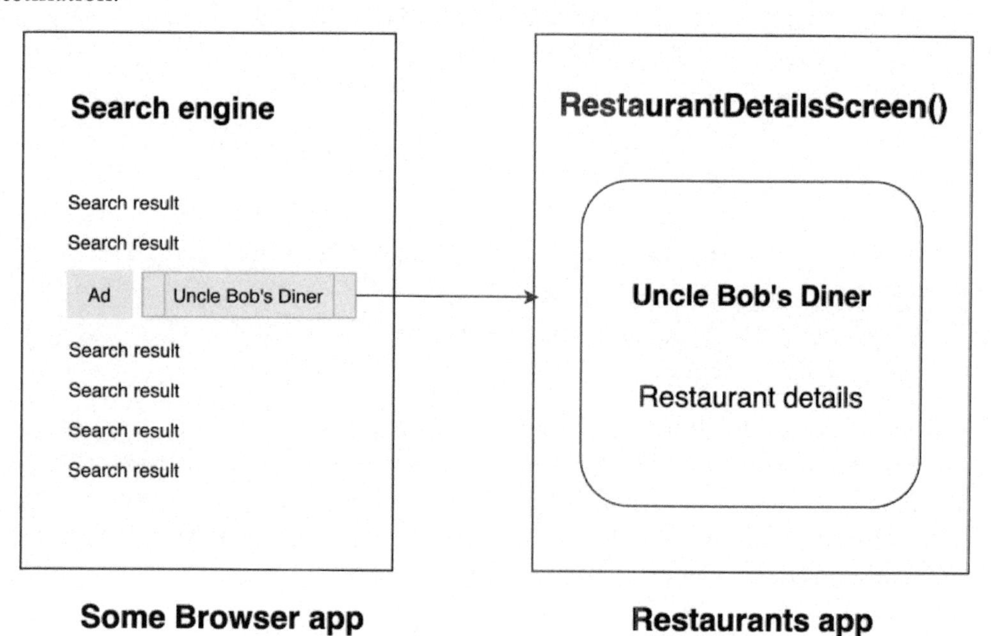

Figure 5.12 – Direct deep link to the screen of interest

By redirecting the user directly to the screen of interest, we improve the user experience and expect our advertising campaign to perform better.

Let's implement such a deep link in our Restaurants application with the help of the Navigation component library:

1. Inside the `RestaurantDetailsScreen()` DSL `composable()` function, apart from `route` and `arguments`, add another parameter called `deepLinks` that expects a list of `NavDeepLink` objects, and pass such an argument using the `navDeepLink` function:

```
NavHost(navController, startDestination = "restaurants")
{
  composable(route = "restaurants") {...}
  composable(
    route = "restaurants/{restaurant_id}",
    arguments = listOf(
      navArgument("restaurant_id") {...}
    ),
    deepLinks = listOf(navDeepLink {
      uriPattern =
    "www.restaurantsapp.details.com/{restaurant_id}"
      })
    ) { RestaurantDetailsScreen() }
}
```

   The `navDeepLink` function expects in turn a `NavDeepLinkDslBuilder` extension function that exposes its own DSL. We've set the `uriPattern` DSL variable to expect our custom URI of `www.restaurantsapp.details.com` but also added our placeholder `"restaurant_id"` argument that will allow the Navigation component to parse and provide us with the ID of the restaurant from the deep link.

   Right now, our application knows how to handle a deep link, but only internally.

2. To make our deep link available externally, inside the `AndroidManifest.xml` file, add the following `<intent-filter>` element within our `MainActivity`'s `<activity>` element:

```
<application ... >
    <activity
        android:name=".MainActivity"
        [...] >
        <intent-filter>
```

```
            <action android:name="[...].action.MAIN" />
            <category android:name="[...].LAUNCHER" />
        </intent-filter>
        <intent-filter>
          <data
                android:host="www.restaurantsapp.
                    details.com"
                android:scheme="https" />
          <action android:name="android.intent.
              action.VIEW" />
          <category android:name="android.intent.
              category.DEFAULT" />
          <category android:name="android.intent.
              category.BROWSABLE" />
        </intent-filter>
    </activity>
</application>
```

Let's break up what we've just added inside the new `<intent-filter>` element:

- A `<data>` element that specifies the following:
  - The `host` parameter as the deep link URI that we've set previously in our navigation graph. This is the URI that our ads should link to.
  - The `scheme` parameter of the deep link as `https`. Every `<data>` element should define a scheme so that the URI is recognized.
- A `<category>` element of `BROWSABLE` that is required for the intent filter to be accessed from web browser apps.
- A `<category>` element of `DEFAULT` that makes the app intercept the deep link's intents implicitly. Without it, the app could be started only if the deep link intent specified the application component name.

To test the deep link, we need to simulate a deep link action. Let's imagine that we want to test a deep link that points to a restaurant that has the ID with the value of `2`. The deep link would look like this: `https://www.restaurantsapp.details.com/2`.

Since we don't have any advertisements that refer to our deep link, we have two options:

- Create a QR code with this URL and then scan it with our device.
- Launch an intent from the command line that simulates the deep link.

Let's go with the second option.

3. Build the project and run the application on an emulator or physical device. This step is needed so that the installed application knows how to respond to our deep link.
4. Close the app or minimize it, but make sure you leave your emulator or device connected to Android Studio.
5. Open the terminal inside Android Studio, paste the following command and enter it:

```
$ adb shell am start -W -a android.intent.action.VIEW -d
"https://www.restaurantsapp.details.com/2"
```

6. The emulator/device that you have connected to Android Studio should now prompt a disambiguation dialog asking you what app you'd like to open the deep link with:

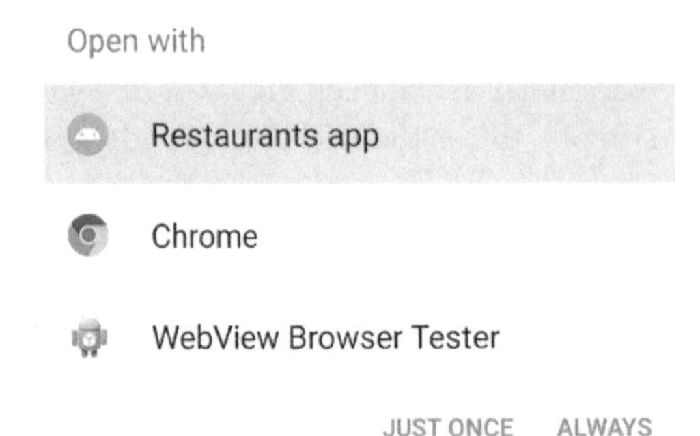

Figure 5.13 – Disambiguation dialog displayed when launching a deep link

Our application is one of those apps and this means that it has been correctly configured to intercept our deep links.

7. Select **Restaurants app** (or whatever you called your app) and press **JUST ONCE**. The application should open our `RestaurantDetailsScreen()` destination and show the details of the desired restaurant.

   Optionally, you can try pressing the system's **Back** button. The Navigation component application knows automatically how to send the user back to the `RestaurantsScreen` composable.

Now that we've also successfully added deep link functionality to our Restaurant application, it's time to wrap this chapter up.

Summary

In this chapter, we learned how to navigate between screens within our Restaurants application. We did that easily with the help of the Jetpack Navigation component library.

We started off by learning the basics of the Jetpack Navigation library and understood how easy our life becomes when having to handle navigation back stacks. Afterward, we created a new screen, implemented the Navigation library, and explored how seamless it is to add navigation between composables. Finally, we added support for deep links and made sure to test such a deep link within our app.

Next up, it's time to focus on improving the quality and architecture of our Restaurants application.

Part 2: A Guide to Clean Application Architecture with Jetpack Libraries

In this part, we will learn how to incorporate clean and modern architectures, add offline capabilities with Room, include Dependency Injection with Hilt, and test UI and application logic by using the demo project from the previous section.

This section comprises the following chapters:

- *Chapter 6, Adding Offline Capabilities with Jetpack Room*
- *Chapter 7, Introducing Presentation Patterns in Android*
- *Chapter 8, Getting Started with Clean Architecture in Android*
- *Chapter 9, Implementing Dependency Injection with Jetpack Hilt*
- *Chapter 10, Test Your App with UI and Unit Tests*

6
Adding Offline Capabilities with Jetpack Room

In this chapter, we're starting our journey of exploring ways to architecture our apps by first making sure that our application can be used without an internet connection.

In the *Introducing Jetpack Room* section, we will briefly note the various caching mechanisms that are on Android. Then, we will introduce the Jetpack Room library and its core elements.

Next, in the *Enabling offline usage by implementing Room* section, we will implement Room in our Restaurants app and allow users to use the application without an internet connection. In the *Applying partial updates to the Room database* section, we will learn how to partially update data inside Room so that we can save selections such as whether the restaurants were favorited by the user.

Finally, in the *Making local data the single source of truth for app content* section, we will understand why having a single source of truth for app data is beneficial, and then we will set the Room database as the single source of content for our app.

To summarize, in this chapter, we're going to cover the following main topics:

- Introducing Jetpack Room
- Enabling offline usage by implementing Room
- Applying partial updates to the Room database
- Making local data the single source of truth for app content

Before jumping in, let's set up the technical requirements for this chapter.

Technical requirements

Usually, building Compose-based Android projects with Jetpack Room will require your day-to-day tools. However, to follow along with the examples smoothly, make sure you have the following:

- The Arctic Fox 2020.3.1 version of Android Studio. You can also use a newer Android Studio version or even Canary builds but note that the IDE interface and other generated code files might differ from the ones used throughout this book.
- The Kotlin 1.6.10, or newer, plugin installed in Android Studio
- The Restaurants app code from the previous chapter.
- Minimal knowledge of SQL databases and queries

The starting point for this chapter is represented by the Restaurants application that was developed in the previous chapter. If you haven't followed the implementation described in the previous chapter, access the starter code for this chapter by navigating to the `Chapter_05` directory of the repository. Then, import the Android project entitled `chapter_5_restaurants_app`.

To access the solution code for this chapter, navigate to the `Chapter_06` directory:

`https://github.com/PacktPublishing/Kickstart-Modern-Android-Development-with-Jetpack-and-Kotlin/tree/main/Chapter_06/chapter_6_restaurants_app`.

Introducing Jetpack Room

Modern applications should be available for use in any conditions, including when the user is missing an internet connection. This allows apps to provide a seamless user experience and usability even when the user's device cannot access the network.

In this section, we will discuss the following:

- Exploring the caching mechanism on Android
- Introducing Jetpack Room as a solution for local caching

So, let's begin!

Exploring the caching mechanism on Android

To cache specific content or application data, reliable Android apps make use of the various offline caching mechanisms that are suitable for different use cases:

- Shared preferences are used to store lightweight data (such as user-related selections) as key-value pairs. This option shouldn't be used to store objects that are part of the app's content.
- Device storage (either internal or external) is used for storing heavyweight data (such as files, pictures, and more).
- SQLite database is used for storing app content in a structured manner inside a private database. **SQLite** is an open source SQL database that stores data in private text files.

In this chapter, we will focus on learning how to cache structured content (which is, usually, held by Kotlin `data class` objects) within a SQLite database. In this way, we allow the user to browse the app's data while remaining offline.

> **Note**
>
> Android comes with a built-in SQLite database implementation that allows us to save structured data.

In our app, we can consider the array of restaurants to be a perfect candidate for app content that can be saved inside a SQLite database. Since the data is structured, with SQLite, we get the advantage of being able to perform different actions such as searching for restaurants within the database, updating particular restaurants, and more.

By caching app content in this way, we can allow users to browse the app's restaurants while offline. However, for this to work, the users need to have previously opened the app using an active internet connection, thereby allowing the app to cache the contents for future offline use.

Now, to save the restaurants to the SQLite private database, we need to make use of the SQLite APIs. These APIs are powerful. However, by using them, you face quite a few disadvantages:

- The APIs are of a low level and are relatively difficult to use.
- The SQLite APIs provide no compile-time verification of SQL queries, which can lead to unwanted runtime errors.
- There is a lot of boilerplate code involved in creating a database, performing SQL queries, and more.

To mitigate these issues, Google provides the Jetpack Room library. This library is nothing more than a wrapper library that simplifies the way we access and interact with the SQLite database.

Introducing Jetpack Room as a solution for local caching

Room is a persistence library that is defined as an abstraction layer over SQLite and provides simplified database access while taking advantage of the power of the SQLite APIs.

As opposed to using the raw SQLite APIs, Room abstracts most of the complexity associated with working with SQLite. The library removes most of the unpleasant boilerplate code that is required to set up and interact with SQLite databases on Android while also providing the compile-time checking of SQL queries.

To make use of the Room library and cache contents using its API, you need to define three primary components:

- **Entities** that define tables within the private database. In our Restaurants app, we will consider the `Restaurant` data class as an entity. This means that we will have a table populated with `Restaurant` objects. In other words, the rows of the table are represented by instances of our restaurants.

- A database class that will contain and expose the actual database.
- **Data Access Objects (DAOs)** that represent an interface. This allows us to get, insert, delete, or update the actual content within the database.

The database class provides us with a reference to the DAO interface associated with the SQLite database:

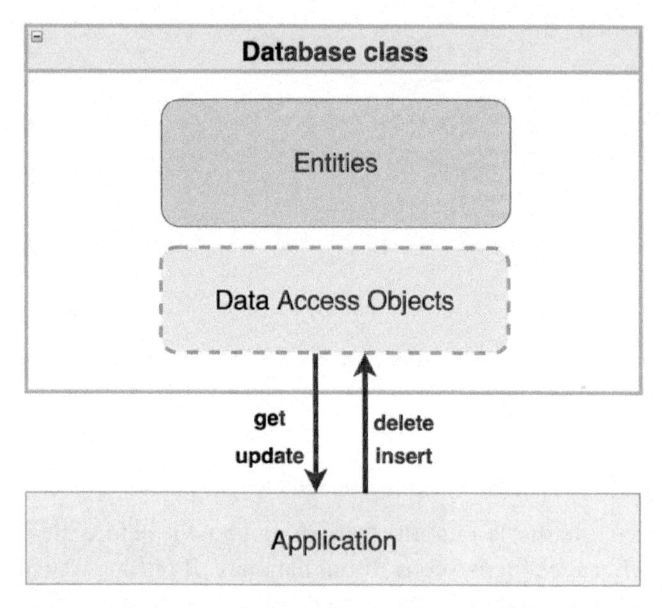

Figure 6.1 – The interaction between the application and the Room database

As previously illustrated, we can use the DAO to retrieve or update the data from the database in the form of entity objects – in our case, the entity is the restaurant, so we will be applying such operations to restaurant objects.

Now that we have a basic understanding of how Room works and how we can interact with it, it's time to see it in action for ourselves and implement Room in our Restaurants app.

Enabling offline usage by implementing Room

We want to locally cache all the restaurants that we receive from our Firebase database. Since this content is structured, we want to use Room to help us with this task.

Essentially, we are trying to save the restaurants when the user is browsing our Restaurants app while online. Then, we will reuse them when the user browses the app while being offline:

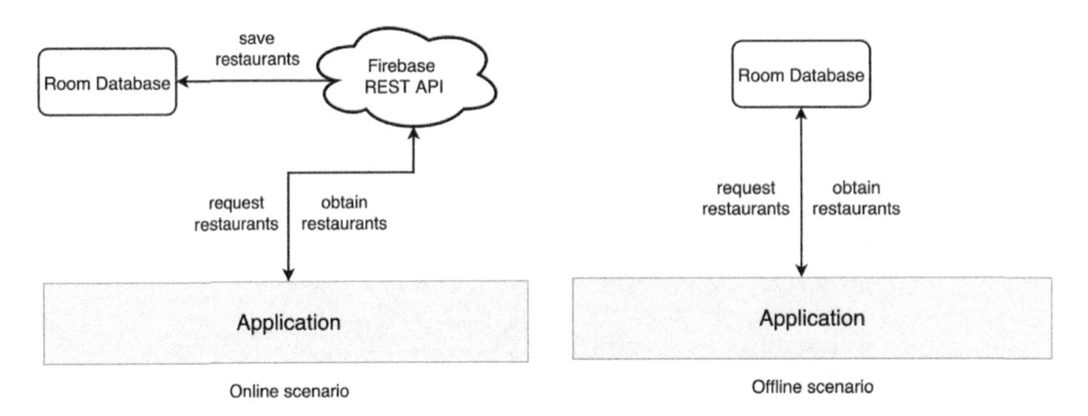

Figure 6.2 – Data retrieval for the Restaurants app with two sources of truth

When online, we retrieve the restaurants from our web API. Before displaying them to the user, first, we will cache them to our Room database. If offline, we will retrieve the restaurants from the Room database and then display them to the user.

Essentially, we are creating two sources of truth for our app:

- The remote API for when the user is online
- The local Room database for when the user is offline

In the next section, we will discuss why this approach is not ideal. However, until then, we are content with the fact that we will be able to use the app while remaining offline.

Let's start implementing Room, and then let's cache those restaurants! Perform the following steps:

1. Inside the `build.gradle` file in the app module, add the dependencies for Room inside the `dependencies` block:

```
implementation "androidx.room:room-runtime:2.4.2"
kapt "androidx.room:room-compiler:2.4.2"
implementation "androidx.room:room-ktx:2.4.2"
```

2. While you are still inside the `build.gradle` file, add the `kotlin-kapt` plugin for Room inside the `plugins` block:

```
plugins {
    id 'com.android.application'
    id 'kotlin-android'
    id 'kotlin-kapt'
}
```

The `kapt` plugin stands for **Kotlin Annotation Processing Tool**. This allows Room to generate annotated code at compile time while hiding most of the associated complexity from us.

After updating the `build.gradle` files, make sure to sync your project with its Gradle files. You can do that by pressing on the **File** menu option and then by selecting **Sync Project with Gradle Files**.

3. Since we want to store restaurant objects inside our local database, let's instruct Room that the `Restaurant` data class is an entity that must be saved. Head inside the `Restaurant.kt` file, and add the `@Entity` annotation on top of the class declaration:

```
@Entity(tableName = "restaurants")
data class Restaurant(…)
```

Inside the `@Entity` annotation, we have passed the name of the table via the `tableName` parameter. We will use this name when making queries.

4. Now that Room will create a table with `Restaurant` objects as rows, it's time to define the columns (or fields) of the entity. While we are still inside the `Restaurant.kt` class, let's add the `@ColumnInfo` annotation on top of each field that we're interested in, and that should represent a column:

```
@Entity(tableName = "restaurants")
data class Restaurant(
    @ColumnInfo(name = "r_id")
    @SerializedName("r_id")
    val id: Int,
    @ColumnInfo(name = "r_title")
    @SerializedName("r_title")
    val title: String,
    @ColumnInfo(name = "r_description")
```

```
        @SerializedName("r_description")
        val description: String,
        var isFavorite: Boolean = false
)
```

For each field we're interested in saving, we've added the `@ColumnInfo` annotation and passed a `String` value to the `name` parameter. These names will correspond to the name of the table's columns. Right now, we are not interested in saving the `isFavorite` field; we will do that a bit later.

5. The entity that represents a table should have a primary key column that ensures uniqueness within the database. For this, we can use the `id` field that was configured from our Firebase database to be unique. While still inside the `Restaurant.kt` class, let's add the `@PrimaryKey` annotation to the `id` field:

```
@Entity(tableName = "restaurants")
data class Restaurant(
        @PrimaryKey()
        @ColumnInfo(name = "r_id")
        @SerializedName("r_id")
        val id: Int,
        ...)
```

Now we have defined the entity for our database and configured the table's columns.

It's time to create a DAO that will serve as the entry point to our database, allowing us to perform various actions on it.

6. Create a DAO by clicking on the application package, selecting **New**, and then selecting **Kotlin Class/File**. Enter `RestaurantsDao` as the name, and select **Interface** as the type. Inside the new file, add the following code:

```
import androidx.room.*

@Dao
interface RestaurantsDao { }
```

Since Room will take care of implementing any actions that we need to interact with the database, the DAO is an interface, just like Retrofit also had an interface for the HTTP methods. To instruct Room that this is a DAO entity, we've added the `@Dao` annotation on top of the interface declaration.

7. Inside the `RestaurantsDao` interface, add two `suspend` functions that will help us to both save the restaurants and retrieve them from the database:

```
@Dao
interface RestaurantsDao {
    @Query("SELECT * FROM restaurants")
    suspend fun getAll(): List<Restaurant>

    @Insert(onConflict = OnConflictStrategy.REPLACE)
    suspend fun addAll(restaurants: List<Restaurant>)
}
```

Now, let's analyze the two methods that we've added:

- `getAll()` is a query statement that returns the restaurants that were previously cached inside the database. Since we need to perform a SQL query when calling this method, we've marked it with the `@Query` annotation and specified that we want all the restaurants (by adding `*`) from the `restaurants` table defined in the `Restaurant` entity data class.
- `addAll()` is an `insert` statement that caches the received restaurants inside the database. To mark this as a SQL `insert` statement, we've added the `@Insert` annotation. However, if the restaurants being inserted are already present in the database, we should replace the old ones with the new ones to refresh our cache. We instructed Room to do so by passing the `OnConflictStrategy.REPLACE` value into the `@Insert` annotation.

Both methods are marked as `suspend` functions because any interaction with the Room database can take time and is an async job; therefore, it shouldn't block the UI.

Now, we have defined an entity class and a DAO class, we must define the last component that Room needs in order to function, the database class.

8. Create a Room database class by clicking on the application package. Select **New**, and then select **Kotlin Class/File**. Enter `RestaurantsDb` as the name, and select **File** as the type. Inside the new file, add the following code:

```
@Database(
    entities = [Restaurant::class],
    version = 1,
    exportSchema = false)
abstract class RestaurantsDb : RoomDatabase() { }
```

Now, let's analyze the code that we've just added:

- `RestaurantsDb` is an abstract class that inherits from `RoomDatabase()`. This will allow Room to create the actual implementation of the database behind the scenes and hide all the heavy implementation details from us.
- For the `RestaurantsDb` class, we've added the `@Database` annotation so that Room knows that this class represents a database and provides an implementation for it. Inside this annotation, we've passed the following:
  - The `Restaurant` class to the `entities` parameter. This parameter tells Room which entities are associated with this database so that it can create corresponding tables. The parameter expects an array, so you can add as many entity classes as you wish, as long as they are annotated with `@Entity`.
  - `1` as the `version` number of the database. We should increment this version number whenever the schema of the database changes. The **schema** is the collection of database objects, such as the tables that correspond to entities. If we change the `Restaurant` class, since it's an entity, we might change the schema of the database, and Room needs to know that for migration purposes.
  - `false` to the `exportSchema` parameter. Room can export the schema of our database externally; however, for simplicity, we chose not to do so.

9. Inside the `RestaurantsDb` class, add an abstract `RestaurantsDao` variable:

```
@Database(…)
abstract class RestaurantsDb : RoomDatabase() {
    abstract val dao: RestaurantsDao
}
```

We know that the database class should expose a DAO object so that we can interact with the database. By leaving it abstract, we allow Room to provide its implementation behind the scenes.

10. Even though we declared a variable to hold our DAO object, we still need to find a way to build the database and obtain a reference to the `RestaurantsDao` instance that Room will create for us. Inside the `RestaurantsDb` class, add `companion object` and then add the `buildDatabase` method:

```
@Database(…)
abstract class RestaurantsDb : RoomDatabase() {
    abstract val dao: RestaurantsDao
    companion object {
```

```
        private fun buildDatabase(context: Context):
            RestaurantsDb =
            Room.databaseBuilder(
                context.applicationContext,
                RestaurantsDb::class.java,
                "restaurants_database")
                .fallbackToDestructiveMigration()
                .build()
    }
}
```

Essentially, this method returns a `RestaurantsDb` instance. To construct a Room database, we need to call the `Room.databaseBuilder` constructor, which expects the following parameters:

- A `Context` object that we provided from the `context` input argument of our `buildDatabase` method.
- The class of the database you're trying to build, that is, the `RestaurantsDb` class.
- A name for the database – we named it `"restaurants_database"`.

The builder returns a `RoomDatabase.Builder` object on which we called `.fallbackToDestructiveMigration()`. This means that, in the case of a schema change (such as performing changes in the entity class and modifying the table columns), the tables would be dropped (or deleted) instead of trying to migrate the contents from the previous schema (which would have been a bit more complex).

Finally, we called `build()` on the builder object so that our `buildDatabase()` method returns a `RestaurantsDb` instance.

It's time to finally get a reference to our DAO so that we can start using the database.

11. While still inside the `companion object` of the `RestaurantsDb` class, add the following code:

```
companion object {
    @Volatile
    private var INSTANCE: RestaurantsDao? = null

    fun getDaoInstance(context: Context): RestaurantsDao
```

```
        {
            synchronized(this) {
                var instance = INSTANCE
                if (instance == null) {
                    instance = buildDatabase(context).dao
                    INSTANCE = instance
                }
                return instance
            }
        }
        private fun buildDatabase(...) = ...
    }
```

Now, let's break down what we've done:

- We added an `INSTANCE` variable of type `RestaurantsDao`. Since this variable is inside the companion object, `INSTANCE` is static. Additionally, we marked it with `@Volatile`. This means that writes to this field are immediately made visible to other threads. Don't worry too much about these multithreading concepts – we will get rid of this boilerplate code soon enough.
- We created a `getDaoInstance()` method where we added a block of code that calls the `buildDatabase()` method and gets the DAO object by calling the `.dao` accessor.

Since we want only one memory reference to our database (and not create other database instances in other parts of the app), we made sure that our `INSTANCE` variable conforms to the singleton pattern. Essentially, the **singleton pattern** allows us to hold a static reference to an object so that it lives as long as our application does.

By following this approach, anytime we need to access the Room database from different parts of the app, we can call the `getDaoInstance()` method, which returns an instance of `RestaurantsDao`. Additionally, we can be sure that it's always the same memory reference and that no concurrency issues will occur since we have wrapped the instance creation code inside a `synchronized` block.

12. You might have noticed that to get a reference to our DAO and cache our restaurants in the database, the `RestaurantsDb.getDaoInstance()` method expects a `Context` object. This is needed to create the instance of the database. However, we want to get our DAO in the `RestaurantsViewModel` class, and we have no context there, so what should we do?

Let's expose the application context from the application class! Create the application class by clicking on the application package, selecting **New**, and then selecting **Kotlin Class/File**. Enter `RestaurantsApplication` as the name, and select **File** as the type. Inside the new file, add the following code:

```
class RestaurantsApplication: Application() {
    init { app = this }
    companion object {
        private lateinit var app: RestaurantsApplication
        fun getAppContext(): Context =
            app.applicationContext
    }
}
```

This class now inherits from `android.app.Application` and exposes its context through the static `getAppContext()` method. The only issue is that even though we have an application class, we still haven't configured the project to recognize it.

13. In the `AndroidManifest.xml` file, inside the `<application>` element, add the `android:name` identifier that sets our `RestaurantsApplication` class as the application class:

```
<application
    android:allowBackup="true"
    android:name=".RestaurantsApplication"
    android:icon="@mipmap/ic_launcher"
    ...
    <activity> … </activity>
</application>
```

It's time to finally start working on caching those restaurants in our database.

14. Inside the `RestaurantsViewModel` class, add a `restaurantsDao` variable. Then, instantiate it via the static `RestaurantsDb.getDaoInstance` method:

```
class RestaurantsViewModel(…) : ViewModel() {
    private var restInterface: RestaurantsApiService
    private var restaurantsDao = RestaurantsDb
        .getDaoInstance(
            RestaurantsApplication.getAppContext()
```

```
            )
        ....
}
```

Make sure that you pass the application context through the newly created `getAppContext()` method inside the application class.

15. Now we're ready to save the restaurants locally! While you are still in the `RestaurantsViewModel` class, inside the `getRemoteRestaurants()` method, add these new lines of code:

```
private suspend fun getRemoteRestaurants():
    List<Restaurant> {
    return withContext(Dispatchers.IO) {
        val restaurants = restInterface.getRestaurants()
        restaurantsDao.addAll(restaurants)
        return@withContext restaurants
    }
}
```

Essentially, what we are doing is the following:

I. Getting the restaurants from the remote API (here, it's the Retrofit `restInterface` variable).

II. Caching those restaurants inside the local database through Room by calling `restaurantsDao.addAll()`.

III. Finally, returning the restaurants to the UI.

16. Run the app while you have a working internet connection.

In terms of the UI, nothing should change – you should still see the restaurants. That said, behind the scenes, the restaurants should now have been cached.

17. Run the app again but without internet.

The chances are that you won't see anything. The restaurants are not there.

This happens because, while we are offline, we never try to get the previously cached restaurants from the Room database. Moreover, when offline, the `restInterface.getRestaurants()` suspending function throws an error because the HTTP call that fetches the restaurants has failed – this exception should arrive inside `CoroutineExceptionHandler`. The exception is thrown by Retrofit because the associated network request has failed.

18. Let's leverage the fact that, while we're offline, the `restInterface.getRestaurants()` function call throws an exception. This is so that we can wrap the whole block of code inside `getRemoteRestaurants()` inside a `try-catch` block:

```
private suspend fun getRemoteRestaurants():
        List<Restaurant> {
    return withContext(Dispatchers.IO) {
        try {
            val restaurants = restInterface
                .getRestaurants()
            restaurantsDao.addAll(restaurants)
            return@withContext restaurants
        } catch (e: Exception) {
            when (e) {
                is UnknownHostException,
                is ConnectException,
                is HttpException -> {
                    return@withContext
                        restaurantsDao.getAll()
                }
                else -> throw e
            }
        }
    }
}
```

Essentially, what happens now is that if the user is offline, we catch the exception thrown by Retrofit. Alternatively, we return the cached restaurants from the Room database by calling `restaurantsDao.getAll()`.

As an extra, we also check whether the exception we've caught has been thrown because of the user's poor or inexistent internet connectivity. If the `Exception` object is of type `UnknownHostException`, `ConnectException`, or `HttpException`, we're loading the restaurants from Room through our DAO; otherwise, we propagate the exception so that it's caught later by `CoroutineExceptionHandler`.

19. Before running the app, let's refactor our `getRemoteRestaurants()` method a bit. Now, the name of the method implies that it retrieves restaurants from a remote source. However, in reality, it also retrieves restaurants from Room if the user is offline. Room is a local data source, so the name of this method is no longer appropriate.

    Rename the `getRemoteRestaurants()` method to `getAllRestaurants()`:

    ```
    private suspend fun getAllRestaurants():
        List<Restaurant> { }
    ```

    Additionally, remember to rename its usage in the `getRestaurants()` method where the coroutine is launched:

    ```
    private fun getRestaurants() {
        viewModelScope.launch(errorHandler) {
            val restaurants = getAllRestaurants()
            state.value = restaurants.restoreSelections()
        }
    }
    ```

20. Run the app again without an internet connection.

    Because the restaurants were previously cached and now the user is offline, we are fetching them from Room. You should see the restaurants even without the internet. Success!

Even though we've come a long way and have managed to make the Restaurants app usable even without internet, there is still something that we've missed. To reproduce it, perform the following steps:

1. Try running the application (either online or offline), and then mark a couple of restaurants as favorites.
2. Disconnect your device from the internet and make sure you are now offline.
3. Restart the application while remaining offline.

You will get to see the restaurants, but your previous selections have been lost. More precisely, even though we have marked some restaurants as favorites, all restaurants now appear as not favorites. It's time to fix this!

Applying partial updates to the Room database

Right now, our application is saving the restaurants that we receive from the remote web API directly inside the Room database.

This is not a bad approach; however, whenever we are marking a restaurant as a favorite, we aren't updating the corresponding restaurant inside Room. If we take a look inside the `RestaurantsViewModel` class and we check its `toggleFavorite()` method, we can see that we're only updating the `isFavorite` flag of a restaurant inside the `state` variable:

```
fun toggleFavorite(id: Int) {
    val restaurants = state.value.toMutableList()
    val itemIndex = restaurants.indexOfFirst { it.id == id }
    val item = restaurants[itemIndex]
    restaurants[itemIndex] = item.copy(isFavorite =
        !item.isFavorite)
    storeSelection(restaurants[itemIndex])
    state.value = restaurants
}
```

We aren't updating the corresponding restaurant's `isFavorite` field value inside Room. So, whenever we use the application offline, the restaurants will no longer appear as favorites, even though when we were online, we might have marked some as favorites.

To fix this, whenever we mark a restaurant as a favorite or not a favorite, we need to apply a partial update on a particular `Restaurant` object inside our Room database. The partial update should not replace the entire `Restaurant` object, but it should only update its `isFavorite` field value.

Let's get started! Perform the following steps:

1. Create a partial entity class by clicking on the application package, selecting **New**, and then selecting **Kotlin Class/File**. Enter `PartialRestaurant` as the name, and select **File** as the type. Inside the new file, add the following code:

```
@Entity
class PartialRestaurant(
    @ColumnInfo(name = "r_id")
    val id: Int,
```

```
    @ColumnInfo(name = "is_favorite")
    val isFavorite: Boolean)
```

In this @Entity annotated class, we've only added two fields:

- An id field with a @ColumnInfo() annotation that has the same value ("r_id") passed to the name parameter as the Restaurant object's id field. This allows Room to match the Restaurant object's id field with the one from PartialRestaurant.
- An isFavorite field with a @ColumnInfo() annotation that has the name set to "is_favorited". So far, Room can't match this field with the one from Restaurant, because inside Restaurant, we haven't annotated the isFavorite field with @ColumnInfo – we'll do that next.

2. Now that our partial entity, called PartialRestaurant, has a column corresponding to the isFavorite field, it's time to also add a @ColumnInfo() annotation with the same value ("is_favorite") for the isFavorite field of the Restaurant entity:

```
@Entity(tableName = "restaurants")
data class Restaurant(
    …
    val description: String,
    @ColumnInfo(name = "is_favorite")
    val isFavorite: Boolean = false
)
```

As a good practice, we've also made the isFavorite field val instead of var to prevent its value from being changed once the object has been created. Because Restaurant is an object passed to a Compose State object, we want to promote immutability across its fields to ensure recomposition events happen.

> **Note**
>
> By having a data class field as var, we can easily change its value at runtime and risk having Compose miss a well-needed recomposition. Immutability ensures that whenever an object field's value changes, a new object is created (just as we do with the .copy() function), and Compose is notified so that it can trigger recomposition.

3. Since the `isFavorite` field is now `val`, the `restoreSelections()` extension function inside `RestaurantViewModel` has broken. Update its code as follows:

```
private fun List<Restaurant>.restoreSelections(): … {
    stateHandle.[…]let { selectedIds ->
        val restaurantsMap = this.associateBy { it.id }
            .toMutableMap()
        selectedIds.forEach { id ->
            val restaurant =
                restaurantsMap[id] ?: return@forEach
            restaurantsMap[id] =
                restaurant.copy(isFavorite = true)
        }
        return restaurantsMap.values.toList()
    }
    return this
}
```

Essentially, what we have done is make sure our `restaurantsMap` of type `Map<Int, Restaurant>` is mutable so that we can replace elements inside it. With this approach, we are now replacing the restaurant at entry `id` by passing a new object reference with the `copy` function. We are not going to go into much detail since this portion of the code will soon be removed.

4. Now that we have a partial entity defined, we need to add another function inside our DAO that will update a `Restaurant` entity through a `PartialRestaurant` entity. Inside `RestaurantsDao`, add the `update()` function:

```
@Dao
interface RestaurantsDao {
    …
    @Insert(onConflict = OnConflictStrategy.REPLACE)
    suspend fun addAll(restaurants: List<Restaurant>)

    @Update(entity = Restaurant::class)
    suspend fun update(partialRestaurant:
        PartialRestaurant)
}
```

Let's understand, step by step, how the new `update()` function works:

I. It's a `suspend` function because, as we know by now, any interaction with the local database is a suspending job that should not run on the main thread.

II. It receives a `PartialRestaurant` entity as an argument and returns nothing. The partial entity's field values correspond to the restaurant that we're trying to update.

III. It's annotated with the `@Update` annotation to which we passed the `Restaurant` entity. The update process has two steps, as follows:

   i. First, `PartialRestaurant` exposes the `id` field, whose value matches the `id` field's value of the corresponding `Restaurant` object.

   ii. Once the match is complete, the `isFavorite` field's value is set to the `isFavorite` field of the matched `Restaurant` object.

These matches are possible because the `id` and `isFavorite` fields of both entities have the same `@ColumnInfo` name values.

5. Now that our DAO knows how to partially update our `Restaurant` entity, it's time to perform the update.

   First, inside `RestaurantsViewModel`, add a new suspending function, called `toggleFavoriteRestaurant()`:

```
private suspend fun toggleFavoriteRestaurant(id: Int,
oldValue: Boolean) =
    withContext(Dispatchers.IO) {
        restaurantsDao.update(
            PartialRestaurant(
                id = id,
                isFavorite = !oldValue
            )
        )
    }
```

Let's understand, step by step, what this new method does:

I. It receives the `id` field of the restaurant that we're trying to update, along with the `oldValue` field which represents the value of the `isFavorite` field just before the user has toggled the heart icon of the restaurant.

II. To partially update a restaurant, it needs to interact with the Room DAO object. This means that the `toggleFavoriteRestaurant` method must be a `suspend` function. As a good practice, we wrapped it inside a `withContext` block that specifies its work must be done inside the `IO` dispatcher. While Room ensures that we wrap our suspending work with a special dispatcher, we explicitly specified the `Dispatchers.IO` dispatcher to better highlight that such heavy work should be done in an appropriate dispatcher.

III. It builds a `PartialRestaurant` object, which it then passes to the DAO's `update()` method that was created earlier. The `PartialRestaurant` object gets the `id` field of the restaurant we're updating, along with the negated value of the `isFavorite` flag. If the user previously didn't have the restaurant marked as favorite, upon clicking the heart icon, we should negate the old (`false`) value and obtain `true`, or vice versa.

Now that we have the method in place to update a restaurant, it's time to call it.

6. While you are still in `RestaurantsViewModel`, make the `toggleFavorite` method launch a coroutine at the end of its body. Then, inside it, call the new `toggleFavoriteRestaurant()` suspending function:

```
fun toggleFavorite(id: Int) {
    ...
    restaurants[itemIndex] = item.copy(isFavorite =
        !item.isFavorite)
    storeSelection(restaurants[itemIndex])
    state.value = restaurants
    viewModelScope.launch {
        toggleFavoriteRestaurant(id, item.isFavorite)
    }
}
```

To the `toggleFavoriteRestaurant()` function, we've passed the following:

- The `id` parameter, which represents the ID of the restaurant the user is trying to mark as favorite or not favorite
- The old value of the favorite status of the restaurant, as defined by the `isFavorite` flag of the `item` field

Now, whenever the user presses on the heart icon, we not only update the UI but also cache this selection inside the local database through a partial update.

7. Build and run the application because it's time to test what we've just implemented! Unfortunately, the app crashes. Can you think of one reason why this happens? If we look at the stack trace of the error, we will see the following message:

```
java.lang.IllegalStateException: Room cannot verify the
data integrity. Looks like you've changed schema but
forgot to update the version number.
```

   This error message makes total sense because we've changed the schema of the database, and now Room doesn't know whether to migrate the old entries or delete them. But how did we change the schema?

   Well, we changed the schema when we defined a new column for the Restaurants table by adding the `@ColumnInfo()` annotation to the `isFavorite` field.

8. To mitigate this issue, we must increase the `version` number of the database. Inside the `RestaurantsDb` class, increase the `version` number from `1` to `2`:

```
@Database(
    entities = [Restaurant::class],
    version = 2,
    exportSchema = false)
abstract class RestaurantsDb : RoomDatabase() { .. }
```

   Now, Room knows that we've changed the schema of the database. In turn, because we haven't provided a migration strategy, and instead, we've called the `fallbackToDestructiveMigration()` method in the `Room.databaseBuilder` constructor when we initially instantiated the database, Room will drop the old contents and tables and provide us with a fresh start.

9. Try running the application online, and then mark a couple of restaurants as favorites.
10. Disconnect your device from the internet and make sure you are now offline.
11. Restart the application while remaining offline.

    Great news! The selections were now kept, and we can see which restaurants were previously marked as favorites!

12. To continue testing, while you are offline, you can try marking other restaurants as favorites.

Then, still in offline mode, restart the app and you will notice that these new selections have also been saved.

13. Connect your device to the internet and run the application – while you are online.

Oops! The restaurants that we have previously marked as favorites no longer appear as such, even though we previously cached these selections inside the Room database.

Essentially, every time we open the application while being connected to the internet, we lose all the previous selections, and no restaurant is marked as favorite anymore.

There are two issues in our code that are causing this! Can you think of why this is happening?

In the next section, we will identify and address them. Additionally, we will make sure that Room is the single source of truth for the content of our application.

Making local data the single source of truth for app content

Whenever we launch the app with the internet, all the restaurants appear as not favorites, even though we previously marked them as favorites and cached the selections in the Room database.

To identify the issue, let's navigate back inside `RestaurantsViewModel` and inspect the `getAllRestaurants()` method:

```
private suspend fun getAllRestaurants(): List<Restaurant> {
    return withContext(Dispatchers.IO) {
        try {
            val restaurants = restInterface.getRestaurants()
            restaurantsDao.addAll(restaurants)
            return@withContext restaurants
        } catch (e: Exception) {
            when (e) {
                is UnknownHostException, [...] -> {
                    return@withContext restaurantsDao.getAll()
                }
                else -> throw e
            }
        }
```

```
    }
}
```

Now, when we launch the app while online, we do three things:

- We load the restaurants from the server by calling `restInterface.getRestaurants()`. For these restaurants, we don't receive the `isFavorite` flag, so we automatically have it set to `false`. This happens because our `Restaurant` class defaults the value of `isFavorite` to false if no value is passed from the Gson deserialization:

  ```
  @Entity(tableName = "restaurants")
  data class Restaurant(
      …
      @ColumnInfo(name = "is_favorite")
      val isFavorite: Boolean = false)
  ```

- Then, we save those restaurants to Room by calling `restaurantsDao.addAll(restaurants)`. However, because we've used the `REPLACE` strategy inside our DAO's `addAll()` function, and because we received the same restaurants from the server, we override the `isFavorite` flags of the corresponding restaurants inside the database to `false`. So, even though our restaurants in Room might have had the `isFavorite` flag set to `true`, because we receive restaurants with the same `id` fields from the server, we end up overriding all those values to `false`.
- Next, we pass the `restaurants` list that we've received from the server to the UI. As we already know, these restaurants have the `isFavorite` field's value of `false`. So, anytime we start the app while connected to the internet, we will always see no restaurants marked as favorites.

If we think about it, there are two main issues here:

- Our application has two sources of truth:
  - When online, it displays the restaurants from the remote server.
  - When offline, it displays the restaurants from the local database.
- Whenever we cache restaurants that already exist inside the local database, we override their `isFavorite` flag to `false`.

If we can fix these two issues by having our UI receive content from a single source of data, we will also be able to remove the need for `SavedStateHandle` and all the special handling related to process recreation – we will see why in a moment.

Essentially, in this section, we will be doing the following:

- Refactoring the Restaurants app to have a single source of truth for data
- Removing the logic of persisting state inside `SavedStateHandle` in the case of process recreation

So, let's begin with the first issue at hand!

Refactoring the Restaurants app to have a single source of truth for data

The approach of having multiple sources of data can lead to many inconsistencies and subtle bugs – just like how our app is now inconsistent in terms of what data it displays when the user is either online or offline.

> **Note**
>
> The concept of designing systems to rely on only one data source used for storing and updating content is related to a practice that is called **Single Source of Truth** (**SSOT**). Having multiple sources of truth for data that the UI consumes can lead to inconsistencies between what's expected to be shown to the UI and what is actually shown. The SSOT concept helps us to structure the data access so that only one data source is trusted to provide the app with data.

Let's make sure that our application only has one source of truth, but which one should we choose?

On the one hand, we cannot control the data that is being sent from our Firebase database, and we also can't update the restaurants stored inside it when the user marks one as a favorite.

On the other hand, we can do that with Room! In fact, we are already doing that – every time a user marks a restaurant as a favorite or not a favorite, we're applying a partial update to that restaurant inside the local database.

So, let's make the local Room database our only source of data:

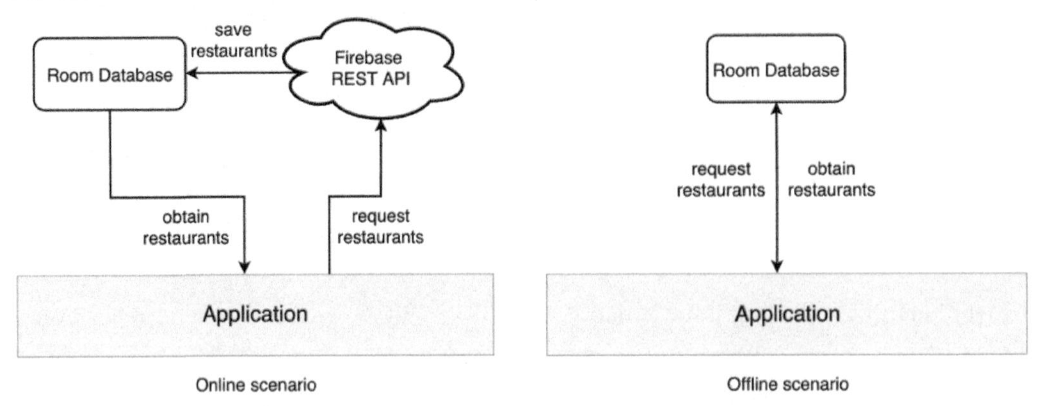

Figure 6.3 – Data retrieval for the Restaurants app with the local database as an SSOT

When the user is online, we should get the restaurants from the server, cache them into Room, and then obtain the restaurants again from Room to finally send them to the UI.

Similarly, if the user is offline, we simply obtain the restaurants from Room and display them.

> **Note**
>
> Alternatively, instead of always asking your Room database for the most up-to-date content, you could update the DAO interface to provide you with a reactive data stream that we can observe. This way, upon every data update, you would automatically be notified with the most up-to-date content in a reactive manner, without having to manually ask for it. To achieve that, you must use special data holders provided by libraries such as Jetpack LiveData, Kotlin Flow, or RxJava. We will explore Kotlin Flow in *Chapter 11, Creating Infinite Lists with Jetpack Paging and Kotlin Flow.*

The similarity between our two scenarios is that now, regardless of the internet connectivity of the user, our UI always displays the restaurants from inside our Room database. In other words, the local database is our SSOT!

Let's start implementing! Perform the following steps:

1. Inside `RestaurantsViewModel`, refactor the `getAllRestaurants()` function to always return the restaurants from the Room database:

```
private suspend fun getAllRestaurants():
        List<Restaurant> {
      return withContext(Dispatchers.IO) {
```

```
        try { … } catch (e: Exception) { […] }
        return@withContext restaurantsDao.getAll()
    }
}
```

Here, our app tries to display the restaurants from the local database in any condition.

2. Now, it's time to refactor the `try - catch` block inside the `getAllRestaurants()` method! Essentially, what we want to do is to get the restaurants from the server and then cache them locally.

   Replace the contents within the `try { }` block with a new `refreshCache()` method:

```
return withContext(Dispatchers.IO) {
    try {
        refreshCache()
    } catch (e: Exception) { […] }
    return@withContext restaurantsDao.getAll()
}
```

3. Additionally, we want to define the `refreshCache()` function to get the restaurants from the remote server and then cache them inside the local database, thereby refreshing their contents:

```
private suspend fun refreshCache() {
    val remoteRestaurants = restInterface
        .getRestaurants()
    restaurantsDao.addAll(remoteRestaurants)
}
```

4. We know that if the refresh of the cache fails, we will still show the local restaurants from Room. But what if the local database is empty?

   Continue refactoring the `getAllRestaurants()` method by updating its `catch` block. You can do this by removing the `return@withContext restaurantsDao.getAll()` call (which is now redundant) from the `is UnknownHostException, is ConnectException, is HttpException` branch and by replacing it with the following code:

```
try { … } catch (e: Exception) {
    when (e) {
```

```
            is UnknownHostException, is ConnectException,
            is HttpException -> {
                if (restaurantsDao.getAll().isEmpty())
                    throw Exception(
                        "Something went wrong. " +
                                "We have no data.")
            }
            else -> throw e
        }
    }
```

Essentially, if a network exception has been thrown, we can check whether we have any local restaurants saved in the Room database:

- If the list is empty, we return from the parent method early by throwing a custom exception to inform the user that we have no data to display.
- However, if the local database has elements, we do nothing and let the `getAllRestaurants()` method return the cached restaurants to the UI.

Now, inside the `toggleFavorite()` function of `ViewModel`, whenever we toggle a restaurant as a favorite or not, we can observe that we're updating the Room database with a partial update. However, we're not fetching the restaurants again from Room and so the UI is never informed of this change:

```
fun toggleFavorite(id: Int) {
    ...
    restaurants[itemIndex] = item.copy(isFavorite =
        !item.isFavorite)
    storeSelection(restaurants[itemIndex])
    state.value = restaurants
    viewModelScope.launch {
        toggleFavoriteRestaurant(id, item.isFavorite)
    }
}
```

Instead, we're updating the `state` variable's value – so the UI receives the updated restaurants in-memory. This means that we are not conforming to the SSOT practice in which we opt to always feed the UI with restaurants from the local database. Let's fix this.

5. Make the `toggleFavoriteRestaurant()` function return the restaurants from our local database. You can do this by calling the `restaurantsDao.getAll()` function from inside the `withContext()` block:

```
private suspend fun toggleFavoriteRestaurant(
    id: Int,
    oldValue: Boolean
) = withContext(Dispatchers.IO) {
        restaurantsDao.update(
            PartialRestaurant(id = id, isFavorite =
                !oldValue))
        restaurantsDao.getAll()
    }
```

6. Inside the `toggleFavorite()` method, store the updated restaurants returned by the `toggleFavoriteRestaurant()` method inside an `updatedRestaurants` variable, and then move the `state.value = restaurants` line from outside the coroutine to inside it while, this time, making it receive the value stored by the `updatedRestaurants` variable:

```
fun toggleFavorite(id: Int) {
    val restaurants = state.value.toMutableList()
    [...]
    storeSelection(restaurants[itemIndex])
    viewModelScope.launch(errorHandler) {
        val updatedRestaurants =
            toggleFavoriteRestaurant(id, item.isFavorite)
        state.value = updatedRestaurants
    }
}
```

Here, we have not updated the `state` object value with the `restaurants` value from the previous state value. Instead, we passed the restaurants from the local database, which were obtained from the `toggleFavoriteRestaurant()` function.

Now that we have made our local database the single source of truth for data, we might assume that our issues have been solved. However, remember that we are still overriding the `isFavorite` field values of the local restaurants whenever we cache restaurants with the same IDs from the server.

That's why the final problem lies in the `refreshCache()` method:

```
private suspend fun refreshCache() {
    val remoteRestaurants = restInterface
        .getRestaurants()
    restaurantsDao.addAll(remoteRestaurants)
}
```

We must find a way to preserve the `isFavorite` field of the restaurants whenever we call `restaurantsDao.addAll(remoteRestaurants)`.

We can fix this issue by complicating the logic that is happening inside the `refreshCache()` function.

7. Inside the `refreshCache()` function, add the following code:

```
private suspend fun refreshCache() {
    val remoteRestaurants = restInterface
        .getRestaurants()
    val favoriteRestaurants = restaurantsDao
        .getAllFavorited()
    restaurantsDao.addAll(remoteRestaurants)
    restaurantsDao.updateAll(
        favoriteRestaurants.map {
            PartialRestaurant(it.id, true)
        })
}
```

Now, let's break down what we've just done:

i. First, just as before, we got the restaurants from the server (which will all have the `isFavorite` fields set to `false` as their default values) by calling `restInterface.getRestaurants()`.

ii. Then, from Room, we obtained all the restaurants that were favorited by calling `restaurantsDao.getAllFavorited()` – we haven't added this function yet so don't worry if your code doesn't compile yet.

iii. Next, just as before, we saved the remote restaurants in Room by calling `restaurantsDao.addAll(remoteRestaurants)`. With this, we override the `isFavorite` field (to `false`) of the existing restaurants that have the same ID as `remoteRestaurants`.

iv. Finally, we partially updated all the restaurants within Room by calling `restaurantsDao.updateAll()`. To this method (which we have yet to implement), we are passing a list of `PartialRestaurant` objects.

These objects resulted from mapping the previously cached `favoriteRestaurants` objects of type `Restaurant` to objects of type `PartialRestaurant`, which have their `isFavorite` fields set to `true`. With this approach, we have now restored the `isFavorite` field's value for those favorited restaurants that were initially cached.

8. Inside `RestaurantsDao`, we must implement the two methods used earlier:

```
@Dao
interface RestaurantsDao {
    [...]
    @Update(entity = Restaurant::class)
    suspend fun updateAll(partialRestaurants:
        List<PartialRestaurant>)
    @Query("SELECT * FROM restaurants WHERE
        is_favorite = 1")
    suspend fun getAllFavorited(): List<Restaurant>
}
```

We have added the following:

- The `updateAll()` method: This is a partial update that works in the same way as the `update()` method. Here, the only difference is that we update the `isFavorite` field for a list of restaurants instead of only one.
- The `getAllFavorited()` method: This is a query just like the `getAll()` method but more specific, as it obtains all the restaurants that have their `isFavorite` field values equal to `1` (which stands for `true`).

We are finally done! It's time to test out the app!

9. Try running the application offline and then mark a couple of restaurants as favorites.
10. Connect your device to the internet and run the application – while you are online.

You should now be able to see the previous selections – all the restaurants that were originally marked as favorites are now persisted across any scenario.

However, we have one more thing to address!

Removing the logic of persisting state in the case of process recreation

Now our application has a single source of truth, that is, the local database:

- Whenever we receive restaurants from the server, we cache them to Room and then refresh the UI with the restaurants from Room.
- Whenever we mark a restaurant as a favorite or not, we cache the selection to Room, and similarly, we then refresh the UI with restaurants from Room.

This means that if a system-initiated process death occurs, we should be able to restore the UI state easily because, now, the restaurants in Room also have the `isFavorite` field cached.

In other words, our app no longer needs to rely on `SavedStateHandle` to restore the restaurants that have been favorited or not; the local source of data for our application will now handle this automatically.

Let's remove our special handling for a system-initiated process death:

1. Inside `RestaurantsViewModel`, remove the `stateHandle: SavedStateHandle` parameter:

```
class RestaurantsViewModel() : ViewModel() { … }
```

2. Inside `RestaurantsViewModel`, remove the `storeSelection()` and the `restoreSelections()` methods.
3. Remove the `companion object` of the `RestaurantsViewModel` class.
4. While you are still inside `ViewModel`, remove all the logic related to the `stateHandle` variable from within the `toggleFavorite()` method. The method should now look like this:

```
fun toggleFavorite(id: Int) {
    viewModelScope.launch(errorHandler) {
        val updatedRestaurants =
            toggleFavoriteRestaurant(id, item.isFavorite)
        state.value = updatedRestaurants
    }
}
```

The issue is that we no longer have the `item` variable, so we don't know what to pass to the `toggleFavoriteRestaurant()` function's `oldValue` parameter instead of `item.isFavorite`. We need to fix this.

5. Add a new parameter to the `toggleFavorite()` method, called `oldValue`:

```
fun toggleFavorite(id: Int, oldValue: Boolean) {
    viewModelScope.launch(errorHandler) {
        val updatedRestaurants =
            toggleFavoriteRestaurant(id, oldValue)
        state.value = updatedRestaurants
    }
}
```

This `Boolean` argument should tell us whether the restaurant was previously marked as favorite or not.

6. Following this, refactor the `getRestaurants()` method to no longer use the `restoreSelections()` method. The method should now look like this:

```
private fun getRestaurants() {
    viewModelScope.launch(errorHandler) {
        state.value = getAllRestaurants()
    }
}
```

7. Next, navigate to the `RestaurantsScreen` file. Then, inside the `RestaurantItem` composable, add another `oldValue` parameter to the `onFavoriteClick` callback function:

```
@Composable
fun RestaurantItem([…],
        onFavoriteClick: (id: Int, oldValue: Boolean)
            -> Unit,
        onItemClick: (id: Int) -> Unit) {
    ...
    Card(…) {
        Row(…) {
            [...]
            RestaurantDetails(...)
            RestaurantIcon(icon, Modifier.weight(0.15f))
```

```
                {
                    onFavoriteClick(item.id, item.isFavorite)
                }
            }
        }
    }
```

Also, make sure that you pass the `item.isFavorite` value to the newly added parameter when the `onFavoriteClick` function is called.

8. Inside the `RestaurantsScreen()` composable, make sure you register and then pass the newly received `oldValue` function parameter to the `toggleFavorite` method of `ViewModel`:

```
@Composable
fun RestaurantsScreen(onItemClick: (id: Int) -> Unit) {
    val viewModel: RestaurantsViewModel = viewModel()
    LazyColumn(…) {
        items(viewModel.state.value) { restaurant ->
            RestaurantItem(
                restaurant,
                onFavoriteClick = { id, oldValue ->
                    viewModel
                        .toggleFavorite(id, oldValue)
                },
                onItemClick = { id -> onItemClick(id) })
        }
    }
}
```

We're done! Now it's time to simulate the system-initiated process death scenario.

9. Build the project and run the application.
10. Mark some restaurants as favorites.
11. Place the app in the background by pressing the home button on the device/emulator.
12. Select the **Logcat** window and then press the red rectangular button on the left-hand side to terminate the application:

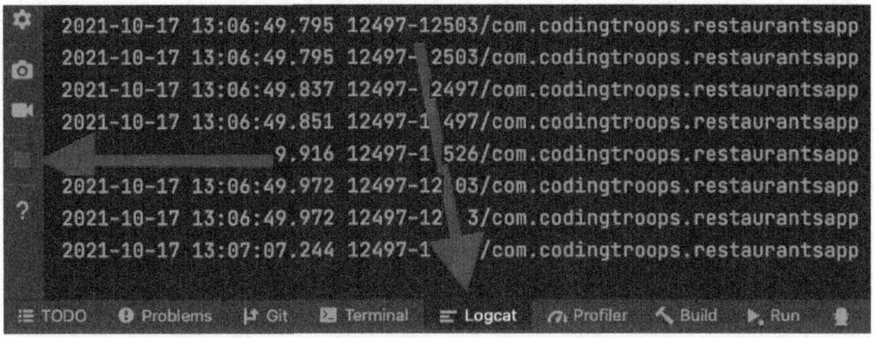

Figure 6.4 – Simulating a system-initiated process death

13. Relaunch the application from the application drawer.

Because the app relies on the content saved in the local database, it should now correctly display the UI state with the previously favorited restaurants from before the system-initiated process death.

> **Assignment**
> In this chapter, we made sure to cache the restaurants in Room so that the first screen of the application could be accessed without the internet.
> As a homework assignment, you can try to refactor the details screen of the application (where the details of a specific restaurant are displayed) to obtain its own data from Room if the user enters the app without the internet.

Summary

In this chapter, we gained an understanding of how Room is an essential Jetpack library because it allows us to offer offline capabilities to our applications.

First, we explored the core elements of Room to see how a private database is set up. Second, we implemented Room inside our Restaurants application and explored how to save and retrieve cached content from the local database.

Afterward, we discovered what partial updates are and how to implement them to preserve a user's selections within the app.

Toward the end of the chapter, we understood why having a single source of truth for the application's content is beneficial and how that helps us in edge cases such as a system-initiated process death.

In the next chapter, we're going to dive deeper into various ways of defining the architecture of our applications by exploring architectural presentation patterns.

7
Introducing Presentation Patterns in Android

In this chapter, we're continuing our journey of exploring ways to architect Android applications. More precisely, we will be making sure that our applications split responsibilities correctly with the introduction of presentation patterns.

In the first section, *Introducing MVC, MVP, and MVVM as presentation patterns*, we will provide a short overview on why we need presentation patterns, and we will explore how most common patterns are implemented in Android projects.

Next up, in the *Refactoring our Restaurants App to fit a presentation pattern* section, we will refactor our Restaurants App to fit the MVVM presentation pattern, while also understanding why MVVM is best suited for our Compose-based app.

In the last section, *Improving state encapsulation in ViewModel*, we will see why it's important for the **user interface** (**UI**) state to be properly encapsulated inside the `ViewModel`, and we will explore how to achieve that.

To summarize, in this chapter, we're going to cover the following main topics:

- Introducing **Model-View-Controller** (**MVC**), **Model-View-Presenter** (**MVP**), and **Model-View-ViewModel** (**MVVM**) as presentation patterns
- Refactoring our Restaurants app to a presentation pattern
- Improving state encapsulation in ViewModel

Before jumping in, let's set up the technical requirements for this chapter.

Technical requirements

Building Compose-based Android projects for this chapter usually requires your day-to-day tools. However, to follow along smoothly, make sure you have the following:

- The Arctic Fox 2020.3.1 version of Android Studio. You can also use a newer Android Studio version or even Canary builds, but note that the IDE interface and other generated code files might differ from the ones used throughout this book.
- Kotlin 1.6.10 or newer plugin installed in Android Studio.
- The Restaurants app code from the previous chapter.

The starting point for this chapter is represented by the Restaurants app developed in the previous chapter. If you haven't followed the implementation from the previous chapter, access the starting point for this chapter by navigating to the `Chapter_06` directory of the repository and importing the Android project entitled `chapter_6_restaurants_app`.

To access the solution code for this chapter, navigate to the `Chapter_07` directory at `https://github.com/PacktPublishing/Kickstart-Modern-Android-Development-with-Jetpack-and-Kotlin/tree/main/Chapter_07/chapter_7_restaurants_app`.

Introducing MVC, MVP, and MVVM as presentation patterns

In the beginning, most Android projects were designed as a bunch of `Activity` or `Fragment` classes that were setting content to their corresponding **Extensible Markup Language** (**XML**) layouts.

As projects grew and new features were requested, developers had to add more logic inside the `Activity` or `Fragment` class, development cycle after development cycle. This means that anything from a new feature, improvement, or bug fix for a particular screen would have to be done inside those `Activity` or `Fragment` classes.

After some time, these classes became larger and larger, and at some point, adding an improvement or fixing a bug could become a nightmare. The reason for this would be that the `Activity` or `Fragment` classes were burdened with all the responsibilities from within a particular project. These classes would be doing the following:

- Defining the UI
- Preparing the data to be displayed and defining different UI states
- Obtaining data from different sources
- Applying different business rules to data

This approach introduces coupling between distinct responsibilities and concerns of a project. For such projects, if—for example—a portion of the UI must be changed, your changes could easily impact other concerns of the app: the way data is presented, the logic of obtaining that data, business rules, and so on.

The worst part of this happening is that when you need to change only a part (say, part of the UI) and you end up changing other parts (say, the presentation, or data logic) you risk breaking unrelated things that worked, therefore possibly introducing new bugs.

Having such an approach where all the code of a project is bundled inside the `Activity` or `Fragment` class, causes your project to develop the following issues:

- **Fragile and difficult to scale**: Adding new features or improvements can break other parts of your app.
- **Difficult to test**: Since all the logic of the app is bundled in one place, testing only one part of the logic is very difficult because all your logic is tangled and tied to platform-related dependencies.
- **Difficult to debug**: When responsibilities are intertwined, then parts of your code base are also intertwined and coupled. Debugging one specific issue becomes extremely difficult because it's hard to track the exact culprit.

To alleviate these issues, we can try to identify the core responsibilities of an app and then separate their corresponding logic and code into distinct components (or classes) that are part of specific layers. This way, we are trying to follow the principle of **separation of concerns** (**SoC**), whereby each layer will contain classes whose responsibilities are tightly related only to their corresponding layer's concern.

To make sure that our projects obey the SoC principle, we can split the app's responsibilities into two major ones and define a layer for each of them, as follows:

- The **Presentation layer** contains classes (or other components) responsible for defining the UI and preparing the data to be presented.
- The **Model layer** contains classes where the application's data is obtained, modeled, and updated.

Even though the two layers seem to do more than one thing, all these actions define a broader dedicated responsibility that encapsulates a specific concern.

In this chapter, while we will be mostly focusing on structuring the Presentation layer, we will also start working on the Model layer. We will continue refactoring the Model layer in *Chapter 8, Getting Started with Clean Architecture in Android.*

To separate concerns within the Presentation layer, you can make use of presentation design patterns. **Presentation design patterns** are architectural patterns that define how the Presentation layer is structured in our applications.

The Presentation layer is a part of our project that is tied to what the user sees: the UI and the presentation of that UI. In other words, the Presentation layer handles two granular, yet related responsibilities associated with two types of logic, as outlined here:

- **UI logic**: Defines the ability to display content on a device in a specific way for one screen or flow. For example, when building an XML layout or a composable hierarchy for a screen, we're defining the UI logic for that specific screen since we're defining its UI elements.
- **Presentation logic**: The logic that defines the state of the UI (for one screen or flow) and how it mutates when the user interacts with our UI, therefore defining how the data is being presented to the UI. We're writing presentation logic when, for example, we must do the following:
    - Ensure that the screen is in a loading state or error state at specific times
    - Present content for a screen in a specific manner by formatting it to some standards

For the Presentation layer to define UI logic and presentation logic, it needs some data to work with. That's why it must be connected to the Model layer, which provides it with raw data, be it from web services, local databases, or other sources. You can see an illustration of this in the following diagram:

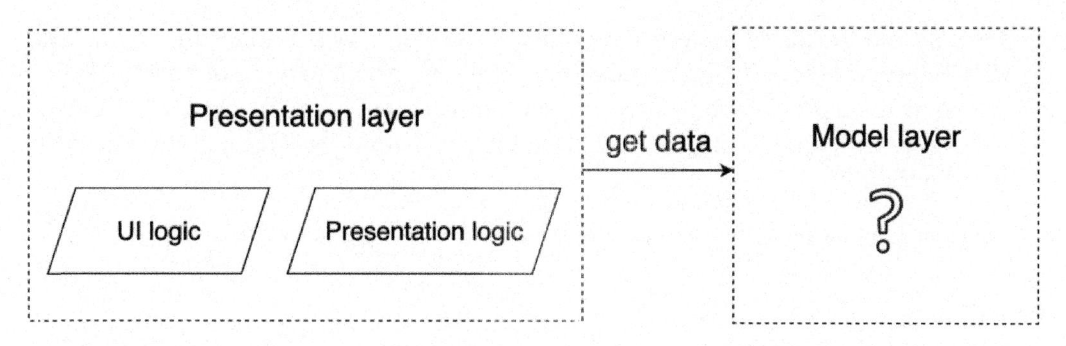

Figure 7.1 – Composition of the Presentation layer and its relation to the Model layer

For now, we will consider the Model layer a black box that just provides us with data.

We can say that such separations allow the UI to become a representation of the model's data through transformations that happen inside the Presentation layer while having components whose responsibilities don't overlap.

In Android, transformations from within the Presentation layer are modeled through three popular presentation patterns that are used in other technology stacks as well, as follows:

- MVC
- MVP
- MVVM

> **Note**
>
> As Android developers, we have adjusted the implementation of these presentation patterns to the specific needs of Android. That's why the way we will exemplify or implement them may vary from their original definitions given by their founders—all this is in pursuit of observing their common usages in Android projects.

These presentation patterns will allow us to separate UI logic from presentation logic for each screen or flow within our app. By doing so, we are ensuring that our Presentation layer has less coupled code that is easier to maintain, easier to scale with new features, and easier to test.

Historically, most Android projects have transitioned from MVC to MVP and, nowadays, to MVVM. Regardless of their structure, though, it's important to mention that the SoC promoted by these presentation patterns often translates into each UI flow being broken into classes or components that are instructed to do something specific, tightly related to their responsibility.

To see what I'm talking about, let's briefly cover them, starting out with MVC.

MVC

A common implementation in Android projects of the MVC pattern defines its layers like so:

- **View**: Views inflated from the XML layouts as a representation of the UI. This layer would only be rendering the content it receives from the Controller onto the screen.
- **Controller**: UI controllers such as `Activity` or `Fragment`. This component would define the state of the UI by preparing data received from the Model layer for presentation, or by intercepting UI events that in turn would mutate the state. Additionally, the Controller would be in charge of setting actual data to the View layer.
- **Model**: The entry point of data. The actual structure doesn't depend on MVC, but we can think of it as the layer that obtains content needed by the Presentation layer, by querying a local database or remote sources such as web **application programming interfaces** (**APIs**).

Let's visualize the actual separation brought by this pattern, as follows:

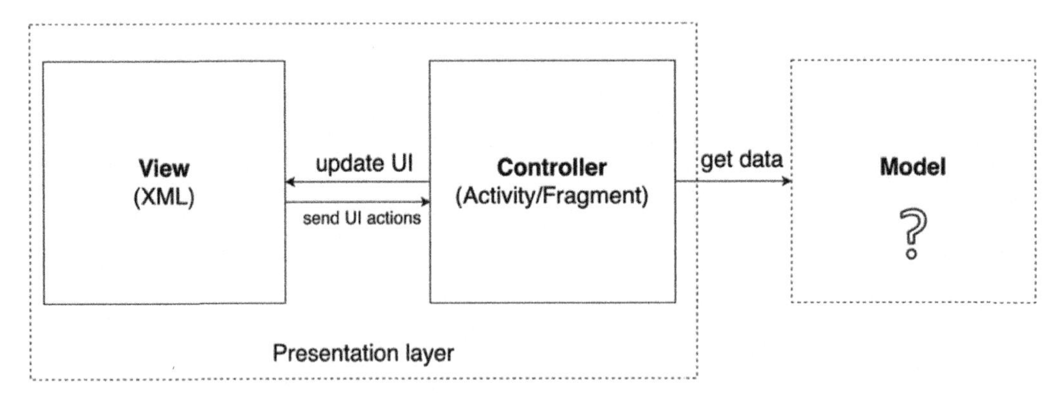

Figure 7.2 – Presentation layer in the MVC pattern

This implementation of the MVC pattern achieves a proper separation between the Presentation layer and the Model layer, therefore liberating `Activity` and `Fragment` controllers from being the ones that obtain data from **REpresentational State Transfer** (**REST**) APIs or local databases. Yet at least in this form factor, MVC doesn't shine where it should because the actual separation within the Presentation layer could be improved.

Disadvantages of this pattern may include the following:

- High coupling between the Controller (`Activity` or `Fragment` controllers) and the View layer. Since the Controller is a component with a lifecycle and it also must provide the infrastructure of building and setting up Android views with content (such as building `Adapter` classes and passing data), testing it becomes difficult because it's tightly coupled with Android APIs.
- The Controller has two responsibilities: it handles the state of the UI (presentation logic) while also providing infrastructure for the View layer to function (UI logic). The two responsibilities become tangled up—when testing one, you would be testing the other too.

Let's move on to another popular presentation pattern in Android.

MVP

A common implementation in Android projects of the MVP pattern defines its layers like so:

- **View**: The UI layer defined by the `Activity` or `Fragment` class and their corresponding inflated views from XML. This layer now encapsulates the entire UI logic: it provides the infrastructure of building and setting up rendered Android views with content.
- **Presenter**: Presents data to the UI by manipulating the View layer indirectly through an interface. With this approach, a one-to-one relationship between a Presenter and a View layer (be it `Activity` or `Fragment`) is established. The interface allows the Presenter to pass data that is ready for presentation to the UI layer and to directly mutate the UI state at the UI level.

  Unlike the Controller in MVC, the Presenter is no longer coupled to lifecycle components or Android View APIs, so it becomes much easier to test the presentation logic that it contains.
- **Model**: The same as in MVC.

Let's visualize the actual separation brought by this pattern, as follows:

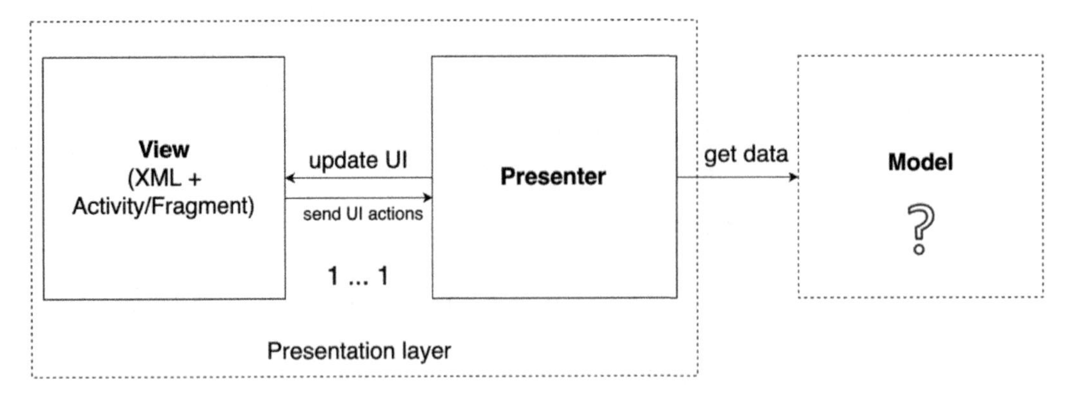

Figure 7.3 – Presentation layer in the MVP pattern

Unlike MVC, `Activity` and `Fragment` are now part of the View layer, which seems more natural because they are both tightly related to the Android UI. This approach allows the Presenter to be the one that prepares data that must be presented, while imperatively mutating the UI.

Since we now have a separate entity that is in charge of presenting data to the UI, we can say that, unlike MVC, MVP performs the SoC inside the Presentation layer somewhat better.

However, there are still some issues with this approach, as outlined here:

- The imperative approach of having the Presenter manually update the UI directly in the `Activity` or `Fragment` class can be prone to bugs and can cause illegal UI states (such as showing an error message and a loading status at the same time) as a project grows and new features are added. This is similar to how a UI controller (such as `Activity`) also imperatively mutates XML views—an approach that we deemed as prone to issues when we introduced Compose with its declarative paradigm.
- If the interface contract between the Presenter and the View layer is not well designed or is missing entirely, the two would become coupled, and reusing the Presenter for other `Activity` or `Fragment` controllers might be difficult.

Let's move on to another important presentation pattern.

MVVM

MVVM is a very popular presentation pattern in Android, mostly because it addresses the concerns stated with the previously mentioned implementation of MVP.

A common implementation in Android projects of MVVM defines its layers like so:

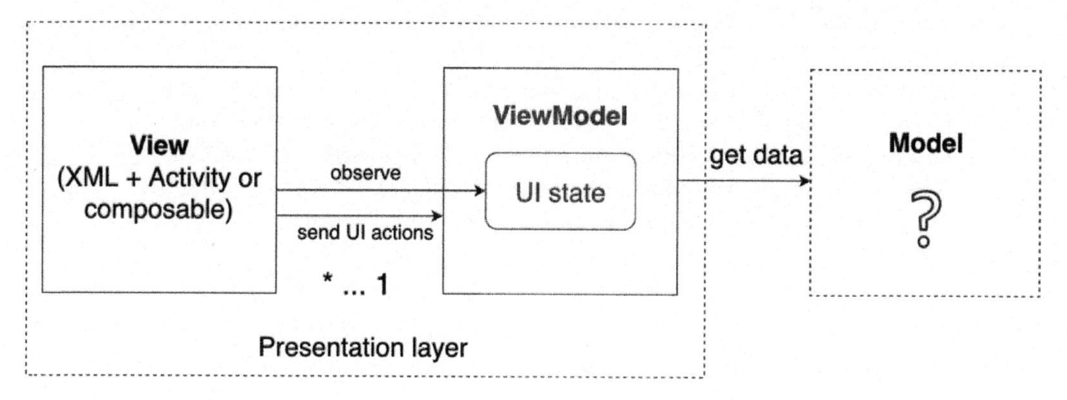

Figure 7.4 – Presentation layer in the MVVM pattern

Let's look at how the layers are defined:

- **View**: The UI layer is the `Activity` or `Fragment` class and its XML views, just as in MVP. Unlike in MVP, though, the View layer observes either an observable state or observable fields from the `ViewModel`, both containing UI data. Whenever new updates are received from those observable entities, the View layer updates the UI with the content received.
- **ViewModel**: This prepares the data received from the Model layer, just as the Presenter in MVP did. Unlike the Presenter, though, the `ViewModel` defines the UI state as an observable property (or multiple observable fields) and is totally decoupled from the View layer as it has no reference to it.
- **Model**: The same as in MVC or MVP.

One advantage of the `ViewModel`, as opposed to the Presenter in MVP, is that it's no longer coupled to the View layer, so it can be reused much more easily. In contrast with MVP, the View layer is responsible for referencing the `ViewModel` for obtaining and observing the observable state, and so the `ViewModel` no longer needs to reference the View layer, becoming totally independent.

In other words, the `ViewModel` in MVVM forces the View layer to subscribe to data, which is different from MVP, where the Presenter was manually setting up the View layer with data. This approach allows multiple Views to bind to the same `ViewModel`, therefore *sharing* the same UI state within the same `ViewModel`.

Another advantage is that since the View layer observes the UI state from the `ViewModel` and binds the received data as an effect, the `ViewModel` doesn't imperatively update the UI as the Presenter did through an interface in MVP. In other words, the View layer obtains the UI state from the `ViewModel` and binds it to the UI—this results in a unidirectional flow of data that is less likely to introduce bugs or illegal states.

> **Note**
>
> While considering the original definition of MVVM, the ViewModel shouldn't be confused with the Jetpack ViewModel component—the ViewModel can be a simple class that presents the data through an observable state. For us on Android, though, it's convenient to consider the Jetpack ViewModel as the actual ViewModel from MVVM because it brings some advantages out of the box.

However, the pattern's implementation that is commonly used in Android considers the Jetpack ViewModel as the ViewModel from MVVM, and this brings both a set of advantages and disadvantages.

Using the Jetpack ViewModel as the `ViewModel` from MVVM is beneficial for the following reasons:

- The Jetpack ViewModel is scoped to the lifetime of the View and provides convenient APIs for canceling work such as the `onCleared()` callback or the `viewModelScope` coroutine scope, therefore providing a convenient API for canceling asynchronous jobs and minimizing the risk of memory leaks.
- The Jetpack ViewModel survives configuration changes, therefore allowing you to preserve the UI state automatically if the user changes the orientation of the device, for example.
- You can easily restore the UI state after system-initiated process death because the Jetpack ViewModel is providing us with a `SavedStateHandle` object.

Unfortunately, this approach comes with the following downsides:

- The `ViewModel` is now a library dependency (the Jetpack ViewModel) that introduces coupling with the Android platform (as it exposes APIs such as `SavedStateHandle`). This prevents us from reusing presentation components for cross-platform projects with **Kotlin Multiplatform** (**KMP**).
- Because the Jetpack ViewModel is a library dependency that handles other responsibilities apart from data presentation, such as restoring the UI state after system-initiated process death, we could argue that the Presentation layer concerns are not very well separated.

Now that we have had a quick overview of presentation patterns, it's time for a practical example.

Refactoring our Restaurants app to fit a presentation pattern

We plan to refactor our Restaurants app to fit a presentation pattern. From our previous comparison, we can consider that MVVM is best suited for our Compose-based app. Don't worry—we will talk about this decision in more detail a bit later.

But before we do that, let's add more functionality inside the application to better highlight how mingling responsibilities can lead to unmaintainable code.

To summarize, in this section, we're going to be doing the following:

- Adding more functionality inside our Restaurants app
- Refactoring our Restaurants app to MVVM

Let's begin!

Adding more functionality inside our Restaurants app

When the Restaurants application is launched, the `RestaurantsScreen()` composable is rendered. Inside this screen, we are loading a bunch of restaurants from the server, and then we're displaying them to the user.

Yet while our app waits for the network request to finish and for the local caching to Room to happen (in order for it to receive restaurants for the UI), the screen remains blank, and the user has no idea what's going on. To provide a better **user experience** (**UX**), we should somehow suggest to the user the fact that we're waiting for content from the server.

We could do that through a loading progress bar! Inside the `RestaurantsScreen()` composable, we could add a loading UI element that is displayed until the `LazyColumn` composable that renders a list of restaurants is populated. When the content arrives, we should hide it, thereby letting the user know that the application has loaded its content.

Let's do that right now, as follows:

1. First, inside the `RestaurantsScreen()` composable, save the restaurant list from the state (retrieved from `RestaurantsViewModel`) inside a `restaurants` variable, like this:

```
@Composable
fun RestaurantsScreen(onItemClick: (id: Int) -> Unit) {
    val viewModel: RestaurantsViewModel = viewModel()
    val restaurants = viewModel.state.value
    LazyColumn(…) {
        items(restaurants) { restaurant ->
            RestaurantItem(…)
        }
    }
}
```

   Make sure to also pass the `restaurants` variable to the `LazyColumn` composable's `items` **domain-specific language** (**DSL**) function.

2. We need to define a condition that lets us know when to show a loading indicator. As a first attempt, we could say that when the `restaurants` variable contains an empty `List<Restaurant>` as a value, which means that restaurants haven't arrived yet, the content is still loading. Add an `isLoading` variable that accounts for this, as follows:

```
@Composable
fun RestaurantsScreen(onItemClick: (id: Int) -> Unit) {
    val viewModel: RestaurantsViewModel = viewModel()
    val restaurants = viewModel.state.value
    val isLoading = restaurants.isEmpty()
    LazyColumn(…) { … }
}
```

   If, however, restaurants arrive from the server, the `state` variable is updated, and the `restaurants` variable no longer contains an empty list of restaurants. At this point, the `isLoading` variable becomes `false`.

3. We want to display a loading indicator while the `isLoading` variable is `true`. To do that, wrap the `LazyColumn` composable in a `Box` composable, and below the `LazyColumn` code, check if the `isLoading` variable is `true` and pass a `CircularProgressIndicator` composable. The code is illustrated in the following snippet:

```
@Composable
fun RestaurantsScreen(onItemClick: (id: Int) -> Unit) {
    ...
    val isLoading = restaurants.isEmpty()
    Box() {
        LazyColumn(...) {...}
        if(isLoading)
            CircularProgressIndicator()
    }
}
```

The `Box` composable allows us to overlay two composables: `LazyColumn` and `CircularProgressIndicator`. Because of the `if` condition that we've added, we now have the following two cases:

- `isLoading` is `true` (the app is waiting for restaurants), so both composables are composed. While the `CircularProgressIndicator` composable is displayed on top of the `LazyColumn` composable, the `LazyColumn` composable contains no elements, so it's not visible.
- `isLoading` is `false` (the app now has restaurants to display), so only the `LazyColumn` composable is composed and visible.

4. To center the `CircularProgressIndicator` composable, add the `Alignment.Center` alignment to the `contentAlignment` parameter of the `Box` composable, while also passing a `Modifier.fillMaxSize()` modifier. The code is illustrated in the following snippet:

```
@Composable
fun RestaurantsScreen(onItemClick: (id: Int) -> Unit) {
    ...
    Box(contentAlignment = Alignment.Center,
        modifier = Modifier.fillMaxSize()) {
        ...
    }
}
```

5. Build and run the app. For a moment (until restaurants are loaded), you should see a loading progress indicator. When restaurants are displayed, this should go away.

Inside the UI layer, we have now added a loading indicator as well as the logic that decides when to display it. In this simple scenario, our logic works, but what happens if the server (or local database) returns an empty list of restaurants? Then the loading indicator will never go away.

Or, what happens if an error occurs? Our `RestaurantsScreen` composable has no idea that an error was generated. This means that not only does it not know when to display the error, but it also doesn't know when to hide the loading indicator if such an error were to occur.

These issues arise from the fact that we're trying to define presentation logic (when to show or hide a loading indicator; when to show an error message) inside the UI layer (where composables reside), thereby mixing UI logic with presentation logic.

We can now see just some limitations that derive from mixing UI logic with presentation logic, yet there's also the fact that in the previous chapters, we've mixed the presentation logic with the data logic. The long-term implications for our current approach are scary: debugging will be difficult, and testing even more so.

It's time to refactor our Restaurants app to MVVM so that we can better separate its responsibilities.

Refactoring our Restaurants app to MVVM

To better separate responsibilities, we will choose the most popular presentation pattern: MVVM. Despite its flaws, when you compare it to MVC and MVP following the definition we previously gave them, it's the best candidate so far for the following reasons:

- It provides a pretty good separation between the UI logic and the presentation logic.
- Our UI layer (the composables) is designed to expect an observable state (more precisely, the Compose `State` object), just like the one the `ViewModel` in MVVM is set to expose.

Now, our Restaurants app already uses the Jetpack ViewModel (that exposes a Compose `State` object that is observed and consumed inside the composables), so we can say that we unknowingly started implementing this modified version of the pattern, whereby the Jetpack ViewModel is the ViewModel from MVVM.

> **Note**
>
> We will consider for now that the advantages of using the Jetpack ViewModel as the `ViewModel` in MVVM are outweighing the disadvantages that it brings, so we will keep it as it is.

However, just because we used a `ViewModel`, that doesn't mean we also implemented the MVVM presentation pattern correctly. Let's first have a look at how we structured our components and classes for the first screen displaying a list of restaurants. You can see how this looks here:

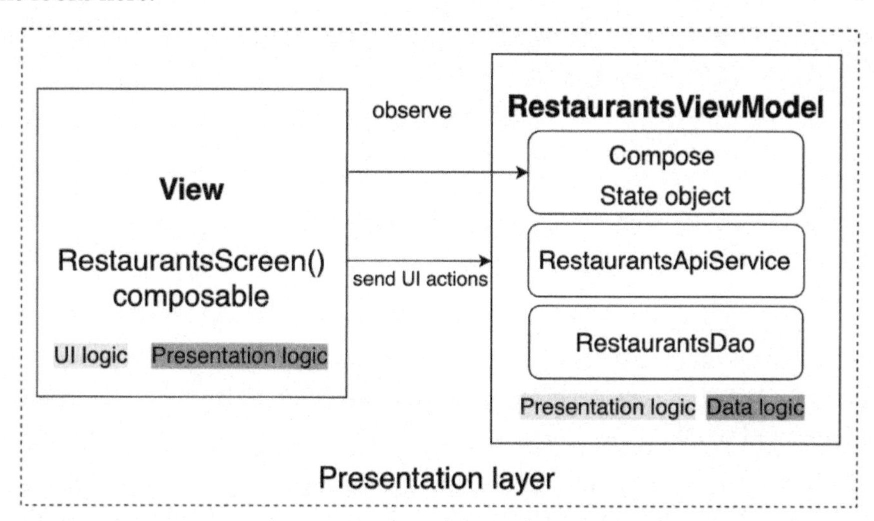

Figure 7.5 – Components with poorly separated responsibilities per layer in the MVVM pattern

For this screen, we notice two violations where layers contain more than one responsibility, as outlined here:

- The View layer (represented by the `RestaurantsScreen()` composable) performs both UI logic and presentation logic. While this composable should only contain UI logic (the stateless composables that consume the state content), some presentation logic lurked in when the `isLoading` variable was calculated, as illustrated in the following code snippet:

```
@Composable
fun RestaurantsScreen(onItemClick: (id: Int) -> Unit) {
    ...
    val isLoading = restaurants.isEmpty()
    ...
}
```

The composables shouldn't be in charge of deciding their own state as in this case—the `RestaurantsScreen()` composable shouldn't hold presentation logic; instead, this should be moved inside the `ViewModel`.

- The `RestaurantsViewModel` class contains both presentation logic (such as holding and updating the state of the UI) and data logic (as it works with the Retrofit service Room **Data Access Object** (**DAO**) when it obtains and caches restaurants), as illustrated in the following code snippet:

```
class RestaurantsViewModel() : ViewModel() {
    private var restInterface: RestaurantsApiService
    private var restaurantsDao = ...
    val state = mutableStateOf(emptyList<Restaurant>())
    private suspend fun getAllRestaurants(): … {…}
        ...
    private suspend fun refreshCache() {...}
}
```

  It's clear that presentation logic occurs when the `state` variable is updated, but there's also a lot of data logic when restaurants are obtained from the `restInterface` variable, then cached and updated in the `restaurantsDao` variable, and so on.

  All this data logic shouldn't reside inside the `ViewModel` but instead inside the Model layer because the `ViewModel` should only present the data and not care to know about the data sources and how they are used—it only knows that it should receive some data.

Now, let's have a look at how we should correctly structure our classes (to follow MVVM) for the first flow of displaying a list of restaurants. The components should look like this:

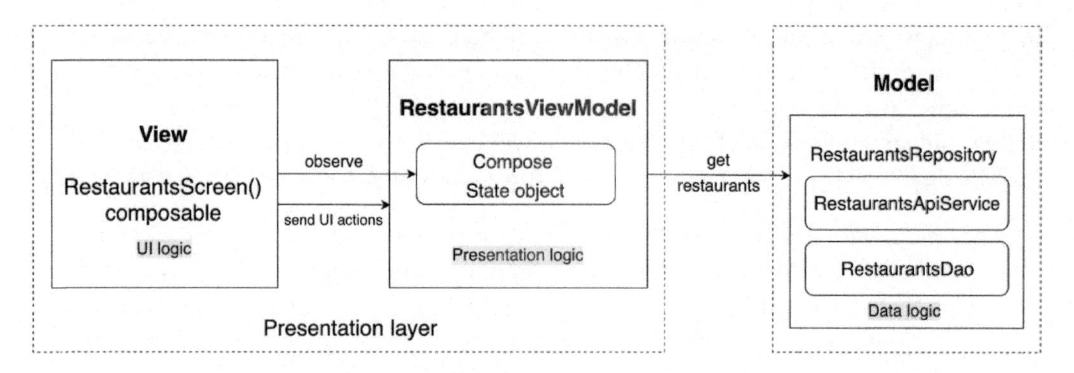

Figure 7.6 – Components with well-separated responsibilities per layer in the MVVM pattern

In the previous diagram, each component handles its own responsibility, as follows:

- The View component contains only composables (`RestaurantsScreen`) with UI logic (consuming the UI state).
- The ViewModel component (`RestaurantsViewModel`) contains only presentation logic (holds the UI state and mutates it).
- The Model component (where we will create a `RestaurantsRepository` class—more on that soon) contains only data logic (obtains restaurants from remote sources, caches them into a local source, and so on).

To achieve this separation, in this section, we will be doing the following:

- Separating UI logic from presentation logic
- Separating presentation logic from data logic

Let's start!

Separating UI logic from presentation logic

The UI logic (rendering composables) is already at the UI level (Compose UI), so we don't have to do anything from this point of view. However, we need to extract the presentation logic from the UI layer to the `ViewModel`, where it should reside.

More specifically, from within the `RestaurantsScreen()` composable, we want to move the calculation of the `isLoading` variable to the `RestaurantsViewModel` class, simply because the `ViewModel` should decide and also know better when the screen should be in a loading state.

To do that, we will create a `state` class that will hold all the information the UI needs in order to render the correct state. This approach is much more efficient because the `ViewModel` is responsible for requesting data and therefore knows better when content arrives, and so on. Because of this, later on, it will be very simple for us to also allow the `ViewModel` to also dictate when the screen must show an error state. Proceed as follows:

1. Create a class that will model the UI state for the `RestaurantsScreen()` composable. Do that by clicking on the application package, selecting **New**, and then **Kotlin Class/File**. Enter `RestaurantsScreenState` as the name and select **Data class** as the type. Inside the new file, add fields that define this screen's state, a `restaurants` list, and an `isLoading` flag. The code is illustrated in the following snippet:

```
data class RestaurantsScreenState(
    val restaurants: List<Restaurant>,
    val isLoading: Boolean)
```

   Since we've used a `data class` instead of a regular `class`, we will be able to easily perform mutation on this object with the `.copy()` function, thereby ensuring that since the Compose `state` object will receive a new object, it will know to trigger recomposition.

2. Inside the `RestaurantsViewModel` class, update the initial state value of the `state` variable and pass a `RestaurantsScreenState` object, as follows:

```
class RestaurantsViewModel() : ViewModel() {
    ...
    val state = mutableStateOf(
        RestaurantsScreenState(
            restaurants = listOf(),
            isLoading = true)
    )
    ...
}
```

   We've marked the `restaurants` field as an empty list, and `isLoading` is `true` because from this point on, we're waiting for restaurants and the UI should render a loading state.

3. Still inside the `RestaurantsViewModel` class, find the `getRestaurants()` method and update the way we update the `state` variable, as follows:

```
private fun getRestaurants() {
    viewModelScope.launch(errorHandler) {
        val restaurants = getAllRestaurants()
        state.value = state.value.copy(
            restaurants = restaurants,
            isLoading = false)
    }
}
```

We first stored restaurants inside a `restaurants` variable. Then, we used the `copy()` function to pass a new restaurants list that we received to the `restaurants` field, and also marked the `isLoading` field to `false` because the data has arrived and the UI should no longer render a loading state.

4. Still in the `RestaurantsViewModel` class, make sure that the `toggleFavorite()` method is correctly updating the `state` variable object using the `copy()` function, as follows:

```
fun toggleFavorite(id: Int, oldValue: Boolean) {
    viewModelScope.launch(errorHandler) {
        val updatedRestaurants = [...]
        state.value = state.value.copy(restaurants =
            updatedRestaurants)
    }
}
```

All right—we've added all the presentation logic within the `ViewModel`, and it's now time to update the UI (our composables) to render new possible UI states.

5. Refactor the `RestaurantsScreen()` composable to consume the new UI state content, as follows:

```
@Composable
fun RestaurantsScreen(onItemClick: (id: Int) -> Unit) {
    val viewModel: RestaurantsViewModel = viewModel()
    val state = viewModel.state.value
    Box(...) {
        LazyColumn(...) {
```

```
                items(state.restaurants) {...}
            }
            if (state.isLoading)
                CircularProgressIndicator()
        }
    }
```

Let's break down what we've done, as follows:

- We renamed the `restaurants` variable as `state` to better suggest that this variable holds the state of this screen.
- We passed `state.restaurants` to the `LazyColumn` composable's `items` DSL function.
- We deleted this line: `val isLoading = restaurants.isEmpty()`.
- We updated the condition for when to show `CircularProgressIndicator()` based on the `state.isLoading` value—no more decision-making logic inside this composable.

6. Build and run the app.

   You should be able to see the loading indicator, just as before, yet the difference is that the presentation logic is better separated and held by the `ViewModel`. With our new approach, if for any reason we receive an empty list from our data sources (Retrofit and Room), the application won't misbehave and show a loading state because the UI is checking whether the list is empty or not.

   To see how simple it is to add a new state to our Compose-based UI, let's continue by setting an error state when any error is thrown inside the `ViewModel`.

7. Inside the `RestaurantsScreenState` class, add an `error: String` parameter that will hold an error message if any error occurs, as follows:

```
data class RestaurantsScreenState(
    val restaurants: List<Restaurant>,
    val isLoading: Boolean,
    val error: String? = null
)
```

   To simplify our work with state handling inside the `ViewModel`, we've set a default value of `null` to the `error` field, since the initial state of the screen shouldn't ever contain an error.

8. Inside the `RestaurantsViewModel` class, find the `errorHandler` variable that we use to catch any exception that might be thrown by our coroutines, and update the `state` object by passing an `exception.message` error message to the `error` field. The code is illustrated in the following snippet:

```
class RestaurantsViewModel() : ViewModel() {
    ...
    private val errorHandler =
        CoroutineExceptionHandler { _, exception ->
            exception.printStackTrace()
            state.value = state.value.copy(
                error = exception.message,
                isLoading = false
            )
        }
    ...
}
```

Additionally, we've set the `isLoading` field to `false` on the new state simply because if an error is thrown, we don't want the UI to be in a loading state.

If, however, you want to add a retry button that is pressed after an error has occurred and was shown, you would have to set the `error` field to `null` when that button is pressed so that the UI won't remain in an error state indefinitely.

9. Inside the `RestaurantsScreen()` composable, add another `if` statement in the `Box` composable. This statement checks whether the `state` object contains an error message to be shown, and if that is `true`, add a `Text` composable that will display the error message. The code is illustrated in the following snippet:

```
@Composable
fun RestaurantsScreen(onItemClick: (id: Int) -> Unit) {
    ...
    Box(...) {
        LazyColumn(...) {...}
        if (state.isLoading)
            CircularProgressIndicator()
        if (state.error != null)
            Text(state.error)
    }
}
```

10. Build the project, and now, let's test the error scenario. Yet to see the error message, we need to simulate an error.

    If you remember, inside our `RestaurantsViewModel` class's `getAllRestaurants()` method, we check if we failed in retrieving restaurants from the server (Retrofit client), and if this happens while the Room DAO is also empty, we throw this error message: `"Something went wrong. We have no data."`.

    To reproduce this scenario, make sure that the following applies:

    - You have cleared the cache of the application. To do that, inside your device or emulator, go to **Settings**, then **Applications**, and search for our Restaurants app and press on it. Then, press **Storage and Cache** and then **Clear Storage**.
    - Your device/emulator is disconnected from the internet.

11. Run the application. You should see this message in the center of the screen: `"Something went wrong. We have no data."`.

> **Note**
>
> For the sake of simplicity, we made sure that the UI logic is separated from the presentation logic only within the first screen of our app. When you're looking to move logic to corresponding classes, thereby ensuring SoC, you need to make sure to do so for all other screens within the app, together with their `ViewModel` classes, and so on.

Now that we've separated UI logic from presentation logic, it's time to separate some data logic.

Separating presentation logic from data logic

While the `RestaurantsViewModel` class contains data logic because it interacts with the Retrofit service and the Room DAO to obtain and cache restaurants, it should only hold presentation logic because its core responsibility is to govern the UI state.

Another sign that our `RestaurantsViewModel` has piled up a lot of logic is that it currently stands at around 90 lines of code—this might not seem much yet, remember that our application is pretty simple and we have little presentation logic, so 90 lines will definitely turn into thousands for production-ready applications.

We want to move the data logic out of the `RestaurantsViewModel` into a different class. Since data logic is part of the Model layer of our application, in this section, we will start exploring how to define the Model layer with the help of Repository classes.

The **Repository** pattern represents a strategy for abstracting data access inside your application. In other words, Repository classes hide away from the caller all the complexity associated with parsing data from the server, storing it in local databases, or performing any caching/refreshing mechanisms.

In our app, the `RestaurantsViewModel` class must decide whether to get data from the `restInterface` (remote) source or from the `restaurantsDao` (local) source, while also making sure to refresh the cache. The following snippet shows the code that is executed:

```
class RestaurantsViewModel() : ViewModel() {
    private var restInterface: RestaurantsApiService
    private var restaurantsDao = [...]
        ...
    private suspend fun refreshCache() {...}
}
```

This is obviously wrong. The `ViewModel` shouldn't care which particular data source to call as it shouldn't need to be the one that initiates caching to local sources. The `ViewModel` should only care about receiving some content that it will prepare for presentation.

Let's lift this burden from the `RestaurantsViewModel` class by creating a Repository class that will abstract all the data logic, as it will be interacting with the two data sources (web API and Room DAO) to do the following:

- Provide a `List<Restaurant>` object to the Presentation layer
- Handle any caching logic such as retrieving restaurants from the web API and caching them to the Room local database
- Define a **single source of truth** (**SSOT**) for data—the Room database

To do that, we must only move the data logic out of the `ViewModel` and separate it in a Repository class. Let's begin, as follows:

1. Create a Repository class by clicking on the application package, selecting **New**, and then **Kotlin Class/File**. Enter `RestaurantsRepository` as the name and select **Class** as the type:

   ```
   class RestaurantsRepository { }
   ```

   Now, let's start moving some code!

2. From inside the `RestaurantsViewModel` class, cut the `restInterface` variable and its initialization logic from the `init` block and paste it inside `RestaurantsRepository`, as follows:

```
class RestaurantsRepository {
    private var restInterface: RestaurantsApiService =
        Retrofit.Builder()
            .addConverterFactory(...)
            .baseUrl(...)
            .build()
            .create(RestaurantsApiService::class.java)
}
```

3. Do the same for the `restaurantsDao` variable, as follows:

```
class RestaurantsRepository {
    private var restInterface: RestaurantsApiService = ...
    private var restaurantsDao = RestaurantsDb
        .getDaoInstance(
            RestaurantsApplication.getAppContext())
}
```

4. Inside the `RestaurantsViewModel` class, add a `repository` variable and instantiate it with the `RestaurantsRepository()` constructor, like this:

```
class RestaurantsViewModel() : ViewModel() {
    private val repository = RestaurantsRepository()
    val state = mutableStateOf(...)
    private val errorHandler = CoroutineExceptionHandler
{ ... }
    init {
        getRestaurants()
    }
     [...]
}
```

Make sure that the `RestaurantsViewModel` no longer contains the `restInterface` variable, the `restaurantsDao` variable, or their initialization code from within the `init` block.

5. Move the `toggleFavoriteRestaurant()`, `getAllRestaurants()`, and `refreshCache()` methods of the `RestaurantsViewModel` class to the `RestaurantsRepository` class, as follows:

```
class RestaurantsRepository {
    private var restInterface: RestaurantsApiService = …
    private var restaurantsDao = […]

    private suspend fun toggleFavoriteRestaurant(…) = […]
    private suspend fun getAllRestaurants(): […] { … }
    private suspend fun refreshCache() { … }
}
```

6. Make sure that apart from the `init { }` block, the `RestaurantsViewModel` class only contains the `toggleFavorite()` and `getRestaurants()` methods, as follows:

```
class RestaurantsViewModel() : ViewModel() {
    […]
    init { getRestaurants() }
    fun toggleFavorite(id: Int, oldValue: Boolean) {…}
    private fun getRestaurants() {…}
}
```

7. Inside the `RestaurantsRepository` class, remove the `private` modifier for the `getAllRestaurants()` and `toggleFavoriteRestaurant()` methods as `RestaurantsViewModel` will need to call them, so they must be public. The code is illustrated in the following snippet:

```
class RestaurantsRepository {
    […]
    suspend fun toggleFavoriteRestaurant(…) = […]
    suspend fun getAllRestaurants(): […] { … }
    private suspend fun refreshCache() { … }
}
```

8. Going back inside the `RestaurantsViewModel` class, update the `getRestaurants()` method to now call `repository.getAllRestaurants()`, as follows:

```
private fun getRestaurants() {
    viewModelScope.launch(errorHandler) {
        val restaurants = repository.getAllRestaurants()
        state.value = state.value.copy(...)
    }
}
```

9. Still inside the `RestaurantsViewModel` class, update the `toggleFavorite()` method to now call `repository.toggleFavoriteRestaurant()`, as follows:

```
fun toggleFavorite(id: Int, oldValue: Boolean) {
    viewModelScope.launch(errorHandler) {
        val updatedRestaurants = repository
            .toggleFavoriteRestaurant(id, oldValue)
        state.value = state.value.copy(...)
    }
}
```

And we're done! While the functionality of the first screen should stay the same, we have now divided the responsibilities within this first flow not only within the Presentation layer but also between the Presentation layer and the Model layer.

> **Assignment**
> You can try to practice what we've learned in this section on the details screen of the Restaurants application.

Next up, let's return for a while to the Presentation layer and inspect how the UI state is exposed from within our `ViewModel`.

Improving state encapsulation in ViewModel

Let's have a look at how the UI state is defined in the RestaurantsViewModel class, as follows:

```
class RestaurantsViewModel() : ViewModel() {
    ...
    val state = mutableStateOf(RestaurantsScreenState(
        restaurants = listOf(),
        isLoading = true))
    ...
}
```

Inside the RestaurantsViewModel, we are holding the state within the state variable with the MutableState<RestaurantsScreenState> inferred type. This variable is public, so inside the UI layer, from within the RestaurantsScreen() composable, we can consume it by accessing the viewModel variable and directly obtaining the state object, as follows:

```
@Composable
fun RestaurantsScreen(onItemClick: (id: Int) -> Unit) {
    val viewModel: RestaurantsViewModel = viewModel()
    val state = viewModel.state.value
    Box(...) {...}
}
```

The problem with this approach might not be obvious, but since the state variable is of type MutableState, not only can we read its value but we can also write its value. In other words, from within the composable UI layer, we have write access to the state variable through the .value accessor.

The danger here is that then we (or other colleagues within our development team) could mistakenly update the UI state from within the UI layer, like so:

```
@Composable
fun RestaurantsScreen(onItemClick: (id: Int) -> Unit) {
    val viewModel: RestaurantsViewModel = viewModel()
    val state = viewModel.state.value
    Box(...) {...}
```

```
    viewModel.state.value = viewModel.state.value.copy(
        isLoading = false)
}
```

You can try to add the previously highlighted line of code but remove it afterwards!

This represents a violation of responsibilities within the Presentation layer: the UI layer shouldn't perform presentation logic. In other words, the UI layer shouldn't be able to mutate its own state that is stored inside the `ViewModel`; instead, only the `ViewModel` should have the right to do so.

This way, the `ViewModel` is the only entity responsible for presentation logic such as defining or mutating the UI state. At the same time, the responsibilities within our presentation patterns would be properly divided and respected.

To fix this, we must somehow force the `RestaurantsViewModel` class to expose a public `state` variable of type `State` instead of `MutableState`. This will prevent the UI layer from accidentally mutating its own state.

We can do this by having the Kotlin **backing property** feature implemented for our `state` variable. This feature states that if a class has two properties that are conceptually the same, yet one of them is part of the public API and the other one is an implementation detail, we can use an underscore to prefix the private property.

Let's see what this means by applying it directly in code, as follows:

1. First, within the `RestaurantsViewModel` class, let's prevent our `state` variable from being accessed because it's of type `MutableState`, as follows:

```
class RestaurantsViewModel() : ViewModel() {
    ...
    private val state = mutableStateOf(...)
    ...
}
```

2. Then, still in the `RestaurantsViewModel` class, rename the `state` variable `_state`. You can do that by selecting the `state` variable, and then pressing *Shift* + *F6*. Make sure that all previous usages of `state` are now called `_state`. The code is illustrated in the following snippet:

```
class RestaurantsViewModel() : ViewModel() {
    ...
    private val _state = mutableStateOf(...)
```

```
    private val errorHandler =
        CoroutineExceptionHandler {
            …
            exception.printStackTrace()
            _state.value = _state.value.copy(…)
        }
    […]
    fun toggleFavorite(id: Int, oldValue: Boolean) {
        viewModelScope.launch(errorHandler) {
            val updatedRestaurants = …
            _state.value = _state.value.copy(…)
        }
    }

    private fun getRestaurants() {
        viewModelScope.launch(errorHandler) {
            val restaurants =
                repository.getAllRestaurants()
            _state.value = _state.value.copy(…)
        }
    }
}
```

The `_state` variable is now the private state of type `MutableState`, so it's the variable that we referred to as the implementation detail. This means that the `ViewModel` can mutate it, but it shouldn't be exposed to the outer world. Yet what should we expose to the UI layer?

3. Still inside the `RestaurantsViewModel`, create another `state` variable called `state` of type `State<RestaurantsScreenState>` and define its custom getter through the `get()` syntax, as follows:

```
class RestaurantsViewModel() : ViewModel() {
    …
    private val _state = mutableStateOf(...)
    val state: State<RestaurantsScreenState>
        get() = _state
    …
}
```

The `state` variable is now the public state of type `State` (so, it's part of the public API), and this means that when the UI layer will try to get its value, the `get()` syntax will be called and the content within the `_state` variable will be returned.

Behind the scenes, the `_state` variable's type `MutableState` is downcasted to type `State` of the `state` variable. This means that composables won't be able to ever mutate the state within the `ViewModel`.

Conceptually, both the `state` variable and the `_state` variable are the same, yet `state` is used as part of a public contract with the outside world (so that it can be consumed by the UI layer), and `_state` is used as an internal implementation detail (a `MutableState` object that can be updated by the `ViewModel`).

4. Finally, inside the `RestaurantsScreen()` composable, make sure that the `state` variable is consumed, like this:

```
@Composable
fun RestaurantsScreen(onItemClick: (id: Int) -> Unit) {
    val viewModel: RestaurantsViewModel = viewModel()
    val state = viewModel.state.value
    Box(…) {…}
}
```

If you now try to mutate the `state` variable's value, as we did at the beginning of this section, then the **Integrated Development Environment** (**IDE**) will show you a compilation error telling you that you need to reassign a `val` variable, as illustrated in the following code snippet:

```
@Composable
fun RestaurantsScreen(onItemClick: (id: Int) -> Unit) {
    val viewModel: RestaurantsViewModel = viewModel()
    val state = viewModel.state.value
    Box(…) {…}
    viewModel.state.value = viewModel.state.value.copy(
        isLoading = false)
}
```

This effectively means that our UI can't mutate its own state by accident anymore.

> **Assignment**
>
> You can try to practice what we've learned in this section on the details screen of the Restaurants application.

Summary

In this chapter, we had a first look at the SoC principle. We understood why we must split an application's responsibilities across several layers and explored how we can do that with the help of presentation design patterns.

In the first part of this chapter, we had a quick look over the implementations for the most common presentation patterns in Android: MVC, MVP, and MVVM.

After that, we established that MVVM might be an appropriate choice for our Compose-based Restaurants application. We understood in which layer each type of logic must reside, and then tried to achieve SoC as well as possible in our application.

In the last part of this chapter, we noticed how easy it is for our UI layer to extend its responsibilities and start performing presentation logic by mutating the UI state within the `ViewModel`. To counter that, we learned how to better encapsulate the UI state by using backed properties.

Let's continue our journey of improving our application's architecture in the next chapter where we will try to adopt some design decisions from the well-known Clean Architecture software design philosophy.

8
Getting Started with Clean Architecture in Android

In this chapter, we're continuing our journey of improving the architectural design of the Restaurants application.

More specifically, we will try to adopt some design decisions from the well-known Clean Architecture. **Clean Architecture** is a software design philosophy that tries to create projects with the best level of the following:

- Separation of concerns
- Testability
- Independence of frameworks or libraries used in peripheral layers, such as the UI or Model layer

By doing so, Clean Architecture tries to allow the business parts of our applications to adapt to changing technologies and interfaces.

Clean Architecture is a very broad and complex topic, so, in this chapter, we will try to focus only on establishing a better separation of concerns by separating existing layers even further, but more importantly, by defining a new layer called the **Domain layer**.

In this chapter, we will on one hand borrow some architectural decisions from Clean Architecture through the *Defining the Domain layer with Use Cases* section and the *Separating the Domain model from Data models* section. On the other hand, we will try to improve project architecture with other techniques through the *Creating a package structure* section and the *Decoupling the Compose-based UI layer from ViewModel* section.

Another essential principle of Clean Architecture is the **Dependency Rule** that we will briefly cover in the *Further reading* section where you will find proper resources to follow up with.

We will cover the following topics in this section:

- Defining the Domain layer with Use Cases
- Separating the Domain model from Data models
- Creating a package structure
- Decoupling the Compose-based UI layer from ViewModel

Before jumping in, let's set up the technical requirements for this chapter.

Technical requirements

Building Compose-based Android projects for this chapter usually requires your day-to-day tools. However, to follow along smoothly, make sure you have the following:

- The Arctic Fox 2020.3.1 version of Android Studio. You can also use a newer Android Studio version or even Canary builds, but note that the IDE interface and other generated code files might differ from the ones used throughout this book.
- Kotlin 1.6.10 or a newer plugin installed in Android Studio
- The Restaurants app code from the previous chapter

The starting point for this chapter is represented by the Restaurants application developed in the previous chapter. If you haven't followed the implementation from the previous chapter, access the starting point for this chapter by navigating to the `Chapter_07` directory of the repository and importing the Android project titled `chapter_7_restaurants_app`.

To access the solution code for this chapter, navigate to the `Chapter_08` directory:

`https://github.com/PacktPublishing/Kickstart-Modern-Android-Development-with-Jetpack-and-Kotlin/tree/main/Chapter_08/chapter_8_restaurants_app`.

Defining the Domain layer with Use Cases

So far, we've talked about the Presentation layer (with UI and presentation logic) and the Model layer (with data logic). Yet, apart from these two layers, most of the time, applications also encapsulate a different type of logic, different from UI, presentation, or data logic.

To identify this type of logic, we must first acknowledge that most applications have a dedicated business scope – for example, a food delivery application could have the business scope of taking orders and generating revenue for the stakeholder. The **stakeholder** is the entity interested in the business, such as the company that owns the restaurant chain.

Such applications can contain business rules imposed by the stakeholders that can vary from minimum order amounts, custom availability ranges for certain restaurants, or predefined time frames for different delivery charges; the list could go on. We can refer to such business rules that are dictated by stakeholders as **business logic**.

For our Restaurants app, let's imagine that the stakeholder (for example, the company we would be building the application for) asked us to always show the restaurants alphabetically, no matter what. This shouldn't be something that the user would know about; instead, it should be a predefined business rule that we must implement.

Now, sorting restaurants alphabetically isn't that big of a deal, so the natural question that arises is, where should we apply this sorting logic?

To figure this out, let's recap the current layering of the project. Right now, the Presentation layer is connected to the Model layer.

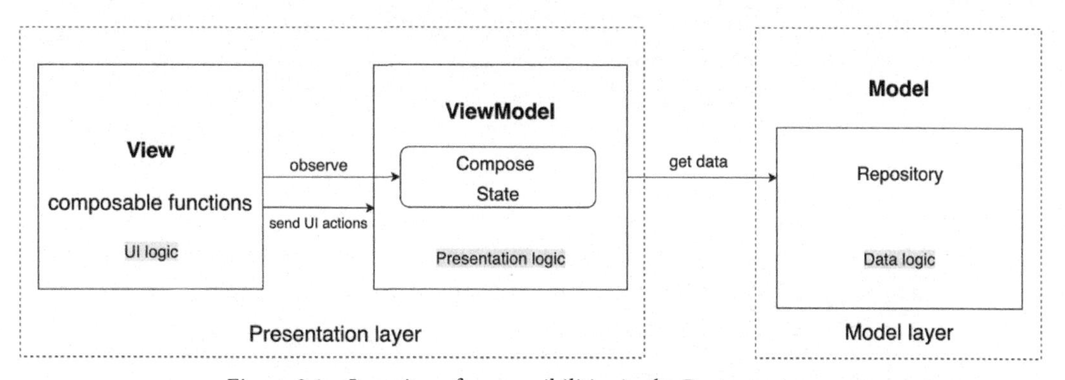

Figure 8.1 – Layering of responsibilities in the Restaurants app

With our existing layer structuring, we could sort the restaurants in the following:

- **UI level (composables)**: Since this sorting logic is business logic, we should try to avoid adding it here.
- **Inside the ViewModel**: If this sorting was a presentation option (so the user could sort restaurants in different ways from the UI by selecting a picker or button), we would have considered this to be presentation logic that can be held inside a `ViewModel` class; yet, remember that this rule is part of the business requirements, and the user shouldn't know about it, so it's probably not a good idea to implement it here.
- **Inside the Repository**: Here, we store data logic (such as caching), which is different from business logic.

None of the options are ideal, and we will see in a moment why this is the case. Until then, let's have a compromise and add this business rule inside the Model layer:

1. Inside `RestaurantsRepository`, refactor the `getAllRestaurants()` method to sort the restaurants by `title` by calling the `sortedBy { }` extension function on the restaurants that are returned:

```
suspend fun getAllRestaurants(): List<Restaurant> {
    return withContext(Dispatchers.IO) {
        try {
            refreshCache()
        } catch (e: Exception) {…}
        return@withContext restaurantsDao.getAll()
            .sortedBy { it.title }
    }
}
```

2. Build and run the application.

   The restaurants are now correctly sorted by their title, yet if you toggle a restaurant as a favorite, you might notice an initial flicker and a re-ordering effect on the list. Can you guess why this has happened?

   The issue here is that in `RestaurantsRepository`, the `toggleFavoriteRestaurant()` method returns the unsorted version of the restaurants from the **Data Access Object** (**DAO**):

```
suspend fun toggleFavoriteRestaurant(…) = withContext(…) {
    ...
```

```
        restaurantsDao.getAll()
    }
```

To fix this, we could repeat the same sorting logic from the `getAllRestaurants()` method.

Yet, this approach is problematic because we would be repeating or duplicating the sorting business rule. Worse than that, since we are in the Model layer, we're mixing data logic with business logic. We shouldn't be mixing data caching logic with business rules.

It's clear that for us to correctly encapsulate business logic and to be able to reuse it, we should extract it to a separate layer. Just like whenever we wanted to prevent any changes impacting the Presentation layer from affecting other layers, such as the UI or Model layers, we want to separate the business logic inside a separate layer so that any changes to the business logic shouldn't impact other layers and their corresponding logic.

According to Clean Architecture concepts, the layer that encapsulates business rules and business logic is referred to as the Domain layer. This layer sits between the Presentation layer and the Model layer. It should process the data from the Model layer by applying the business rules that it incorporates, and then feed the Presentation layer with the business-compliant content.

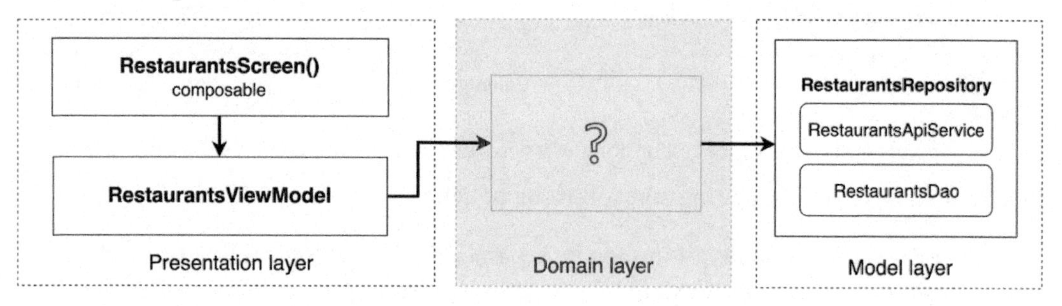

Figure 8.2 – Layering of responsibilities in the Restaurants app, including the Domain layer

In other words, in a particular flow (as in the screen with the list of restaurants), the Presentation layer through the `ViewModel` would connect to the Domain layer instead of the Model layer. In turn, the Domain layer would get the data from the Model layer.

> **Note**
> Not all applications, screens, or flows contain business logic. For these cases, the Domain layer is optional. The Domain layer should hold business logic, but, if there is no such logic, there should be no such layer.

But what should the Domain layer contain?

According to Clean Architecture concepts, repeatable business logic that is related to a specific application action or flow should be encapsulated in a Use Case. In other words, **Use Cases** are classes that extract repeatable business rules related to a single functionality of your application as a single unit of business logic.

For example, an online ordering app can have business logic related to displaying only stores in the near proximity of the user. To encapsulate this business rule, we could create a `GetStoresInProximityUseCase` class. Or, maybe there is some business logic associated with the logout action triggered by the user (such as executing some user benefits or points calculation behind the scenes); then, we could implement `LogOutUserUseCase`.

So, in our Restaurants app, any business logic must be encapsulated in a Use Case that sits between the Presentation layer and the Model layer:

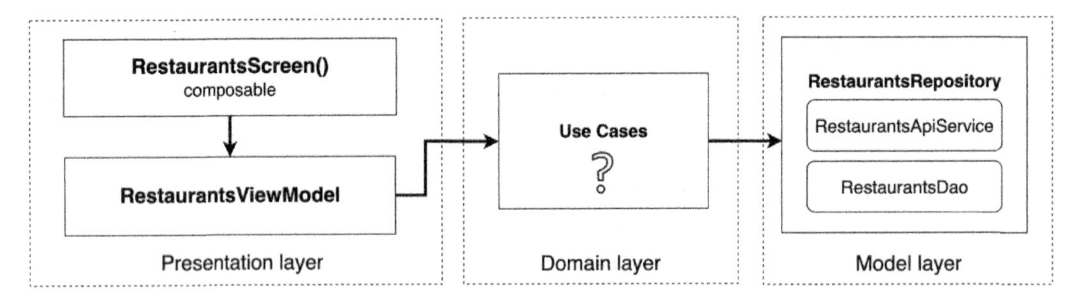

Figure 8.3 – Layering of responsibilities where the Domain layer contains Use Cases

A separated Domain layer brings the following benefits:

- Improves the testability of the app by separating business logic into its own classes. This way, business responsibilities are separated from other components and their logic can be tested separately without having to care about components from other layers.
- By separating business logic inside Use Cases, we avoid code duplication, and we improve the re-usability of business rules and their corresponding logic.
- Improves the readability of the classes that contain Use Cases dependencies. This is because each unit of business is now extracted separately and provides developers with valuable insights into the business actions each screen or flow executes.

Before jumping into a practical example, let's briefly cover a few important aspects of Use Cases:

- They can use (or depend on) other Use Cases. Since Use Cases define a single unit of reusable business logic, then Use Cases can use other Use Cases to define complex business logic.
- They usually obtain their data from the Model layer but are not conditioned to only one `Repository` class – in other words, you can access multiple repositories from within your Use Case.
- They usually have only one public method, mostly because Use Cases encapsulate business rules related to a single functionality of your app (like `LogOutUserUseCase` does).
- They should follow a naming convention. A popular convention for the Use Case class is a verb in the present tense that defines the action, usually followed by a few words that express the *what*, and that ends with the UseCase suffix. Some examples could be `GetStoresInProximityUseCase` or `CalculateOrderTotalUseCase`.

It's time to see what a Use Case class looks like. In our Restaurants app, the business logic of sorting restaurants alphabetically is a good match for it being extracted to a Use Case because of the following:

- It's a business rule dictated by the stakeholder.
- It's repeated twice.
- It's part of a specific action of the app (getting the restaurants).

Let's define our first Use Case class!

1. Click on the application package, select **New**, and then **Kotlin Class/File**. Enter `GetRestaurantsUseCase` as the name, select **Class**, and add this code:

```
class GetRestaurantsUseCase {
    private val repository: RestaurantsRepository =
        RestaurantsRepository()
    suspend operator fun invoke(): List<Restaurant> {
        return repository.getAllRestaurants()
                        .sortedBy { it.title }
    }
}
```

Functionally, this Use Case class gets the restaurants from `RestaurantsRepository`, applies the business rule of sorting the restaurants alphabetically, just like `RestarauntsViewModel` did, and then returns the list. In other words, `GetRestaurantsUseCase` is now the one responsible for applying business rules.

This Use Case does that with only one public method, which is also a `suspend` function because the `repository.getAllRestaurants()` call is a suspending function call. But, more importantly, why did we name the function of the Use Case as `invoke()` while also specifying the `operator` keyword?

We did that because Kotlin allows us to define an `invoke` operator on a class so we can call it on any instances of the class without a method name. This is how we will call the `invoke()` operator of `GetRestaurantsUseCase`:

```
val useCase = GetRestaurantsUseCase()
val result = useCase()
```

This syntax is especially useful for us because our Use Case classes have only one method, and the name of the class is already suggestive enough, so we don't need a named function.

2. Make sure to remove the sorting logic that we initially added in the `getAllRestaurants()` method in `RestaurantsRepository`. The returned data of the method should look like this:

```
suspend fun getAllRestaurants(): List<Restaurant> {
    return withContext(Dispatchers.IO) {
        try { … } catch (e: Exception) {…}
        return@withContext restaurantsDao.getAll()
    }
}
```

3. Inside `RestaurantsViewModel`, add a new dependency to the `GetRestaurantsUseCase` class:

```
class RestaurantsViewModel() : ViewModel() {
  private val repository = RestaurantsRepository()
  private val getRestaurantsUseCase =
GetRestaurantsUseCase()
  [...]
}
```

4. Then, inside the `getRestaurants()` method of the `ViewModel`, remove the call for restaurants to the `repository` variable, and instead, call the `invoke()` operator for the `getRestaurantsUseCase` variable:

```
private fun getRestaurants() {
    viewModelScope.launch(errorHandler) {
        val restaurants = getRestaurantsUseCase()
        _state.value = _state.value.copy(
            restaurants = restaurants, [...])
    }
}
```

Before building and running the app, let's try to identify any other business rules for this particular flow of the app.

If we have a look inside `RestaurantsRepository`, the `toggleFavoriteRestaurant()` method takes in an `oldValue: Boolean` parameter, and negates it before passing it to `PartialRestaurant`:

```
suspend fun toggleFavoriteRestaurant(
    id: Int,
    oldValue: Boolean
) =
    withContext(Dispatchers.IO) {
        restaurantsDao.update(
            PartialRestaurant(
                id = id,
                isFavorite = !oldValue
            )
        )
        restaurantsDao.getAll()
    }
```

This happens every time we mark a restaurant as a favorite or not favorite. The rule of negating `oldValue` of the favorite status of the restaurant (by passing `!oldValue`) can be considered a business rule imposed by the stakeholder: *whenever a user presses on the heart icon of a restaurant, we must toggle its favorite status to the opposite value.*

To be able to reuse this business logic and not have it done by `RestaurantsRepository`, let's also extract this rule to a Use Case.

5. First, inside `RestaurantsRepository`, rename the `oldValue` parameter to `value` and make sure to not negate it anymore when passing it to the `isFavorite` field of `PartialRestaurant`:

```
suspend fun toggleFavoriteRestaurant(id: Int, value:
Boolean) =
    withContext(Dispatchers.IO) {
        restaurantsDao.update(
            PartialRestaurant(id = id, isFavorite = value)
        )
        restaurantsDao.getAll()
    }
```

6. Click on the application package, select **New**, and then **Kotlin Class/File**. Enter `ToggleRestaurantUseCase` as the name, select **Class**, and add this code:

```
class ToggleRestaurantUseCase {
    private val repository: RestaurantsRepository =
        RestaurantsRepository()
    suspend operator fun invoke(
        id: Int,
        oldValue: Boolean
    ): List<Restaurant> {
        val newFav = oldValue.not()
        return repository
            .toggleFavoriteRestaurant(id, newFav)
    }
}
```

This Use Case now encapsulates the business rule of negating the favorite flag of a restaurant with the `val newFav = oldValue.not()` line. While the business logic here is rather slim, in production apps, things tend to get more complex. This Use Case should be called whenever we mark a restaurant as a favorite or not favorite.

7. Inside `RestaurantsViewModel`, add a new dependency to the `ToggleRestaurantUseCase` class:

```
class RestaurantsViewModel() : ViewModel() {
    private val getRestaurantsUseCase =
GetRestaurantsUseCase()
```

```
    private val toggleRestaurantsUseCase =
ToggleRestaurantUseCase()
    [...]
}
```

At this step, you can also safely remove the `RestaurantsViewModel` class's dependency to the `RestaurantsRepository` class by removing the `repository` variable.

8. Then, inside the `toggleFavorite()` method of the `ViewModel`, remove the call for toggling the restaurant on the `repository` variable, and instead, call the `invoke()` operator for the `toggleRestaurantUseCase` variable:

```
fun toggleFavorite(id: Int, oldValue: Boolean) {
    viewModelScope.launch(errorHandler) {
        val updatedRestaurants =
            toggleRestaurantsUseCase(id, oldValue)
        _state.value = _state.value.copy(...)
    }
}
```

Now, the business rule of toggling a restaurant as a favorite or not is done inside `ToggleRestaurantUseCase`.

9. Now that we have extracted business logic into Use Case classes, build the app and run it. The application should behave the same.

Yet, if you try toggling a restaurant as a favorite, the list of restaurants still flickers, and their order seems to change. Can you think of why this happens?

Let's circle back to `RestaurantsRepository` and check out the `toggleFavoriteRestaurant` method:

```
suspend fun toggleFavoriteRestaurant(...)= withContext(...) {
    restaurantsDao.update(
        PartialRestaurant(id = id, isFavorite = value)
    )
    restaurantsDao.getAll()
}
```

The problem with this method is that it returns the restaurants obtained from the Room DAO by calling `restaurantsDao.getAll()`. These restaurants are not sorted alphabetically, as our business rules now indicate. So, every time we toggle a restaurant as favorite, we update the UI with the unsorted list of restaurants.

We need to somehow reuse the sorting logic from `GetRestaurantsUseCase`:

1. First, from within `RestaurantsRepository`, remove the `restaurantsDao.getAll()` call from the `toggleFavoriteRestaurant` method:

```
suspend fun toggleFavoriteRestaurant(…)= withContext(…) {
    restaurantsDao.update(
        PartialRestaurant(id = id, isFavorite = value)
    )
}
```

   This way, this method no longer returns a list of restaurants; it just updates a specific restaurant. As of now, the `toggleFavoriteRestaurant` method doesn't return anything anymore.

2. Then, inside the `ToggleRestaurantUseCase` class, remove the return statement for the `repository.toggleFavoriteRestaurant()` line, and instead return the sorted list of restaurants by directly instantiating and calling the `invoke()` operator on the `GetRestaurantsUseCase` class:

```
class ToggleRestaurantUseCase {
    private val repository: … = RestaurantsRepository()
    suspend operator fun invoke(…): List<Restaurant> {
        val newFav = oldValue.not()
        repository.toggleFavoriteRestaurant(id, newFav)
        return GetRestaurantsUseCase().invoke()
    }
}
```

This approach fixes our issue – whenever we toggle a restaurant as a favorite or not, the UI no longer flickers because the UI is updated with the correctly sorted list – yet this happens with a lengthy delay.

Unfortunately, this functionality is not efficient at all because whenever we toggle a restaurant as a favorite or not, the `GetRestaurantsUseCase` calls the `RestaurantsRepository` class's `getAllRestaurants()` method that, in turn, triggers a request to get the restaurants again from the Web API, attempts to cache them into `Room`, and only then provides us with a list, hence the delay we've just experienced.

In a good application architecture, a network request that gets the new list of items shouldn't be done after every UI interaction with an item. Let's fix this by refactoring our code and by creating a new Use Case that only retrieves the cached restaurants, sorts them, and returns them:

1. First, inside `RestaurantsRepository`, add a new method called `getRestaurants()` that only retrieves the restaurants from our Room DAO:

```
suspend fun getRestaurants() : List<Restaurant> {
    return withContext(Dispatchers.IO) {
        return@withContext restaurantsDao.getAll()
    }
}
```

2. Click on the application package, select **New**, and then **Kotlin Class/File**. Enter `GetSortedRestaurantsUseCase` as the name, select **Class**, and add this code:

```
class GetSortedRestaurantsUseCase {
    private val repository: RestaurantsRepository =
        RestaurantsRepository()
    suspend operator fun invoke(): List<Restaurant> {
        return repository.getRestaurants()
            .sortedBy { it.title }
    }
}
```

   The `GetSortedRestaurantsUseCase` class now retrieves the restaurants from the `RestaurantsRepository` by calling the previously created `getRestaurants()` method (without triggering any network request or caching), applies the sorting business rule, and finally, returns the list of restaurants.

3. Use the newly created `GetSortedRestaurantsUseCase` class inside `ToggleRestaurantUseCase` so that we only get the cached restaurants every time we toggle a restaurant as a favorite or not:

```
class ToggleRestaurantUseCase {
    private val repository: ... = RestaurantsRepository()
    private val getSortedRestaurantsUseCase =
        GetSortedRestaurantsUseCase()
    suspend operator fun invoke(...): List<Restaurant> {
        val newFav = oldValue.not()
```

```
        repository.toggleFavoriteRestaurant(id, newFav)
        return getSortedRestaurantsUseCase()
    }
}
```

Now, we must refactor `GetRestaurantsUseCase` to reuse the sorting business logic from within `GetSortedRestaurantsUseCase` because the alphabetical sorting logic is now duplicated in both Use Cases:

1. First, inside `RestaurantsRepository`, update the `getAllRestaurants` method to no longer return the restaurants by no longer returning `restaurantsDao.getAll()`, while also removing the function's return type:

```
suspend fun getAllRestaurants() {
    return withContext(Dispatchers.IO) {
        try { … } catch (e: Exception) { … }
    }
}
```

2. Rename the `getAllRestaurants` method to `loadRestaurants()` to better reflect its responsibility:

```
suspend fun loadRestaurants() {
    return withContext(Dispatchers.IO) {
        try { … } catch (e: Exception) { … }
    }
}
```

3. Inside `GetRestaurantsUseCase`, add a new dependency to the `GetSortedRestaurantUseCase` class and refactor the class as follows:

```
class GetRestaurantsUseCase {
    private val repository: … = RestaurantsRepository()
    private val getSortedRestaurantsUseCase =
        GetSortedRestaurantsUseCase()
    suspend operator fun invoke(): List<Restaurant> {
        repository.loadRestaurants()
        return getSortedRestaurantsUseCase()
    }
}
```

Inside the `invoke()` function, we made sure to first call the newly renamed `loadRestaurants()` method of the `RestaurantsRepository` and then, in addition, to invoke `GetSortedRestaurantsUseCase`, which is now also returned.

4. To better reflect its purpose, rename the `GetRestaurantsUseCase` class to `GetInitialRestaurantsUseCase`:

```
class GetInitialRestaurantsUseCase {
    private val repository: ... = RestaurantsRepository()
    private val getSortedRestaurantsUseCase =
        GetSortedRestaurantsUseCase()
    suspend operator fun invoke(): List<Restaurant> {...}
}
```

5. As a consequence, inside `RestaurantsViewModel`, update the type for the `getRestaurantsUseCase` variable:

```
class RestaurantsViewModel() : ViewModel() {
  private val repository = RestaurantsRepository()
  private val getRestaurantsUseCase =
      GetInitialRestaurantsUseCase()
  ...
}
```

6. Build the app and run it. The application should now behave correctly when marking a restaurant as a favorite or not; the restaurants remain sorted alphabetically.

Let's now move on to another way of improving the architecture of our app.

Separating the Domain model from Data models

Inside the Domain layer, apart from Use Cases, another essential business component in our app is the **Domain model component**. The Domain model components are those classes that represent core business data or concepts used throughout the application.

> **Note**
>
> Since the Domain models reside inside the Domain layer, they should be agnostic of any third-party library or dependency – ideally, they should be pure Java or Kotlin classes.

For example, in our Restaurants app, the core entity used throughout the app (retrieved, updated, and displayed) is the `Restaurant` data class, which contains data such as `title` and `description`.

If we think about it, our Restaurants app's core business entity is represented by the restaurant itself: that's what the application is about, so it's only natural that we would consider the `Restaurant` class as a business entity.

> **Note**
>
> In Clean Architecture, Domain model classes are often referred to as Entity classes. However, it's important to mention that the Room database `@Entity` annotation has nothing to do with Clean Architecture; any class annotated with the Room `@Entity` annotation doesn't automatically become an entity. In fact, as per Clean Architecture, Entity classes should have no library dependencies such as database annotations.

If we have a look at our `Restaurant` data class though, we can identify a serious issue:

```
import androidx.room.ColumnInfo
    …
import com.google.gson.annotations.SerializedName
@Entity(tableName = "restaurants")
data class Restaurant(
    @PrimaryKey()
    @ColumnInfo(name = "r_id")
    @SerializedName("r_id")
    val id: Int,
    @ColumnInfo(name = "r_title")
    @SerializedName("r_title")
    val title: String,
    …
)
```

Can you spot the problem?

While, in the beginning, the `Restaurant` data class was a pure Kotlin data class with some fields, in time, it grew to something more than that.

We first added Retrofit to our app so we could get the restaurants from a Web API, and had to mark the fields we obtained with `@SerializedName` annotations so that the GSON (Google Gson) deserialization would work. Then we added Room to the mix because we wanted to cache the restaurants, so we had to add an `@Entity` annotation to the class, and other annotations, such as `@PrimaryKey` and `@ColumnInfo`, to its fields.

While it was convenient for us to use only one Data model class throughout the app, we have now coupled a Domain model class (`Restaurant.kt`) to library dependencies, such as GSON or Room. This means that our Domain model is coupled to the Data or Model layer that is responsible for obtaining data.

According to Clean Architecture, the Domain model classes should reside inside the Domain layer and be agnostic of any libraries tightly related to the way we retrieve or cache data from several sources.

In other words, we need to make a separation between Domain models and **Data Transfer Objects** (**DTOs**) by creating separate classes for both types. While Domain models are plain Kotlin classes, DTOs are classes that contain both the fields needed for a specific data operation, such as caching items to a local source, but also dependencies such as library annotations.

With such a separation, the Domain model is now a business entity that doesn't care about implementation details (such as libraries), so every time we might have to replace a library (such as Retrofit or Room) with another library, we must only update the DTOs (hence, the Model layer) and not classes within the Domain model.

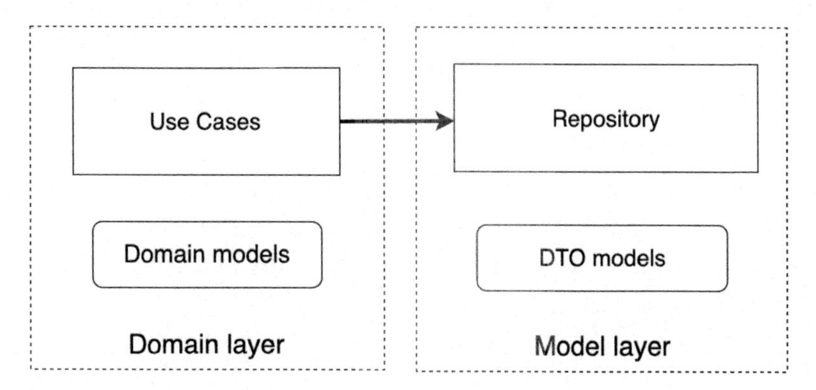

Figure 8.4 – Separating Domain models from DTO models

To achieve such a separation in our Restaurants app, we must split our `Restaurant` class into three classes. We must do the following:

- Create two DTOs as `data class` classes that will be used for transferring data:
    - A `RemoteRestaurant` class that will contain the fields received from the Web API. These fields will also be annotated with GSON serialization annotations required by Retrofit to parse the response.
    - A `LocalRestaurant` class that will contain the fields and their corresponding annotations required by Room to cache restaurants.
- Refactor the `Restaurant` data class to be a plain Kotlin data class, without any third-party dependencies. This way, the `Restaurant` data class will be a proper Domain model class, independent of the Model layer that is tightly coupled to third-party libraries.

Let's begin!

1. Click on the application package, select **New**, and then **Kotlin Class/File**. Enter `RemoteRestaurant` as the name, select **Class**, and add this code to define the DTO for our remote source (Firebase remote database):

```
data class RemoteRestaurant(
    @SerializedName("r_id")
    val id: Int,
    @SerializedName("r_title")
    val title: String,
    @SerializedName("r_description")
    val description: String)
```

   Inside this class, we have added all the fields received from the Web API, along with their corresponding serialization fields. You can get these annotations and their imports from the `Restaurant` class.

   Another advantage of having a separate DTO class is that it now contains only the necessary fields – for instance, unlike `Restaurant`, `RemoteRestaurant` no longer contains an `isFavorite` field because we don't receive it from the REST API of our Firebase Database.

2. Click on the application package and create a new file called `LocalRestaurant`. Add this code to define the DTO for our local source (Room local database):

```
@Entity(tableName = "restaurants")
data class LocalRestaurant(
    @PrimaryKey()
    @ColumnInfo(name = "r_id")
    val id: Int,
    @ColumnInfo(name = "r_title")
    val title: String,
    @ColumnInfo(name = "r_description")
    val description: String,
    @ColumnInfo(name = "is_favorite")
    val isFavorite: Boolean = false)
```

You can get the fields, annotations, and their imports from the `Restaurant` class.

3. Now, navigate to the `Restaurant` class. It's time to remove all its third-party dependencies to Room and GSON and keep it as a simple Domain model class containing the fields that define our restaurant entity. It should now look like this:

```
data class Restaurant(
    val id: Int,
    val title: String,
    val description: String,
    val isFavorite: Boolean = false)
```

Make sure to also remove any imports for the GSON and Room annotations.

4. Inside the `RestaurantsDb` class, update the entity used in Room to our newly created `LocalRestaurant`, while also updating the schema version to `3`, just to be sure that Room will provide a fresh start:

```
@Database(
    entities = [LocalRestaurant::class],
    version = 3,
    exportSchema = false)
abstract class RestaurantsDb : RoomDatabase() {
    abstract val dao: RestaurantsDao
    …
}
```

5. Rename the `PartialRestaurant` class to `PartialLocalRestaurant` to better clarify that this class is used by our local data source, Room:

```
@Entity
class PartialLocalRestaurant(
@ColumnInfo(name = "r_id")
val id: Int,
@ColumnInfo(name = "is_favorite")
val isFavorite: Boolean)
```

6. Inside the `RestaurantsDao` interface, replace the `Restaurant` class usages with `LocalRestaurant`, and the `PartialRestaurant` class usages with `PartialLocalRestaurant`:

```
@Dao
interface RestaurantsDao {
    @Query("SELECT * FROM restaurants")
    suspend fun getAll(): List<LocalRestaurant>

    @Insert(onConflict = OnConflictStrategy.REPLACE)
    suspend fun addAll(restaurants:
        List<LocalRestaurant>)

    @Update(entity = LocalRestaurant::class)
    suspend fun update(partialRestaurant:
       PartialLocalRestaurant)

    @Update(entity = LocalRestaurant::class)
    suspend fun updateAll(partialRestaurants:
        List<PartialLocalRestaurant>)

    @Query("SELECT * FROM restaurants WHERE
        is_favorite = 1")
    suspend fun getAllFavorited(): List<LocalRestaurant>
}
```

7. Inside `RestaurantsRepository`, navigate to the `toggleFavoriteRestaurant()` method, and replace the `PartialRestaurant` usage with `PartialLocalRestaurant`:

```
suspend fun toggleFavoriteRestaurant(
    ...
) = withContext(Dispatchers.IO) {
    restaurantsDao.update(
      PartialLocalRestaurant(id = id, isFavorite = value)
    )
}
```

8. Still inside `RestaurantsRepository`, navigate to the `getRestaurants()` method, and map the `LocalRestaurant` objects (received by the `restaurantsDao.getAll()` method call) to `Restaurant` objects:

```
suspend fun getRestaurants() : List<Restaurant> {
    return withContext(Dispatchers.IO) {
        return@withContext restaurantsDao.getAll().map {
            Restaurant(it.id, it.title,
                it.description, it.isFavorite)
        }
    }
}
```

We have mapped `List<LocalRestaurant>` to `List<Restaurant>` by using the `.map { }` extension function. We did that by constructing and returning a `Restaurant` object from `LocalRestaurant`, represented by the `it` implicit variable name.

> **Note**
>
> Your Model layer (represented by the `Repository` here), should only return Domain model objects to the Domain entity. In our case, `RestaurantsRepository` should return `Restaurant` objects, and not `LocalRestaurants` objects, simply because the Use Case classes (so, the Domain layer) that use this `Repository` shouldn't have any knowledge of DTO classes from the Model layer.

9. Navigate to the `RestaurantsApiService` interface (the Retrofit interface) and replace the usages of the `Restaurant` class with `RemoteRestaurant`:

```
interface RestaurantsApiService {
    @GET("restaurants.json")
     suspend fun getRestaurants(): List<RemoteRestaurant>

    @GET("restaurants.json?orderBy=\"r_id\"")
     suspend fun getRestaurant(…):
         Map<String, RemoteRestaurant>
}
```

10. Going back to `RestaurantsRepository`, navigate to the `refreshCache()` method and map the `remoteRestaurants` list from Retrofit to `LocalRestaurant` objects so that `restaurantsDao` can cache them:

```
private suspend fun refreshCache() {
    val remoteRestaurants = restInterface
        .getRestaurants()
    val favoriteRestaurants = restaurantsDao
        .getAllFavorited()
    restaurantsDao.addAll(remoteRestaurants.map {
        LocalRestaurant(
            it.id,
            it.title,
            it.description,
            false
        )
    })
    restaurantsDao.updateAll(
        favoriteRestaurants.map {
            PartialLocalRestaurant(
                id = it.id,
                isFavorite = true
            )
        })
}
```

Additionally, make sure to update the usage of `PartialRestaurant` to `PartialLocalRestaurant` in the `restaurantsDao.updateAll()` method call.

11. Navigate to `RestaurantsDetailsViewModel` and, inside the `getRemoteRestaurant()` method, map the `RemoteRestaurant` object received from the Retrofit API to a `Restaurant` object by using the `?.let{ }` extension function:

```
private suspend fun getRemoteRestaurant(id: Int):
Restaurant {
    return withContext(Dispatchers.IO) {
        val response =  restInterface.getRestaurant(id)
        return@withContext response.values.first().let {
            Restaurant(
                id = it.id,
                title = it.title,
                description = it.description
            )
        }
    }
}
```

Remember that in the restaurant details screen, we don't have any business logic or Use Cases, or even a `Repository`, so we have directly added a variable for the Retrofit interface inside the `ViewModel` – and that's why we are mapping the Domain model inside the `ViewModel`.

12. Build and run the app. The app should behave the same.

Let's now take a break from creating classes and let's organize our project a bit.

Creating a package structure

Our Restaurants app has come a long way. As we tried to separate responsibilities and concerns as much as possible, new classes emerged – quite a few actually.

If we have a look on the left of Android Studio, on the **Project** tab, we have an overview of the classes we've defined in our project.

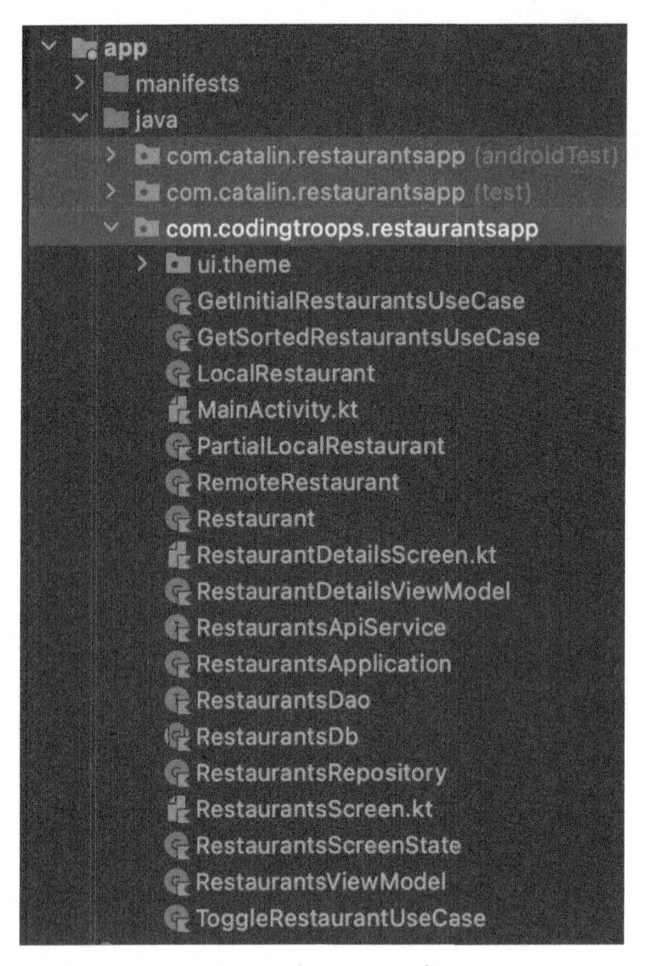

Figure 8.5 – Project structure without any package structuring strategy

It's clear that our project has no folder structure at all – all files and classes are tossed around inside the `restaurantsapp` root package.

> **Note**
>
> The name of the root package might differ if you selected a different name for your app.

Because we've opted to throw any new class inside the root package, it's difficult to have clear visibility over the project. Our approach is similar to adding dozens of files and assets on the desktop of our PC – in time, it becomes impossible to find anything on the screen.

To alleviate this issue, we can opt for a **packaging strategy** for our project in which each class belongs to a folder. A clear folder structure allows developers to have good visibility and to gain valuable insight into the application's components, there by allowing easier access and navigation through the project files.

The most common package organizing strategies are as follows:

- **Organize packages by category or layer**: For this strategy, each package contains classes that are of the same type or belong to the same layer. The following are examples:
    - A `presentation` package would contain all the files related to the Presentation layer, regardless of the feature they belong to, such as all the files with composables, and all the `ViewModel` classes.
    - Similarly, a `data` package would contain all files related to the Model layer, regardless of the feature they belong to, such as repositories, Retrofit interfaces, or Room DAO interfaces.
- **Organize packages by feature**: For this strategy, the root packages represent and reflect a specific feature of the app. For example, a `restaurants` package would contain all the classes related to the `restaurants` feature, from UI classes to `ViewModel` classes, Use Cases, and repositories.

Both approaches have their pros and cons, but most notably, the package organization by layer doesn't scale well if the app has a lot of features, as there is no way to differentiate between classes from different features.

On the other hand, the package organization by feature can be problematic if, in each feature package, all classes are thrown around without any distinct categorization.

For our Restaurants app, we will use a mix of these two strategies. More specifically, we will do the following:

- Keep `RestaurantsApplication.kt` inside the root package.
- Create a root package for the only feature our application has, named `restaurants`. This package will contain the functionality for displaying both the list of restaurants and the detail screen.
- Create sub-packages inside the `restaurants` package for each layer:
  - `Presentation`: For composables and `ViewModel` classes. Inside this package, we can also break the screens that we have into separate packages: `list` for the first screen with the list of restaurants, and `details` for the second screen with the details of one restaurant. Additionally, we will keep the `MainActivity` class inside the `presentation` package since it's the host component for the UI.
  - `Data`: For classes within the Model layer. Here, we will not only add `RestaurantsRepository,` but we'll also create two sub-packages for the two different data sources: `local` (for caching classes such as `RestaurantsDao` and `LocalRestaurant`), and `remote` (for classes related to the remote source such as `RestaurantsApiService` and `RemoteRestaurant`).
  - `Domain`: For business-related classes, the Use Case classes, and also the `Restaurant.kt` Domain model class.

With this approach, if we were to add a new feature, maybe related to ordering (which we could call `ordering`), the package structure would provide us with immediate information about the features our application contains. When expanding a certain feature package, we can expand the package of the layer we're interested in working with and have a clear overview of the components we need to update or modify.

To achieve such a packaging structure, you will have to perform the following actions a few times:

1. Create a new package. To do that, left-click on a certain existing package (such as the `restaurantsapp` package), select **New**, then **Package**, and finally, enter the name of the package.
2. Move an existing class into an existing package. To do that, simply drag the file and drop it into the desired package.

In the end, the package structure that we described and that we want to achieve is the following:

Figure 8.6 – Project structure after applying our package structuring strategy

Keep in mind, however, that when moving the `MainActivity.kt` file from its initial location to the `presentation` package, you might have to update the `Manifest.xml` file to reference the new correct path to the `MainActivity.kt` file:

```
<manifest [...]>
    [...]
    <application
        [...]
        <activity
            android:name=".restaurants.presentation.
                MainActivity"
            android:exported="true"
            android:label="@string/app_name"
            android:theme="@style/Theme.RestaurantsApp.
                NoActionBar">
            <intent-filter>
                [...]
            </intent-filter>
            <intent-filter>
                [...]
            </intent-filter>
        </activity>
    </application>
</manifest>
```

Some versions of Android Studio do that out of the box for you; however, if they don't, you might end up with a nasty compilation error because the `Manifest.xml` file is no longer detecting our `Activity`.

Now that we have refactored the structure of our project, we can say that the packages structure provides us with immediate information about the features of the app (in our case, there is only one feature related to restaurants) and also with a clear overview of the components corresponding to a specific feature.

> **Note**
>
> The autogenerated files for Compose projects (`Color.kt`, `Shape.kt`, `Theme.kt`, and `Type.kt`) were left inside the `theme` package that resides inside the `ui` package. This is because theming should be consistent across features.

Let's now move on to another way of improving the decoupling inside the UI layer between the composables and the `ViewModel`.

Decoupling the Compose-based UI layer from ViewModel

Our UI layer (represented by the composable functions) is tightly coupled to the `ViewModel`. This is natural, since the screen composables instantiate their own `ViewModel` to do the following:

- Obtain the UI state and consume it
- Pass events (such as clicking on a UI item) up to the `ViewModel`

As an example, we can see how the `RestaurantsScreen()` composable uses an instance of `RestaurantsViewModel`:

```
@Composable
fun RestaurantsScreen(onItemClick: (id: Int) -> Unit) {
    val viewModel: RestaurantsViewModel = viewModel()
    val state = viewModel.state.value
    Box(…) { … }
}
```

The problem with our approach is that if we want to later test the UI layer, then, inside the test, the `RestaurantsScreen` composable will instantiate `RestaurantsViewModel`, which in turn will get data from Use Case classes, which in turn will trigger heavy I/O work in `RestaurantsRepository` (like the network request to obtain the restaurants, or the operation of saving them inside the local database).

When we have to test the UI, we should not care whether the `ViewModel` obtains the data correctly and translates it into a proper UI state. The effect of separating concerns is to facilitate testing a target class (or composable in this discussion) without having to care about other layers doing their work.

Right now, our screen composables are tied to a library dependency, the `ViewModel`, and it's ideal to decouple such dependencies as much as possible to promote reusability and testability.

In order to decouple the `RestaurantsScreen()` composable as much as possible from its `ViewModel`, we will refactor it so that the following happens:

- It will no longer reference a `ViewModel` class (the `RestaurantsViewModel` class).
- Instead, it will receive a `RestaurantsScreenState` object as a parameter.
- It will also define new function parameters to expose callbacks to its caller – we will see who the caller is in a minute.

> **Note**
>
> By extracting the `ViewModel` instantiation from screen composables, such as `RestaurantsScreen()`, we're promoting reusability in the sense that we can much easier replace the ViewModel type that creates the state for this composable. This approach also enables us to port the Compose-based UI layer much easier to **Kotlin Multiplatform** (**KMP**) projects.

Let's begin!

1. Inside the `RestaurantsScreen` file, update the `RestaurantsScreen()` composable by removing its `viewModel` and `state` variables, while also making sure it receives a `RestaurantsScreenState` object as a `state` parameter and an `onFavoriteClick` function:

```
@Composable
fun RestaurantsScreen(
    state: RestaurantsScreenState,
    onItemClick: (id: Int) -> Unit,
    onFavoriteClick: (id: Int, oldValue: Boolean) -> Unit
) {
    Box(…) {
        LazyColumn(…) {
            items(state.restaurants) { restaurant ->
                RestaurantItem(
                    restaurant,
                    onFavoriteClick = { id, oldValue ->
                        onFavoriteClick(id, oldValue)
                    },
                    onItemClick = { id ->
                        onItemClick(id)
```

```
                        }
                    )
                }
            }
            [...]
        }
    }
```

Additionally, make sure to remove the `viewModel.toggleFavorite()` call and instead, call the newly added `onFavoriteClick()` function inside the `RestaurantItem` corresponding callback.

2. Since we changed the signature of the `RestaurantsScreen()` function, we must also update the `DefaultPreview()` composable to correctly call the `RestaurantsScreen()` composable:

```
@Preview(showBackground = true)
@Composable
fun DefaultPreview() {
    RestaurantsAppTheme {
        RestaurantsScreen(
            RestaurantsScreenState(listOf(), true),
            {},
            { _, _ -> }
        )
    }
}
```

3. In the `MainActivity` class and inside the `RestaurantsApp()` composable, make the destination composable for `RestaurantsScreen()` responsible for wiring up the screen composable with its `ViewModel`, thereby ensuring good communication between `RestaurantsScreen()` and `RestaurantsViewModel`:

```
@Composable
private fun RestaurantsApp() {
    val navController = rememberNavController()
    NavHost(navController, startDestination =
        "restaurants") {
        composable(route = "restaurants") {
```

```
            val viewModel: RestaurantsViewModel =
                viewModel()
            RestaurantsScreen(
                state = viewModel.state.value,
                onItemClick = { id ->
                    navController
                        .navigate("restaurants/$id")
                },
                onFavoriteClick = { id, oldValue ->
                    viewModel.toggleFavorite(id, oldValue)
                })
        }
        composable(
            route = "restaurants/{restaurant_id}",
            [...]) { RestaurantDetailsScreen() }
        }
```

With this approach, the destination `composable()` with the initial route of `"restaurants"` is the composable that manages and wires up the `RestaurantsScreen()` composable to its content by doing the following:

- Instantiating `RestaurantsViewModel`
- Getting and passing the state to `RestaurantsScreen()`
- Handling the `onItemClick()` and `onFavoriteClick()` callbacks

4. Build and run the application. The app should behave the same.
5. You will notice that if you rebuild the project and navigate back to the `RestaurantsScreen()` composable, the preview will now function correctly because the `RestaurantsScreen()` composable is no longer tied to a `ViewModel`, and so Compose can very easily preview its content.

> **Assignment**
> In this chapter, we have better decoupled the first screen of the app (the `RestaurantScreen()` composable) from its `ViewModel` to promote reusability and testability. As homework, you can practice doing the same for the `RestaurantDetailScreen()` composable.

Summary

In this chapter, we have dipped our toes into Clean Architecture in Android. We started by understanding a bit about what Clean Architecture means and some of the best ways we can achieve this in our Restaurants app, while also covering the main benefits of following such a software design philosophy.

We started with Clean Architecture in the first section, where we defined the Domain layer with Use Cases, and continued refactoring in the second section, where we separated the Domain model from Data models.

Then, we improved the architecture of the app by creating a package structure and by decoupling the Compose-based UI layer from the `ViewModel` classes even further.

In the next chapter, we will continue our journey of improving the architecture of our application by adopting dependency injection.

Further reading

Clean Architecture is a very complex subject, and one chapter is simply not enough to cover it. However, one of the most important concepts that Clean Architecture brings is the Dependency Rule. The Dependency Rule states that within a project, dependencies can only point inward.

To understand what the Dependency Rule is about, let's visualize the layer dependencies of our Restaurants app through a simplified version of concentric circles. Each concentric circle represents different areas of software with their corresponding layer dependencies (and libraries).

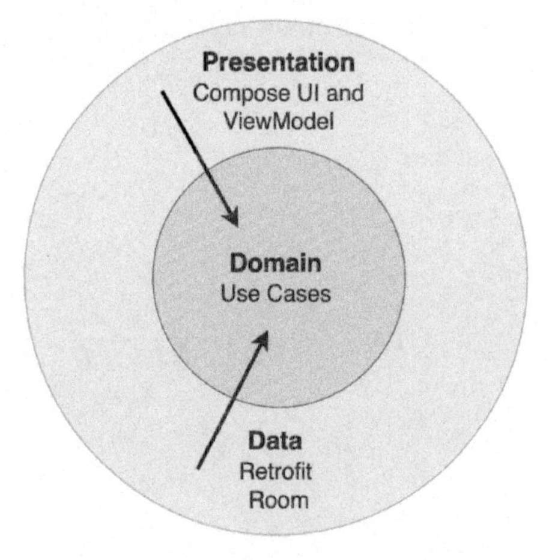

Figure 8.7 – The Dependency Rule with layers and components

This representation dictates that implementation details should be placed in *outer* circles (just as Compose is an implementation detail of the UI layer or Retrofit is an implementation detail for the Data layer), while business policies (Use Cases from the Domain layer) are placed within the *inner* circle.

The purpose of this representation is to enforce the Dependency Rule that states how dependencies should only be pointing inward.

The Dependency Rule (expressed with the inward-pointing arrows) showcases the following:

- The Presentation layer depends inward on the Domain layer (just like the `ViewModel` classes in our app correctly depend on Use Case classes) and how the Data layer should also depend inward on the Domain layer (in our app, Use Cases depend on `Repository` classes, while it should be the other way around – more on this in a second).
- The Domain layer should not depend on an outer layer – in our app, the Use Cases depend on `Repository` classes, which violates the Dependency Rule.

The approach of having the Presentation and Data layers (that contain details of implementation such as the Compose, Room, and Retrofit libraries) depend on the inner Domain layer is beneficial because it allows us to effectively separate the business policies (from within the inner circle, that is, the Domain layer) from outer layers. Outer layers can frequently change their implementation and we don't want these changes to impact the inner Domain layer.

In our Restaurants app though, the Domain layer depends on the Data layer because Use Case classes depend on `Repository` classes. In other words, the Dependency Rule is violated because the inner circle (the Domain layer) depends on an outer circle.

To fix this, we could define an `interface` class for the Data layer (for the `Repository` classes) and consider it part of the Domain layer (for now, by moving it inside the `domain` package).

This way, the Use Cases depend on an interface defined within the Domain layer, so now, the Domain layer has no outer dependencies. On the other hand, the `Repository` class (the Data layer) implements an interface provided by the Domain layer, so the Data layer (from the outer circle) now depends on the Domain layer (from the inner circle), thereby correctly adhering to the Dependency Rule.

> **Note**
>
> Another way of separating concerns (or layers) and making sure to respect the Dependency Rule is to modularize the app into layers, where each layer is a Gradle module.

I encourage you to study more about the Dependency Rule in Robert C. Martin's blog, while also checking out other strategies for achieving Clean Architecture: `https://blog.cleancoder.com/uncle-bob/2012/08/13/the-clean-architecture.html`.

9 Implementing Dependency Injection with Jetpack Hilt

In this chapter, we're continuing our journey of improving the architectural design of the Restaurants app. More precisely, we will be incorporating **dependency injection** (**DI**) in our project.

In the first section, *What is DI?*, we will start by defining DI and understanding its basic concepts, from what a dependency is, the types of dependencies, and what injection represents, through to concepts such as dependency containers and manual injection.

Afterward, in the *Why is DI needed?* section, we will focus in more detail on the benefits that DI brings to our projects.

In the last section, *Implementing DI with Hilt*, we will first understand how the Jetpack Hilt DI library works, and how to use it, and finally, with its help, we will incorporate DI in our Restaurants app.

To summarize, in this chapter we will be covering the following sections:

- What is DI?
- Why is DI needed?
- Implementing DI with Hilt

Before jumping in, let's set up the technical requirements for this chapter.

Technical requirements

Building Compose-based Android projects for this chapter would usually require your day-to-day tools; however, to follow along smoothly, make sure you have the following:

- The Arctic Fox 2020.3.1 version of Android Studio. You can also use a newer Android Studio version or even Canary builds but note that IDE interface and other generated code files might differ from the ones used throughout this book.
- Kotlin 1.6.10 or newer plugin installed in Android Studio
- The Restaurants app code from the previous chapter

The starting point for this chapter is represented by the Restaurants app developed in the previous chapter. If you haven't followed the implementation from the previous chapter, access the starting point for this chapter by navigating to the `Chapter_08` directory of the repository and importing the Android project entitled `chapter_8_restaurants_app`.

To access the solution code for this chapter, navigate to the `Chapter_09` directory: `https://github.com/PacktPublishing/Kickstart-Modern-Android-Development-with-Jetpack-and-Kotlin/tree/main/Chapter_09/chapter_9_restaurants_app`.

What is DI?

In simple terms, **DI** represents the concept of providing the instances of the dependencies that a class needs, instead of having it construct them itself. But, what are dependencies?

Dependencies are other classes that a certain class *depends on*. For example, an `ExampleViewModel` class could contain a `repository` variable of type `Repository`:

```
class ExampleViewModel {
    private val repository: Repository = Repository()
    fun doSomething() {
```

```
        repository.use()
    }
}
```

That's why `ExampleViewModel` depends on `Repository`, or `Repository` is a dependency for `ExampleViewModel`. Most of the time, classes have many more dependencies, but we'll stick with only one for the sake of simplicity. In this case, the `ExampleViewModel` provides its own dependencies so it's very easy to create an instance of it:

```
fun main() {
    val vm = ExampleViewModel()
    vm.doSomething()
}
```

Now, the previous example doesn't incorporate DI, mainly because `ExampleViewModel` provides instances for its own dependencies. It does that by instantiating a `Repository` instance (through the `Repository()` constructor) and by passing it to the `repository` variable.

To incorporate DI, we must create a component that provides `ExampleViewModel` with its dependencies:

```
object DependencyContainer {
    val repo: Repository = Repository()
}
```

The `DependencyContainer` class will act, as the name suggests, as a **dependency container**, as it will provide instances for all the dependencies our classes need. When a class needs an instance for its dependency, this container will provide it. This way, we centralize the creation of the instances of dependencies so we can handle this process (which can become elaborate for complex projects where each dependency has other dependencies, for example) within a single place in our project.

> **Note**
>
> Apart from the DI technique, you can also use the **service locator** pattern to construct classes. Unlike DI, if you try to follow the service locator pattern, then the class that needs to be constructed will be responsible for creating its own dependencies with the help of a `ServiceLocator` component. Both DI and the service locator pattern are useful; however, we will only cover DI in this chapter.

Getting back to incorporating DI, we then must allow `DependencyContainer` to provide a `Repository` instance to `ExampleViewModel`:

```
class ExampleViewModel {
    private val repository: Repository =
        DependencyContainer.repo
    fun doSomething() {
        repository.use()
    }
}
```

This technique of having dependencies declared as variables (for example, `ExampleViewModel` contains a `repository` variable) and then providing their instances through a container is a form of DI called **field injection**.

There are several issues with this approach, mainly caused by the fact that we have declared dependencies as field variables. The most notable ones are as follows:

- The `ExampleViewModel` class is tightly coupled to our `DependencyContainer` and we cannot use the `ViewModel` without it.
- The dependencies are **implicit**, which means they are hidden from the outside world. In other words, whoever is instantiating `ExampleViewModel` doesn't know about the `ViewModel` class's dependencies or their creation.

  This won't allow us to reuse the same `ExampleViewModel` with other implementations of its dependencies (given its dependencies, such as `Repository`, are interfaces that can be implemented by different classes).
- Since `ExampleViewModel` has hidden dependencies, it becomes hard for us to test it. As we will instantiate the `ExampleViewModel` and put it under test, it will create its own `Repository` instance that will probably make real I/O requests for every test. We want our tests to be fast and reliable and not dependent on real third-party APIs.

To alleviate these issues, we must first refactor `ExampleViewModel` to expose its dependencies through its public API to the outside world. The most appropriate way to do that is through its public `constructor`:

```
class ExampleViewModel constructor(private val repo:
Repository) {
    fun doSomething() { repo.use() }
}
```

Now, `ExampleViewModel` exposes its dependencies to the outside world through its constructor, making those dependencies **explicit**. Yet, who's going to provide the dependencies from outside?

When we need to instantiate `ExampleViewModel`, `DependencyContainer` will provide it with the necessary dependencies from the outside:

```
fun main() {
    val repoDependency = DependencyContainer.repository
    val vm = ExampleViewModel(repoDependency)
    vm.doSomething()
}
```

In the previous example, instead of field injection, we have used **constructor injection**. This is because we have provided and injected the dependencies to `ExampleViewModel` from the outside world through its constructor.

As opposed to field injection, constructor injection allows us to do the following:

- Decouple our classes from the DI container, just like `ExampleViewModel` no longer depends on `DependencyContainer`.
- The dependencies are exposed to the outside world, so we can reuse the same `ExampleViewModel` with other implementations of `Repository` (given `Repository` is an interface).
- The `ExampleViewModel` class can no longer decide which dependency implementation to get and use as was the case with field injection, so we have now inverted this responsibility from `ExampleViewModel` to the outside world.
- `ExampleViewModel` is easier to test, as we can easily pass a mock or a fake `Repository` implementation (given `Repository` is an interface) that will behave the way we're expecting it to in a test.

So far, with the help of a dependency container, we have incorporated DI by ourselves by allowing `DependencyContainer` to provide instances of dependencies to our classes (that is, an instance of `ExampleViewModel`). This technique is called **manual DI**.

Apart from manual DI, you can have DI done automatically through frameworks that relieve you from the burden of the following:

- Providing instances of dependencies to the classes that need them. More specifically, frameworks help you wire up complex object relationships for the required dependencies, so you don't have to write boilerplate code to generate instances and pass them to appropriate objects. This infrastructure code is often cumbersome for large-sized apps, so a framework that automates that for you can be quite handy.
- Scoping dependencies to certain lifetime scopes, such as the `Application` scope or `Activity` scope. For example, if you want a certain dependency to be a singleton (to be scoped to the lifetime of the application), you must manually make sure that only one instance is created in memory while also avoiding concurrency issues due to concurrent access. A framework can do that for you behind the scenes.

In Android, a very simple DI library is **Hilt**, and we will explore it in the *Implementing DI with Hilt* section. But until then, let's better understand why DI is needed in the first place.

Why is DI needed?

DI is not a must for all projects. Until now, our Restaurants app worked just fine without any DI incorporated. Yet, while not including DI might not seem like a big issue, by incorporating it you bring a lot of benefits to your project; the most notable advantages are that you can do the following:

- Write less boilerplate code.
- Write testable classes.

Let's cover these two next.

Write less boilerplate code

Let's circle back to our Restaurants app, and let's have a look at how we instantiate the Retrofit interface within the `RestaurantsRepository` class:

```
class RestaurantsRepository {
    private var restInterface: RestaurantsApiService =
        Retrofit.Builder()
            .addConverterFactory(
                GsonConverterFactory.create())
            .baseUrl("your_firebase_database_url")
```

```
                .build()
                .create(RestaurantsApiService::class.java)
        [...]
    }
```

Now, let's have a look at how we similarly instantiate the Retrofit interface within the `RestaurantsDetailsViewModel` class:

```
class RestaurantDetailsViewModel(…): ViewModel() {
    private var restInterface: RestaurantsApiService
    [...]
    init {
        val retrofit: Retrofit = Retrofit.Builder()
            .addConverterFactory(GsonConverterFactory.create())
            .baseUrl("your_firebase_database_url")
            .build()
        restInterface = retrofit
            .create(RestaurantsApiService::class.java)
        [...]
    }
    [...]
}
```

While the code seems different, in essence, it's the same code needed to instantiate a concrete instance of `RestaurantsApiService`. Unfortunately, we have duplicated this instantiation code in two places, both in the `RestaurantsRepository` class and in the `RestaurantsDetailsViewModel` class.

In medium to large-sized production apps, the relationship between objects is often much more complex, making such infrastructure code plague every class, mostly because, without any DI, every class builds the instances of the dependencies it needs. Such code is often duplicated throughout the project and ultimately becomes difficult to manage.

DI will help us centralize this infrastructure code and will eliminate all the duplicated code needed to provide instances of dependencies, wherever we need them throughout the project.

Going back to our Restaurants app, if we were to use manual DI, all this instantiation code could be extracted into a `DependencyContainer` class that would provide us with a `RestaurantsApiService` instance wherever we need it, so we would have no more duplicated code! Don't worry, we will incorporate DI soon, in the upcoming *Implementing DI with Hilt* section.

Now that we touched upon how DI helps us with containing and organizing the code related to building instances of classes, it's time to check out another essential advantage of DI.

Write testable classes

Let's suppose that we want to test the behavior of `RestaurantsRepository` to make sure that it performs as expected. But first, let's have a quick look at the existing implementation of `RestaurantsRepository`:

```
class RestaurantsRepository {
    private var restInterface: RestaurantsApiService =
        Retrofit.Builder()
            .[...]
            .create(RestaurantsApiService::class.java)
    private var restaurantsDao = RestaurantsDb
        .getDaoInstance(
            RestaurantsApplication.getAppContext()
        )
    suspend fun toggleFavoriteRestaurant(…) = {…}
    suspend fun getRestaurants(): List<Restaurant> {…}
    [...]
}
```

We can see that no DI is currently incorporated, as `RestaurantsRepository` has two implicit dependencies: an instance of `RestaurantsApiService` and an instance of `RestaurantsDao`. The `RestaurantsRepository` provides instances to its own dependencies, first by constructing a `Retrofit.Builder()` object and creating the concrete instance by calling `.create(…)`.

Now, let's say we want to test this `RestaurantsRepository` class, and make sure that it behaves correctly by running different verifications. Let's imagine how such a test class would look:

```
class RestaurantsRepositoryTest {
    @Test
    fun repository_worksCorrectly() {
        val repo = RestaurantsRepository()
        assertNotNull(repo)
        // Perform other verifications
    }
}
```

The previous test structure is simple: we created a `RestaurantsRepository` instance by using its constructor and then we saved it inside a `repo` variable. We then asserted that the instance of the `Repository` is not `null`, so we can proceed with testing its behavior.

This is optional, yet if you're trying to write the previous test class and follow this process, make sure that the `RestaurantsRepositoryTest` class is placed inside the `test` directory of the application:

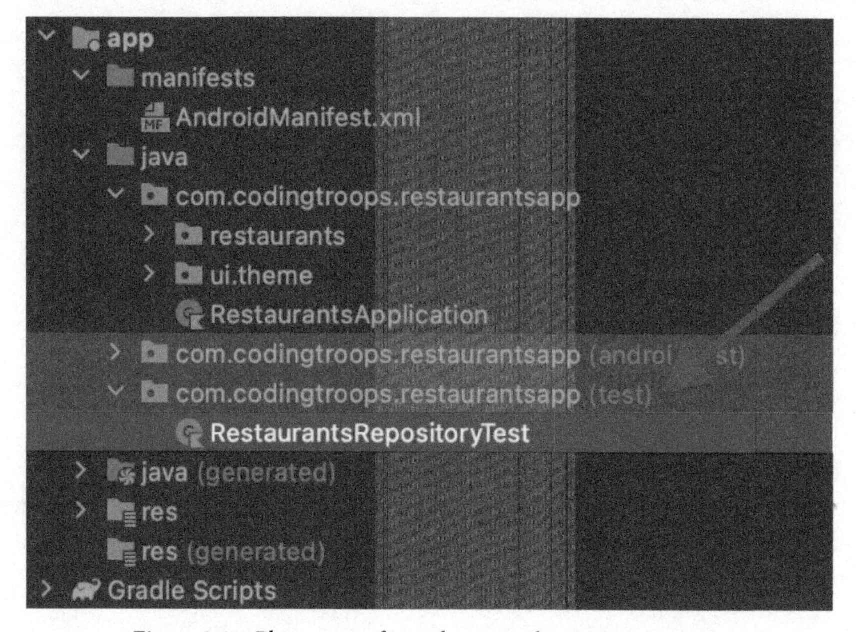

Figure 9.1 – Placement of test classes in the project structure

Now, if we would to run this test, it will throw an exception before having the chance to verify anything. The stack trace would look like this:

```
lateinit property app has not been initialized
kotlin.UninitializedPropertyAccessException: lateinit property app has not been initialized
    at com.codingtroops.restaurantsapp.RestaurantsApplication$Companion.getAppContext(RestaurantsApplication.kt:10)
    at com.codingtroops.restaurantsapp.restaurants.data.RestaurantsRepository.<init>(RestaurantsRepository.kt:25)
    at com.codingtroops.restaurantsapp.RestaurantsRepositoryTest.addition_isCorrect(RestaurantsRepositoryTest.kt:16)
```

Figure 9.2 – Stack trace of running invalid test

This happens because we're trying to write a small test for `RestaurantsRepository` but this class is not yet testable (in fact, we're trying to perform a Unit test – we will tackle this in more detail in *Chapter 10, Test Your App with UI and Unit Tests*).

But, why is our simple test throwing `UninitializedPropertyAccessException`?

If we have a look at the stack trace, we can see that the crash is caused because our test is trying to obtain the application context through `getAppContext()` from the `RestaurantsApplication` class.

It makes sense because, if we have another look at `RestaurantsRepository`, we can see that to obtain the `restaurantsDao` instance, the `Repository` calls `RestaurantsDb.getDaoInstance()` that initializes the Room database, and it needs an instance of `Context` to do that:

```
class RestaurantsRepository {
    [...]
    private var restaurantsDao = RestaurantsDb
        .getDaoInstance(
            RestaurantsApplication.getAppContext()
        )
    suspend fun toggleFavoriteRestaurant(...) = {...}
    suspend fun getRestaurants(): List<Restaurant> {...}
    [...]
}
```

Our small test shouldn't need a `Context` object, simply because it should neither try to create a Room database nor to create a Retrofit client instance; it shouldn't even depend on these concrete implementations. This is not efficient for small tests simply because such operations are memory-expensive and will do nothing but slow down our tests.

Moreover, we don't want our small test (that should run with much ease and very fast, several times in a short time frame) to make Room queries or, even worse, network requests through Retrofit, simply because the tests are dependent on the external world and so they become expensive and difficult to automate.

If, however, we would have had DI in place with constructor injection, we could have created our own classes that *fake* the behavior, ultimately making our `Repository` class easy to test and independent of concrete implementations that perform heavy I/O operations. We'll cover more about tests and *faking* in *Chapter 10, Test Your App with UI and Unit Tests*.

Going back to our app, we're not yet ready to write tests, because as you could see, we're lacking DI in our project. Now that we've seen that, without DI, life is somehow tough, let's learn how we can incorporate DI in the Restaurants app with the help of the Hilt library!

Implementing DI with Hilt

DI libraries are often used to simplify and accelerate the incorporation of DI in our projects, especially when the infrastructure code required by manual DI gets difficult to manage in large projects.

Hilt is a DI library that is part of Jetpack, and it removes the unnecessary boilerplate involved in manual dependency injection in Android apps by generating the code and the infrastructure that you otherwise would have had to develop manually.

> **Note**
> Hilt is a DI library based on another popular DI framework called **Dagger**, meaning that they are strongly related, so we will often refer to Hilt as *Dagger Hilt* in this chapter. Due to the steep learning curve of the Dagger APIs, Hilt was developed as an abstraction layer over Dagger to allow easier adoption of automated DI in Android projects.

Dagger Hilt relies on annotation processors to automatically generate code at build time, making it able to create and optimize the process of managing and providing dependencies throughout your project. Because of that, its core concepts are strongly connected to the use of annotations, so before we start adding and implementing Hilt in our Restaurants app, we must first cover a few concepts to better understand how Dagger Hilt works.

To summarize, in this section we will be doing the following:

- Understanding the basics of Dagger Hilt
- Setting up Hilt
- Using Hilt for DI

Let's begin!

Understanding the basics of Dagger Hilt

Let's analyze the three most important concepts and their corresponding annotations that we're required to work with to enable automatic DI in our project:

- Injection
- Modules
- Components

Let's start with injection!

Injection

Dagger Hilt needs to know the type of instances we want it to provide us with. When we discussed manual constructor injection, we initially wanted `ExampleViewModel` to be injected wherever we needed it, and we used a `DependencyContainer` class for that.

If we want Dagger Hilt to inject instances of a class somewhere, we must first declare a variable of that type and annotate it with the `@Inject` annotation.

Let's say that inside the `main()` function used for the manual DI example, we no longer want to use manual DI to get an instance of `ExampleViewModel`. Instead, we want Dagger to instantiate this class. That's why we will annotate the `ExampleViewModel` variable with the Java `@Inject` annotation and refrain from instantiating the `ViewModel` class by ourselves. Dagger Hilt should do that for us now:

```
import javax.inject.Inject

@Inject
```

```
val vm: ExampleViewModel

fun main() {
    vm.doSomething()
}
```

Now, for Dagger Hilt to know how to provide us with an instance of the `ExampleViewModel` class, we must also add the `@Inject` annotation to the dependencies of `ExampleViewModel` so that Dagger knows how to instantiate the `ViewModel` class.

Since the dependencies of `ExampleViewModel` are inside the constructor (from when we used manual constructor injection), we can directly add the `@Inject` annotation to `constructor`:

```
class ExampleViewModel @Inject constructor(private val repo:
Repository) {
    fun doSomething() { repo.use() }
}
```

Now, Dagger Hilt also needs to know how to inject the dependencies of `ExampleViewModel`, more precisely the `Repository` class.

Let's consider that `Repository` has only one dependency, a `Retrofit` constructor variable. For Dagger to know how to inject a `Repository` class, we must annotate its constructor with `@Inject` as well:

```
class Repository @Inject constructor(val retrofit: Retrofit){
    fun use() { retrofit.baseUrl() }
}
```

Until now, we got away with `@Inject` annotations because we had access to the classes and dependencies that we were trying to inject, but now, how can Dagger know how to provide us with a `Retrofit` instance? We have no way of tapping inside the `Retrofit` class and annotating its constructor with `@Inject`, since it's in an external library.

To instruct Dagger on how to provide us with specific dependencies, let's learn a bit about modules!

Modules

Modules are classes annotated with `@Module` that allow us to instruct Dagger Hilt on how to provide dependencies. For example, we need Dagger Hilt to provide us with a `Retrofit` instance in our `Repository`, so we could define a `DataModule` class that tells Dagger Hilt how to do so:

```
@Module
object DataModule {
    @Provides
    fun provideRetrofit(): Retrofit {
        return Retrofit.Builder().baseUrl("some_url").build()
    }
}
```

To tell the library how to provide us with a dependency, we must create a method inside the `@Module` annotated class where we manually build that class instance.

Since we don't have access to the `Retrofit` class and we need it injected, we've created a `provideRetrofit()` method (you can call it any way you want) annotated with the `@Provides` annotation, and that returns a `Retrofit` object. Inside the method, we manually created the `Retrofit` instance the way we needed it to be built.

Now, Dagger Hilt knows how to provide us with all the dependencies our `ExampleViewModel` needs (its direct `Repository` dependency and `Repository` `Retrofit` dependency). Yet, Dagger will complain that it needs a component class in which the module we've created must be installed.

Let's have a brief look at components next!

Components

Components are interfaces that represent the container for a certain set of dependencies. A component takes in modules and makes sure that the injection of its dependencies happens with respect to a certain lifecycle.

For our example with the `ExampleViewModel`, `Repository`, and `Retrofit` dependencies, let's say that we create a component that manages the creation for these dependencies.

With Dagger Hilt, you can define a component with the `@DefineComponent` annotation:

```
@DefineComponent()
interface MyCustomComponent(…) { /* component build code */ }
```

Afterward, we could install our `DataModule` in this component:

```
@Module
@InstallIn(MyCustomComponent::class)
object DataModule {
    @Provides
    fun provideRetrofit(): Retrofit { […] }
}
```

In practice though, the process of defining and building a component is more complex than that. This is because a component must scope its dependencies to a certain lifetime scope (such as the lifetime of the application) and have a pre-existent parent component.

Luckily, Hilt provides components for us out of the box. Such predefined components allow us to install modules in them and to scope dependencies to their corresponding lifetime scope.

Some of the most important predefined components are as follows:

- `SingletonComponent`: Allows us to scope dependencies to the lifetime of the application, as singletons, by annotating them with the `@Singleton` annotation. Every time a dependency annotated with `@Singleton` is requested, Dagger will provide the same instance.
- `ActivityComponent`: Allows us to scope dependencies to the lifetime of an `Activity`, with the `@ActivityScoped` annotation. If the `Activity` is recreated, a new instance of the dependency will be provided.
- `ActivityRetainedComponent`: Allows us to scope dependencies to the lifetime of an `Activity`, surpassing its recreation upon orientation change, with the `@ActivityRetainedScoped` annotation. If the `Activity` is recreated upon orientation change, the same instance of the dependency is provided.
- `ViewModelComponent`: Allows us to scope dependencies to the lifetime of a `ViewModel`, with the `@ViewModelScoped` annotation.

As the lifetime scope of these components varies, this also translates into the fact that each component derives its lifetime scope from each other, from the widest `@Singleton` lifetime scope (of the application) to narrower scopes such as `@ActivityScoped` (of an `Activity`):

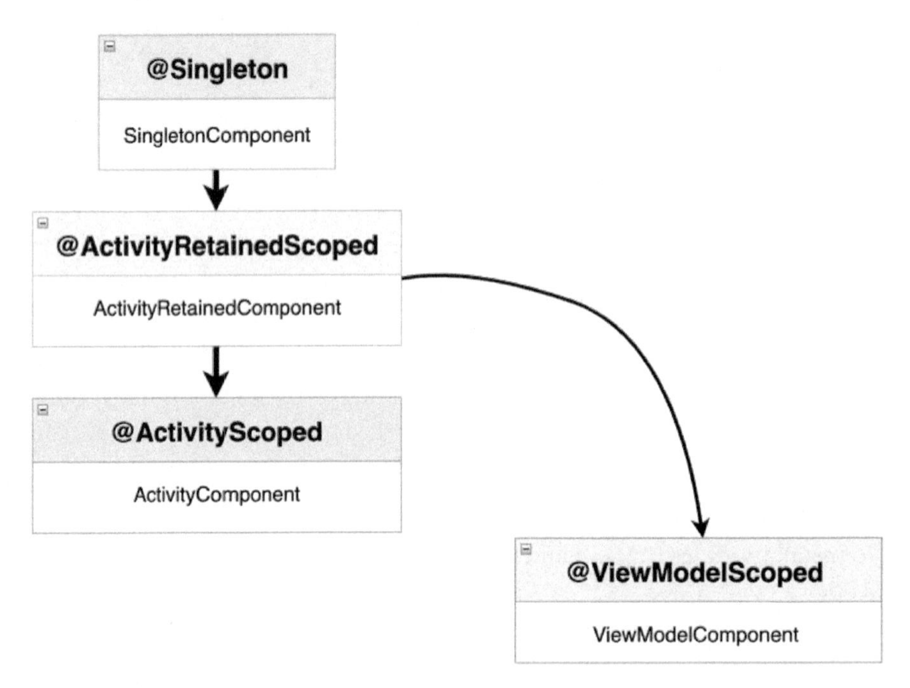

Figure 9.3 – Simplified version of Dagger Hilt scope annotations and their corresponding components

While in our Restaurants app, we will mostly be using `SingletonComponent` and its `@Singleton` scope annotation; it's important to note that Dagger Hilt exposes a broader variety of predefined components and scopes. Check them out in the documentation here: `https://dagger.dev/hilt/components.html`.

Now that we've briefly covered components, it's time to add Hilt to our Restaurants app!

Setting up Hilt

Before injecting dependencies with Hilt, we must first set up Hilt. Let's begin!

1. In the project-level `build.gradle` file, inside the `dependencies` block, add the Hilt-Android Gradle dependency:

```
buildscript {
    ...
    dependencies {
```

```
        ...
        classpath 'com.google.dagger:hilt-android-
            gradle-plugin:2.40.5'
    }
}
```

2. Moving inside the application-level `build.gradle` file, add the Dagger Hilt plugin inside the `plugins` block:

```
plugins {
    [...]
    id 'kotlin-kapt'
    id 'dagger.hilt.android.plugin'
}
```

3. Still inside the application-level `build.gradle`, inside the `dependencies` block, add the Android-Hilt dependencies:

```
dependencies {
    [...]
    implementation "com.google.dagger:hilt-
        android:2.40.5"
    kapt "com.google.dagger:hilt-compiler:2.40.5"
}
```

The `kapt` keyword stands for **Kotlin Annotation Processor Tool** and is required by Dagger Hilt to generate code based on the annotations we will be using.

After updating the `build.gradle` files, make sure to sync your project with its Gradle files. You can do that by pressing on the **File** menu option and then by selecting **Sync Project with Gradle Files**.

4. Annotate the `RestaurantsApplication` class with the `@HiltAndroidApp` annotation:

```
@HiltAndroidApp
class RestaurantsApplication: Application() { [...] }
```

To make use of automated DI with Hilt, we must annotate our `Application` class with the `HiltAndroidApp` annotation. This annotation allows Hilt to generate DI-related boilerplate code, starting with the application-level dependency container.

5. Build the project to trigger Hilt's code generation.
6. Optionally, if you want to check out the generated classes, first, expand the **Project** tab on the left, and then expand the package for the generated code. These classes are the proof that Hilt generates a lot of code behind the scenes so we can incorporate DI much easier:

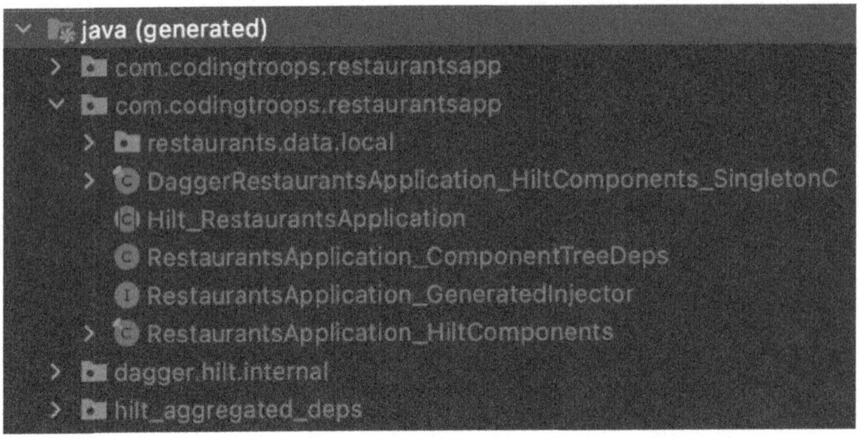

Figure 9.4 – Automatically generated classes by Hilt

Let's move on to the actual implementation!

Using Hilt for DI

In this sub-section, we will implement DI with Hilt for the first screen of our app where the list of restaurants is displayed. In other words, we want to inject all the dependencies that `RestaurantsScreen()` needs or depends on.

To have a starting point, let's have a look inside the `RestaurantsApp()` composable for the `RestaurantsScreen()` destination and see what we have to inject first:

```
@Composable
private fun RestaurantsApp() {
    val navController = rememberNavController()
    NavHost(navController, startDestination = "restaurants") {
        composable(route = "restaurants") {
            val viewModel: RestaurantsViewModel = viewModel()
            RestaurantsScreen(state = viewModel.state.value, [...])
        }
```

```
        composable(...) { RestaurantDetailsScreen() }
    }
}
```

It's clear that `RestaurantsScreen()` depends on `RestaurantsViewModel` to obtain its state and consume it.

This means that we must first inject an instance of `RestaurantsViewModel` inside the `composable()` destination where the `RestaurantsScreen()` resides:

1. Since we cannot add the `@Inject` annotation inside a composable function, we must use a special composable function to inject a `ViewModel`. To do that, first, add the `hilt-navigation-compose` dependency inside the `dependencies` block of the app-level `build.gradle` file:

```
dependencies {
    [...]
    implementation "com.google.dagger:hilt-
        android:2.40.5"
    kapt "com.google.dagger:hilt-compiler:2.40.5"
    implementation 'androidx.hilt:hilt-navigation-
        compose:1.0.0'
}
```

After updating the `build.gradle` file, make sure to sync your project with its Gradle files. You can do that by pressing on the **File** menu option and then by selecting **Sync Project with Gradle Files**.

2. Then, going back inside the `RestaurantsApp()` composable, in the DSL `composable()` destination for our `RestaurantsScreen()` composable, replace the `viewModel()` constructor of `RestaurantsViewModel` with the `hiltViewModel()` composable:

```
@Composable
private fun RestaurantsApp() {
    val navController = rememberNavController()
    NavHost(navController, startDestination =
            "restaurants") {
        composable(route = "restaurants") {
            val viewModel: RestaurantsViewModel =
                hiltViewModel()
```

```
            RestaurantsScreen(...)
        }
        composable(...) { RestaurantDetailsScreen() }
    }
}
```

The `hiltViewModel()` function injects an instance of `RestaurantsViewModel` scoped to the lifetime of the `RestaurantsScreen()` navigation component destination.

3. Since now our composable hierarchy injects a `ViewModel` at some point with the help of Hilt, we must annotate the Android component that is the host of the `RestaurantsApp()` root composable with the `@AndroidEntryPoint` annotation. In our case, the `RestaurantsApp()` composable is hosted by the `MainActivity` class, so we must annotate it with the `@AndroidEntryPoint` annotation:

```
@AndroidEntryPoint
class MainActivity : ComponentActivity() {
    override fun onCreate(savedInstanceState: Bundle?) {
        super.onCreate(savedInstanceState)
        setContent {
            RestaurantsAppTheme { RestaurantsApp() }
        }
    }
}
```

The `@AndroidEntryPoint` annotation generates another component for our `Activity` with a lifetime narrower than the lifetime of the application. More precisely, this component allows us to scope dependencies to the lifetime of our `Activity`.

4. In the `RestaurantsViewModel` class, first refactor it to explicitly declare its dependencies by moving them inside its constructor so that testability is promoted through constructor injection:

```
class RestaurantsViewModel constructor(
   private val getRestaurantsUseCase:
       GetInitialRestaurantsUseCase,
    private val toggleRestaurantsUseCase:
        ToggleRestaurantUseCase
```

```
) : ViewModel() {
    private val _state = mutableStateOf(...)
    [...]
}
```

Notice that, while we extracted the two Use Case variables into the constructor, we're no longer instantiating them – we will leave that to Hilt.

5. To get Hilt to inject `RestaurantsViewModel` for us, mark the `ViewModel` with the `@HiltViewModel` annotation, while also annotating its constructor with the `@Inject` annotation so that Hilt understands which dependencies of the `ViewModel` must be provided:

```
@HiltViewModel
class RestaurantsViewModel @Inject constructor(
    private val getRestaurantsUseCase: [...] ,
    private val toggleRestaurantsUseCase: [...]) :
        ViewModel() {
    [...]
}
```

Now that our `ViewModel` is annotated with `@HiltViewModel`, instances of `RestaurantsViewModel` will be provided by `ViewModelComponent` that respects the lifecycle of a `ViewModel` (bound to the lifetime of the composable destination while also surviving configuration changes).

6. Now that we instructed Hilt how to provide `RestaurantsViewModel`, we might think we're done; yet, if we build the application, we will get this exception:

.GetInitialRestaurantsUseCase cannot be provided
ructor or an @Provides-annotated method.

Figure 9.5 – Hilt compilation error

The issue lies in the fact that, while we instructed Hilt to inject `RestaurantsViewModel` and its dependencies, we never made sure that Hilt knows how to provide those dependencies: neither the `GetInitialRestaurantsUseCase` dependency nor the `ToggleRestaurantsUseCase` dependency.

In other words, if we want `RestaurantsViewModel` to be injected, we need to make sure that its dependencies can be provided by Hilt, and their dependencies too, and so on.

7. Let's first make sure that Hilt knows how to provide `GetInitialRestaurantsUseCase` to `RestaurantsViewModel`. Inside the `GetInitialRestaurantsUseCase` class, move its dependencies inside the constructor and mark it with `@Inject`, just like we did with `RestaurantsViewModel`:

```
class GetInitialRestaurantsUseCase @Inject constructor(
    private val repository: RestaurantsRepository,
    private val getSortedRestaurantsUseCase:
        GetSortedRestaurantsUseCase) {
    suspend operator fun invoke(): List<Restaurant> { … }
}
```

After you add the `repository` and `getSortedRestaurantsUseCase` variables inside the constructor, remember to remove the old member variables as well as their instantiation code from the body of `GetInitialRestaurantsUseCase`.

Note that we aren't annotating the `GetInitialRestaurantsUseCase` class with any Hilt scope annotations, simply because we don't want it to be tied to a certain lifetime scope.

Now, Hilt knows how to inject the `GetInitialRestaurantsUseCase` class, yet we must also instruct Hilt how to provide its dependencies as well: `RestaurantsRepository` and `GetSortedRestaurantsUseCase`.

We need to make sure that Hilt knows how to provide instances of `RestaurantsRepository`. We can see that its dependencies are `RestaurantsApiService` (the Retrofit interface) and `RestaurantsDao` (the Room Data Access Object interface):

```
class RestaurantsRepository {
    private var restInterface: RestaurantsApiService =
        Retrofit.Builder()
        [...]
        .create(RestaurantsApiService::class.java)
    private var restaurantsDao = RestaurantsDb
        .getDaoInstance(
            RestaurantsApplication.getAppContext()
```

```
            )
        [...]
}
```

The issue here is that once we place these dependencies inside the constructor and inject them, Hilt will have no idea how to provide them – simply because we cannot tap into the internal workings of Room or Retrofit and inject their dependencies too, like we did with `RestaurantsViewModel`, `GetInitialRestaurantsUseCase`, and now with `RestaurantsRepository`.

For Hilt to know how to provide dependencies out of our reach, we must create a `module` class where we will instruct Hilt on how to provide us with instances of `RestaurantsApiService` and `RestaurantsDao`:

8. Expand the `restaurants` package, then right click on the `data` package, and create a new package called `di` (short for dependency injection). Inside this package, create a new `object` class called `RestaurantsModule` and add the following code inside:

```
@Module
@InstallIn(SingletonComponent::class)
object RestaurantsModule { }
```

`RestaurantsModule` will allow us to instruct Hilt on how to provide Room and Retrofit dependencies to `RestaurantsRepository`. Since this is a Hilt module, we have done the following:

- Annotated it with `@Module` so that Hilt recognizes it as a module that provides instances of dependencies.
- Annotated it with `@InstallIn()` and passed the predefined `SingletonComponent` component provided by Hilt. Since our module is installed in this component, the dependencies that are contained can be provided anywhere throughout the application since `SingletonComponent` is an application-level dependency container.

9. Next up, inside `RestaurantsModule`, we need to tell Hilt how to provide our dependencies, so we will start with `RestaurantsDao`. For us to obtain an instance to `RestaurantsDao`, we must first instruct Hilt on how to instantiate a `RestaurantsDb` class.

Add a provideRoomDatabase method annotated with @Provides that will instruct Hilt how to provide an RestaurantsDb object by borrowing part of the instantiation code of the database class from the companion object of the RestaurantsDb class:

```
@Module
@InstallIn(SingletonComponent::class)
object RestaurantsModule {
    @Singleton
    @Provides
    fun provideRoomDatabase(
        @ApplicationContext appContext: Context
    ): RestaurantsDb {
        return Room.databaseBuilder(
            appContext,
            RestaurantsDb::class.java,
            "restaurants_database"
        ).fallbackToDestructiveMigration().build()
    }
}
```

First off, we've annotated the provideRoomDatabase() method with the @Singleton instance so that Hilt will create only one instance of RestaurantsDb for the whole application, allowing us to save memory.

Then, we can see that the provideRoomDatabase() method builds a RestaurantsDb instance, yet for this to work, we needed to provide the application-wide context to the Room.databaseBuilder() method. To achieve this, we have passed a Context object as a parameter of provideRoomDatabase() and annotated it with @ApplicationContext.

To understand how Hilt provides us with the application Context object, we must first note that each Hilt container comes with a set of default bindings that we can inject as dependencies. The SingletonComponent container provides us with the application-wide Context object wherever we need it by defining the @ApplicationContext annotation.

10. Now that Hilt knows to provide us with `RestaurantsDb`, we can create another `@Provides` method that takes in a `RestaurantsDb` variable (which Hilt will now know how to provide) and return a `RestaurantsDao` instance:

```
@Module
@InstallIn(SingletonComponent::class)
object RestaurantsModule {
  @Provides
  fun provideRoomDao(database: RestaurantsDb):
      RestaurantsDao  {
        return database.dao
  }
  @Singleton
  @Provides
  fun provideRoomDatabase(
      @ApplicationContext appContext: Context
  ): RestaurantsDb { ... }
}
```

11. Still inside `RestaurantsModule`, we now have to tell Hilt how to provide us with an instance of `RestaurantsApiService`. Do the same as before, but this time add a `@Provides` method for an instance of `Retrofit`, and one for an instance of `RestaurantsApiService`. Now, `RestaurantsModule` should look like this:

```
@Module
@InstallIn(SingletonComponent::class)
object RestaurantsModule {
    @Provides
    fun provideRoomDao(database: RestaurantsDb): [...] {
        return database.dao
    }
    @Singleton
    @Provides
    fun provideRoomDatabase(@ApplicationContext
        appContext: Context): RestaurantsDb {  [...]  }
    @Singleton
    @Provides
```

```
    fun provideRetrofit(): Retrofit {
        return Retrofit.Builder()
            .addConverterFactory([...])
            .baseUrl("[...]")
            .build()
    }

    @Provides
    fun provideRetrofitApi(retrofit: Retrofit):
        RestaurantsApiService {
    return retrofit
        .create(RestaurantsApiService::class.java)
    }
}
```

Remember that all this instantiation code resides in `RestaurantsRepository`, so you can get it from there.

12. Now that Hilt knows how to provide both dependencies of `RestaurantsRepository`, head back in the `RestaurantsRepository` class and apply constructor injection with Hilt by adding the `@Inject` annotation to the constructor while moving its `RestaurantsApiService` and `RestaurantsDao` dependencies inside the constructor:

```
@Singleton
class RestaurantsRepository @Inject constructor(
    private val restInterface: RestaurantsApiService,
    private val restaurantsDao: RestaurantsDao
) {
    suspend fun toggleFavoriteRestaurant(...) = [...]
        [...]
    }
```

Usually, `Repository` classes have a static instance so that only one instance is re-used throughout the app. This is useful when different data is stored in memory globally in `Repository` classes (be cautious with system-initiated process death because that will wipe anything in memory!).

Finally, to have only one instance of `RestaurantsRepository` that can then be reused across the app, we have annotated the class with the `@Singleton` annotation. This annotation is provided by the Hilt `SingletonComponent` container and allows us to scope instances of classes to the lifetime of the application.

13. Now that Hilt knows how to inject `RestaurantsRepository`, let's get back to the other remaining dependency of `GetInitialRestaurantsUseCase`: the `GetSortedRestaurantsUseCase` class. Head inside this class and make sure to inject its dependencies by moving the `repository` variable inside the constructor as we did before with other classes:

```
class GetSortedRestaurantsUseCase @Inject constructor(
    private val repository: RestaurantsRepository
) {
    suspend operator fun invoke(): List<Restaurant> {
        return repository.getRestaurants()
            .sortedBy { it.title }
    }
}
```

While we have annotated `RestaurantsRepository` with a scope annotation, we haven't added any scope annotation for this Use Case class simply because we don't want the instance to be preserved across a specific lifetime.

Now, we have instructed Hilt how to provide all the dependencies for the first dependency of `RestaurantsViewModel`, which is `GetInitialRestaurantsUseCase`!

14. Next up, let's tell Hilt how to provide the dependencies for the second and last dependency of `RestaurantsViewModel`, the `ToggleRestaurantUseCase` class. Head inside this class and make sure to inject its dependencies by moving the `repository` and `getSortedRestaurantsUseCase` variables inside the constructor as we did before with other classes:

```
class ToggleRestaurantUseCase @Inject constructor(
    private val repository: RestaurantsRepository,
    private val getSortedRestaurantsUseCase:
        GetSortedRestaurantsUseCase
) {
    suspend operator fun invoke(id: Int, oldValue:
        Boolean): List<Restaurant> {
```

```
            val newFav = oldValue.not()
            repository.toggleFavoriteRestaurant(id, newFav)
            return getSortedRestaurantsUseCase()
        }
}
```

15. Optionally, you can head inside the `RestaurantsDb` class and delete the entire `companion object` that was in charge of providing a singleton instance for our `RestaurantsDao`. The `RestaurantsDb` class should now be much slimmer and look like this:

```
@Database(
    entities = [LocalRestaurant::class],
    version = 3,
    exportSchema = false
)
abstract class RestaurantsDb : RoomDatabase() {
    abstract val dao: RestaurantsDao
}
```

    It's safe to delete this instantiation code because from now on, Hilt will do that for us out of the box.

16. Also, if you followed the previous step of cleaning up the `RestaurantsDb` class, inside `RestaurantsApplication`, you can also remove all the logic inside this class that was related to obtaining the application-wide `Context` object. From now on, Hilt will do that for us out of the box.

    The `RestaurantsApplication` class should be much slimmer and look like this:

```
@HiltAndroidApp
class RestaurantsApplication: Application()
```

17. Build and run the application. Now, the build should be successful because Hilt is in charge of providing the dependencies that we required it to provide.

With the help of DI, we have now promoted testability while also extracting the boilerplate associated with building class instances.

> **Assignment**
>
> We have integrated DI with Hilt for the first screen of `RestaurantsApplication`. However, the project is still not incorporating DI entirely because the second destination of our app (represented by the `RestaurantDetailsScreen()` composable) has neither its `RestaurantDetailsViewModel` injected nor this `ViewModel` class's dependencies injected. As a take-home assignment, incorporate DI in this second screen. This will allow you to get rid of the redundant Retrofit client instantiation inside `RestaurantDetailsViewModel` – remember that you can now inject a `RestaurantsApiService` instance directly with Hilt!

Summary

In this chapter, we improved the architecture of the Restaurants App by incorporating DI.

We discussed what DI is and covered its basic concepts: dependency with its implicit or explicit types, injection, dependency containers, and manual injection.

We then examined the main benefits that DI brings to our projects: testable classes and less boilerplate code.

Finally, we covered how DI frameworks can help us with the injection of dependencies, and explored the Jetpack Hilt library as a viable solution for DI on Android. Afterward, we practiced what we learned as we incorporated DI with Hilt in our Restaurants app.

Since we incorporated DI, it's a bit clearer that our classes can be easily tested, so it's time we start writing some tests in the next chapter!

Further reading

Knowing how to work with the basics of Hilt is usually enough for most projects. However, sometimes you might need to use more advanced features of Hilt or Dagger. To learn more about Dagger and how the framework automatically creates the dependencies for you by building a dependency graph, check this article: `https://medium.com/android-news/dagger-2-part-i-basic-principles-graph-dependencies-scopes-3dfd032ccd82`.

On the same note, apart from the `@Singleton` scope that was the most used scope throughout our app, Dagger Hilt exposes a broader variety of predefined components and scopes that allow you to scope different classes to various lifecycles. Check out more about components and their scopes in the official documentation: `https://dagger.dev/hilt/components.html`.

Leaving components and their scopes aside, in some projects, you might need to allow injection of dependencies in other Android classes than `Activity`. To see which Android classes can be annotated with `@AndroidEntryPoint`, check out the documentation: `https://dagger.dev/hilt/android-entry-point`.

10
Test Your App with UI and Unit Tests

In the previous chapters, one of our main focuses was to have a testable architecture. We tried to achieve that by decoupling different components from each other.

In this chapter, because of the architecture we put in place, we will see how easy it is to test in isolation different parts of the Restaurants app.

In the *Exploring the fundamentals of testing* section, we will be understanding the benefits of testing and exploring various types of tests. In the *Learning the basics of testing your Compose UI* section, we will learn how to test our Compose UI.

Finally, in the *Covering the basics of unit-testing your core logic* section, we will learn how to test the core functionality of your Restaurants app.

To summarize, in this chapter we will be covering the following sections:

- Exploring the fundamentals of testing
- Learning the basics of testing your Compose UI
- Covering the basics of unit-testing your core logic

Before jumping in, let's set up the technical requirements for this chapter.

Technical requirements

Building Compose-based Android projects for this chapter usually requires your day-to-day tools. However, to follow along smoothly, make sure you also have the following:

- The Arctic Fox 2020.3.1 version of Android Studio. You can also use a newer Android Studio version or even Canary builds but note that the IDE interface and other generated code files might differ from the ones used throughout this book.
- The Kotlin 1.6.10 or newer plugin installed in Android Studio.
- The Restaurants app code from the previous chapter.

The starting point for this chapter is represented by the Restaurants app developed in the previous chapter. If you haven't followed the implementation from the previous chapter, access the starting point for this chapter by navigating to the `Chapter_09` directory of the repository and import the Android project entitled `chapter_9_restaurants_app`.

To access the solution code for this chapter, navigate to the `Chapter_10` directory: `https://github.com/PacktPublishing/Kickstart-Modern-Android-Development-with-Jetpack-and-Kotlin/tree/main/Chapter_10/chapter_10_restaurants_app`

Exploring the fundamentals of testing

In this section, we will briefly cover the basics of testing. More precisely, we will be doing the following:

- Understanding the benefits of testing
- Exploring the types of tests

Let's start with the benefits of testing!

Understanding the benefits of testing

Testing our code is essential. Through tests, we ensure that our app's functional behavior is correct and as expected, while also making sure that it's usable, just as it was designed. By performing tests, we can release stable and functional apps to end users.

More importantly, if we develop an app and then test it consistently, we ensure that new updates with new functionality won't break the existing functionality, and no bugs will arise. This is often referred to as **regression testing**.

You can test your app manually by navigating through it on your device or emulator and making sure that every piece of data is displayed correctly, while also being able to interact correctly with every UI component.

However, manual testing is neither efficient nor fast. With manual testing, you must traverse every user flow, generate every user interaction, and verify the integrity of data displayed at any moment. Also, you must do this, consistently, on every application update. Moreover, manual testing scales poorly, as with every new update that contains a new functionality, the manual workload of testing the entire application increases.

Over time, manual testing becomes a burden for medium- and large-sized applications. Also, manual testing involves a human tester, which generates a human factor – this basically means that a tester may or may not in some circumstances overlook some bugs.

To alleviate these issues, in this chapter, we will be writing automated tests. Practically, we will define some scripted tests and then allow tools to run them, automatically. This approach is faster, consistent, and more efficient, as it scales better with the size of the project.

In other words, we will write other chunks of code that will test the code of our application. While this might sound weird, the approach of having automated tests is much more productive and reliable, and less time-consuming than manual testing.

Next up, let's cover the different types of tests that we can write.

Exploring types of tests

To better understand how to write tests, we must first decide *what exactly can be tested* in our apps. From this perspective, let's cover the most important types of tests:

- **Functional tests**: Is the app doing what is expected? We already touched upon functional tests and their benefits in the *Understanding the benefits of testing* section.
- **Compatibility tests**: Is the app working correctly on all devices and Android API levels? The Android ecosystem makes this particularly difficult if you consider the variety of devices and manufacturers.
- **Performance tests**: Is the app fast or efficient enough? Sometimes, apps can suffer from bottlenecks and UI stutters that can be identified via performance benchmarks.
- **Accessibility tests**: Is the app working well with accessibility services? Such services are used to assist users with disabilities in using our Android application.

In this chapter, we will be mainly focusing on functional tests in an attempt to ensure the functional integrity of our application.

Now, apart from deciding what has to be tested, we must also think about the *scope or size of the tests*. The scope indicates the size of the app's portion we're testing. From the perspective of the scope of the tests, we have the following:

- **Unit tests**: Often referred to as small tests, these test the functional behavior of methods, classes, or groups of classes in an isolated environment. Usually, unit tests target small portions of the app without interacting with the real-world environment; hence, they are more reliable than tests that depend on external input.
- **Integration tests**: Often referred to as medium tests, these test whether multiple units interact and function correctly together.
- **End-to-end tests**: Often referred to as big tests, these test large portions of the application, from multiple screens to entire user flows.

Depending on the size of the tests, each type has a degree of isolation. The **degree of isolation** is tightly related to the scope of the tests, as it measures how dependent the component we're testing is on other components. As the size of the test increases, from small to big, the isolation level of the tests decreases.

In this chapter, we will be mainly focusing on unit tests, as they are fast, with the simplest setup, and most reliable in helping us validate the functionality of our application. These traits are tightly related to the higher isolation level of unit tests from external components.

Lastly, we must also classify tests based on the system they will be running on:

- **Local tests**: Run on your workstation or development system (used in practices such as **Continuous Integration** (**CI**)) without the need of an Android device or emulator. They are usually small and fast, isolating the component under test from the rest of the application. Most of the time, unit tests are local tests.
- **Instrumented tests**: Run on an Android device, be it a physical device or emulator. Most of the time, UI tests are considered instrumented tests, since they allow the automated testing of an application on an Android device.

In this chapter, our unit tests will be local when we will be testing the core logic of some components in isolation and instrumented when we will be performing UI unit tests for a specific screen in isolation.

Let's proceed with local UI tests first!

Learning the basics of testing your Compose UI

UI tests allow us to evaluate the behavior of our Compose code against what is expected to be correct. This way, we can catch bugs early in our UI development process.

To test our UI, we must first decide what we are aiming to evaluate. To keep it simple, in this section, we will unit-test our UI in an isolated environment. In other words, we want to test the following:

- That our composable screens consume the received state as expected. We want to make sure that the UI correctly represents the different state values that it can receive.
- For our composable screens, that user-generated events are correctly forwarded to the caller of the composable.

To keep our tests simple, we will define these tests as unit tests and try to isolate screen composables from their `ViewModel` or from other screen composables; otherwise, our test will become an integration or an end-to-end test.

In other words, we will test separately each screen, with total disregard of anything outside of their composable function definition. Even though our tests will run on an Android device, they will be testing only one unit – a screen composable.

> **Note**
>
> Some UI tests can also be considered unit tests, as long as they are testing only one part of the UI of your application, as we will do in this section.

For starters, we need to test the first screen of our application, represented by the `RestaurantsScreen()` composable. Let's begin!

1. First, add the following testing dependencies inside the `dependencies` block of the app-level `build.gradle` file:

```
dependencies {
    [...]
    androidTestImplementation "androidx.compose.ui:ui-
        test-junit4:$compose_version"
    debugImplementation "androidx.compose.ui:ui-test-
        manifest:$compose_version"
}
```

These dependencies will allow us to run our Compose UI tests on an Android device.

After updating the `build.gradle` file, make sure to sync your project with its Gradle files. You can do that by pressing on the **File** menu option and then by selecting **Sync Project with Gradle Files**.

2. Before creating a test class, locate the `androidTest` package that is suited for instrumented tests:

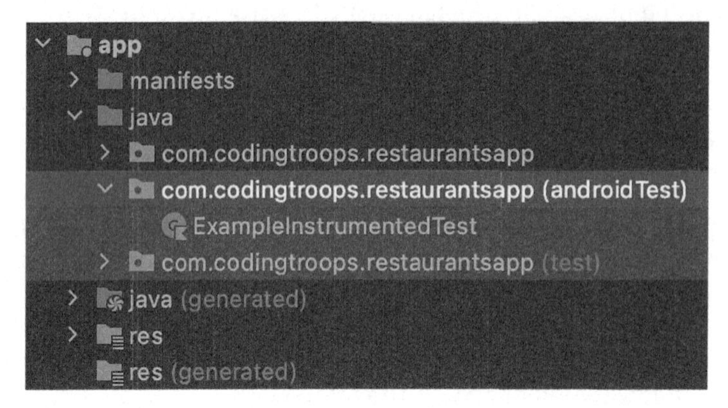

Figure 10.1 – Observing the androidTest package for UI tests

In Android projects, this directory stores source files for UI tests. Also note that the pre-built `ExampleInstrumentedTest` class resides in this directory.

3. Create an empty Kotlin class named `RestaurantsScreenTest` inside the `androidTest` package.

Inside this class, we will define a method for each independent test. Behind the scenes, every method will become a standalone UI test that can pass or fail.

4. Before creating our first test method, inside the `RestaurantsScreenTest` class, add the following code:

```
import androidx.compose.ui.test.junit4.*
import org.junit.Rule

class RestaurantsScreenTest {
    @get:Rule
    val testRule: ComposeContentTestRule =
        createComposeRule()
}
```

To run our Compose UI tests, we are using the JUnit testing framework that will allow us to write repeatable unit tests in an isolated environment with the help of a test rule. **Test rules** allow us to add functionality to all the tests within a test class.

In our case, we need to test Compose UI in every test method, so we had to use a special `ComposeContentTestRule` object. To access this rule, we have previously imported a special JUnit rule dependency so that our test class now defines a `testRule` variable and instantiates it by using the `createComposeRule()` method.

`ComposeContentTestRule` will not only allow us to set the Compose UI under test but also host tests on an Android device, while also giving us the ability to interact with the composables under test or perform UI assertions.

Before writing our first test method though, we need to clearly understand what behavior we are trying to test.

Let's have a look at how our `RestaurantsScreen()` composable consumes a `RestaurantsScreenState` instance from its `state` parameter, and how it forwards events to its caller through the `onItemClick` and `onFavoriteClick` function parameters:

```
@Composable
fun RestaurantsScreen(
    state: RestaurantsScreenState,
    onItemClick: (id: Int) -> Unit,
    onFavoriteClick: (id: Int, oldValue: Boolean) -> Unit
) {
    Box(…) {
        LazyColumn(…) {
            items(state.restaurants) { restaurant ->
                RestaurantItem(restaurant,
                   onFavoriteClick = { id, oldValue ->
                        onFavoriteClick(id, oldValue) },
                   onItemClick = { id ->
                        onItemClick (id) })
            }
        }
        if(state.isLoading)
            CircularProgressIndicator()
        if(state.error != null)
```

```
                Text(state.error)
        }
    }
```

By looking at the previous snippet, we see that we can test how the `onItemClick` and `onFavoriteClick` functions are called, based on different UI interactions, and also that we can test whether the state is consumed correctly or not. Yet we can't infer very well the possible values of the state that our composable is receiving.

To get an overview of the possible states that we want to feed into our `RestaurantsScreen()` so that we can test its behavior, we need to have a look at its state producer, `RestaurantsViewModel`:

```
class RestaurantsViewModel @Inject constructor(…) :
ViewModel() {
    private val _state = mutableStateOf(
        RestaurantsScreenState(
            restaurants = listOf(),
            isLoading = true
        )
    )
    […]
    private val errorHandler = CoroutineExceptionHandler
    { ... ->
        exception.printStackTrace()
        _state.value = _state.value.copy(
            error = exception.message,
            isLoading = false)
    }
    init { getRestaurants() }
    fun toggleFavorite(itemId: Int, oldValue: Boolean) {
        […]
    }
    private fun getRestaurants() {
        viewModelScope.launch(errorHandler) {
            val restaurants = getRestaurantsUseCase()
            _state.value = _state.value.copy(
                restaurants = restaurants,
                isLoading = false)
```

```
            }
        }
    }
```

We can say that our screen should have three possible states:

- **Initial loading state**: At this point, we're waiting for restaurants, thus rendering a loading status. You can see this initial state declared at the top of the `ViewModel` class in the initialization of the `_state` variable, where the `restaurants` parameter of `RestaurantsScreenState` is set to `emptyList()` and the `isLoading` parameter is set to `true`.
- **State with content**: The restaurants have arrived, so we reset the loading status and render them. You can see how this state is created inside the coroutine launched in the `getRestaurants()` method where we mutated the initial state and set the `isLoading` parameter to `false`, while also passing the list of restaurants to the `restaurants` parameter.
- **Error state**: Something went wrong when the app tried to fetch its content – that is, restaurants. You can see how this state is created inside the block of code exposed by `CoroutineExceptionHandler` where the `isLoading` parameter is set to `false` to reset the loading status, while also passing the message of `Exception` to the `error` parameter.

Now that we know what behavior the `RestaurantsScreen` composable should exhibit and what input we should pass to it in order to produce such a behavior, it's time to actually put our composable screen under test.

Let's begin by verifying whether the `RestaurantsScreen` composable correctly renders the first state – that is, the initial loading state.

5. Inside the `RestaurantsScreenTest` class, add an empty test function named `initialState_isRendered()` that will later test whether our `RestaurantsScreen()` composable properly renders the initial state:

```
class RestaurantsScreenTest {
    @get:Rule
    val testRule: ComposeContentTestRule =
        createComposeRule()

    @Test
    fun initialState_isRendered() {  }
}
```

To tell the JUnit testing library to run an individual test for this method, we've annotated it with the `@Test` annotation.

Also, note that we named this method around the specific behavior it's trying to test, going from what we're testing (the initial state) to how it's supposed to behave (to be rendered correctly), while separating these two with an underscore. For unit tests, there are a lot of naming conventions, yet we will try to stick to the simple version mentioned before.

> **Note**
>
> Each test method annotated with `@Test` should focus on only one specific behavior, just as `initialState_isRendered()` will test whether the `RestaurantsScreen()` properly renders the initial state, and no other pieces. This allows us to focus on only one behavior on each test method so that we can better identify later which specific behavior is no longer working as expected.

6. Prepare the `initialState_isRendered()` method to set the Compose UI by calling `testRule.setContent()`, just as our `MainActivity` did with its own `setContent()` method:

```
@Test
fun initialState_isRendered() {
    testRule.setContent { }
}
```

7. Inside the block of code exposed by the `setContent()` method, we must pass the **unit under test**, which is nothing else than the composable we're trying to test.

In our case, we will pass the `RestaurantsScreen()` composable, not before wrapping it inside the `RestaurantsAppTheme()` theme function so that the Compose UI that is under test mimics what our app is actually displaying in the production code:

```
@Test
fun initialState_isRendered() {
    testRule.setContent {
        RestaurantsAppTheme {
            RestaurantsScreen()
        }
    }
}
```

If you have named your app name differently, then the theme composable might have a different definition.

8. Now, the `RestaurantsScreen()` composable is expecting a `RestaurantsScreenState` object into its `state` parameter and two functions for its `onFavoriteClick()` and `onItemClick()` parameters. Let's add these while also passing the expected initial state from the screen's `ViewModel`:

```
@Test
fun initialState_isRendered() {
    testRule.setContent {
        RestaurantsAppTheme {
            RestaurantsScreen(
                state = RestaurantsScreenState(
                    restaurants = emptyList(),
                    isLoading = true),
                onFavoriteClick =
                    { _: Int, _: Boolean -> },
                onItemClick = { })
        }
    }
}
```

Since we're looking to test whether `RestaurantsScreen()` is correctly rendering the initial state, we have passed an instance of `RestaurantsScreenState` that had the `restaurants` parameter set to `emptyList()`, and the `isLoading` parameter is set to `true` while the `error` parameter is by default set to `null`.

We have now finished setting up the `RestaurantsScreen()` composable and fed it with the expected initial state. It's time to perform the assertion of whether our composable is correctly consuming this initial state or not.

In the `RestaurantsScreen()` composable, the initial state is a state mainly defined by the loading indicator that expresses how the app is waiting for content:

```
@Composable
fun RestaurantsScreen(…) {
    Box(…) {
        LazyColumn(…) {…}
        if(state.isLoading)
```

```
                CircularProgressIndicator()
            if(state.error != null)
                Text(state.error)
        }
    }
```

That's why we can check whether the `CircularProgressIndicator()` is visible on the screen. But how can we assert whether this composable is visible or not?

Compose provides us with several testing APIs to help us find elements, verify their attributes, and even perform user actions. For UI tests with Compose, we consider pieces of UI as **nodes** that we can identify with the help of semantics. **Semantics** give meaning to a UI element, and for an entire composable hierarchy, a semantics tree is generated to describe it.

In other words, we should be able to identify anything that is described on the screen with the help of its exposed semantics.

To give an example, a `Text` composable that displays a `String` object such as `"Hello"` will become a node in the semantics tree that we can identify by its `text` property value – `"Hello"`. Similarly, composables such as `Image` expose a mandatory `contentDescription` parameter whose value will allow us to identify the corresponding node in the semantics tree inside our tests. Don't worry – we'll see a practical example of this in a second.

> **Note**
>
> While the semantics attributes are mainly used for accessibility purposes (`contentDescription`, for example, is a parameter that allows people with disabilities to better understand what the visual element it describes is about), it's also a great tool that exposes semantics used to identify nodes in our tests.

Now that we have briefly covered how we can use semantics information to identify UI elements as nodes, it's time to get back to our test, which should validate if, upon an initial state consumed by `RestaurantsScreen()`, its `CircularProgressIndicator()` is visible.

However, if we look again at the usage of `CircularProgressIndicator()`, we can see that it exposes no semantics that we can use to identify it later in our test:

```
@Composable
fun RestaurantsScreen(…) {
    Box(…) {
        LazyColumn(…) {…}
        if(state.isLoading)
            CircularProgressIndicator()
        […]
    }
}
```

There is no `contentDescription` parameter and no visual text displayed. To be able to identify the node of `CircularProgressIndicator()` we must manually add a semantics `contentDescription` property.

9. For a moment, let's head out of the `androidTest` directory and go back inside the main package where our production code resides. Inside the `presentation` package, create a new `object` class named `Description` and define a constant description `String` variable for our loading composable:

```
object Description {
    const val RESTAURANTS_LOADING =
            "Circular loading icon"
}
```

10. Inside the `RestaurantsScreen()` composable, pass a `semantics` modifier to the `CircularProgressIndicator()` composable and set its `contentDescription` property to the previously defined `RESTAURANTS_LOADING`:

```
@Composable
fun RestaurantsScreen(…) {
    Box(…) {
        LazyColumn(…) { … }
        if (state.isLoading)
            CircularProgressIndicator(
                Modifier.semantics {
                    this.contentDescription =
                       Description.RESTAURANTS_LOADING
```

```
                    })
            [...]
        }
}
```

Now, we will be able to identify the node represented by the `CircularProgressIndicator()` composable inside our UI tests by using the `contentDescription` semantics property.

11. Now, go back inside the `androidTest` directory and navigate to the `RestaurantsScreenTest` class, and in the `initialState_isRendered()` test method, use the `testRule` variable to identify the node with the `RESTAURANT_LOADING` content description with the help of the `onNodeWithContentDescription()` method, and finally, verify that the node is displayed with the `assertIsDisplayed()` method:

```
@Test
fun initialState_isRendered() {
    testRule.setContent {
        RestaurantsAppTheme { RestaurantsScreen(...) }
    }
    testRule.onNodeWithContentDescription(
        Description.RESTAURANTS_LOADING
    ).assertIsDisplayed()
}
```

> **Note**
>
> As you can see with the `initialState_isRendered()` method, every test method has two parts – the setup of the expected behavior and then the assertions that verify that the resultant behavior is correct.

12. Inside the **Project** tab on the left, right-click on the `RestaurantsScreenTest` class and select **Run RestaurantsScreenTest**.

This command will run all the tests inside this class (only one in our case) on an Android device (either your physical Android device or your emulator).

If we switch to the **Run** tab, we will see that our test where we checked whether the initial state of `RestaurantsScreen()` was rendered correctly has passed:

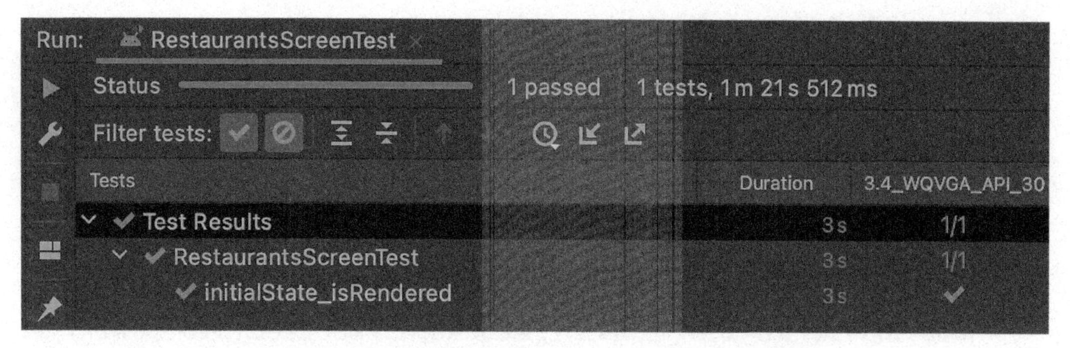

Figure 10.2 – Observing the UI tests that have passed

> **Note**
>
> Although we have defined a test where UI elements are identified via semantic properties, it's also possible to match a piece of UI by making it incorporate a `testTag` modifier that is later identified via the `hasTestTag()` matcher. However, you should avoid this practice, as you will be polluting your Compose UI production code with testing identifiers used only for tests.

While your test ran on an Android device or emulator, you might have noticed that no UI was shown on its screen. This happens because the UI tests are really fast. If you want to see the UI that you're testing, you can add a `Thread.sleep()` call at the end of the test method; however, you should avoid such a practice in your production test code.

Now, it's time to test whether the `RestaurantsScreen()` composable is rendering another state correctly – the state with content. In this state, the restaurants have arrived, so we reset the loading status to `false` and render the restaurants.

13. Inside the `RestaurantsScreenTest` class, add another test function named `stateWithContent_isRendered()`, which should test whether the state with content is rendered correctly:

```
@Test
fun stateWithContent_isRendered() {
    testRule.setContent {
        RestaurantsAppTheme {
            RestaurantsScreen(
                state = RestaurantsScreenState(
                    restaurants =,
                    isLoading = false),
```

```
                    onFavoriteClick =
                        { _: Int, _: Boolean -> },
                    onItemClick = { }
                )
            }
        }
    }
```

Inside this test method, we have set the `RestaurantsScreen()` composable with a state whose `isLoading` field is `false` (as the restaurants have arrived) but haven't passed a list of restaurants yet. We need to create a dummy list of restaurants to mimic some restaurants from our data layer.

14. For a moment, let's head out of the `androidTest` directory and go back inside the main package where our production code resides. Inside the `restaurants` package, create a new `object` class named `DummyContent`, and inside this class, add a `getDomainRestaurants()` method that will return a dummy array list of `Restaurant` objects:

```
object DummyContent {
    fun getDomainRestaurants() = arrayListOf(
        Restaurant(0, "title0", "description0", false),
        Restaurant(1, "title1", "description1", false),
        Restaurant(2, "title2", "description2", false),
        Restaurant(3, "title3", "description3", false))
}
```

15. Now, go back inside the `androidTest` directory and navigate to the `RestaurantsScreenTest` class. Inside the `stateWithContent_isRendered()` method, declare a `restaurants` variable that will hold the dummy restaurants from the `DummyContent` class and pass it to the `restaurants` parameter of `RestaurantsScreenState`:

```
@Test
fun stateWithContent_isRendered() {
    val restaurants = DummyContent.getDomainRestaurants()
    testRule.setContent {
        RestaurantsAppTheme {
            RestaurantsScreen(
```

```
                state = RestaurantsScreenState(
                    restaurants = restaurants,
                    isLoading = false), [...])
            }
        }
    }
```

Now that we have finished the setup part of this test method, it's time to perform our assertions. Since we are testing that `RestaurantsScreen()` is correctly rendering the state that contains restaurants, let's have another quick look at the composable under test:

```
@Composable
fun RestaurantsScreen(state: RestaurantsScreenState, [...])
{
    Box(...) {
        LazyColumn(...) {
            items(state.restaurants) { restaurant ->
                RestaurantItem(...)
            }
        }
        if(state.isLoading)
            CircularProgressIndicator()
        if(state.error != null)
            Text(state.error)
    }
}
```

We can deduct that the two conditions we can assert are as follows:

- The restaurants from `RestaurantsScreenState` are displayed on the screen.
- The `CircularProgressIndicator()` composable is not rendered, so its node is not visible on the screen.

Let's start off with the first assertion. Instead of relying on the `contentDescription` semantic property, we can use another semantic property that is more obvious – the text displayed on the screen. Since `LazyColumn` will render a list of `RestaurantItem()` composables, each one will call a `Text` composable that will render the title and the description of the restaurant passed to its `text` parameter. With the help of our `ComposeContentTestRule`, we can identify a node with a certain text value by calling the `onNodeWithText()` method.

16. Back in the `stateWithContent_isRendered()` method, let's assert that `title` of the first `Restaurant` object from our dummy list is visible.

    Do that by passing the title of the first element from the `restaurants` variable to the `onNodeWithText()` method, thereby identifying its corresponding node. Finally, call the `assertIsDisplayed()` method to verify whether this node is displayed:

```
@Test
fun stateWithContent_isRendered() {
    val restaurants = DummyContent.getDomainRestaurants()
    testRule.setContent {
        RestaurantsAppTheme {
            RestaurantsScreen(
                state = RestaurantsScreenState(
                    restaurants = restaurants,
                    isLoading = false
                ),
                [...])
        }
    }
    testRule.onNodeWithText(restaurants[0].title)
        .assertIsDisplayed()
}
```

17. Similarly, to assert whether the node of the title of the first restaurant from our dummy list is displayed, verify whether the node of the description of the first restaurant is displayed:

```
@Test
fun stateWithContent_isRendered() {
    val restaurants = DummyContent.getDomainRestaurants()
    testRule.setContent { ... }
    testRule.onNodeWithText(restaurants[0].title)
        .assertIsDisplayed()
    testRule.onNodeWithText(restaurants[0].description)
        .assertIsDisplayed()
}
```

You might be wondering why we aren't asserting whether `title` or `description` of all the elements from the `DummyContent` class is visible. It's important to understand that our test is asserting whether some nodes are displayed on the screen.

That's why, if our `restaurants` list contained 10 or 15 elements and we tested whether all titles and description nodes are visible, we could have had this test method pass on tall devices, since all the restaurants would fit and would be *composed* on the screen, but it could have failed if the test device was small and only some of the restaurants fitted on the screen and were composed.

This would have made our test flaky. To prevent our test from being flaky, we only asserted whether the first restaurant is visible, therefore minimizing the chance of having the test run and fail on an incredibly small screen.

Another interesting tactic that you can employ in order to test that content is correctly rendered would be to emulate a scroll action inside your test to the bottom of the list and check whether the last element is visible. This, however, is more complex, so we will proceed with the simpler version that we have implemented.

18. Lastly, let's assert that the node corresponding to the `CircularProgressIndicator()` composable does not exist, therefore ensuring that the app is not loading anything anymore. Do that by calling the `assertDoesNotExist()` method on the node with the `RESTAURANTS_LOADING` content description:

```
@Test
fun stateWithContent_isRendered() {
    val restaurants = DummyContent.getDomainRestaurants()
    testRule.setContent { … }
    testRule.onNodeWithText(restaurants[0].title)
        .assertIsDisplayed()
    testRule.onNodeWithText(restaurants[0].description)
        .assertIsDisplayed()
    testRule.onNodeWithContentDescription(
        Description.RESTAURANTS_LOADING
    ).assertDoesNotExist()
}
```

19. Now that we have finished writing our second test method asserting whether the `RestaurantsScreen()` composable is correctly rendering the state with content, inside the **Project** tab on the left, right-click on the `RestaurantsScreenTest` class and select **Run RestaurantsScreenTest**.

    The tests should run and pass.

> **Assignment**
>
> Try writing a test method on your own that asserts whether the `RestaurantsScreen()` composable renders the error state correctly. As a hint, you should be passing an error text to the `error` parameter of the `RestaurantsScreen()`, and then you should be asserting whether a node with that particular text is visible, while also verifying that the node corresponding to the `CircularProgressIndicator()` composable does not exist.

Finally, let's write a test method where we can verify whether upon clicking on a restaurant element from our dummy list, the correct callback is exposed by the parent `RestaurantsScreen()` composable:

20. Inside the `RestaurantsScreenTest` class, add another test function named `stateWithContent_ClickOnItem_isRegistered()`. Inside this method, store the dummy list inside a `restaurants` variable, and then store the first restaurant that we will click upon inside the `targetRestaurant` variable:

```
@Test
fun stateWithContent_ClickOnItem_isRegistered() {
    val restaurants = DummyContent.getDomainRestaurants()
    val targetRestaurant = restaurants[0]
}
```

21. Then, set `RestaurantsScreen()` under test and feed it with a state with content by passing the contents of the `restaurants` variable to the `restaurants` parameter of `RestaurantsScreenState`:

```
@Test
fun stateWithContent_ClickOnItem_isRegistered() {
    val restaurants = DummyContent.getDomainRestaurants()
    val targetRestaurant = restaurants[0]
    testRule.setContent {
        RestaurantsAppTheme {
            RestaurantsScreen(
                state = RestaurantsScreenState(
                    restaurants = restaurants,
                    isLoading = false),
                onFavoriteClick = { _, _ -> },
                onItemClick = { id ->  })
        }
    }
}
```

22. Then, identify the node that contains the `title` text of `targetRestaurant` and then simulate a user click on this node by calling the `performClick()` method:

```
@Test
fun stateWithContent_ClickOnItem_isRegistered() {
    val restaurants = DummyContent.getDomainRestaurants()
    val targetRestaurant = restaurants[0]
    testRule.setContent {
        RestaurantsAppTheme {
            RestaurantsScreen(
                state = RestaurantsScreenState(
                    restaurants = restaurants,
                    isLoading = false),
                onFavoriteClick = { _, _ -> },
                onItemClick = { id -> })
        }
    }
    testRule.onNodeWithText(targetRestaurant.title)
        .performClick()
}
```

23. Now that we have simulated a user-click interaction, let's assert that the `id` value from the `onItemClick` callback exposed by the `RestaurantsScreen()` composable matches with the `id` value of the restaurant we have clicked on:

```
@Test
fun stateWithContent_ClickOnItem_isRegistered() {
    val restaurants = DummyContent.getDomainRestaurants()
    val targetRestaurant = restaurants[0]
    testRule.setContent {
        RestaurantsAppTheme {
            RestaurantsScreen(
                state = RestaurantsScreenState(
                    restaurants = restaurants,
                    isLoading = false),
                onFavoriteClick = { _, _ -> },
                onItemClick = { id ->
                    assert(id == targetRestaurant.id)
```

```
                    }
                )
            }
        }
        testRule.onNodeWithText(targetRestaurant.title)
            .performClick()
    }
```

24. Inside the **Project** tab on the left, right-click on the `RestaurantsScreenTest` class and select **Run RestaurantsScreenTest**.

    The three tests should run and pass.

> **Note**
>
> You might have noticed that we haven't given any attention to testing how the UI updates when a user toggles a restaurant as a favorite or not a favorite. The only way we could have done that is by adding a dedicated semantic property to the heart icon of each restaurant from the list and then testing the value of that property. However, we would have tested a semantic property value and not the UI – for such cases, it's better to look into **screenshot testing** strategies. Screenshot testing is a UI testing practice that generates screenshots of your app, which are then compared to the initially defined *correct* versions.

Now that we briefly covered UI testing with Compose, it's time to unit-test our app's behind-the-scenes functionality!

Covering the basics of unit-testing your core logic

Apart from testing our UI layer, we must also test the core logic of our application. This means that we should try to verify as much behavior as possible in terms of presentation logic (testing `ViewModel` classes), business logic (testing `UseCase` classes), or even data logic (testing `Repository` classes).

The easiest way of validating such logic is by writing unit tests for each class or group of classes whose behavior we're trying to verify.

In this section, we will be writing unit tests for the `RestaurantsViewModel` class and the `ToggleRestaurantUseCase` class. Since these components don't interact directly with the UI, their unit tests will run directly on your local workstation's **Java Virtual Machine (JVM)**, rather than running on an Android device, as our UI tests did.

To summarize, in this section, we will be doing the following:

- Testing the functionality of a `ViewModel` class
- Testing the functionality of a `UseCase` class

Let's begin by testing the `RestaurantsViewModel` class!

Testing the functionality of a ViewModel class

We want to test the functionality of our `RestaurantsViewModel` so that we can make sure that it's correctly performing the role of state producer for the `RestaurantsScreen()` composable.

To achieve that, we will write unit tests for this `ViewModel` class in isolation. Let's begin:

1. First, locate the `test` package that is suited for regular unit tests:

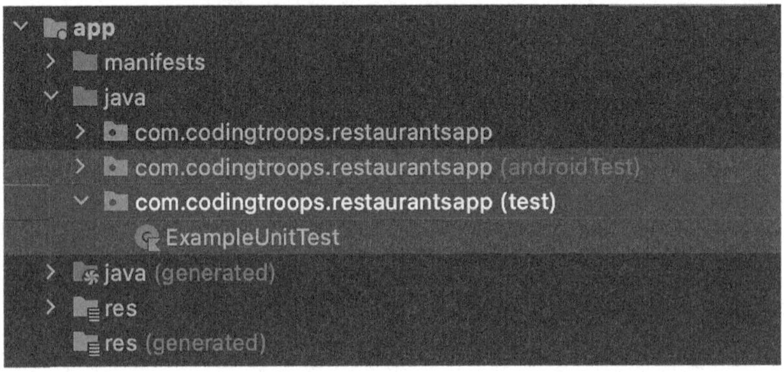

Figure 10.3 – Observing the test package used for regular unit tests

Also, note that the pre-built `ExampleUnitTest` class resides inside this package.

2. Create an empty Kotlin class named `RestaurantsViewModelTest` inside the `test` package. Inside this class, we will define a method for each independent test. Behind the scenes, every method will become a standalone unit test that can pass or fail.

Before starting to write our first test method, let's have another look at our `RestaurantsViewModel` class so that we can remind ourselves which cases we're looking to test:

```
class RestaurantsViewModel @Inject constructor(…) :
ViewModel() {
    private val _state = mutableStateOf(
        RestaurantsScreenState(
```

```
                restaurants = listOf(),
                isLoading = true
            )
        )
        [...]
        private val errorHandler = CoroutineExceptionHandler
        { ... ->
            exception.printStackTrace()
            _state.value = _state.value.copy(
                error = exception.message,
                isLoading = false)
        }
        init { getRestaurants() }
        fun toggleFavorite(itemId: Int, oldValue: Boolean) {
            [...]
        }
        private fun getRestaurants() {
            viewModelScope.launch(errorHandler) {
                val restaurants = getRestaurantsUseCase()
                _state.value = _state.value.copy(
                    restaurants = restaurants,
                    isLoading = false)
            }
        }
    }
```

We can say that our `RestaurantsViewModel` should produce the exact three states that we fed to the `RestaurantsScreen()` composable in its own UI tests:

- **Initial loading state**: At this point, we're waiting for restaurants, thus rendering a loading status. You can see this initial state declared at the top of the `ViewModel` class in the initialization of the `_state` variable, where the `restaurants` parameter of `RestaurantsScreenState` is set to `emptyList()` and the `isLoading` parameter is set to `true`.
- **State with content**: The restaurants have arrived. This state is produced inside the coroutine launched in the `getRestaurants()` method, where we mutated the initial state and set the `isLoading` parameter to `false` while also passing the list of restaurants to the `restaurants` parameter.

- **Error state**: Something went wrong when the app tried to fetch its content. You can see how this state is created inside `CoroutineExceptionHandler`, where the `isLoading` parameter is set to `false` to reset the loading status while also passing the message of `Exception` to the `error` parameter.

In the end, what we basically have to do is assert that the value of the `state` variable (of type `RestaurantsScreenState`), which is exposed to the UI, evolves correctly over time, from the initial state to all possible states.

Let's begin with a test method that asserts whether the initial state is produced as expected:

1. Inside the `RestaurantsViewModelTest` class, add an empty test function named `initialState_isProduced()` that will later test whether our `RestaurantsViewModel` class properly produces the initial state:

```
@Test
fun initialState_isProduced() {  }
```

   As with the UI tests, we will make use of the JUnit testing library to define and run individual unit tests for each method annotated with the `@Test` annotation.

   Again similar to the UI tests, we named this method around the specific behavior it's trying to test, going from what we're testing (the initial state) to what should happen (the state being correctly produced).

2. Inside the `initialState_isProduced()` method, we must create an instance of the subject under test – that is, `RestaurantsViewModel`. Define a `viewModel` variable and instantiate it with the value returned by the `getViewModel()` method, which we will define in a second:

```
@Test
fun initialState_isProduced() {
    val viewModel = getViewModel()
}
```

3. Still inside the `RestaurantsViewModelTest` class, define the `getViewModel()` method, which will return an instance of `RestaurantsViewModel`:

```
private fun getViewModel(): RestaurantsViewModel {
    return RestaurantsViewModel()
}
```

The problem now is that the `RestaurantsViewModel` constructor needs an instance of `GetInitialRestaurantsUseCase` and `ToggleRestaurantsUseCase`. In turn, these two classes also have other dependencies that we must instantiate. Let's have a clearer look at what classes we need to instantiate:

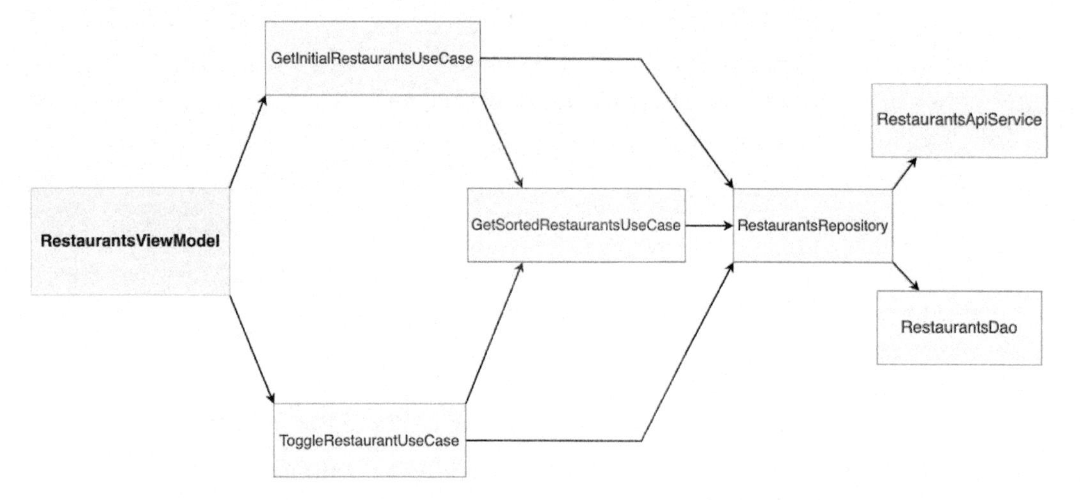

Figure 10.4 – Observing the direct and transitive dependencies of RestaurantsViewModel

We can see that both `GetInitialRestaurantsUseCase` and `ToggleRestaurantsUseCase` depend on `GetSortedRestaurantsUseCase` and `RestaurantsRepository`. The latter then depends on two library interfaces – `RestaurantsApiService` and `RestaurantsDao`.

Essentially, we must instantiate all these classes to test our `RestaurantsViewModel`.

4. Inside the `RestaurantsViewModelTest` class, refactor the `getViewModel()` method to construct all the necessary dependencies of `RestaurantsViewModel`:

```
private fun getViewModel(): RestaurantsViewModel {
    val restaurantsRepository =
        RestaurantsRepository(?, ?)
    val getSortedRestaurantsUseCase =
        GetSortedRestaurantsUseCase(restaurantsRepository)
    val getInitialRestaurantsUseCase =
        GetInitialRestaurantsUseCase(
            restaurantsRepository,
```

```
                getSortedRestaurantsUseCase)
        val toggleRestaurantUseCase =
            ToggleRestaurantUseCase(
                restaurantsRepository,
                getSortedRestaurantsUseCase
            )
        return RestaurantsViewModel(
            getInitialRestaurantsUseCase,
            toggleRestaurantUseCase
        )
    }
```

If you read the previous snippet from bottom to top, you will notice that we were able to construct all the dependencies of the `RestaurantsViewModel`, and their dependencies, and so on until we hit `RestaurantsRepository`. This depends on two library interfaces, `RestaurantsApiService` and `RestaurantsDao`, whose implementations are provided by the Retrofit and Room libraries.

In our production code, these two interfaces cross the boundary to the *real world* because their implementations, provided by the Retrofit and Room libraries, communicate with a real Firebase REST API and a real Room local database:

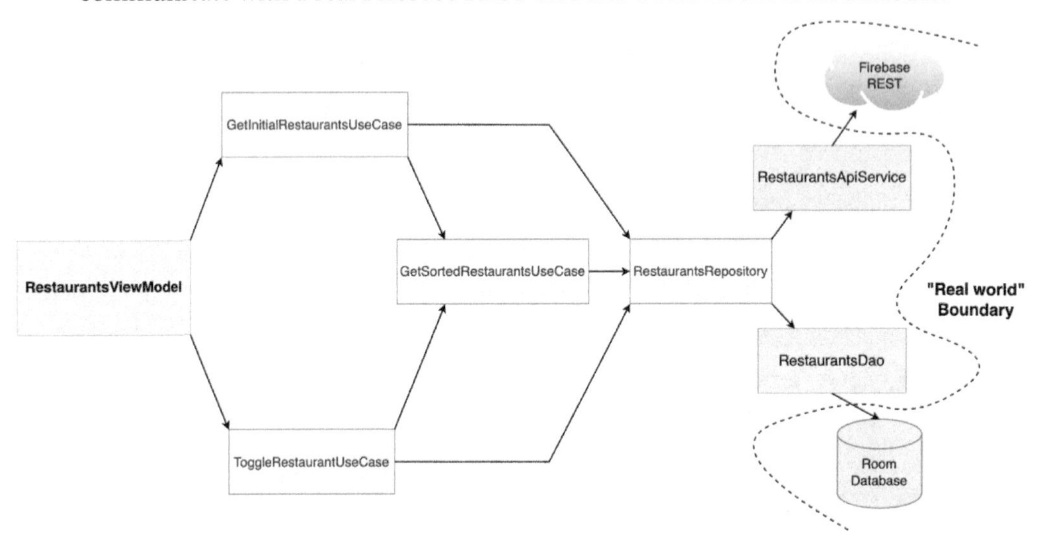

Figure 10.5 – Observing the real-world boundary crossed by the transitive dependencies of RestaurantsViewModel

If we were to use the existing implementations of these two interfaces provided by Retrofit and Room in our test code, the `RestaurantsViewModel` instance will communicate with the external world and our tests won't be isolated. Instead, our test code will be slow and not reliable because it will be dependent on our web REST API and a real local database.

Yet how can we make our `RestaurantsViewModel` tests isolated, fast, and reliable? We can simply make sure that instead of having Retrofit and Room provide the implementations for `RestaurantsApiService` and `RestaurantsDao`, we define dummy implementations for these interfaces that won't communicate with the real world.

These dummy implementations are often called fakes. **Fakes** are simplified implementations of the interfaces that we're looking to interact with in our tests. Such implementations mimic the behavior of the production implementations in a very simplified manner, often by returning dummy data. Fakes will only be used in our tests, so we can ensure that our testing environment is isolated.

Apart from fakes, to mimic the functionality of components that cross the boundary to the real world, you can also use mocks. **Mocks** are objects that also simulate the behavior of a real object; however, you can configure their output on the fly without any additional classes.

In this chapter, we will only focus on fakes, since most of the time, to create mocks, you need to use special mocking frameworks. Also, fakes tend to be more practical and can be reused across tests, whereas mocks tend to clutter your tests, as they bring a lot of boilerplate code.

> **Note**
>
> Whenever you have a component that interacts with the *real world*, be it a web API, local database, or other production systems, you should define an interface for it. This way, in your production code, your other components interact with a real implementation of that interface, while your tests interact with a fake implementation of it.

Let's see how we can implement fakes. In our case, `RestaurantsRepository` needs fake implementations of the `RestaurantsApiService` and `RestaurantsDao` interfaces. Let's begin with a fake implementation of the `RestaurantsApiService` interface:

1. To create a fake for the `RestaurantsApiService` interface, we must define a class that will implement the interface and simulate the functionality of a REST API. Inside the `test` package, create a Kotlin class named `FakeApiService` that implements the `RestaurantsApiService` interface and add the following code inside:

```
class FakeApiService : RestaurantsApiService {
    override suspend fun getRestaurants()
            : List<RemoteRestaurant> {
        delay(1000)
        return DummyContent.getRemoteRestaurants()
    }

    override suspend fun getRestaurant(id: Int)
            : Map<String, RemoteRestaurant> {
        TODO("Not yet implemented")
    }
}
```

Our `FakeApiService` overrides the required methods and returns some dummy restaurants from the `DummyContent` class. In the `getRestaurants()` method, we also call a coroutine-based `delay()` function of 1,000 milliseconds to better simulate an asynchronous response. Since we will not be using the `getRestaurant()` method in our tests right now, we haven't added any implementation inside it.

Going back to the dummy content that is returned, note that the `getRestaurants()` method must return a list of `RemoteRestaurant` objects, so we called a non-existent `getRemoteRestaurants()` method on the `DummyContent` class. Let's define this method up next.

2. Head back inside the main source set where our production code resides. Inside the `DummyContent` class, add a new method called `getRemoteRestaurants()` that maps the list of `Restaurant` objects returned by the `getDomainRestaurants()` method to `RemoteRestaurant` objects:

```
object DummyContent {
    fun getDomainRestaurants() = arrayListOf(…)
    fun getRemoteRestaurants() = getDomainRestaurants()
        .map {
            RemoteRestaurant(
                it.id,
                it.title,
                it.description
            )
        }
}
```

3. Now, head back inside the `test` package. We've created a fake for the `RestaurantsApiService` interface, but we must also create one fake for the `RestaurantsDao` interface that will implement the interface and simulate the functionality of a local database. Inside the `test` package, create a Kotlin class named `FakeRoomDao` that implements the `RestaurantsDao` interface and add the following code inside:

```
class FakeRoomDao : RestaurantsDao {
    private var restaurants =
                HashMap<Int, LocalRestaurant>()
    override suspend fun getAll()
            : List<LocalRestaurant> {
        delay(1000)
        return restaurants.values.toList()
    }
    override suspend fun addAll(
        restaurants: List<LocalRestaurant>
    ) {
        restaurants.forEach {
            this.restaurants[it.id] = it
        }
    }
```

```
    override suspend fun update(
        partialRestaurant: PartialLocalRestaurant
    ) {
        delay(1000)
        updateRestaurant(partialRestaurant)
    }
    override suspend fun updateAll(
        partialRestaurants: List<PartialLocalRestaurant>
    ) {
        delay(1000)
        partialRestaurants.forEach {
            updateRestaurant(it)
        }
    }
    override suspend fun getAllFavorited()
            : List<LocalRestaurant> {
        return restaurants.values.toList()
            .filter { it.isFavorite }
    }
}
```

Our `FakeRoomDao` class mimics the functionality of a real Room database, yet instead of storing restaurants in the local SQL database, it stores them in memory in the `restaurants` variable. We will not cover each method implementation of `FakeRoomDao`.

However, we will conclude that each method simulates the interaction with a persistent storage service. Additionally, as our `FakeRoomDao` simulates interaction with a real local database, each of its actions will cause a delay triggered by the pre-built suspending `delay()` function.

However, our `FakeRoom` class makes use of an `updateRestaurant()` method that we haven't defined so far. Let's do that now.

4. At the end of the body of the `FakeRoom` class, add the missing `updateRestaurant()` method that toggles the value of the `isFavorite` field:

```
class FakeRoomDao : RestaurantsDao {
    [...]
    override suspend fun getAllFavorited()
```

```
                : List<LocalRestaurant> { ... }
    private fun updateRestaurant(
        partialRestaurant: PartialLocalRestaurant
    ) {
        val restaurant =
            this.restaurants[partialRestaurant.id]
        if (restaurant != null)
            this.restaurants[partialRestaurant.id] =
                restaurant.copy(
                    isFavorite =
                        partialRestaurant.isFavorite
                )
    }
}
```

5. Now that we have finished implementing the fakes for our `RestaurantsApiService` and `RestaurantsDao` interfaces, it's time to pass them where we need them in our tests. Remember that the last missing piece was to provide fake implementations of the `RestaurantsRepository` dependencies so that our test is isolated.

   Head back inside the `RestaurantsViewModelTest` class and update the `getViewModel()` function to pass instances of the `FakeApiService` and `FakeRoomDao` classes to `RestaurantsRepository`:

```
private fun getViewModel(): RestaurantsViewModel {
    val restaurantsRepository = RestaurantsRepository(
        FakeApiService(), FakeRoomDao())
    [...]
    return RestaurantsViewModel(...)
}
```

   Now that the `getViewModel()` method is able to return an instance of `RestaurantsViewModel` that we can easily test, let's get back to our `initialState_isProduced()` test method, which currently looks like this:

```
@Test
fun initialState_isProduced() {
    val viewModel = getViewModel()
}
```

Remember that the scope of this test method is to verify that when our `RestaurantsViewModel` is initialized, it produces a correct initial state. Let's do that now.

6. First, inside the `initialState_isProduced()` test method, store the initial state inside an `initialState` variable:

```
@Test
fun initialState_isProduced() {
    val viewModel = getViewModel()
    val initialState = viewModel.state.value
}
```

7. Next, by using the built-in `assert()` function, verify whether the content of `initialState` is as expected:

```
@Test
fun initialState_isProduced() {
    val viewModel = getViewModel()
    val initialState = viewModel.state.value
    assert(
        initialState == RestaurantsScreenState(
            restaurants = emptyList(),
            isLoading = true,
            error = null)
    )
}
```

In this test method, we're asserting whether the value of the `initialState` variable is a `RestaurantsScreenState` object with a `false` `isLoading` field and an `emptyList()` value inside the `restaurants` field. Additionally, we're testing that there is no value stored inside the `error` field.

8. Now that we have defined our first test method, it's time to run the test!

Inside the **Project** tab on the left, right-click on the `RestaurantsViewModelTest` class and select **Run RestaurantsViewModelTest**. This command will run all the tests inside this class (only one in our case) directly on your local JVM, rather than running on an Android device, as our UI tests did.

If you switch to the **Run** tab, you will see that our test has failed:

```
java.lang.IllegalStateException Create breakpoint : Module with the Main dispatcher had failed to
 initialize. For tests Dispatchers.setMain from kotlinx-coroutines-test module can be used
    at kotlinx.coroutines.internal.MissingMainCoroutineDispatcher.missing(MainDispatchers.kt:113)
    at kotlinx.coroutines.internal.MissingMainCoroutineDispatcher.isDispatchNeeded(MainDispatchers
.kt:94)
```

Figure 10.6 – Observing how the test inside the RestaurantsViewModelTest class has failed

This exception is thrown because our Restaurants app handles asynchronous work with the help of coroutines, and our test code doesn't know how to interact with them.

For instance, our `RestaurantsViewModel` launches coroutines that call several suspend functions, and all of these happen on `viewModelScope`, which has the `Dispatchers.Main` dispatcher set by default:

```
@HiltViewModel
class RestaurantsViewModel @Inject constructor(...) : [...]
{
    [...]
    fun toggleFavorite(itemId: Int, oldValue: Boolean) {
        viewModelScope.launch(errorHandler) { ... }
    }
    private fun getRestaurants() {
        viewModelScope.launch(errorHandler) { ... }
    }
}
```

The main issue here is that our coroutines are launched on the Main thread on our local JVM, which can't work with the UI thread.

> **Note**
>
> The `Dispatchers.Main` dispatcher uses the Android `Looper.getMainLooper()` function to run code in the UI thread. That method is available in UI tests but not in the regular unit tests that run on our JVM.

To make our testing code compliant with the usage of coroutines, we need to use the Kotlin coroutines testing library, which will provide us with scopes and dispatchers that are dedicated to testing coroutines. If our test code is run from coroutines that are built with these dedicated scopes and dispatchers, our test will no longer fail.

Let's add the Kotlin coroutines testing library!

1. In the app-level `build.gradle` file, add a `testImplementation` dependency to the Kotlin coroutines testing package:

```
dependencies {
    [...]
    testImplementation "com.google.truth:truth:1.1.2"
    testImplementation 'org.jetbrains.kotlinx:kotlinx-
        coroutines-test:1.6.1'
}
```

2. Synchronize your project with its Gradle files by clicking on the **Sync your project with Gradle files** button in Android Studio or by pressing on the **File** menu option and then by selecting **Sync Project with Gradle Files**.
3. Head back inside the `RestaurantsViewModelTest` class and define a variable for a `StandardTestDispatcher` object and a variable for a `TestScope` object based on the previously defined dispatcher:

```
@ExperimentalCoroutinesApi
class RestaurantsViewModelTest {
    private val dispatcher = StandardTestDispatcher()
    private val scope = TestScope(dispatcher)
    @Test
    fun initialState_isProduced() {…}
    private fun getViewModel(): RestaurantsViewModel {…}
}
```

   Additionally, we've added the `@ExperimentalCoroutinesApi` annotation to the `RestaurantsViewModelTest` class, since these testing APIs are still experimental.

4. Next up, make sure that all the code from within the body of the `initialState_isProduced()` test method is run inside a test-specific coroutine. To do that, launch a coroutine that wraps this method's body by calling the `runTest()` coroutine builder on our `scope` variable of type `TestScope`:

```
@Test
fun initialState_isProduced() = scope.runTest {
    val viewModel = getViewModel()
```

```
        val initialState = viewModel.state.value
        assert(
            initialState == RestaurantsScreenState(
                restaurants = emptyList(),
                isLoading = true,
                error = null))
    }
```

5. Run the `RestaurantsViewModelTest` class. If you switch to the **Run** tab, you will see that our test has failed again, with the same exception as before. Since we wrapped the body of our test method inside a test coroutine, our test code still throws an exception, telling us that we still need to change the dispatcher of the coroutine.

   If we have another look at `RestaurantsViewModel`, we can note that both the coroutines launched with `viewModelScope` have no dispatcher set, so they're using `Dispatchers.Main` behind the scenes:

```
@HiltViewModel
class RestaurantsViewModel @Inject constructor(...) : [...]
{
    [...]
    fun toggleFavorite(itemId: Int, oldValue: Boolean) {
        viewModelScope.launch(errorHandler) { ... }
    }
    private fun getRestaurants() {
        viewModelScope.launch(errorHandler) { ... }
    }
}
```

   However, in our test, all coroutines that are launched should use `StandardTestDispatcher` defined in our test class. So, how can we pass a test dispatcher to the coroutines launched in our `RestaurantsViewModel`?

   We can inject the dispatcher inside the `RestaurantsViewModel` class by using its constructor and making it accept a `CoroutineDispatcher` object, which will be passed to all the coroutines that are launched.

   This way, in our production code, `RestaurantsViewModel` will receive and use the `Dispatchers.Main` dispatcher, and inside our test code, it will receive and use the `StandardTestDispatcher` dispatcher.

> **Note**
>
> The practice of injecting dispatchers into our coroutine-based classes is encouraged, as it allows us to have better isolation and control over the testing environment of our unit tests.

6. Head back inside the main source set where our production code resides. Inside `RestaurantsViewModel`, add a `dispatcher` constructor parameter of type `CoroutineDispatcher` and pass it to the `viewModelScope()` calls:

```
@HiltViewModel
class RestaurantsViewModel @Inject constructor(
    private val getRestaurantsUseCase: [...],
    private val toggleRestaurantsUseCase: [...],
    private val dispatcher: CoroutineDispatcher) :
        ViewModel(){
     [...]
     fun toggleFavorite(itemId: Int, oldValue: Boolean) {
         viewModelScope.launch(errorHandler
             + dispatcher) { … }
     }
     private fun getRestaurants() {
         viewModelScope.launch(errorHandler
             + dispatcher) { … }
     }
}
```

However, if we build the project now, we will get an error because Hilt doesn't know how to provide an instance of `CoroutineDispatcher` to `RestaurantsViewModel`.

To instruct Hilt on how to provide our `ViewModel` with the dispatcher it needs (that is, `Dispatchers.Main`), we must create a Hilt module.

7. Inside the `di` package, create a new class called `DispatcherModule` and add the following code that tells Hilt how to provide any `CoroutineDispatcher` dependencies with `Dispatchers.Main`:

```
@Module
@InstallIn(SingletonComponent::class)
object DispatcherModule {
```

```
    @Provides
    fun providesMainDispatcher(): CoroutineDispatcher
        = Dispatchers.Main
}
```

However, right now, Hilt will always provide `Dispatchers.Main` to any `CoroutineDispatcher` dependencies. What if we need later to obtain a dispatcher different than `Dispatchers.Main`? Let's see how we can prepare for that.

8. At the top of the body of `DispatcherModule`, define an annotation class called `MainDispatcher` annotated with the `@Qualifier` annotation:

```
@Qualifier
@Retention(AnnotationRetention.BINARY)
annotation class MainDispatcher

@Module
@InstallIn(SingletonComponent::class)
object DispatcherModule {…}
```

The `@Qualifier` annotation allows us to provide different dispatchers to the `CoroutineDispatcher` dependencies. In our case, we defined that a `@MainDispatcher` annotation will provide the `Dispatchers.Main` dispatcher.

9. Add the `@MainDispatcher` annotation to the `providesMainDispatcher()` method so that Hilt will know what dispatcher to provide when such an annotation is used on a dependency:

```
@Qualifier
@Retention(AnnotationRetention.BINARY)
annotation class MainDispatcher
@Module
@InstallIn(SingletonComponent::class)
object DispatcherModule {
    @MainDispatcher
    @Provides
    fun providesMainDispatcher(): CoroutineDispatcher
        = Dispatchers.Main
}
```

10. Then, inside `RestaurantsViewModel`, annotate the `dispatcher` parameter with the newly created `@MainDispatcher` annotation so that Hilt will provide us with the `Dispatchers.Main` dispatcher:

```
@HiltViewModel
class RestaurantsViewModel @Inject constructor(
    private val getRestaurantsUseCase: […],
    private val toggleRestaurantsUseCase: […],
    @MainDispatcher private val dispatcher:
        CoroutineDispatcher
) : ViewModel() { ... }
```

11. Now that the `RestaurantsViewModel` uses the `Dispatcher.Main` dispatcher in our production code, head back inside the `test` source set and inside the `RestaurantsViewModelTest` class, update its `getViewModel()` method by passing the `dispatcher` member field to the `RestaurantsViewModel` constructor call:

```
@ExperimentalCoroutinesApi
class RestaurantsViewModelTest {
    private val dispatcher = StandardTestDispatcher()
    private val scope = TestScope(dispatcher)
    @Test
    fun initialState_isProduced() = scope.runTest {…}
    private fun getViewModel(): RestaurantsViewModel {
        […]
        return RestaurantsViewModel(
            getInitialRestaurantsUseCase,
            toggleRestaurantUseCase,
            dispatcher)
    }
}
```

Now, in our test code, `RestaurantsViewModel` will use the `StandardTestDispatcher` dispatcher for all the launched coroutines.

12. Now, run the `RestaurantsViewModelTest` class again. If you switch to the **Run** tab, you will see that our test has now passed:

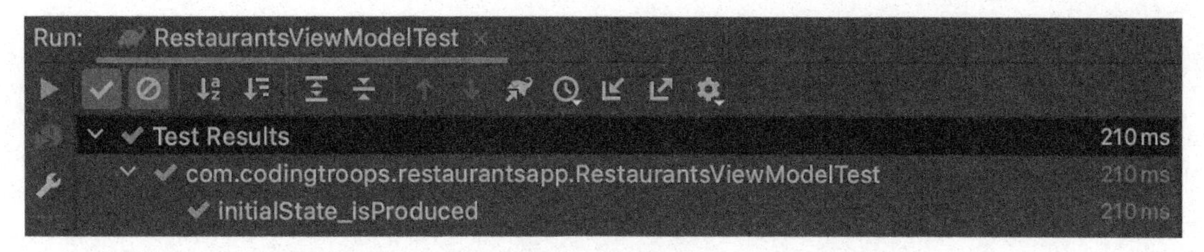

Figure 10.7 – Observing how the test inside the RestaurantsViewModelTest class has succeeded

Since our test uses the `runTest()` coroutine builder, any `delay()` calls in our fake implementations are skipped, making our test run fast, in just a few hundred milliseconds.

Now that we have tested whether our `ViewModel` produces a correct initial state, it's time to test the state that comes after this initial state – the state with content. This state is produced when the restaurants have arrived (from our data layer), so the `isLoading` field should be reset to `false`, while the `restaurants` field should contain a list of restaurants.

13. Add a new testing method inside `RestaurantsViewModelTest` called `stateWithContent_isProduced()` that asserts whether the state with restaurants is produced as expected:

```
@Test
fun stateWithContent_isProduced() = scope.runTest {
    val testVM = getViewModel()
    val currentState = testVM.state.value
    assert(
        currentState == RestaurantsScreenState(
            restaurants =
                    DummyContent.getDomainRestaurants(),
            isLoading = false,
            error = null)
    )
}
```

Since the `FakeApiService` returns the dummy list of `RemoteRestaurant` from the `DummyContent` class, it's only natural that we're expecting to get the same content in `ViewModel` but in the shape of the `Restaurant` objects – so we're asserting that the `restaurants` field of `currentState` contains the restaurants from `DummyContent`.

Unfortunately, if we run the `RestaurantsViewModelTest` class, the `stateWithContent_isProduced()` test will fail, telling us that `currentState` has the `isLoading` field's value of `true` and there are no restaurants inside the `restaurants` field.

This issue makes sense because we're basically obtaining the initial state and expecting it to be the state with content, which, in fact, comes later on. Because there are several `delay()` calls in our `FakeApiService` and `FakeRoomDao` implementations, we must allow time to pass so that `ViewModel` produces the second state – the one with restaurants. But how can we do that?

Inside a test, to immediately execute all pending tasks (such as the launched coroutine to get restaurants in our `ViewModel`) and to advance the virtual clock until after the last delay, we can call the `advanceUntilIdle()` function exposed by the coroutines test library.

14. Inside the `stateWithContent_isProduced()` test method, after `RestaurantsViewModel` is instantiated but before our assertion, add the `advanceUntilIdle()` method call:

```
@Test
fun stateWithContent_isProduced() = scope.runTest {
    val testVM = getViewModel()
    advanceUntilIdle()
    val currentState = testVM.state.value
    assert(
        currentState == RestaurantsScreenState(
            restaurants =
                DummyContent.getDomainRestaurants(),
            isLoading = false,
            error = null)
    )
}
```

When we call `advanceUntilIdle()` inside our `scope` variable of type `TestScope`, we're advancing the virtual clock of `TestCoroutineScheduler` featured in the `StandardTestDispatcher` that we've initially passed to our `scope`.

15. Now, run the `RestaurantsViewModelTest` class again. If you switch to the **Run** tab, you will see that the `stateWithContent_isProduced()` test still failed.

The main issue here is that while we're trying to advance the virtual clock of our test by leveraging the fact that our test instance of `RestaurantsViewModel` now launches its coroutines on the `StandardTestDispatcher` instance that we've passed to it, we have another class that is passing its own `CoroutineDispatcher`.

If we have a closer look inside our `RestaurantsRepository`, we can see that it's passing a production-use `Dispatchers.IO` dispatcher to all its `withContext()` calls:

```
@Singleton
class RestaurantsRepository @Inject constructor(...) {
    suspend fun toggleFavoriteRestaurant(...) =
        withContext(Dispatchers.IO) {...}
    suspend fun getRestaurants() : List<Restaurant> {
        return withContext(Dispatchers.IO) {...}
    }
    suspend fun loadRestaurants() {
        return withContext(Dispatchers.IO) {...}
    }
    private suspend fun refreshCache() {...}
}
```

Because the `RestaurantsRepository` instance that our `RestaurantsViewModel` indirectly depends on uses the `Dispatchers.IO` dispatcher and not the `StandardTestDispatcher` one, the virtual clock of our test is not advanced as expected. Let's fix this issue by injecting the dispatcher in the `RestaurantsRepository`, just as we did for `RestaurantsViewModel`.

16. However, before performing the injection, we must first define a new type of `CoroutineDispatcher` that Hilt should know how to inject – the `Dispatchers.IO` dispatcher.

    Head inside the `DispatchersModule` class and, just as we did for the `Dispatchers.Main` dispatcher, instruct Hilt on how to provide us with the `Dispatchers.IO` dispatcher:

```
@Qualifier
@Retention(AnnotationRetention.BINARY)
annotation class MainDispatcher
@Qualifier
@Retention(AnnotationRetention.BINARY)
```

```
annotation class IoDispatcher

@Module
@InstallIn(SingletonComponent::class)
object DispatcherModule {
    @MainDispatcher
    @Provides
    fun providesMainDispatcher(): CoroutineDispatcher =
        Dispatchers.Main
    @IoDispatcher
    @Provides
    fun providesIoDispatcher(): CoroutineDispatcher =
        Dispatchers.IO
}
```

17. Head back inside the main source set where our production code resides. Inside the `RestaurantsRepository` class, inject `CoroutineDispatcher`, annotate it with the `@IoDispatcher` qualifier, and then pass the injected `dispatcher` to all the `withContext()` calls:

```
@Singleton
class RestaurantsRepository @Inject constructor(
    private val restInterface: RestaurantsApiService,
    private val restaurantsDao: RestaurantsDao,
    @IoDispatcher private val dispatcher:
        CoroutineDispatcher
) {
    suspend fun toggleFavoriteRestaurant(…) =
        withContext(dispatcher) {…}
    suspend fun getRestaurants() : List<Restaurant> {
        return withContext(dispatcher) {…}
    }
    suspend fun loadRestaurants() {
        return withContext(dispatcher) {…}
    }
    private suspend fun refreshCache() {…}                }
```

18. Then, heading back inside our `test` package, inside the `RestaurantsViewModelTest` class, update the `getViewModel()` method to pass our `dispatcher` field of type `StandardTestDispatcher` to the `RestaurantsRepository` constructor:

```
private fun getViewModel(): RestaurantsViewModel {
    val restaurantsRepository = RestaurantsRepository(
        FakeApiService(),
        FakeRoomDao(),
        dispatcher)
    [...]
    return RestaurantsViewModel(
        getInitialRestaurantsUseCase,
        toggleRestaurantUseCase,
        dispatcher)
}
```

19. Now, run the `RestaurantsViewModelTest` class again. If you switch to the **Run** tab, you will see that both our tests have now passed.

> **Assignment**
>
> Try testing on your own that `RestaurantsViewModel` is correctly producing an error state. As a tip, make sure to throw an instance of the `Exception` class inside `FakeApiService` but just for this specific test method where you're verifying the error state. To achieve that, you can configure a constructor parameter in `FakeApiService` so that it can throw an exception if needed.

Now that we tested how `RestaurantsViewModel` is producing the UI state, let's briefly have a look at how we could test a business component.

Testing the functionality of a UseCase class

Aside from unit-testing the presentation layer of our application, it's very important to also test the business rules present in the app. In our Restaurants app, the business logic is encapsulated in `UseCase` classes.

Let's see say that we want to test `ToggleRestaurantUseCase`. Essentially, we want to make sure that when we execute this `UseCase` class for a specific restaurant, the business logic of negating the `isFavorite` field of the `Restaurant` is working.

In other words, if one restaurant was not marked as favorite, after executing `ToggleRestaurantUseCase` for that specific restaurant, its `isFavorite` field should become `true`. While this business logic is indeed slim, in medium to large-sized applications, such business logic can become much more complex.

Let's see how a unit test for `ToggleRestaurantUseCase` would look:

```
@ExperimentalCoroutinesApi
class ToggleRestaurantUseCaseTest {
    private val dispatcher = StandardTestDispatcher()
    private val scope = TestScope(dispatcher)
    @Test
    fun toggleRestaurant_IsUpdatingFavoriteField() =
            scope.runTest {
        // Setup useCase
        val restaurantsRepository = RestaurantsRepository(
            FakeApiService(),
            FakeRoomDao(),
            dispatcher)
        val getSortedRestaurantsUseCase =
            GetSortedRestaurantsUseCase(restaurantsRepository)
        val useCase = ToggleRestaurantUseCase(
            restaurantsRepository,
            getSortedRestaurantsUseCase)

        // Preload data
        restaurantsRepository.loadRestaurants()
        advanceUntilIdle()

        // Execute useCase
        val restaurants = DummyContent.getDomainRestaurants()
        val targetItem = restaurants[0]
        val isFavorite = targetItem.isFavorite
        val updatedRestaurants = useCase(
            targetItem.id,
            isFavorite
        )
        advanceUntilIdle()
```

```
        // Assertion
        restaurants[0] = targetItem.copy(isFavorite =
            !isFavorite)
        assert(updatedRestaurants == restaurants)
    }
}
```

This unit test is similar to the ones we wrote for `RestaurantsViewModel` in the sense that it's also using `StandardTestDispatcher` and `TestScope`, simply because the `invoke()` operator of `ToggleRestaurantUseCase` is a `suspending` function.

The structure of the test is split into three parts, delimited by the suggestive comments:

- **Setup**: In this first phase, we have constructed a `ToggleRestaurantUseCase` instance and its direct and transitive dependencies, while passing our test dispatcher to the dependencies that need it.
- **Preload data**: For `ToggleRestaurantUseCase` to be able to execute its business logic on a specific restaurant, we first had to make sure that our `RestaurantsRepository` instance had loaded the dummy restaurants. We then called `advancedUntilIdle()`, allowing any suspending (blocking) work related to obtaining and caching dummy restaurants to finish.
- **Execute Use Case**: We defined the restaurant whose `isFavorite` field we want to toggle as `targetItem`, obtained its current `isFavorite` field value, and executed `ToggleRestaurantUseCase`, storing the resultant restaurants inside the `updatedRestaurants` variable. Since this operation refreshes and re-obtains the restaurants from the fake local database, we then called `advancedUntilIdle()`, allowing any suspending work to finish.
- **Assertion**: We've first updated the dummy list we're expecting to be correct by manually toggling the first restaurant's `isFavorite` field. Finally, we asserted that the resultant `updatedRestaurants` list is the same as the one we would expect to be correct – that is, `restaurants`.

If you run this test, it should pass.

> **Assignment**
> Try testing the behaviour of other Use Case classes such as `GetSortedRestaurantsUseCase` or even classes from the data layer such as `RestaurantsRepository`.

Summary

In this chapter, we first had a look at the benefits of testing and classified tests based on different aspects. Afterward, we took a shot at testing our Compose-based UI and learned how to write UI unit tests by leveraging the power of the semantics modifiers.

Finally, we learned how to write regular – non-UI – unit tests in order to validate the core functionality of our application. In this part, we learned how to test our coroutine-based code and how important it is to inject the `CoroutineDispatcher` objects.

In the next chapter, we're steering away from the architectural side of Android development, and we will be incorporating data pagination with the help of yet another interesting library called Jetpack Paging.

Further reading

In this chapter, we've briefly covered the basics of UI and unit testing, so the core concepts taught here should give you a solid starting point. However, there are several other topics that you might need while you continue your testing adventure:

- For UI tests, we used semantics modifiers to identify UI elements from our node hierarchy. When testing Compose UI, you should also be aware of the merged and unmerged semantics tree. Learn more about this topic by reading the official docs: `https://developer.android.com/jetpack/compose/semantics`.
- With UI tests, we only scratched the surface in terms of testing APIs. Make sure to check out this official testing cheat sheet: `https://developer.android.com/jetpack/compose/testing-cheatsheet`.
- Our unit tests are based on the JUnit testing framework. To discover the power and flexibility of Junit, check out its official docs: `https://junit.org/junit4/`.
- In your coroutine-based tests, apart from the `advanceUntilIdle()` API, you can also use the `advancetimeBy()` API to fast-forward the virtual clock of the test by a certain amount. Learn more about this function from the official Coroutines docs: `https://kotlin.github.io/kotlinx.coroutines/kotlinx-coroutines-test/kotlinx.coroutines.test/-delay-controller/advance-time-by.html`.
- Your unit tests must be deterministic in the sense that every run of one test for the same revision of code should always yield the same result. Learn more about deterministic and non-deterministic tests from Martin Fowler: `https://martinfowler.com/articles/nonDeterminism.html`.

Part 3: Diving into Other Jetpack Libraries

In this final part, we will explore and utilize other important Jetpack libraries, including Paging and Lifecycle, while making use of Kotlin Flow and creating a new demo project.

This section comprises the following chapters:

11
Creating Infinite Lists with Jetpack Paging and Kotlin Flow

In the previous chapters, we built the great Restaurants App that displayed content from our own backend. However, the number of restaurants displayed in the Restaurants App was fixed, and the user was only able to browse through the few restaurants that we added to our Firebase database.

In this chapter, we will understand how pagination can help us display large datasets of items without putting pressure on our backend and without huge network bandwidth consumption. We will create the impression of an infinite list of items inside a new app that we will be working on called the Repositories App, and we will achieve that with the help of yet another Jetpack library called **Paging**.

In the first section, *Why do we need pagination?*, we will explore what data pagination is and how it can help us break large datasets into pages of data, thereby optimizing the communication between our app and the backend server. Up next, in the *Importing and exploring the Repositories App* section, we will explore a project in which we will integrate pagination: the Repositories App that displays information about GitHub repositories.

Then, in the *Using Kotlin Flow to handle streams of data* section, we will cover how paginated content can be expressed as a data stream and how Kotlin Flow is a great solution to handle such content. In the last section, *Exploring pagination with Jetpack Paging*, we will first explore the Jetpack Paging library as a solution to working with paginated content in our Android app, and then, with the help of this new library, we will integrate paging in our Repositories App to create the illusion of an infinite list of repositories.

To summarize, in this chapter, we will be covering the following sections:

- Why do we need pagination?
- Importing and exploring the Repositories App
- Using Kotlin Flow to handle streams of data
- Exploring pagination with Jetpack Paging

Before jumping in, let's set up the technical requirements for this chapter.

Technical requirements

Building Compose-based Android projects for this chapter usually requires your day-to-day tools. However, to follow along smoothly, make sure you have the following:

- The Arctic Fox 2020.3.1 version of Android Studio. You can also use a newer Android Studio version or even Canary builds but note that IDE interface and other generated code files might differ from the ones used throughout this book.
- Kotlin 1.6.10 or newer plugin installed in Android Studio
- The existing Repositories App from the GitHub repository of the book

The starting point for this chapter is represented by the Repositories App that you can find by navigating to the `Chapter_11` directory of the GitHub repository of the book, and then by importing the `repositories_app_starting_point_ch11` directory from within Android Studio. Don't worry, as we will do this together later in this chapter.

To access the solution code for this chapter, navigate to the `Chapter_11` directory and then import the `repositories_app_solution_ch11` directory from within Android Studio.

You can find the `Chapter_11` directory by following this link:

`https://github.com/PacktPublishing/Kickstart-Modern-Android-Development-with-Jetpack-and-Kotlin/tree/main/Chapter_11`

Why do we need pagination?

Let's say we have an Android application that allows you to explore GitHub repositories by displaying a list of projects. It does that by querying the GitHub **REpresentational State Transfer** (**REST**) **application programming interface** (**API**) with Retrofit and obtaining a fixed number of repositories inside the app. While the REST API serves the application with detailed information for each repository, the app only uses and displays the title and description of the repository.

> **Note**
>
> Don't confuse the Repository classes in our project architecture that abstract data logic with the GitHub repositories that are displayed in our Repositories App.

Now, let's imagine that this application retrieves and displays 20 repository elements. Because of this, the user will be able to scroll the content until the 20th element, and therefore will be able to visualize no more than 20 elements.

But what if we wanted to allow the user to explore more repositories inside our list? In the end, the purpose of the app is to browse a larger number of repositories and not just 20.

We could update the network call and request a larger list of elements from one single shot. In other words, we could refactor our app to obtain and display a list of 10,000 repositories on one occasion—that is, when the app is launched.

However, with such an approach, we can think of three main issues, as outlined here:

- **The user interface (UI) of the app could become unresponsive**—If our app tried to render all 10,000 elements, our UI would most likely freeze and become sluggish. However, this issue can be avoided by reusing or rendering only items that are visible on the screen. In fact, until now, we used the `LazyColumn` composable to render UI elements in a lazy manner (when needed), so we can conclude that this issue can be easily fixed.
- **The app would put a lot of pressure on the backend**—Imagine what would happen if every Android application client requested 10,000 database records from the backend server—these services would have to consume quite some resources to query and return so many elements.

- Such a **HyperText Transfer Protocol** (**HTTP**) request and response would cause a high network bandwidth consumption caused by the huge **JavaScript Object Notation** (**JSON**) payload that would have to be transferred. All 10,000 elements could contain a lot of fields and nested information—it's clear that having such a payload sent around between our apps and the server would be highly inefficient.

While we can easily address the first issue, we can conclude that the second and third issues are very concerning. Many real-world applications and systems face these problems, and in order to alleviate them, the concept of pagination was adopted for most client-server communication-based relationships where large datasets had to be displayed to the end user.

Pagination is a server-friendly communication approach that breaks a huge result into multiple smaller chunks. In other words, if your backend supports pagination, your application can request only a portion of data (often called a **page**) and receive a partial response, thereby allowing the transfer to be faster and more efficient on both sides.

When the application needs more results, it just requests another page, and another page, and so on. This approach is beneficial both for the app and backend service since only small portions of data are served and interpreted at a certain moment in time.

With pagination, if the user decides to visualize only a small portion of items and then switch to another app, your app would have requested only this small portion of data. Without pagination, in the same case, your backend would have served your app with the entire collection of items, while some of your users wouldn't have had a chance to see all of them. This would be a waste of resources from the perspective of your app, but especially from the perspective of your backend service. Also, only a small portion out of the huge payload sent over the internet was needed.

To implement such a pagination behavior on the UI, there are two well-known UI approaches for mobile apps, as follows:

- A fixed number of items are displayed on a screen that resembles a web page. On this page, there is a fixed amount of scrolling space because if the user wants to see new items, a button must be pressed to switch pages (often representing the number of a specific page), and then a new set of data is loaded and displayed, replacing the existing content.

  From a mobile **user experience** (**UX**) perspective, this is a poor design choice because, as opposed to monitor screens used for web pages, scrolling over contents is more natural on smaller-sized devices such as phones.

- The list of items displayed grows as the user scrolls, thereby creating the impression that the list is infinite—such an approach is often referred to as infinite scrolling. While there is no such thing as an infinite list, this approach mimics one. It starts with a few requests for the initial page/s, and as the user scrolls to see more elements, it requests more pages with more content on the fly. This approach relies heavily on scrolling and usually creates a better UX.

In this chapter, we will go for the second option—in other words, we will implement paging in an attempt to mimic the infinite list effect. Let's also try to visualize how the app could request more items as the user scrolls in the following simplified example, where **Page 1** contains only six elements:

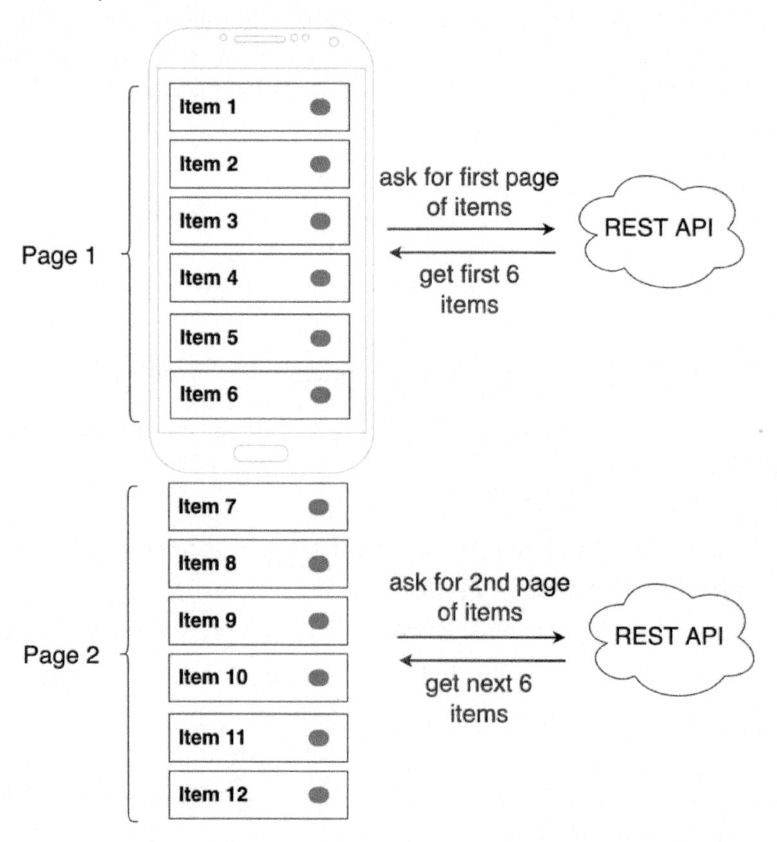

Figure 11.1 – Observing how infinite lists can be achieved with pagination

For the app to request the second page with items, the users must scroll further down, thereby informing the app about their intention of wanting to see more elements.

When the app catches on to this intention (because the user reached the end of the list), it asks for the second page with items from the backend, making the list of repositories grow and allowing the user to browse through the new content. This process repeats on and on, as the user keeps on reaching the end of the list.

Before implementing this pagination approach, let's first get to know our starting point—the GitHub Repositories App!

Importing and exploring the Repositories App

The Repositories App project is a simple application that displays a list of repositories obtained from the GitHub Search API. This project is a simplified version of a Compose-based application that incorporates only a few concepts from the previous chapters as it tries to be a good candidate for implementing pagination with the Jetpack Paging library rather than being a fully-fledged sample app that applies all the concepts taught in the book.

Nevertheless, we will see how the Repositories App follows a **Model-View-ViewModel** (**MVVM**) presentation pattern, uses Retrofit to obtain data, a `ViewModel` class to hold state and present data, coroutines for the **asynchronous** (**async**) operation of obtaining data from the server, and Compose for the UI layer.

Let's start off by importing this project into Android Studio, as follows:

1. Navigate to the GitHub repository page of the book, located at `https://github.com/PacktPublishing/Kickstart-Modern-Android-Development-with-Jetpack-and-Kotlin`.
2. Download the repository files. You can do that by pressing the **Code** button and then by selecting **Download zip**.
3. Unzip the downloaded files and remember the location where you did this.
4. Open Android Studio, press on the **File** tab option, and then select **Open**.
5. Search for the directory where you unzipped the project files. Once you have found it, navigate to the `Chapter_11` directory, select the `repositories_app_starting_point_ch11` directory, and press **Open**.
6. Run the application on your test device.

You should notice that our Repositories App displays a list of repositories, and the index of each repository item from the list is displayed on the left side, as illustrated in the following screenshot:

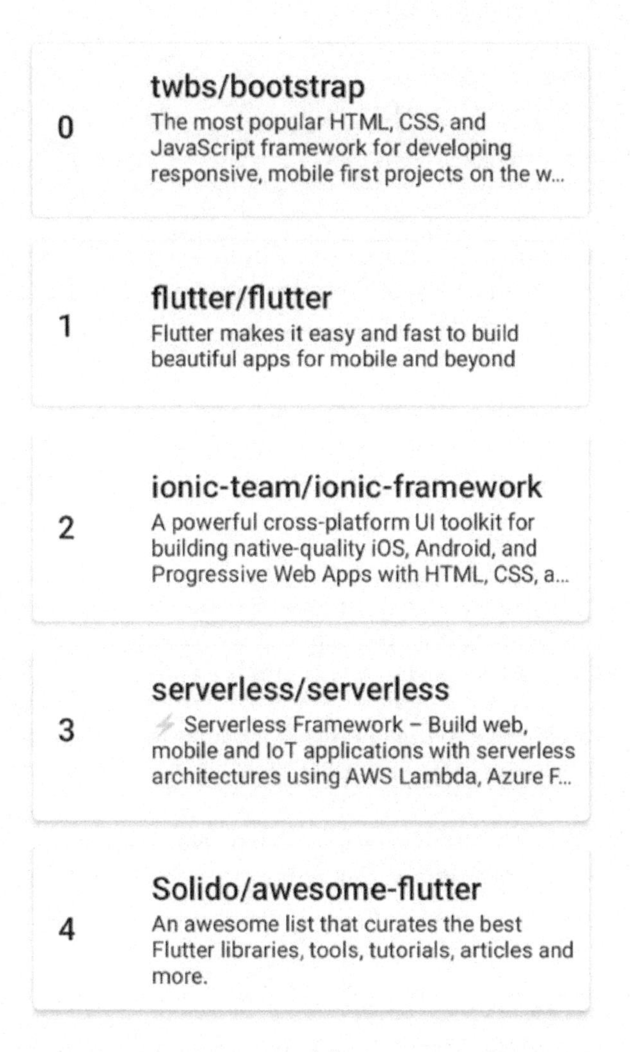

Figure 11.2 – Observing the Repositories App without pagination

If you scroll further down, you will notice that only 20 elements can be viewed. This means that our app doesn't support paging and the user can only browse through 20 repositories.

If we have a look inside the `RepositoriesApiService.kt` file, we will notice that our app instructs the REST API through the `@GET()` endpoint **Uniform Resource Locator** (**URL**) to obtain the first page of repositories while fetching only 20 items per page, as illustrated in the following code snippet:

```
interface RepositoriesApiService {
    @GET("repositories?q=mobile&sort=stars&page=1&per_page=20")
    suspend fun getRepositories(): RepositoriesResponse
}
```

If you have a look at the parameters hardcoded within the request, you will notice that our app always requests the first page of repositories. Also, because it can specify the page number, this clearly means that the backend we're accessing supports pagination, but because we always ask for page `1`, our app doesn't take advantage of it.

More specifically, when the app performs this request, it will always retrieve 20 records from the backend from the page with index `1`. Later in this chapter, we will learn how to make multiple network calls requesting different page numbers, therefore adopting pagination.

> **Note**
>
> If you're looking to build an app that supports pagination, you must first make sure that your backend supports pagination, just as the GitHub Search API does. Remember that the whole purpose of pagination is to ease the workload of the backend API and to minimize the network bandwidth consumption associated with retrieving a huge JSON payload, so if your backend doesn't support pagination, you can't implement pagination in your app.

Let's have a brief look over the response we receive from the GitHub API by navigating to the `Repository.kt` file. Basically, we get a list of `Repository` objects, and we parse the `id`, `name`, and `description` values of the repository, as illustrated in the following code snippet:

```
data class RepositoriesResponse(
    @SerializedName("items") val repos: List<Repository>
)
data class Repository(
    @SerializedName("id")
    val id: String,
    @SerializedName("full_name")
    val name: String,
```

```
    @SerializedName("description")
    val description: String)
```

As mentioned before, our app makes use of the GitHub Search API, and this can be better observed inside the `DependencyContainer.kt` class where the Retrofit `RepositoriesApiService` dependency is manually constructed, and the base URL of this API is passed. You can view the code for this process in the following snippet:

```
object DependencyContainer {
    val repositoriesRetrofitClient: RepositoriesApiService =
        Retrofit.Builder()
            .addConverterFactory(GsonConverterFactory.create())
            .baseUrl("https://api.github.com/search/")
            .build().create(RepositoriesApiService::class.java)
}
```

If you're looking to find out more about the API we're using in this chapter, head over to the official documentation of the GitHub Search API, at `https://docs.github.com/en/rest/search#search-repositories`.

Now, going back to our Repositories App, if we navigate to the `RepositoriesViewModel.kt` file, we will see that our `ViewModel` class uses the `RepositoriesApiService` dependency to obtain a list of repositories by launching a coroutine and setting the result to a Compose `State` object holding a list of `Repository` objects. The code is illustrated in the following snippet:

```
class RepositoriesViewModel(
    private val restInterface: RepositoriesApiService
    = DependencyContainer.repositoriesRetrofitClient
) : ViewModel() {
    val repositories = mutableStateOf(emptyList<Repository>())
    init {
        viewModelScope.launch {
            repositories.value =
                restInterface.getRepositories().repos
        }
    }
}
```

The approach of having a Jetpack ViewModel launch a coroutine to obtain data with the help of Retrofit is very similar to what we've done in the Restaurants App.

The UI level is also similar to the Restaurants App. If we navigate to the `MainActivity.kt` file, we can see that our `Activity` class creates a `ViewModel` instance, retrieves a Compose `State` object, obtains its value of type `List<Repository>`, and passes it to a composable function to consume it, as illustrated in the following code snippet:

```
class MainActivity : ComponentActivity() {
    override fun onCreate(savedInstanceState: Bundle?) {
        super.onCreate(savedInstanceState)
        setContent {
            RepositoriesAppTheme {
                val viewModel: RepositoriesViewModel =
                    viewModel()
                val repos = viewModel.repositories.value
                RepositoriesScreen(repos)
            }
        }
    }
}
```

The composable function that consumes the list of `Repository` objects resides inside the `RepositoriesScreen.kt` file, as illustrated in the following code snippet:

```
@Composable
fun RepositoriesScreen(repos: List<Repository>) {
    LazyColumn(
        contentPadding = PaddingValues(
            vertical = 8.dp,
            horizontal = 8.dp)
    ) {
        itemsIndexed(repos) { index, repo ->
            RepositoryItem(index, repo)
        }
    }
}
```

Just as in the Restaurants App, our screen-level composable uses the `LazyColumn` composable to optimize the way the UI renders elements in the list.

`LazyColumn` usage is important for our use case of trying to implement pagination because we don't want our UI to render thousands of UI elements. Luckily, as we know already, `LazyColumn` has us covered because it only composes and lays out visible elements on the screen.

Now, you might have noticed that the `RepositoriesScreen` composable uses the `itemsIndexed()` **domain-specific language (DSL)** function instead of the `items()` function that we used in the Restaurants App. This is because, since our app will support pagination, we want to paint the index of the element displayed on the screen to better understand where we are at right now. To get the index of the composable item visible on the screen, the `itemsIndexed()` function provides us with this information out of the box.

Finally, let's have a brief look over the structure of the `RepositoryItem` composable that displays the contents of a `Repository` object, while also rendering the index of the repository, as follows:

```
@Composable
fun RepositoryItem(index: Int, item: Repository) {
    Card(
        elevation = 4.dp,
        modifier = Modifier.padding(8.dp).height(120.dp)
    ) {
        Row(
            verticalAlignment = Alignment.CenterVertically,
            modifier = Modifier.padding(8.dp)
        ) {
            Text(
                text = index.toString(),
                style = MaterialTheme.typography.h6,
                modifier = Modifier
                    .weight(0.2f)
                    .padding(8.dp))
            Column(modifier = Modifier.weight(0.8f)) {
                Text(
                    text = item.name,
                    style = MaterialTheme.typography.h6)
                Text(
```

```
                text = item.description,
                style = MaterialTheme.typography.body2,
                overflow = TextOverflow.Ellipsis,
                maxLines = 3)
            }
        }
    }
}
```

Now that we have briefly covered the current state of the Repositories App, we can conclude that it could really use pagination to show more repositories, especially when the GitHub Search API supports that. It's time to cover another important aspect that pagination forces us to be aware of, and that's the concept of streams of data.

Using Kotlin Flow to handle streams of data

If we want our app to support pagination in the form of an infinite list, it's clear that our existing approach of having a single one-shot request to the backend that results in one UI update will not suffice.

Let's first have a look in the following code snippet at how our `RepositoriesViewModel` class requests data:

```
class RepositoriesViewModel(
    private val restInterface: RepositoriesApiService =  [...]
) : ViewModel() {
    val repositories = mutableStateOf(emptyList<Repository>())
    init {
        viewModelScope.launch {
            repositories.value =
                restInterface.getRepositories().repos
        }
    }
}
```

When the `ViewModel` is initialized, it executes the `getRepositories()` suspending function inside a coroutine. The suspending function returns a list of `Repository` objects that is passed to the `repositories` variable. This means that our `ViewModel` performs a one-shot request for data in the form of a one-time call to the suspending function—no other request is done over time to get new repositories as the user scrolls through the list. That's why our app receives a single event with data (an initial list of objects) from the backend as a single result.

We can imagine that calling a similar `getRepositories()` suspending function with the one in our app would just as well return a one-time response as its return type would be `List<Repository>`, as illustrated in the following screenshot:

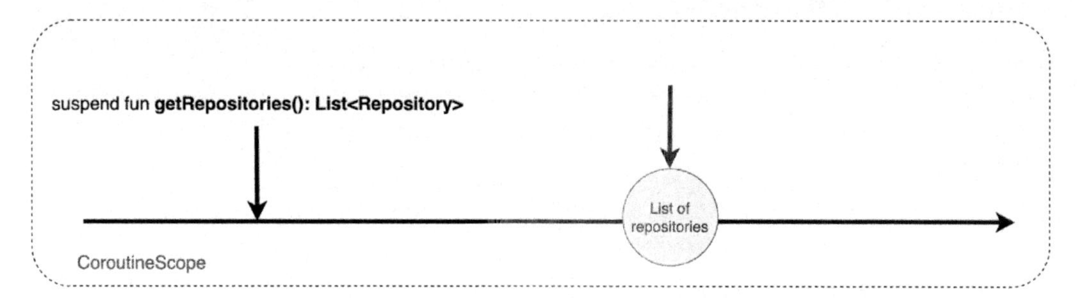

Figure 11.3 – Observing one-shot data result with suspending function

> **Note**
>
> While our `ViewModel` contains a `repositories` variable whose type is `MutableState`, meaning that it can change its value over time, we aren't going to use Compose `State` objects to observe changes coming from the data layer as this would break the responsibilities of layers. Right now, in our code, we are calling a suspending function that returns only one result or one set of data asynchronously. This result is passed to the `repositories` variable, so even though our UI state can change over time, it only receives one update.

To support an infinite list, we must somehow design our app to receive multiple results over time, just as with a stream of data. In other words, our app must request new `Repository` objects as the user scrolls, thereby receiving multiple events with data, and not just one. With every new data event coming in, our app should get a new list of `Repository` objects that now contains the newly received repositories as well.

To make our `ViewModel` receive multiple events of data in the form of a stream of data, we can use Flow. Kotlin **Flow** is a data type built on top of coroutines that exposes a stream of multiple, asynchronously computed values.

As opposed to suspending functions, which emit a single result, Flow allows us to emit multiple values sequentially over time. However, just as a suspending function emits a result in an asynchronous manner that you can later obtain from within a coroutine, Flow also emits results asynchronously, so you must observe its results from within a launched coroutine.

You could use Flow to listen for events coming from various sources; for example, you could use Flow to get location updates every time the location of the user changes. Or, you could use Flow to get sequential updates from your Room database—instead of manually querying the database every time you insert or update items, you can tell Room to return a flow that will emit updates with its most up-to-date content whenever you perform insertions, updates, and so on.

Getting back to our example with repositories, let's imagine that our `getRepositories()` function is no longer a suspending function, but instead returns a flow whose contained data is of type `List<Repository>`, as illustrated in the following screenshot:

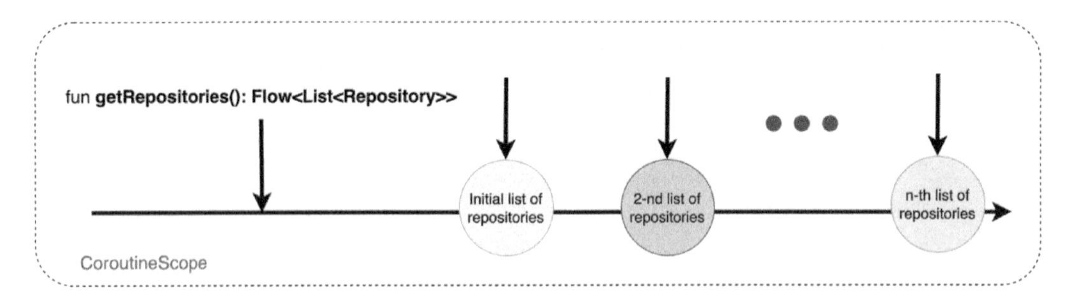

Figure 11.4 – Observing multiple results over time with Kotlin Flow

Just as the Compose `State` object holds data of a certain type (for example, `State<Int>` emits values of type `Int`), Flow also holds data of a certain type; in our previous example, that type was the data we're interested in emitting—that is, `List<Repository>`.

But how can we observe the emitted values of a flow?

Let's take the previous example where the `getRepositories()` method returned a `Flow<List<Repository>>` instance, and let's imagine that we're trying to observe its values in a UI component, as follows:

```
class SomeViewModel(…) : ViewModel() {
    init {
        viewModelScope.launch {
            getRepositories().collect { repos ->
```

```
                    // Update UI
                }
            }
        }
        [...]
}
```

Since a flow emits values asynchronously, we obtained the `Flow<List<Repository>>` instance inside a launched coroutine and then called the `.collect()` method, which in turn provided us with a block of code where we can consume the `List<Repository>` values.

As opposed to obtaining such a list from a suspending function call, it's important to remember that the values emitted by the flow change (or, at least, should change) over time. In other words, for every callback that provides us with a value stored in the `repos` variable, the content of its value of type `List<Repository>` could be different, allowing us to update the UI on every new emission.

In this section, we have explored what a flow is and how we can consume it. However, Kotlin Flow is a very complex subject; for example, we aren't going to cover the manner in which you can create a flow, or how you can modify the produced stream. If you're looking to find out more about Flow, check the official Android documentation at `https://developer.android.com/kotlin/flow`.

Let's now explore the last missing piece of the puzzle—the Paging library.

Exploring pagination with Jetpack Paging

To implement an infinite list of repositories in our Repositories App, we must find a way to request more repositories as the user scrolls through the existing list and reaches its bottom, thereby adding new elements on the fly. Instead of manually deciding when the user is approaching the bottom of the current list of repositories and then triggering a network request to get new items, we can use the Jetpack Paging library, which hides all this complexity from us.

Jetpack Paging is a library that helps us load and display pages of data from a large set of data, either through network requests or from our local data storage, thereby allowing us to save network bandwidth and optimize the usage of system resources.

In this chapter, for simplicity, we will use the Paging library to display an infinite list of repositories obtained from a network source (that is, the GitHub Search API), without involving the local cache.

> **Note**
>
> The Jetpack Paging library is now at its third implementation iteration, which is often referred to as Paging 3 or Paging v3. In this chapter, we will be using this latest version, so even though we will simply call it Jetpack Paging, we are in fact referring to Jetpack Paging 3.

The Jetpack Paging library abstracts most of the complexity associated with requesting the correct page at the correct time, depending on the scroll position of the user. Practically, it brings a lot of benefits to the table, such as the following:

- Avoidance of data request duplication—your app will request data only when needed; for example, when the user reaches the end of the list and more items must be rendered.
- Paged data is cached in memory out of the box. During the lifetime of the app process, once a page was loaded, your app will never request it again. If you cache the paginated data in a local database, then your application will not need to request a specific page for cases such as after an app restart.
- Paginated data is exposed as a data stream of the type that fits your need: Kotlin Flow, LiveData, or RxJava. As you might have guessed, we will use Flow.
- Out-of-the-box support for View System or Compose-based UI components that request data automatically when the user scrolls toward the end of the list. With such support, we don't have to know when to request new pages with data as the UI layer will trigger that for us out of the box.
- Retry and refresh capabilities triggered directly by the UI components.

Before moving to the actual integration of the Paging library, let's spend a bit of time looking over the main components part of the Paging API. To ensure paging in your application with the Jetpack Paging API, you must use the following:

- A `PagingSource` component—Defines the source of data for the paginated content. This object decides which page to request and loads it from your remote or local data source. If you're looking to have both a local and remote data source for your paginated content, you could use the built-in `RemoteMediator` API of the Paging library. Check out the *Further reading* section for more information on this.
- A `Pager` component—Based on the defined `PagingSource` component, you can construct a `Pager` object that will expose a stream of `PagingData` objects. You can configure the `Pager` object by passing a `PagingConfig` object to its constructor and specifying the page size of your data, for example.

The PagingData class is a wrapper over your paginated data containing a set of items part of the corresponding page. The PagingData object is responsible for triggering a query for a new page with items that is then forwarded to the PagingSource component.

- A dedicated UI component that supports pagination—To consume the stream of paginated content, your UI must make use of dedicated UI components that can handle paginated data. If your UI is based on the traditional View System, you could use the PagingDataAdapter component. Since our UI layer is based on Compose, LazyColumn has us covered as it knows how to consume paginated data (more on that in the next section).

To get a visual understanding of how all these components should fit, let's take the following example of a possible implementation of the Paging library inside our Repositories App:

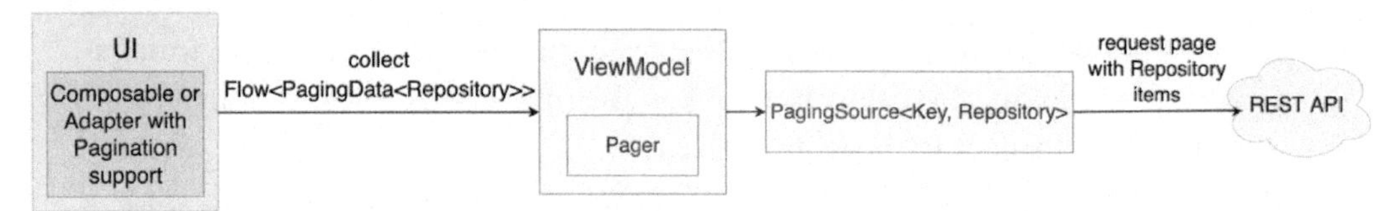

Figure 11.5 – Observing how Paging library APIs can be used in the Repositories App

At the UI level, our composable collects a flow that contains a stream of PagingData<Repository> objects. The PagingData object contains a list of Repository objects, and behind the scenes, it's responsible for forwarding requests for new pages to PagingSource, which in turn asks for new items from our REST API.

Inside ViewModel, we will have a Pager object that will use an instance of PagingSource. We will define a PagingSource object so that it knows which page to ask for and where to ask for it—that is, the GitHub Search API.

Now that we have covered the theoretical aspects of our pagination integration with Jetpack Paging, let's see which practical tasks we will be working on in this section. We will be doing the following:

- Implementing pagination with Jetpack Paging
- Implementing loading and error states plus retry functionality

Let's proceed with the first task: integrating pagination in our Repositories App.

Implementing pagination with Jetpack Paging

In this section, we will integrate paging in our Repositories App and create an infinite list of repositories with the help of Jetpack Paging. To achieve that, we will implement and add all the components described in the previous section.

Let's get cracking! Proceed as follows:

1. First, inside the app-level `build.gradle` file, in the `dependencies` block, add the Compose Gradle dependency for Jetpack Paging, as follows:

```
dependencies {
    [...]
    implementation "androidx.paging:
        paging-compose:1.0.0-alpha14"
}
```

   After updating the `build.gradle` file, make sure to sync your project with its Gradle files. You can do that by pressing on the **File** menu option and then by selecting **Sync Project with Gradle Files**.

2. Next up, let's refactor our Retrofit `RepositoriesApiService` interface by removing the hardcoded page index of `1` within the `@GET()` request annotation, and by adding a query `page` parameter of type `Int` representing the page index we're looking to acquire. The code is illustrated in the following snippet:

```
interface RepositoriesApiService {
    @GET("repositories?q=mobile&sort=stars&per_page=20")
    suspend fun getRepositories(@Query("page") page:Int):
        RepositoriesResponse
}
```

   Before these changes, we were always obtaining the first page of repository results. Now, we have updated our network request to harvest the power of paginated REST APIs—that is, the capability to ask for a different page index based on the scrolling position of the user.

   To achieve this, we used the Retrofit `@Query()` annotation, which basically will insert the value of the `page` parameter we have defined in the `getRepositories()` method into the `GET` request. As the GitHub Search API expects a `"page"` query key in the URL request, we have passed the `"page"` key to the `@Query()` annotation.

3. It's now time to build a `PagingSource` component that will request new pages through our `RepositoriesApiService` dependency and will keep track of which page to ask for, while also keeping an in-memory cache of the previously retrieved pages.

   Inside the root package of the app, create a new class named `RepositoriesPagingSource` and paste the following code below it:

```
class RepositoriesPagingSource(
    private val restInterface: RepositoriesApiService
    = DependencyContainer.repositoriesRetrofitClient,
) : PagingSource<Int, Repository>() {
    override suspend fun load(params: LoadParams<Int>)
            : LoadResult<Int, Repository> {
    }

    override fun getRefreshKey(
        state: PagingState<Int, Repository>,
    ): Int? {
        return null
    }
}
```

   Let's break down the code we have just added. This component is doing the following:

   - It is in charge of requesting new pages, so it has a dependency on `RepositoriesApiService` as the `restInterface` constructor field.
   - It is a `PagingSource` component, so it inherits from the `PagingSource` class while also defining the following:
     - A key as the type of the page index—in our case, the GitHub Search API requires an integer representing the index of the page, so we set the key as `Int`.
     - Type of the loaded data—in our case, `Repository` objects.

- Implementing the following two mandatory functions:
    - The `load()` suspending function, which is called automatically by the Paging library and should fetch more items asynchronously. This method takes in a `LoadParams` object that keeps track of information such as what is the key (index) of the page that must be requested, or the initial load size of items. Also, this method returns a `LoadResult` object indicating if a specific query result was successful or has failed.
    - The `getRefreshKey()` function, which is called to obtain and return the most recent page key in case of a refresh event so that the user is returned to the latest known page (and not the first one). A refresh event can come from a variety of sources, such as a manual UI refresh triggered by the user, a database cache invalidation event, system events, and so on.

For simplicity, and also because we will not implement refresh capabilities, we will skip implementing the `getRefreshKey()` method, so we just returned `null` inside the body of this method. However, if you're looking to also support such behavior, check out the *Further reading* section where additional resources are listed to help you provide an implementation for this method.

4. Now that we have covered the purpose of the two mandatory methods, let's implement the one we're really interested in—the `load()` function.

This method should return a `LoadResult` object, so first, add a `try-catch` block, and inside the `catch` block, return an `Error()` instance of `LoadResult` by passing the `Exception` object that was caught, as illustrated in the following code snippet:

```
class RepositoriesPagingSource(…) : […] {
    override suspend fun load(params: LoadParams<Int>)
    : LoadResult<Int, Repository> {
        try {
        } catch (e: Exception) {
            return LoadResult.Error(e)
        }
    }
    override fun getRefreshKey(…): Int? { … }
}
```

With this approach, if the request for a new page fails, we let the Paging library know that an error event occurred by returning the `LoadResult.Error` object.

5. Next up, inside the `try` block, we must first obtain and store the next page we're interested in. Store the index of the next page inside the `nextPage` variable, as follows:

```
class RepositoriesPagingSource(…) : […] {
    override suspend fun load(params: LoadParams<Int>)
    : LoadResult<Int, Repository> {
        try {
            val nextPage = params.key ?: 1
        } catch (e: Exception) {
            return LoadResult.Error(e)
        }
    }
    override fun getRefreshKey(…): Int? { … }
}
```

We obtained the index for the next page by tapping into the `params` parameter and getting its `key` field—this field will always give us the index of the next page that must be loaded. If this is the first time a page is requested, the `key` field will be `null`, so we default to the value of `1` in that case.

6. Since we now know the index of the next page of repositories that we need, let's query our REST API for that specific page by calling the `getRepositories()` method of `restInterface` and by passing in the newly defined `nextPage` parameter, as follows:

```
class RepositoriesPagingSource(…) : […] {
    override suspend fun load(params: LoadParams<Int>)
            : LoadResult<Int, Repository> {
        try {
            val nextPage = params.key ?: 1
            val repos = restInterface
                .getRepositories(nextPage).repos
        } catch (e: Exception) {
            return LoadResult.Error(e)
        }
    }
    override fun getRefreshKey(…): Int? { … }
}
```

In this step, we also store a list of `Repository` objects from within the response inside the `reposResponse` variable.

7. Next up, we must return a `LoadResult` object, as the request to our REST API is successful at this point. Let's instantiate and return a `LoadResult.Page` object, as follows:

```
class RepositoriesPagingSource(...) : [...] {
    override suspend fun load(params: LoadParams<Int>)
            : [...] {
        try {
            val nextPage = params.key ?: 1
            val repos = restInterface
                .getRepositories(nextPage).repos
            return LoadResult.Page(
                data = repos,
                prevKey = if (nextPage == 1) null
                          else nextPage - 1,
                nextKey = nextPage + 1)
        } catch (e: Exception) {
            return LoadResult.Error(e)
        }
    }
    override fun getRefreshKey(...): Int? { ... }
}
```

We had to pass the following to the `LoadResult.Page()` constructor:

- A list of `Repository` objects from the newly requested page to the `data` parameter.
- The previous key of the newly requested page to the `prevKey` parameter. This key is important if, for some reason, the previous pages are invalidated and must be reloaded when the user starts scrolling up. Most of the time, we would deduct `1` from the `nextPage` value, yet we also made sure that if we had just requested the first page (the value of `nextPage` would be `1`), we would pass `null` to the `prevKey` parameter.
- The next key after `nextPage` to the `nextKey` parameter. This is a simple one as we have just added `1` to the value of `nextPage`.

Now that we finished the `PagingSource` implementation, it's time to build the `Pager` component and get a stream of paginated data.

8. Inside `RepositoriesViewModel`, replace the `RepositoriesApiService` dependency with the newly created `RepositoriesPagingSource` class, as follows:

```
class RepositoriesViewModel(
    private val reposPagingSource:
    RepositoriesPagingSource = RepositoriesPagingSource()
) : ViewModel() {
}
```

At the same time, we make sure to remove any existing implementation inside the `RepositoriesViewModel`, leaving it blank for the upcoming step.

9. Still inside the `RepositoriesViewModel`, define a `repositories` variable that will hold our flow of paginated data, like this:

```
import kotlinx.coroutines.flow.Flow

class RepositoriesViewModel(
    private val reposPagingSource:
    RepositoriesPagingSource = RepositoriesPagingSource()
) : ViewModel() {
    val repositories: Flow<PagingData<Repository>>
}
```

The paginated content with `Repository` items is held within a `PagingData` container, making our stream of data to be of type `Flow<PagingData<Repository>>`.

Now, we must instantiate our `repositories` variable. However, creating a flow is not trivial, especially when the data (the list of repositories) must grow as the user scrolls. The Paging library has us covered, as it will hide this complexity from us and will provide us with a flow that emits data as we would expect it to: when the user scrolls to the end of the list, new requests are made to the backend, and new `Repository` objects are appended to the list.

10. As the first step to obtaining our flow of paginated data, we must create an instance of the `Pager` class based on the previously created `PagingSource` object, like so:

```
class RepositoriesViewModel(
    private val reposPagingSource:
    RepositoriesPagingSource = RepositoriesPagingSource()
) : ViewModel() {
    val repositories: Flow<PagingData<Repository>> =
        Pager(
            config = PagingConfig(pageSize = 20),
            pagingSourceFactory = {
                reposPagingSource
            })
}
```

To create an instance of a `Pager`, we called the `Pager()` constructor and passed the following:

- A `PagingConfig` object with a `pageSize` value of `20` (to match this value with the number of repositories we're requesting from the backend) to the `config` parameter.
- The `reposPagingSource` instance of type `RepositoriesPagingSource` to the `pagingSourceFactory` parameter. By doing so, the Paging library will know which `PagingSource` object to query for new pages.

11. Finally, to obtain a flow with data from the newly created `Pager` instance, we must simply access the `flow` field exposed by the resulted `Pager` instance, as follows:

```
class RepositoriesViewModel(...) : ViewModel() {
    val repositories: Flow<PagingData<Repository>> =
        Pager(
            config = PagingConfig(pageSize = 20),
            pagingSourceFactory = {
                reposPagingSource
            }).flow.cachedIn(viewModelScope)
}
```

On the resulting flow, we also called the `cachedIn()` extension function that makes sure that the stream of data is kept alive as long as the passed `CoroutineScope` object is alive and then returns back the same flow it's called upon. Since we wanted the paginated content to be cached as long as the `ViewModel` is kept in memory, we passed the `viewModelScope` scope to this extension function. This makes sure that the flow is also preserved upon events where the `ViewModel` survives—for example, configuration change.

12. Now, we must obtain the flow in our Compose-based UI, so inside the `RepositoriesAppTheme()` composable call from within `MainActivity`, replace the `repos` variable with the `reposFlow` variable that holds a reference to the `repositories` flow variable of the `ViewModel`, as follows:

```
class MainActivity : ComponentActivity() {
    override fun onCreate(savedInstanceState: Bundle?) {
        super.onCreate(savedInstanceState)
        setContent {
            RepositoriesAppTheme {
                val viewModel: RepositoriesViewModel =
                    viewModel()
                val reposFlow = viewModel.repositories
                RepositoriesScreen()
            }
        }
    }
}
```

13. Next up, we must use a special collection function (similar to the `collect()` function used in the previous section) that can consume and remember the paginated data from within `reposFlow` in the context of Compose.

    Declare a new variable called `lazyRepoItems` and instantiate it with the result returned from the `collectAsLazyPagingItems()` call on `reposFlow`, as follows:

```
class MainActivity : ComponentActivity() {
    override fun onCreate(savedInstanceState: Bundle?) {
        super.onCreate(savedInstanceState)
        setContent {
            RepositoriesAppTheme {
```

```
                    val viewModel: [...] = viewModel()
                    val reposFlow = viewModel.repositories
                    val lazyRepoItems
                        : LazyPagingItems<Repository> =
                        reposFlow.collectAsLazyPagingItems()
                    RepositoriesScreen(lazyRepoItems)
                }
            }
        }
}
```

The `collectAsLazyPagingItems()` function returned a `LazyPagingItems` object filled with `Repository` objects. The `LazyPagingItems` object is responsible for accessing `Repository` objects from the flow so that they can be consumed by our `LazyColumn` component later on—that's why, in the end, we passed `lazyRepoItems` to the `RepositoriesScreen()` composable.

14. Moving to the last piece of the puzzle, the `RepositoriesScreen()` composable, make sure that it accepts the `LazyPagingItems` object returned by our flow by adding the `repos` parameter, as follows:

```
@Composable
fun RepositoriesScreen(
    repos: LazyPagingItems<Repository>
) {
    LazyColumn (...) {
    }
}
```

Also, while you're at this step, remove all the code inside the DSL `content` block exposed by `LazyColumn` as we will re-add it in a different structure in the next step.

15. Finally, still inside `RepositoriesScreen()`, pass the `repos` input parameter to another `itemsIndexed()` DSL function that accepts `LazyPagingItems`, as follows:

```
@Composable
fun RepositoriesScreen(
    repos: LazyPagingItems<Repository>
) {
    LazyColumn(...) {
```

```
            itemsIndexed(repos) { index, repo ->
                if (repo != null) {
                    RepositoryItem(index, repo)
                }
            }
        }
    }
```

The `LazyColumn` API knows how to consume paginated data and how to report back to our instances of `Pager` and `PagingSource` when a new page should be loaded, and that's why we made use of an overloaded variant of the `itemsIndexed()` DSL function that accepts `LazyPagingItems` as content.

Also, because the returned `repo` value can be `null`, we added a null check before passing it to our `RepositoryItem()` composable.

16. Finally, build and run the application. Try to scroll to the bottom of the repositories list. This should trigger a request to get new items, and therefore you should be able to scroll and browse through an *endless* list of repositories.

> **Note**
> If you make too many requests to the GitHub Search API, you might be temporarily limited, and the application will stop loading new items and throw an error. To make our application express such an event, we will learn how to display error states, up next.

Next up, let's improve the UI and UX of our application by adding loading and error states in the context of an infinite list.

Implementing loading and error states plus retry functionality

While our application now features an infinite list that the user can scroll through, it doesn't express any sort of loading or error state. The good news is that the Paging library tells us exactly when loading states or error states must be shown.

However, before jumping into the actual implementation, we should first cover the possible loading states and error states that emerge from interacting with an app that features pagination. Luckily, all these cases are already covered by the Paging API.

While the `LazyPagingItems` API provides us with several `LoadState` objects, the most common ones—and the ones we will need in this section—are the `refresh` and `append` types, as explained in more detail here:

- The `LoadState.refresh` instance of `LoadState` represents initial states that occur after the first request of paginated items or after a refresh event. The two values that we're interested in for this object are these:
    - `LoadState.Loading` — This state means that the app is expressing the initial loading status. When this status arrives for the first time after an app launch, no content would be painted on the screen at that point.
    - `LoadState.Error` — This state means that the app is expressing the initial error status. Just as with the previous state, if this status arrives for the first time after an app launch, no content is present.
- The `LoadState.append` instance of `LoadState` represents states that occur at the end of a subsequent request of paginated items. The two values we're interested in for this object are similar to type `refresh` but have different significance, as outlined here:
    - `LoadState.Loading` — This state means that the app is in a loading status at the end of a subsequent request for a page with repositories; in other words, the app has requested another page with repositories and it's waiting for the results to arrive. At this point, there should be content rendered from the previous pages.
    - `LoadState.Error` — This state means that the app reached an error status after a subsequent request for a page with repositories. In other words, the app has requested another page with repositories but the request has failed. Just as with the previous state, there should be content rendered from the previous pages.

Let's listen for these states in our app and start with type `LoadState.refresh`, as follows:

1. Inside the `RepositoriesScreen()` composable, below the `itemsIndexed()` call, store the `refresh` load state instance inside the `refreshLoadstate` variable, as follows:

```
@Composable
fun RepositoriesScreen(
    repos: LazyPagingItems<Repository>
) {
    LazyColumn(...) {
```

```
            itemsIndexed(repos) { index, repo ->
                if (repo != null) {
                    RepositoryItem(index, repo)
                }
            }
            val refreshLoadState = repos.loadState.refresh
        }
    }
```

Every time this refreshes, `LoadState` will change; the values within `refreshLoadState` will be the latest ones and will correspond to the page where they occurred.

2. Next up, create a `when` expression and verify whether `refreshLoadState` is of type `LoadState.Loading`, and if it is, inside a new `item()` call, pass a `LoadingItem()` composable that we will define in a bit. The code is illustrated in the following snippet:

```
@Composable
fun RepositoriesScreen(
    repos: LazyPagingItems<Repository>
) {
    LazyColumn(…) {
        itemsIndexed(repos) { index, repo ->
            if (repo != null) {
                RepositoryItem(index, repo)
            }
        }
        val refreshLoadState = repos.loadState.refresh
        when {
            refreshLoadState is LoadState.Loading -> {
                item {
                    LoadingItem(
                        Modifier.fillParentMaxSize())
                }
            }
        }
    }
}
```

Since we are adding another `item()` call below the `itemsIndexed()` DSL call, we are actually adding another composable below the list of composables from the `itemsIndexed()` call. However, since `refreshLoadState` can be of type `LoadState.Loading` on the first request for a page of items, this means that the screen is empty at this time, so we also passed a `fillParentMaxSize` modifier to the `LoadingItem()` composable, thus making sure that this composable will take up the entire size of the screen.

3. Next up, at the bottom of the `RepositoriesScreen.kt` file, let's quickly define a `LoadingItem()` function that will feature a `CirculatorProgressIndicator()` composable, as follows:

```
@Composable
fun LoadingItem(
    modifier: Modifier = Modifier
) {
    Column(
        modifier = modifier.padding(24.dp),
        verticalArrangement = Arrangement.Center,
        horizontalAlignment =
            Alignment.CenterHorizontally
    ) { CircularProgressIndicator() }
}
```

4. Now, run the app, and notice how the progress indicator animation is running before the first page of repositories is loaded and how it is occupying the entire screen, as illustrated in the following screenshot:

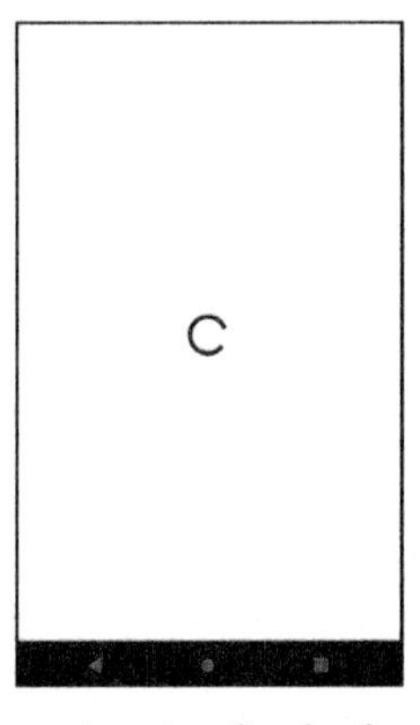

Figure 11.6 – Adding a loading animation for the first request of paginated content

5. Now, let's cover the case where `refreshLoadState` is of type `Loadstate.Error`. Back inside the `LazyColumn` component of the `RepositoriesScreen()` composable, below the first `when` branch, add another check for the state to be `LoadState.Loading`—and if that's the case, add an `ErrorItem()` composable that we will define in a bit. The code that you must add is illustrated in the following snippet:

```
@Composable
fun RepositoriesScreen(
    repos: LazyPagingItems<Repository>
) {
    LazyColumn(...) {
        itemsIndexed(repos) { index, repo -> [...] }
        val refreshLoadState = repos.loadState.refresh
        when {
            refreshLoadState is LoadState.Loading -> {
                item { LoadingItem(...) }
            }
            refreshLoadState is LoadState.Error -> {
                val error = refreshLoadState.error
                item {
                    ErrorItem(
                        message = error.localizedMessage
                            ?: "",
                        modifier =
                            Modifier.fillParentMaxSize()
                    )
                }
            }
        }
    }
}
```

The `ErrorItem()` composable requires an error message to display, so we stored the `Throwable` object from `LoadState` in the `error` variable and passed its `localizedMessage` value to the `message` parameter of the composable.

Similar to the `LoadState.Loading` case from before, we are adding another `item()` call below the `itemsIndexed()` DSL call, so we are actually adding another composable below the list of composables from the `itemsIndexed()` call. Also, since `refreshLoadState` can be of type `LoadState.Error` on the request for the first page of items, this means that the screen is empty at this time, so we also passed a `fillParentMaxSize` modifier to the `ErrorItem()` composable, thus making sure that this composable is taking up the entire size of the screen.

6. Next up, at the bottom of the `RepositoriesScreen.kt` file, let's quickly define an `ErrorItem()` function that will feature a `Text()` composable displaying a red error message, as follows:

```
@Composable
fun ErrorItem(
    message: String,
    modifier: Modifier = Modifier) {
    Row(
        modifier = modifier.padding(16.dp),
        horizontalArrangement =
            Arrangement.SpaceBetween,
        verticalAlignment = Alignment.CenterVertically
    ) {
        Text(
            text = message,
            maxLines = 2,
            modifier = Modifier.weight(1f),
            style = MaterialTheme.typography.h6,
            color = Color.Red)
    }
}
```

7. To mimic an error state, run the app on your emulator or physical device without an internet connection, and you should see a similar error occupying the entire screen, as illustrated in the following screenshot:

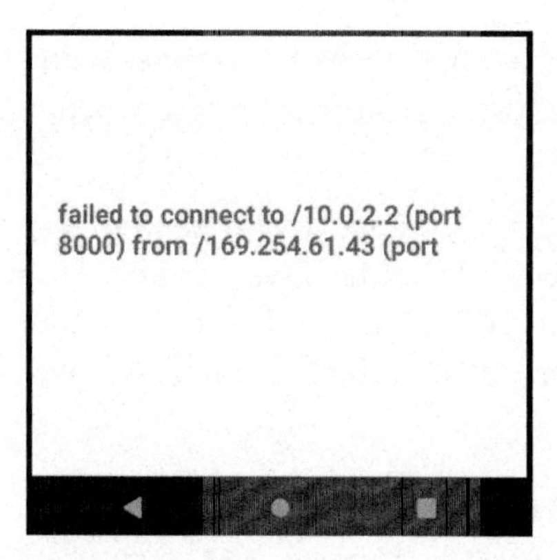
failed to connect to /10.0.2.2 (port
8000) from /169.254.61.43 (port

Figure 11.7 – Adding an error message for the first request of paginated content

Note that the error message could be different depending on the circumstances of the error scenario that you have created.

Before moving on to the append type of `LoadState`, let's briefly cover the retry functionality that is provided out of the box by the Paging library. In other words, we want to give the user the option to retry obtaining the data in case something went wrong, such as with our forced-error case of disconnecting the test device from the internet.

Let's do that next.

8. Refactor the `ErrorItem()` composable to accept an `onClick()` function parameter that will be triggered by the `onClick` event caused by the press of a new retry `Button()` composable, as follows:

```
@Composable
fun ErrorItem(
    message: String,
    modifier: Modifier = Modifier,
    onClick: () -> Unit) {
    Row(...) {
        Text(...)
        Button(
            onClick = onClick,
            modifier = Modifier.padding(8.dp)
        ) { Text(text = "Try again") }
    }
}
```

Also, inside the `Row()` composable that was displaying the error message, we have now added a `Button()` composable that when pressed, forwards the event to its caller.

9. Then, back inside the `LazyColumn` component of `RepositoriesScreen()`, find the case where `LoadState` is of type `LoadState.Error` and implement the `onClick` parameter of the `ErrorItem()` composable that will now trigger a reload. The code is illustrated in the following snippet:

```
@Composable
fun RepositoriesScreen(
    repos: LazyPagingItems<Repository>
) {
    LazyColumn(...) {
        itemsIndexed(repos) { index, repo -> [...] }
        val refreshLoadState = repos.loadState.refresh
        when {
            refreshLoadState is LoadState.Loading -> {
                ...
            }
            refreshLoadState is LoadState.Error -> {
                val error = refreshLoadState.error
                item {
                    ErrorItem(
                        message = error.localizedMessage
                            ?: "",
                        modifier =
                           Modifier.fillParentMaxSize(),
                        onClick = { repos.retry() })
                }
            }
        }
    }
}
```

To trigger a reload, we called the `retry()` function provided by our `LazyPagingItems` instance. Behind the scenes, when the `retry()` function is called, the Paging library notifies `PagingSource` to request the problematic page again—in this case, for us, the first page with repositories.

10. Run the app on your emulator or physical device without an internet connection. You should now see the error state occupying the entire screen containing the error message, but also a retry button. The following screenshot provides a depiction of this:

failed to connect to /
10.0.2.2 (port 8000)

Try again

Figure 11.8 – Adding error message and retry button for the first request of paginated content

Don't press the retry button just yet.

11. Reconnect your device to the internet and then press the retry button. As an effect of this action, the content should now load successfully.

Now that we have covered the possible `LoadState` values for the `refresh` state, it's time to also cover the values for the `append` state. As we previously stated, type `LoadState.append` represents states that occur at the end of a subsequent request of paginated items.

The possible states we're interested in for this scenario are the `LoadState.Loading` state—meaning the user has scrolled toward the end of the list and the app is waiting for another page with repositories—and the `LoadState.Error` state—meaning that the user has scrolled toward the end of the list but the request to get a new page with repositories has failed.

12. Inside the block of code exposed by the `itemsIndexed()` call from within the `RepositoriesScreen()` composable, just as we did with the `refresh` state, store the `append` state inside a new `appendLoadState` variable, and then add two corresponding branches inside the `when` expression treating the `LoadState.Loading` and the `LoadState.Error` cases. The code is illustrated in the following snippet:

```
@Composable
fun RepositoriesScreen(
    repos: LazyPagingItems<Repository>
) {
    LazyColumn(...) {
        itemsIndexed(repos) { [...] }
        val refreshLoadState = repos.loadState.refresh
        val appendLoadState = repos.loadState.append
        when {
            refreshLoadState is LoadState.Loading -> {
                item {
```

```
                    LoadingItem(...)
                }
            }
            refreshLoadState is LoadState.Error -> {
                val error = refreshLoadState.error
                item {
                    ErrorItem(
                        message = error.localizedMessage
                            ?: "",
                        modifier = ...,
                        onClick = { repos.retry() })
                }
            }
            appendLoadState is LoadState.Loading -> {
                item {
                    LoadingItem(
                        Modifier.fillMaxWidth())
                }
            }
            appendLoadState is LoadState.Error -> {
                val error = appendLoadState.error
                item {
                    ErrorItem(
                        message = error.localizedMessage
                            ?: "",
                        onClick = { repos.retry() })
                }
            }
        }
    }
}
```

The way we treated the possible values of `appendLoadState` is very similar to how we treated the possible values of `refreshLoadState`. However, the notable difference is that `appendLoadState` state values occur when the app has already loaded some pages and the user has scrolled toward the end of our list, meaning that our app is either waiting for a new page with repositories or failed to load it.

That's why, in the `LoadState.Loading` case, we have passed the `Modifier.fillMaxWidth()` modifier to the `LoadingItem()` composable, therefore making sure that the loading indicator item appears at the bottom of the list as a list element. In other words, the loading element will take only the available width and it will not cover the entire screen like we did when `refreshLoadState` was of type `LoadState.Loading`.

Similarly, for the `LoadState.Error` case, we passed the `Modifier.fillMaxWidth()` modifier to the `ErrorItem()` composable, therefore making sure that the error element appears as a list element and doesn't cover the entire screen like we did when `refreshLoadState` was of type `LoadState.Error`.

Let's see these two cases in practice, and let's start with the case when our `appendLoadState` instance has a value of `LoadState.Loading`.

13. First, run the app while your test device is connected to the internet. If you scroll down to the bottom of the list with repositories, you should see the loading indicator animation displayed until a new page with repositories is loaded, as illustrated in the following screenshot:

Figure 11.9 – Adding a loading animation for a subsequent request of paginated content

Unlike the loading indicator that is shown initially, this indicator appears as an item within the list, thereby indicating that the app is waiting for a new page with repositories.

> **Note**
>
> If your network speed is very fast, you might miss the loading spinner as you are scrolling through new pages. To simulate a slower connection, you can change the network speed of your Android emulator by going into **AVD Manager**, pressing the **Edit** button of your emulator, and then selecting **Show Advanced Settings**. Inside this menu, you can slow down the internet speed of your emulator so that you can see the loading spinner.

Now, let's test the case when our `appendLoadState` instance is of type `LoadState.Error`.

14. First, run the app while your test device is connected to the internet.
15. Then, disconnect your test device from the internet and scroll down to the bottom of the list with repositories. Initially, you might see the loading indicator, yet after a short period of time, you should see the error element appearing at the bottom of the list, as illustrated in the following screenshot:

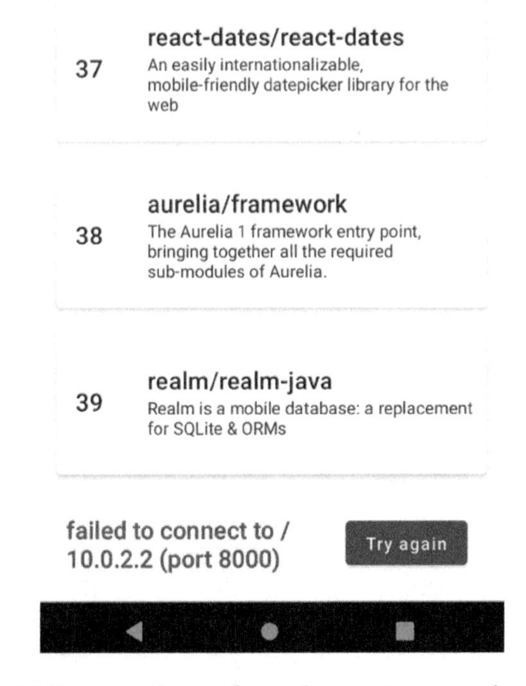

Figure 11.10 – Adding error element for a subsequent request of paginated content

Unlike the error message that is shown initially, this error element appears as an item in the list, thereby indicating that the app has failed to obtain the next page with repositories.

16. Optionally, you can reconnect your device to the internet and press the retry button—the new page with repositories should now load, so you can continue browsing and scrolling for more items.

Summary

In this chapter, we first understood what pagination is and how pagination can be used to expose large datasets of items to users in a more efficient manner.

Then, we got to meet the Repositories App, a simple Android project where a fixed amount of GitHub repositories was displayed. At that point, we took the decision that users should be able to browse through a huge number of repositories that the GitHub Search API is exposing, so the only solution for that was to integrate paging within our app.

However, we then realized that we needed to first understand the concept of data streams in the context of pagination, so we learned a few things about Kotlin Flow and how it can be a simple solution to consume paginated content.

Then, we explored how the Jetpack Paging library is an elegant solution to adding pagination to our apps, culminating with the practical task of integrating paging in our Repositories App with the help of this library. Finally, we transformed our Repositories App into a modern application that creates the illusion of an infinite list of repositories, with initial and intermediary loading or error states, as well as retry functionality.

In the next chapter, we will tackle yet another Jetpack subject—Lifecycle components!

Further reading

In this chapter, we briefly covered how you can integrate Jetpack Paging into an Android application. However, in the context of pagination and Jetpack Paging, there are a couple of more advanced topics that you might end up wondering about, as outlined here:

- **Having both a local and remote source for paginated content**—For such a case, you will need a component that manages communication between the two data sources. For this task, you could use the built-in `RemoteMediator` API of the Paging library. You can learn more about it from its official documentation at `https://developer.android.com/topic/libraries/architecture/paging/v3-network-db#implement-remotemediator`.

- **Adding support for content refresh or invalidation**—If you're looking to support pull-to-refresh functionality, or you're interested in making sure that the user is returned to the appropriate page upon various system events that could restart the paginated content, you need to obtain the refresh keys of the `PagingSource` component. Learn more about this from the official documentation at `https://developer.android.com/topic/libraries/architecture/paging/v3-migration#refresh-keys`.

As you know by now, testing is very important. In the context of paging, testing can get a little trickier. If you're interested in learning how to test your paging app, check out the official documentation at `https://developer.android.com/topic/libraries/architecture/paging/test`.

12
Exploring the Jetpack Lifecycle Components

In this chapter, we're adding a countdown timer component to our Repositories app from *Chapter 11*, *Creating Infinite Lists with Jetpack Paging and Kotlin Flow*, while also exploring the Jetpack Lifecycle components.

In the first section, *Introducing the Jetpack Lifecycle components*, we want to explore how the lifecycle events and states are tied to Android components such as `Activity` or `Fragment`, and then how predefined components from the `Lifecycle` package can react to them.

Next, in the *Adding a countdown component in the Repositories app* section, we will be creating and adding a countdown timer component to the Repositories app. When a 60-second countdown finishes, we will award users with a fictional prize.

However, we will want the countdown to run as long as the timer is visible on the screen; otherwise, users could cheat by minimizing the application and having the countdown run in background. In the *Creating your own lifecycle-aware component* section, we will prevent users from cheating by making our timer component aware of the different lifecycle events and states that our Android components traverse.

In the *Making our countdown component aware of the lifecycle of composables* section, we will realize that users can also cheat on the countdown contest by scrolling and hiding the timer countdown UI element. To prevent them from doing that, we will also make sure that our countdown component knows how to react to composition cycles that our Compose UI features.

To summarize, in this chapter, we will be covering the following sections:

- Introducing the Jetpack Lifecycle components
- Adding a countdown component in the Repositories app
- Creating your own lifecycle-aware component
- Making our countdown component aware of the lifecycle of composables

Before jumping in, let's set up the technical requirements for this chapter.

Technical requirements

Building Compose-based Android projects for this chapter usually requires your day-to-day tools. However, to follow along with this chapter smoothly, make sure that you also have the following:

- The Arctic Fox 2020.3.1 version of Android Studio. You can also use a newer Android Studio version or even Canary builds but note that the IDE interface and other generated code files might differ from the ones used throughout this book.
- A Kotlin 1.6.10 or newer plugin installed in Android Studio.
- The existing Repositories app from the GitHub repository of the book.

The starting point for this chapter is represented by the Repositories app developed in the previous chapter. If you haven't followed the implementation from the previous chapter, access the starting point for this chapter by navigating to the `Chapter_11` directory of the repository and importing the Android project entitled `repositories_app_solution_ch11`.

To access the solution code for this chapter, navigate to the `Chapter_12` directory: `https://github.com/PacktPublishing/Kickstart-Modern-Android-Development-with-Jetpack-and-Kotlin/tree/main/Chapter_12/repositories_app_ch12`.

Introducing the Jetpack Lifecycle components

It's no secret by now that components within the Android framework have certain lifecycles that we must respect when we need to interact with them. The most common components that own a lifecycle are `Activity` and `Fragment`.

As programmers, we cannot control the lifecycle of Android components because their lifecycle is defined and controlled by the system or the way Android works.

Going back to Lifecycle components, a very good example is the entry point to our Android application, represented by the `Activity` component, which, as we know, possesses a lifecycle. This means that in order to create a screen in our Android application, we need to create an `Activity` component – from this point on, all our components must be aware of its lifecycle to not leak any memory.

Now, when we say that `Activity` has a system-defined lifecycle, this actually translates into our `Activity` class inheriting from `ComponentActivity()`, which in turn contains a `Lifecycle` object. If we have a look at our `MainActivity` class from the Repositories app, we can see that it inherits from `ComponentActivity()`:

```
class MainActivity : ComponentActivity() {
    override fun onCreate(savedInstanceState: Bundle?) {
        super.onCreate(savedInstanceState)
        [...]
    }
}
```

Now, if we dig into the source code of the `ComponentActivity.java` class, we can see that it implements the `LifecycleOwner` interface:

```
95    public class ComponentActivity extends androidx.core.app.ComponentActivity implements
96            ContextAware,
97            LifecycleOwner,
98            ViewModelStoreOwner,
99            HasDefaultViewModelProviderFactory,
100           SavedStateRegistryOwner,
101           OnBackPressedDispatcherOwner,
102           ActivityResultRegistryOwner,
103           ActivityResultCaller {
```

Figure 12.1 – Observing how ComponentActivity implements the LifecycleOwner interface

In other words, the `ComponentActivity` class is an owner of a lifecycle. If we check out the implementation of the `LifecycleOwner` interface a few hundreds of lines downward in the source code, we can see that the `LifecycleOwner` interface contains a single method called `getLifecycle()` that returns a `Lifecycle` object:

```
467    @NonNull
468    @Override
469    public Lifecycle getLifecycle() {
470        return mLifecycleRegistry;
471    }
472
```

Figure 12.2 – Observing the implementation of the LifecycleOwner interface method

From these findings, we can deduct that our `Activity` classes have a system-defined lifecycle, as they implement the `LifecycleOwner` interface, which in turn means that they own a `Lifecycle` object.

> **Note**
>
> There are several other components in Android that have a lifecycle. In the context of the `Activity` classes, there are other classes inheriting directly or indirectly from `ComponentActivity`, therefore owning a `Lifecycle` object – see `AppCompatActivity` or `FragmentActivity`. Alternatively, just as `Activity` classes have a lifecycle, so do `Fragment` components. If you check out the source code of the `Fragment` class, you will notice that it also implements the `LifecycleOwner` interface, and so it also contains a `Lifecycle` object.

Simply put, the concept of a component having a lifecycle boils down to the idea of it providing a concrete implementation of the `Lifecycle` interface. This brings the idea that components with a lifecycle, such as `Activity`, expose information related to their lifecycle.

To better understand what we can find out about a component's lifecycle, we must explore the source code of the `Lifecycle` abstract class. If we do that, we will learn that the `Lifecycle` class contains information about the lifecycle state of the component that it's bound to, such as `Activity` or `Fragment`. The `Lifecycle` class features two main tracking pieces of information in the form of enumerations:

- **Event**: The events represented by the lifecycle callbacks that are triggered by the system and that we are all familiar with by now (`onCreate()`, `onStart()`, `onResume()`, `onPause()`, `onStop()`, and `onDestroy()`).
- **State**: The current state of the component tracked – `INITIALIZED`, `DESTROYED`, `CREATED`, `STARTED`, and `RESUMED`. If our `Activity` just received the `onResume()` callback, it means that until a new event arrives, it will stay in the `RESUMED` state. Upon every new event (the lifecycle callback), the state changes.

While we were already pretty familiar with the lifecycle events (callbacks), we might need to better understand how lifecycle states are defined.

Let's take a practical example and explore what information a `Lifecycle` object can provide about an `Activity` component. As previously mentioned, the information is structured in the form of events and states:

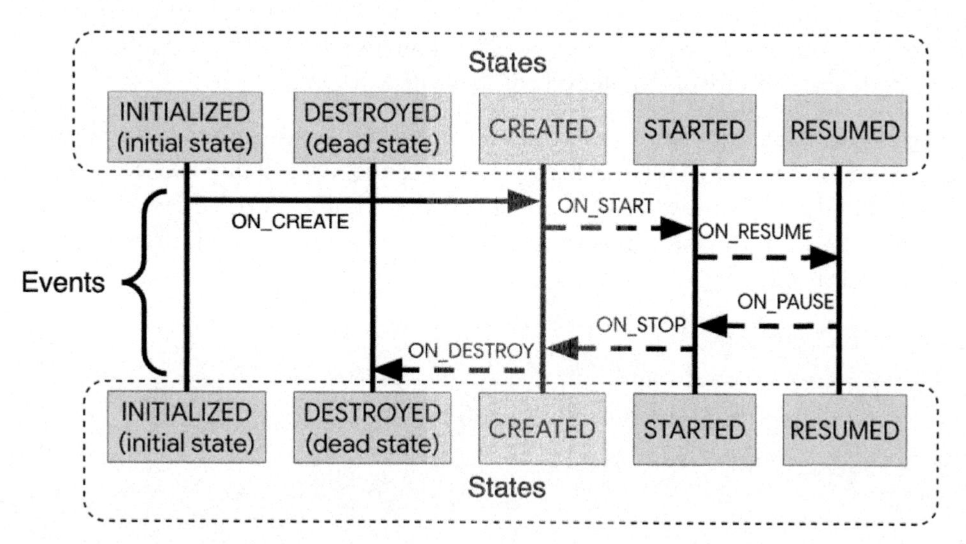

Figure 12.3 – The lifecycle of an Activity picturing its lifecycle events and states

In the preceding diagram, we were able to dissect the lifecycle of an `Activity` component by its events and states. We also now have a better overview of how lifecycle events trigger transitions between lifecycle states.

But why do all these events and states matter to us?

In fact, most of our code is driven with respect to lifecycle information. To avoid potential crashes, memory leaks, or wasting resources, it's essential to perform actions only in the correct state or on the correct lifecycle event.

When we think of lifecycle events, we can say that different types of functionalities can and should only be executed at appropriate times, or after certain lifecycle callbacks. For example, we wouldn't want to update our UI components with data after the `onDestroy()` callback in our `Activity`, as it's very likely that our app would crash simply because the UI has been scrapped by this time. Another example would be that when the `onResume()` event is called in our `Activity`, we would know that our `Activity` has gained (or regained) focus, so we can perform certain actions in our code such as initializing our camera component.

When we think of lifecycle states, we can say that different continuous actions can and should be running only during certain lifecycle periods – for example, we would want to start observing database changes if the state is `RESUMED` because that's when the user can interact with the screen and mutate data. When this state transitions to a different one, such as `CREATED` or `DESTROYED`, we might want to stop observing database changes so that we avoid memory leaks and don't waste resources.

From the previous examples, it's clear that our code should be aware of the lifecycle of Android components. When we write code based on lifecycle events or states, we're writing code that is aware of the lifecycle of a specific component.

Let's take an example and use our imagination a bit – the `Presenter` class features a data stream produced by several network requests. That data stream is observed and passed to the UI. However, any ongoing network requests must be canceled in the `cancelOngoingNetworkRequests()` method, as our UI no longer needs to consume their response:

```
class Presenter() {
    // observe data and pass it to the UI
    fun cancelOngoingNetworkRequests() {
        // stop observing data
    }
}
```

Let's say that an instance of our `Presenter` class is used inside `MainActivity`. Naturally, it must respect the lifecycle of the `MainActivity` class. That's why we should stop any ongoing network requests from within the `Presenter` class by calling the `cancelOngoingNetworkRequests()` method of the `Presenter` class inside the `onDestroyed()` lifecycle callback of the `MainActivity` class:

```
class MainActivity : ComponentActivity() {
    val presenter = Presenter()

    override fun onStart() {
        super.onStart()
        //consume data from presenter
    }
    override fun onDestroy() {
        super.onDestroy()
        presenter.cancelOngoingNetworkRequests()
    }
}
```

We can say that our `Presenter` is aware of the lifecycle of its host, `MainActivity`.

If a component respects the lifecycle of an Android component such as `Activity`, then we can consider that component to be **lifecycle-aware**.

However, we manually made our `Presenter` class be lifecycle-aware by manually calling a certain cleanup method from the `MainActivity` lifecycle callback. In other words, we had our `MainActivity` manually tell `Presenter` that it must stop its ongoing work.

Also, whenever we need to use our `Presenter` in some other `Activity` or `Fragment` classes, that component will need to remember to call the `cancelOngoingNetworkRequests()` method of `Presenter` on a certain lifecycle callback, therefore producing boilerplate code. If `Presenter` needed multiple actions on certain lifecycle callbacks, then that boilerplate code would have multiplied.

With the **Jetpack Lifecycle package**, we no longer need to manually force our Android components to call methods on every other class that cares about their lifecycle events or states. We can create lifecycle-aware components without having `Activity` or `Fragment` components manually inform our classes that a certain lifecycle event was triggered, or a certain state was reached – the `Lifecycle` package will help us receive the callbacks directly inside our components in a more efficient manner.

The Jetpack `Lifecycle` package provides us with the following:

- Predefined lifecycle-aware components with different purposes that require less boilerplate or work from our side. Such components are two Jetpack libraries:
    - `ViewModel`
    - `LiveData`
- A Lifecycle API that allows us to create a custom lifecycle-aware component much easier with less boilerplate code.

Before creating our own lifecycle-aware component, we should briefly cover the two predefined lifecycle-aware components that the Jetpack `Lifecycle` package provides us with. Let's begin with `ViewModel`.

ViewModel

In this book, we have already covered Jetpack's `ViewModel` as a class where our UI state resides and where most of the presentation logic is found. However, we also learned that in order to properly cancel data streams or ongoing network requests, `ViewModel` is aware of the lifecycle of its host `Activity`, `Fragment`, and even its composable destination (in conjunction with the Jetpack Navigation component).

In contrast to our `Presenter` class, whose lifecycle we have manually tied to the lifecycle of a host `Activity`, Jetpack's `ViewModel` is a lifecycle-aware component that we can use to eliminate any boilerplate calls from `Activity` or `Fragment` components.

To be more precise, `ViewModel` knows when its host component with a lifecycle reaches the end of its lifecycle and provides us with a callback method that we can use by overriding the `onCleared()` method. Inside this callback, we can cancel any pending work whose result we're no longer interested in to avoid memory leaks or wasting resources.

As an example, if our `ViewModel` is hosted by an `Activity`, then it knows when in the lifecycle of that `Activity` the `onDestroy()` event was called, and so it automatically triggers the `onCleared()` callback:

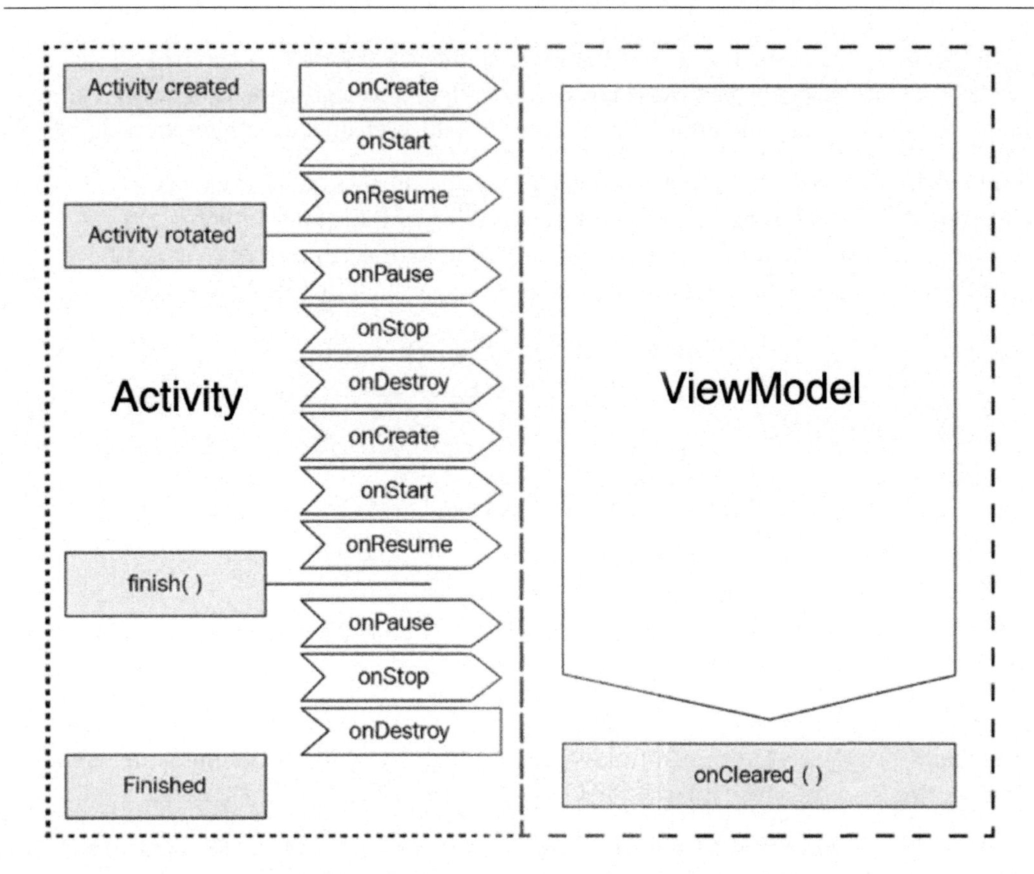

Figure 12.4 – The lifecycle of ViewModel is tied to the lifecycle of an Activity

This basically means that instead of manually having our `Activity` inform the `ViewModel` that its lifecycle has ended so that it can stop its work, `ViewModel` is a lifecycle-aware component that does that out of the box for you by providing a handle for that event – that is, the `onCleared()` callback:

```
class MyViewModel(): ViewModel() {
    override fun onCleared() {
        super.onCleared()
        // Cancel work
    }
}
```

Additionally, in the context of an `Activity` host, the `ViewModel` component is also aware of any lifecycle callbacks caused by events such as a configuration change, so it knows how to outlive those and helps us maintain the UI state, even after a configuration change.

But how does `ViewModel` know about the lifecycle callbacks of an `Activity` component? To answer that, we can look at a traditional way of instantiating a `ViewModel` inside an `Activity` by using the `ViewModelProvider` API and specifying the type of `ViewModel` that must be retrieved – that is, `MyViewModel`:

```
class MyActivity: ComponentActivity() {
    override fun onCreate(savedInstanceState: Bundle?) {
        super.onCreate(savedInstanceState)
        val vm =
          ViewModelProvider(this)[MyViewModel::class.java]
         // Perform operations
    }
}
```

To get an instance of `MyViewModel`, we used the `ViewModelProvider()` constructor and passed the `this` instance of the `MyActivity` class to the `owner` parameter that expected a `ViewModelStoreOwner` object. `MyActivity` indirectly implements the `ViewModelStoreOwner` interface because `ComponentActivity` does so.

To control the lifetime of the instance of our `ViewModel`, `ViewModelProvider` needs an instance of `ViewModelStoreOwner` because when it instantiates our `MyViewModel`, it will *link* the lifetime of this instance to the lifetime of the `ViewModelStoreOwner` – that is, `MyActivity`.

But how does `ViewModel` know when it must be cleared? In other words, what triggers the `onCleared()` method of the `MyViewModel` class?

`ComponentActivity` will wait for its `onDestroy()` lifecycle callback, and when that event is triggered, it will call the `getViewModelStore()` method of the `ViewModelStoreOwner` interface and obtain a `ViewModelStore` object. On this object, it will then call the `clear()` method to clear the `ViewModel` instance that was linked to `ComponentActivity` – in our case, the `MyViewModel` instance.

If you check out the source code of the `ComponentActivity` class, you will find the following implementation, which proves the previous points we're trying to express:

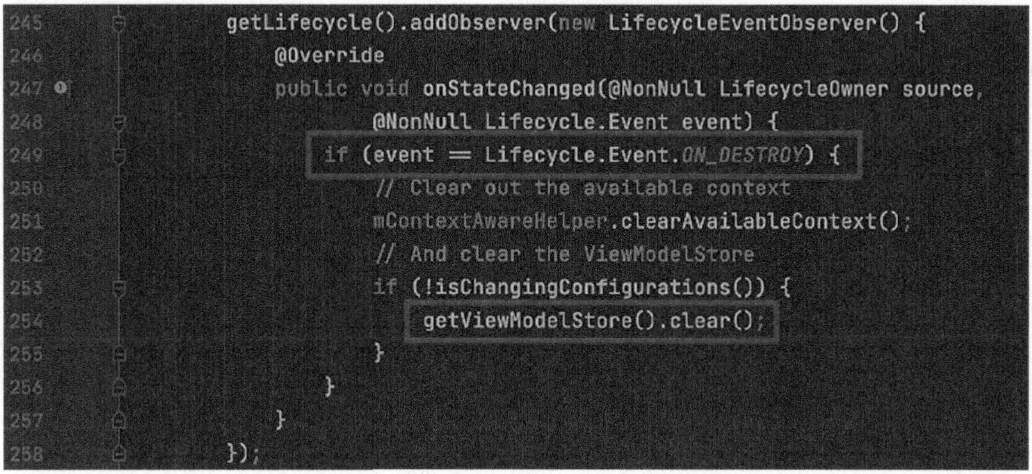

```
245        getLifecycle().addObserver(new LifecycleEventObserver() {
246            @Override
247            public void onStateChanged(@NonNull LifecycleOwner source,
248                    @NonNull Lifecycle.Event event) {
249                if (event == Lifecycle.Event.ON_DESTROY) {
250                    // Clear out the available context
251                    mContextAwareHelper.clearAvailableContext();
252                    // And clear the ViewModelStore
253                    if (!isChangingConfigurations()) {
254                        getViewModelStore().clear();
255                    }
256                }
257            }
258        });
```

Figure 12.5 – ViewModel is cleared on the onDestroy() callback of ComponentActivity

Now, the `ViewModel` lifecycle-aware component is helpful because it allows us to easily stop pending work and also persist UI state across configuration changes.

However, there is another important lifecycle-aware component that we haven't covered in this book and that we should briefly mention, and that is `LiveData`.

LiveData

`LiveData` is an observable data holder class that allows us to get data updates in a lifecycle-aware manner inside our Android components, such as `Activity` and `Fragment`. While specific implementations of Kotlin Flow data streams are similar to `LiveData` because both allow us to receive multiple data events over time, `LiveData` presents the advantage of being a lifecycle-aware component.

> **Note**
>
> In this section, we won't cover `LiveData` extensively to understand its API. Instead, we will try to highlight its lifecycle-aware character. Right now, you don't have to code along.

Without going into too much detail, let's see a simple usage of a `LiveData` object kept inside a `ViewModel` class and consumed from an `Activity` component.

Inside `ViewModel`, we instantiated a `MutableLiveData` object that will hold values of type `Int`, passed an initial value of `0`, and then in the `init{}` block launched a coroutine, where we've set the value to `100` after a `5000`-millisecond delay:

```
class MyViewModel(): ViewModel() {
    val numberLiveData: MutableLiveData<Int> =
        MutableLiveData(0)
    init {
        viewModelScope.launch {
            delay(5000)
            numberLiveData.value = 100
        }
    }
}
```

`numberLiveData` is now a data holder that will first notify any components observing it of the value `0` and, after 5 seconds, the value `100`.

Now, an `Activity` can be observing these values by first obtaining an instance of `MyViewModel`, tapping into its `numberLiveData` object, and then starting to observe the changes through the `observe()` method:

```
class MyActivity: ComponentActivity() {
    override fun onCreate(savedInstanceState: Bundle?) {
        super.onCreate(savedInstanceState)
        val vm =
          ViewModelProvider(this)[MyViewModel::class.java]
        vm.numberLiveData.observe(this, object: Observer<Int> {
            override fun onChanged(t: Int?) {
                // Consume values
            }
        })
    }
}
```

Now, to the `observe()` method, we've passed the following:

- First, the `this` instance of the `MyActivity` class to the `owner` parameter that expected a `LifecycleOwner` object. This worked because `MyActivity` indirectly implements (through `ComponentActivity`) the `LifecycleOwner` interface and therefore owns a `Lifecycle` object. The `observe()` method expected a `LifecycleOwner` as its first parameter, so that the observing feature is lifecycle-aware of the lifecycle of `MainActivity`.
- An `Observer<Int>` Kotlin inner `object` that allows us to receive the data events (holding the `Int` values) from the `MutableLiveData` object inside the `onChanged()` callback. Each time a new value is propagated, this callback will be triggered, and we will receive the latest value.

Now that we have briefly covered how to use `LiveData`, let's better understand the whole reason why we are talking about `LiveData`. As we've mentioned, `LiveData` is a lifecycle-aware component, but how does it achieve that?

When we passed our `MainActivity` as `LifecycleOwner` to the `owner` parameter of the `observe()` method, behind the scenes, `LiveData` started an observing process dependent on the `Lifecycle` object of the provided `owner`.

More precisely, the `Observer` object provided as the second parameter to the `observe()` method will only receive updates if the owner – that is, `MainActivity` – is in the `STARTED` or `RESUMED` lifecycle state.

This behavior is essential, as it allows Activity components to only receive UI updates from ViewModel components when they are visible or in focus, therefore making sure that the UI can safely handle the data events and not waste resources.

If, however, updates would have occurred in other states when the UI would not have been initialized, our app could have misbehaved or, even worse, crashed or introduced memory leaks. To be sure that such behavior doesn't occur, if the owner moves to the `DESTROYED` state, the `Observer` object will be automatically removed.

In the following diagram, you will be able to visualize how `LiveData` updates only come when the `Activity` component is in the `RESUMED` or `STARTED` state, while also automatically removing the `Observer` object when the state becomes `DESTROYED`:

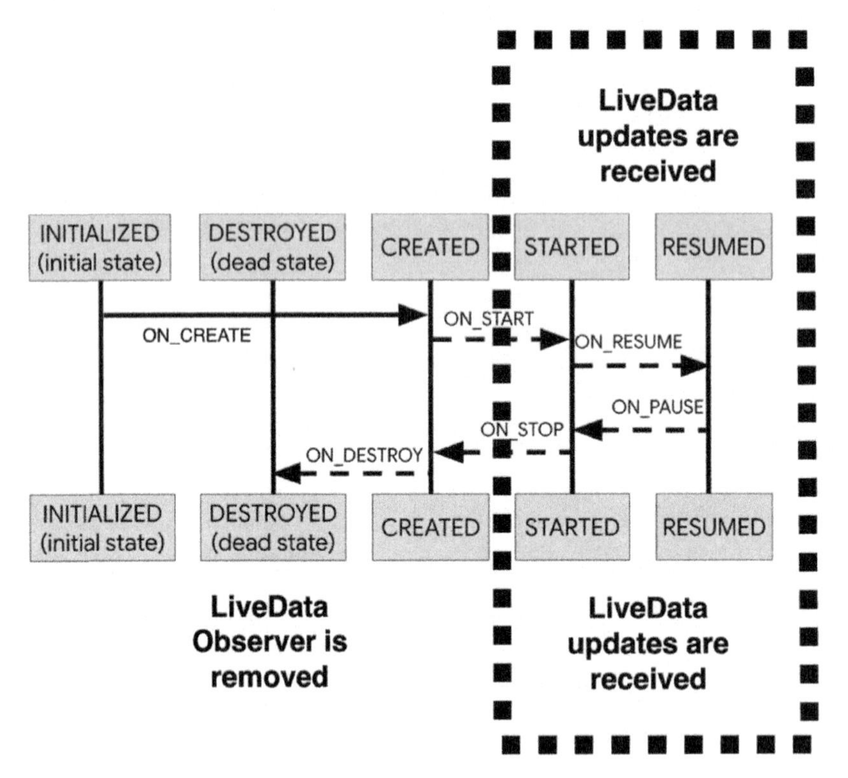

Figure 12.6 – Lifecycle states and events when LiveData updates are received and the LiveData Observer is removed

With such behavior, `LiveData` becomes a lifecycle-aware component in the sense that any `LifecycleOwner` must be in an active lifecycle state to be receiving updates from it.

Now that we have covered the two predefined lifecycle-aware components (`ViewModel` and `LiveData`) that are part of the `Lifecycle` package, it's time to add a countdown timer component in our Repositories app so that later on, we can transform it into a custom lifecycle-aware component with the help of the Lifecycle APIs.

Adding a countdown component in the Repositories app

Our plan is to learn how to create our own lifecycle-aware component. However, before we can do that, we must first create a normal component that, by default, is not aware of the lifecycle of any Android component.

To do that, we can create a countdown timer component inside our Repositories app that will track whether the user has spent at least 60 seconds on the app, and if so, we will award the user with a fictional prize.

More precisely, our plan is to create a countdown timer widget inside the `RepositoriesScreen()` that will award the user with a prize upon a 60-second countdown. However, for the countdown to work and the prize to be awarded, the user must be inside `RepositoriesScreen()` and have the countdown composable visible.

The countdown will behave like so:

- It will start from 60 and finish when the countdown reaches 0. Upon every second, the timer will decrease by 1 unit.
- When the countdown has finished, a prize message will be displayed.
- It will be paused if the countdown composable is not visible. In other words, if the user is not inside the `RepositoriesScreen()` composable or the timer composable is not visible or hidden within `RepositoriesScreen()`, then the countdown should be paused.

Now that we have a plan, let's implement a countdown timer component:

1. Inside the root package, create a new class called `CustomCountdown` and define its constructor to feature two function parameters that will be called as the countdown timer functions:

```
class CustomCountdown(
    private val onTick: ((currentValue: Int) -> Unit),
    private val onFinish: (() -> Unit),
) {
}
```

   We will have to call the `onTick()` function after every second has passed and the `onFinish()` function when the countdown has ended.

2. Now, inside the `CustomCountdown` class, let's create an inner class called `InternalTimer` that will inherit from the built-in Android `android.os.CountDownTimer` class and handle the actual countdown sequence:

```
class CustomCountdown(
    private val onTick: ((currentValue: Int) -> Unit),
    private val onFinish: (() -> Unit),
) {
    class InternalTimer(
        private val onTick: ((currentValue: Int) -> Unit),
        private val onFinish: (() -> Unit),
        millisInFuture: Long,
        countDownInterval: Long
    ) : CountDownTimer(millisInFuture,
                       countDownInterval){
    }
}
```

While the constructor of `InternalTimer` also accepts two identical function parameters, as `CustomCountdown` does, it's essential to note its `millisInFuture` and `countDownInterval` parameters that it forwards to the built-in Android `CountDownTimer` class. These two parameters will configure the core functionality of the timer – the countdown starting point in time and the time period that passes between timer ticks.

3. Next up, let's finish the implementation of the `InternalTimer` class:

```
class CustomCountdown(
    private val onTick: ((currentValue: Int) -> Unit),
    private val onFinish: (() -> Unit),
) {
    class InternalTimer(
        private val onTick: ((currentValue: Int) -> Unit),
        private val onFinish: (() -> Unit),
        millisInFuture: Long,
        countDownInterval: Long
    ) : CountDownTimer(millisInFuture,
        countDownInterval) {
```

```
            init {
                this.start()
            }
            override fun onFinish() {
                onFinish.invoke()
            }
            override fun onTick(millisUntilFinished: Long) {
                onTick(millisUntilFinished.toInt())
            }
        }
    }
```

To make sure the timer works as expected, we have done the following:

- Called the `start()` method provided by the inherited parent, `CountDownTimer`, inside the `init{}` block. This should automatically start the timer upon inception.
- Implemented the two mandatory `onFinish()` and `onTick()` methods of the inherited parent, `CountDownTimer`, and propagated the events to the caller of `InternalTimer` by calling its `onFinish()` and `onTick()` function parameters.

4. Then, back in the `CustomCountdown` class, let's create an instance of `InternalTimer` and configure it to work like a 60-second countdown timer that starts from `60` and finishes at `0`.

   To do that, let's pass to its constructor not only the `onFinish` and `onTick` function parameters but also 60 seconds (as `60000` milliseconds) to the `millisInFuture` parameter and 1 second (as `1000` milliseconds) to the `countDownInterval` parameter:

```
class CustomCountdown(
    private val onTick: ((currentValue: Int) -> Unit),
    private val onFinish: (() -> Unit),
) {
    var timer: InternalTimer = InternalTimer(
        onTick = onTick,
        onFinish = onFinish,
        millisInFuture = 60000,
        countDownInterval = 1000)
```

```
    class InternalTimer(
        private val onTick: ((currentValue: Int) -> Unit),
        private val onFinish: (() -> Unit),
        millisInFuture: Long,
        countDownInterval: Long
    ): CountDownTimer(millisInFuture, countDownInterval)
    { … }
}
```

5. Still inside `CustomCountdown`, to provide a way for canceling the countdown, add a `stop()` method that will allow us to call the `cancel()` method inherited by `InternalTimer` from the Android `CountDownTimer` class:

```
class CustomCountdown(…) {
    var timer: InternalTimer = InternalTimer(…)
    fun stop() {
        timer.cancel()
    }
    class InternalTimer(
        […]
    ): CountDownTimer(millisInFuture, countDownInterval)
    { … }
}
```

6. Then, in `RepositoriesViewModel`, add not only a `timerState` variable that will hold the text state displayed by our countdown composable but also a `timer` variable that will hold a `CustomCountdown` object:

```
class RepositoriesViewModel(…) : ViewModel() {
    val repositories: Flow<PagingData<Repository>> = […]
    val timerState = mutableStateOf("")
    var timer: CustomCountdown = CustomCountdown(
        onTick = { msLeft ->
            timerState.value =
                (msLeft / 1000).toString() +
                    " seconds left"
        },
        onFinish = {
            timerState.value = "You won a prize!"
```

```
            })
    }
```

Inside the `onTick` callback, we are computing the remaining seconds and setting a `String` message about our countdown to `timerState`. Then, in the `onFinish` callback, we're setting a prize message to `timerState`.

7. As a good practice, inside `RepositoriesViewModel`, make sure to stop the timer inside the `onCleared()` callback if the user moves to a different screen. This would mean that `RepositoriesScreen()` wouldn't be composed anymore, so this `ViewModel` would be cleared and the countdown should be stopped so that it doesn't send events and waste resources:

```
class RepositoriesViewModel(…) : ViewModel() {
    val repositories: Flow<PagingData<Repository>> = […]
    val timerState = mutableStateOf("")
    var timer: CustomCountdown = CustomCountdown(…)
    override fun onCleared() {
        super.onCleared()
        timer.stop()
    }
}
```

8. Now, move to `MainActivity` and make sure that just as the repositories are consumed and passed to the `RepositoriesScreen()` composable, the countdown timer text produced by `ViewModel` is also consumed and passed to `RepositoriesScreen()`:

```
class MainActivity : ComponentActivity() {
    override fun onCreate(savedInstanceState: Bundle?) {
        super.onCreate(savedInstanceState)
        setContent {
            RepositoriesAppTheme {
                val viewModel: RepositoriesViewModel = …
                val reposFlow = viewModel.repositories
                val timerText =
                    viewModel.timerState.value
                val lazyRepoItems: […] = […]
                RepositoriesScreen(
                    lazyRepoItems,
```

```
                        timerText
                    )
                }
            }
        }
    }
```

9. Then, at the end of the `RepositoriesScreen.kt` file, create a simple `CountdownItem()` composable function that takes in a `timerText: String` parameter and sets its value to a `Text` composable:

```
@Composable
private fun CountdownItem(timerText: String) {
    Text(timerText)
}
```

10. Next, in the `RepositoriesScreen()` composable, add a new parameter for the countdown text called `timerText`, and inside the `LazyColumn` scope, before the `itemsIndexed()` call, add a singular `item()` **Domain-Specific Language (DSL)** function call where you should add the `CountdownItem()` composable while passing the `timerText` variable to it:

```
@Composable
fun RepositoriesScreen(
    repos: LazyPagingItems<Repository>,
    timerText: String
) {
    LazyColumn(...) {
        item {
            CountdownItem(timerText)
        }
        itemsIndexed(repos) { index, repo -> [...] }
        [...]
    }
}
```

By doing so, we make sure that the countdown timer is displayed at the top of the screen as the first item within the list of repositories.

11. Build and run the application. You should first see the countdown timer telling you how much time you need to wait, and after approximately 1 minute, you should see the prize message displayed:

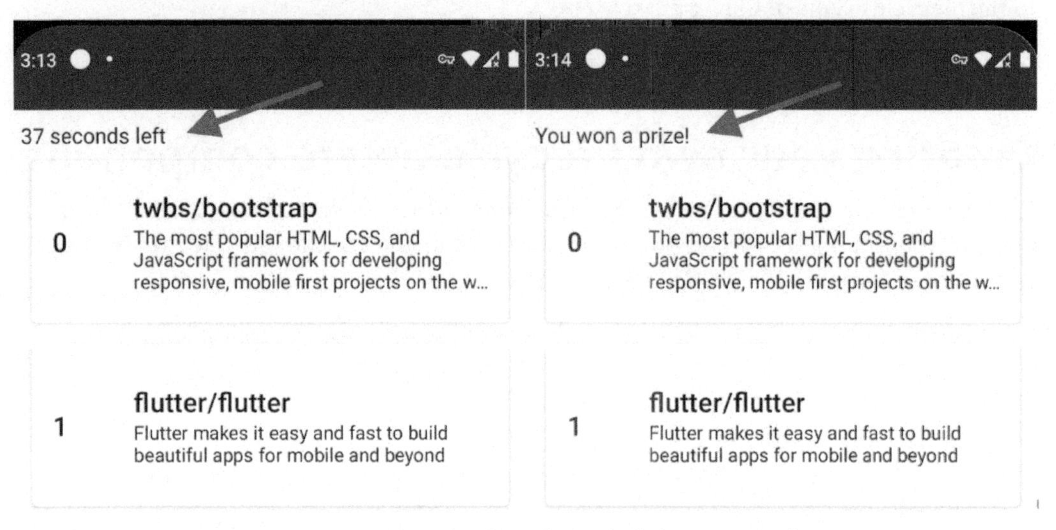

Figure 12.7 – Observing how the countdown timer works

We have now finished incorporating the countdown timer that ends by awarding the user with a fictional prize.

However, there is a scenario where our timer doesn't work as expected. Let's identify it:

1. Restart the application. You can do that by closing the current instance of the app and reopening it.

   The countdown should have started from 60 again at this point.

2. Before the countdown finishes, remember or write down somewhere the current countdown value and then put the app in background.
3. Wait for a few seconds and then bring the app back to the foreground.

You should notice that while the app was in the background, the countdown kept going. We wanted the timer to be paused when the app was put in the background and then resumed when the app was brought back to the foreground – this would have allowed us to award the prize to users that actively use the app and have the countdown timer visible. This behavior didn't occur, as the timer kept on counting while the app was not visible or in focus.

This is happening because we didn't do anything to pause the timer when the app goes into the background or resume it when the app comes back to the foreground. In other words, our countdown timer is not lifecycle-aware, so it doesn't get notified and can't react to the lifecycle events of the `Activity` host.

Next, let's make our countdown timer a lifecycle-aware component.

Creating your own lifecycle-aware component

We need to make our `CustomCountdown` aware of the lifecycle of `MainActivity`. In other words, our countdown logic should observe and react to the lifecycle events of our `LifecycleOwner` – that is, `MainActivity`.

To make our `CustomCountdown` lifecycle-aware, we must force it to implement the `DefaultLifecycleObserver` interface. By doing so, the `CustomCountdown` will be observing the lifecycle events or states defined by the `Lifecycle` object that `LifecycleOwner` provides.

Our main goal is to pause the countdown when the app is put in the background and to resume it when the app is brought back into the foreground. More precisely, our `CustomCountdown` must react to the following lifecycle events of `MainActivity`:

- `onPause()`: When the `onPause()` callback comes in `MainActivity`, `CustomCountdown` must pause its countdown.
- `onResume()`: When the `onResume()` callback comes in `MainActivity`, `CustomCountdown` must resume its countdown.

With this behavior, we can award the prize to users that actively use the app and have the countdown timer visible and in focus.

Now that we have a plan, let's start coding.

1. Make the `CustomCountdown` class implement the `DefaultLifecycleObserver` interface and then override the two lifecycle callbacks we're interested in, `onResume()` and `onPause()`:

```
class CustomCountdown(
    [...]
): DefaultLifecycleObserver {
    var timer: InternalTimer = InternalTimer(
        onTick = onTick,
        onFinish = onFinish,
```

```
        millisInFuture = 60000,
        countDownInterval = 1000)
    override fun onResume(owner: LifecycleOwner) {
        super.onResume(owner)
    }
    override fun onPause(owner: LifecycleOwner) {
        super.onPause(owner)
    }
    fun stop() { timer.cancel() }
    class InternalTimer(…) {…}
}
```

Once we make our `CustomCountdown` observe the lifecycle of `MainActivity`, its `onResume(owner: LifecycleOwner)` callback will be called when the `onResume()` callback of `MainActivity` is called, and similarly, its `onPause(owner: LifecycleOwner)` callback will be called when the `onPause()` callback of `MainActivity` is called.

2. Now that we know when to pause and resume our countdown timer, we need to find ways to actually pause and resume it.

   First, let's pause the countdown in the `onPause()` callback by calling the `cancel()` method of the `timer` variable:

```
class CustomCountdown(
    […]
): DefaultLifecycleObserver {
    var timer: InternalTimer = InternalTimer(…)
    override fun onResume(owner: LifecycleOwner) {
        super.onResume(owner)
    }
    override fun onPause(owner: LifecycleOwner) {
        super.onPause(owner)
        timer.cancel()
    }
    fun stop() { timer.cancel() }

    class InternalTimer(…) : CountDownTimer(…) {…}
}
```

With this behavior, when `MainActivity` is paused, we are stopping the countdown run by the `InternalTime` instance held inside the `timer` variable.

3. Next up, we need to resume the `timer` in the `onResume()` callback. However, to resume it, we need to know the value of the last countdown before the `onPause()` callback was triggered and the timer was canceled. With that last known countdown value, we can reinitiate our timer in the `onResume()` callback.

   Inside the inner `InternalTimer` class, create a `lastKnownTime` variable, initiate it with the value of `millisInFuture`, and then make sure to update it in the `onFinish()` and `onTick()` timer callbacks:

```
class CustomCountdown(
    [...]
): DefaultLifecycleObserver {
    var timer: InternalTimer = InternalTimer(
        [...]
        millisInFuture = 60000,
        countDownInterval = 1000)
    override fun onResume(owner: LifecycleOwner) { ... }
    override fun onPause(owner: LifecycleOwner) { ... }
    fun stop() { timer.cancel() }

    class InternalTimer(...) : CountDownTimer(...) {
        var lastKnownTime: Long = millisInFuture
        init { this.start() }
        override fun onFinish() {
            lastKnownTime = 0
            onFinish.invoke()
        }
        override fun onTick(millisUntilFinished: Long) {
            lastKnownTime = millisUntilFinished
            onTick(millisUntilFinished.toInt())
        }
    }
}
```

While in the `onFinish()` callback, we've set `lastKnownTime` to `0` because the countdown has finished, in the `onTick()` callback, we've made sure to save inside the `lastKnownTime` variable the latest value received from the `onTick()` callback – that is, `millisUntilFinished`.

4. Now, going back in the parent `CustomCountdown` class, resume the countdown in the `onResume()` callback of `CustomCountdown` by first canceling the countdown of the previous timer and then by storing inside the `timer` variable another instance of `InternalTimer`, which now starts the countdown from the `lastKnownTime` value of the previous `InternalTimer` instance:

```
class CustomCountdown(
    [...]
): DefaultLifecycleObserver {
    var timer: InternalTimer = InternalTimer(
        onTick = onTick,
        onFinish = onFinish,
        millisInFuture = 60000,
        countDownInterval = 1000)
    override fun onResume(owner: LifecycleOwner) {
        super.onResume(owner)
        if (timer.lastKnownTime > 0) {
            timer.cancel()
            timer = InternalTimer(
                onTick = onTick,
                onFinish = onFinish,
                millisInFuture = timer.lastKnownTime,
                countDownInterval = 1000)
        }
    }
    override fun onPause(owner: LifecycleOwner) { [...] }
    fun stop() { timer.cancel() }

    class InternalTimer(...) : CountDownTimer(...) {...}
}
```

With this behavior, when MainActivity is resumed, we are creating a new InternalTimer instance that starts off the countdown from the value that the previous timer recorded before being paused. Also, note that the new instance of InternalTimer receives the same parameters as the first initialization of the timer variable – the same onTick() and onFinish() callbacks and the same countDownInterval – the only difference is the starting point of the countdown, which should now be less than 60 seconds.

For the onPause() and onResume() callbacks of the CustomCountdown class to be called when their corresponding lifecycle events are called inside MainActivity, we must effectively bind our DefaultLifecycleObserver – that is, the CustomCountdown instance – to the lifecycle of our LifecycleOwner – that is, MainActivity.

Let's do that next.

5. Go back inside the RepositoriesScreen.kt file, and inside the CountdownItem() composable, first obtain the LifecycleOwner instance that the composable function belongs to by tapping into the LocalLifeCycleOwner API and then get the owner by accessing its current variable:

```
@Composable
private fun CountdownItem (timerText: String) {
    val lifecycleOwner: LifecycleOwner  =
        LocalLifecycleOwner.current
    Text(timerText)
}
```

Finally, we've stored the LifecycleOwner instance into the lifecycleOwner variable.

It's important to mention that since the parent composable of CountdownItem() – that is, RepositoriesScreen() – is hosted by MainActivity, it's only natural that the LifecycleOwner instance that we have obtained is in fact MainActivity.

6. Then, we need to make sure that the Lifecycle instance of our lifecycleOwner adds and removes our DefaultLifecycleObserver timer.

To achieve that, we need to first create a composition side effect that allows us to know when the CountdownItem() composable first entered composition so that we can add the observer, and then when it was removed from composition so that we can remove the observer.

For such a case, we can use the `DisposableEffect()` composable, which provides us with a block of code where we can perform actions when the composable enters composition, and then perform other actions when the composable leaves composition through its inner `onDispose()` block:

```
@Composable
private fun CountdownItem (timerText: String) {
    val lifecycleOwner: LifecycleOwner =
        LocalLifecycleOwner.current
    DisposableEffect(key1 = lifecycleOwner) {
        onDispose {

        }
    }
    Text(timerText)
}
```

Since this is a side effect, anything we add inside the block of code exposed by the `DisposableEffect` function will not be re-executed upon recomposition. However, this effect will be restarted if the value provided to the `key1` parameter changes. In our case, we want this effect to be restarted if the value of `lifecycleOwner` changes - this will allow us to have access to the correct `lifecycleOwner` instance inside this side-effect composable.

7. Now that we know when and where we can add and then remove the observer, let's first obtain the `Lifecycle` object from the `lifecycleOwner` variable so that we can store it inside the `lifecycle` variable:

```
@Composable
private fun CountdownItem(timerText: String) {
    val lifecycleOwner: LifecycleOwner =
        LocalLifecycleOwner.current
    val lifecycle = lifecycleOwner.lifecycle
    DisposableEffect(key1 = lifecycleOwner) {
        onDispose {

        }
    }
    Text(timerText)
}
```

Next, on the `Lifecycle` object from within the `lifecycle` variable, we will add and remove the observer.

8. Inside the block of code exposed by the `DisposableEffect()` composable, add the observer on the `lifecycle` variable by calling its `addObserver()` method, and then inside its exposed `onDispose()` callback, remove it with the `removeObserver()` method:

```
@Composable
private fun CountdownItem(timerText: String) {
    val lifecycleOwner: LifecycleOwner
        = LocalLifecycleOwner.current
    val lifecycle = lifecycleOwner.lifecycle
    DisposableEffect(key1 = lifecycleOwner) {
        lifecycle.addObserver()
        onDispose {
            lifecycle.removeObserver()
        }
    }
    Text(timerText)
}
```

With this approach, when the `CountdownItem()` composable is first composed, we will make our countdown component observe the lifecycle events of `MainActivity`. Then, when the `CountdownItem()` leaves composition, our countdown component will no longer observe such events.

However, you might have noticed that both the `addObserver()` and `removeObserver()` methods expect a `LifecycleObserver` object, but we didn't provide any.

In fact, we should have passed the `CustomCountdown` instance to the `addObserver()` and `removeObserver()` methods because `CustomCountdown` is the component that implements `DefaultLifecycleObserver` and that we want to react to the lifecycle changes of our `MainActivity`.

Next, let's obtain the `CustomCountdown` instance.

9. Update the `CountdownItem()` function definition to receive a `getTimer()` function parameter that returns a `CustomCountdown` timer. This callback method should be called to provide the `addObserver()` and `removeObserver()` methods with a `LifecycleObserver` instance:

```
@Composable
private fun CountdownItem(timerText: String,
    getTimer: () -> CustomCountdown) {
    val lifecycleOwner: LifecycleOwner
        = LocalLifecycleOwner.current
    val lifecycle = lifecycleOwner.lifecycle
    DisposableEffect(key1 = lifecycleOwner) {
        lifecycle.addObserver(getTimer())
        onDispose {
            lifecycle.removeObserver(getTimer())
        }
    }
    Text(timerText)
}
```

Since the `CustomCountdown` class implements `DefaultLifecycleObserver`, which extends `FullLifecycleObserver`, which in turn extends `LifecycleObserver`, the `addObserver()` and `removeObserver()` methods accept our `CustomCountdown` instance as an observer to the `Lifecycle` object of our `lifecycleOwner` – that is, `MainActivity`.

10. Since `CountdownItem()` now expects a `getTimer: () -> CustomCountdown` callback function, we must also force our `RepositoriesScreen()` composable to accept such a callback function as well and then pass it to our `CountdownItem()` composable:

```
@Composable
fun RepositoriesScreen(
    repos: LazyPagingItems<Repository>,
    timerText: String,
    getTimer: () -> CustomCountdown
) {
    LazyColumn(...) {
        item {
            CountdownItem(timerText, getTimer)
```

```
            }
            itemsIndexed(repos) { … }
            […]
        }
    }
```

11. Lastly, inside `MainActivity`, update the `RepositoriesScreen()` composable call to provide a `getTimer()` function implementation, where we will get the `CustomCountdown` instance from the `viewModel` variable through its `timer` field:

```
class MainActivity : ComponentActivity() {
    override fun onCreate(savedInstanceState: Bundle?) {
        super.onCreate(savedInstanceState)
        setContent {
            RepositoriesAppTheme {
                […]
                RepositoriesScreen(
                    lazyRepoItems,
                    timerText,
                    getTimer = {viewModel.timer}
                )
            }
        }
    }
}
```

We have finally tied our `DefaultLifecycleObserver` – that is, the `CustomCountdown` instance – to the lifecycle of our `LifecycleOwner` – that is, `MainActivity`. Now that the `CustomCountdown` class should react to the lifecycle events of our `MainActivity`, let's test our problematic scenario from before.

12. Build and run the app. The countdown should have started from 60 again at this point.
13. Before the countdown finishes, remember or write down somewhere the current countdown value and put the app in background.
14. Wait for a few seconds and then bring the app back to foreground.

You should now notice that while the app was in background, the countdown was paused. We wanted the timer to be paused when the app was put in background and then resumed when the app was brought back to foreground – and now this is happening! We can now award the prize to users that actively use the app.

However, there is still an edge case that we haven't covered. Let's discover it:

1. Build and run the app. The countdown should have started from 60 again at this point.
2. Before the countdown finishes, remember or write down somewhere the current countdown value and then quickly scroll down past four or five repositories within the list until the countdown is not visible anymore.
3. Wait for a few seconds and then scroll back up to the top of the list so that the countdown is visible again.

Note that after we scrolled down, while the timer wasn't visible, the countdown kept going. We wanted the timer to be paused when the timer isn't visible anymore and then resumed when the timer is visible again – this would have allowed us to award the prize to users that have the countdown timer visible so that they didn't cheat on our contest. This behavior didn't occur, as the timer kept on counting while the timer wasn't visible.

This is happening because we didn't do anything to pause the timer when the timer composable leaves composition or resume it when the timer composable is composed again. In other words, our countdown timer is not aware of the lifecycle of our timer composable.

Next, let's make our countdown timer aware of Compose composition cycles so that users don't cheat in our contest.

Making our countdown component aware of the lifecycle of composables

The main issue is that our `CustomCountdown` component still runs its countdown even after the `CountdownItem()` composable leaves composition. We want to pause the timer when its corresponding composable is not visible anymore. With such an approach, we can prevent users from cheating, and we can award the prize only to users that have had the countdown timer visible for the full amount of time. Basically, if the timer is not visible anymore, the countdown should stop.

To pause the timer when its corresponding composable function leaves composition, we must somehow call the `stop()` function exposed by `CustomCountdown`. But when should we do that?

If you look inside the body of the `CountdownItem()` composable, you will notice that we have already registered a `DisposableEffect()` composable that notifies us when the `CountdownItem()` composable leaves composition by exposing the `onDispose()` callback:

```
@Composable
private fun CountdownItem(…) {
    val lifecycleOwner: […] = LocalLifecycleOwner.current
    val lifecycle = lifecycleOwner.lifecycle
    DisposableEffect(key1 = lifecycleOwner) {
        lifecycle.addObserver(getTimer())
        onDispose {
            lifecycle.removeObserver(getTimer())
        }
    }
    Text(timerText)
}
```

When the composable leaves composition, inside the `onDispose()` callback, we are already removing the `CustomCountdown` as an observer to the lifecycle of our `MainActivity`. Exactly at this point, we can also pause the timer because the composable leaves composition:

1. Update the `CountdownItem()` function definition to accept a new `onPauseTimer()` callback function and then make sure to call it inside the `onDispose()` callback of `DisposableEffect()`:

```
@Composable
private fun CountdownItem(timerText: String,
    getTimer: () -> CustomCountdown,
    onPauseTimer: () -> Unit) {
    val lifecycleOwner: […] = LocalLifecycleOwner.current
    val lifecycle = lifecycleOwner.lifecycle
    DisposableEffect(key1 = lifecycleOwner) {
        lifecycle.addObserver(getTimer())
        onDispose {
            onPauseTimer()
            lifecycle.removeObserver(getTimer())
        }
```

```
        }
        Text(timerText)
    }
```

2. Since `CountdownItem()` now expects an `onPauseTimer: () -> Unit` callback function, we must also force our `RepositoriesScreen()` composable to accept such a callback function and then pass it to our `CountdownItem()` composable:

```
@Composable
fun RepositoriesScreen(
    repos: LazyPagingItems<Repository>,
    timerText: String,
    getTimer: () -> CustomCountdown,
    onPauseTimer: () -> Unit
) {
    LazyColumn(...) {
        item {
            CountdownItem(
                timerText,
                getTimer,
                onPauseTimer
            )
        }
        itemsIndexed(repos) { ... }
        [...]
    }
}
```

3. Lastly, inside `MainActivity`, update the `RepositoriesScreen()` composable call to provide an `onPauseTimer()` function implementation, where we will pause the timer by calling the `stop()` method of the `CustomCountdown` instance obtained from the `viewModel` variable through its `timer` field:

```
class MainActivity : ComponentActivity() {
    override fun onCreate(savedInstanceState: Bundle?) {
        super.onCreate(savedInstanceState)
        setContent {
            RepositoriesAppTheme {
```

```
                [...]
                RepositoriesScreen(lazyRepoItems,
                    timerText,
                    getTimer = { viewModel.timer },
                    onPauseTimer =
                        { viewModel.timer.stop() }
                )
            }
        }
    }
}
```

4. Build and run the app. The countdown should have started from 60 again at this point.
5. Before the countdown finishes, remember or write down somewhere the current countdown value and then quickly scroll down past four or five repositories within the list until the countdown is not visible anymore. Make sure to scroll past a few repositories so that Compose removes the node of the timer composable – if you scroll just a bit, the node of the timer won't be removed.
6. Wait for a few seconds and then scroll back up to the top of the list so that the countdown is visible again.

Note that the timer was now paused while the `CountdownItem()` composable was not visible. We have now achieved the desired effect!

But how come the countdown is resumed when the composable becomes visible again? We didn't do anything to cover that case – we only stopped the timer when the `CountdownItem()` composable left composition, but we didn't resume it when it became visible again as it re-entered composition.

Fortunately, the timer is resumed out of the box when the `CountdownItem()` composable re-enters composition – but why is this happening?

This behavior is exhibited because of an interesting side effect provided by the Lifecycle APIs. More precisely, as soon as we're binding the `LifecycleObserver` instance to the `Lifecycle` instance of our `LifecycleOwner`, the observer instantly receives as a first event the event corresponding to the current state of `LifecycleOwner`.

Let's have a look inside the `CountdownItem()` composable and see how this could be happening:

```
@Composable
private fun CountdownItem(timerText: String,
    getTimer: () -> CustomCountdown,
    onPauseTimer: () -> Unit) {
    val lifecycleOwner: LifecycleOwner
                = LocalLifecycleOwner.current
    val lifecycle = lifecycleOwner.lifecycle
    DisposableEffect(key1 = lifecycleOwner) {
        lifecycle.addObserver(getTimer())
        onDispose {
            onPauseTimer()
            lifecycle.removeObserver(getTimer())
        }
    }
    Text(timerText)
}
```

In our case, as soon as we're binding the `DefaultLifecycleObserver` instance - that is, `CustomCountdown` - to the `Lifecycle` of the `LifecycleOwner` instance - that is, `MainActivity` - the observer receives as a first event the event corresponding to the current state.

In other words, as soon as our timer composable is visible, we're adding the timer as an observer to the lifecycle of our `MainActivity` class. At that point, the `RESUMED` state is the current state of `MainActivity`, so the `onResume()` callback is triggered inside the `CustomCountdown` component, which effectively resumes the timer countdown in our specific scenario:

```
class CustomCountdown([…]): DefaultLifecycleObserver {
    var timer: InternalTimer = InternalTimer(…)
    override fun onResume(owner: LifecycleOwner) {
        super.onResume(owner)
        if (timer.lastKnownTime > 0) {
            timer.cancel()
            timer = InternalTimer(
                onTick = onTick,
```

```
                    onFinish = onFinish,
                    millisInFuture = timer.lastKnownTime,
                    countDownInterval = 1000)
            }
        }
        override fun onPause(owner: LifecycleOwner) { [...] }
        fun stop() { timer.cancel() }
        class InternalTimer(...) : CountDownTimer(...) {...}
}
```

We have now made our countdown timer aware of the Compose composition cycles as well.

Summary

In this chapter, we understood what a lifecycle-aware component is and how we can create one.

We first explored how the lifecycle events and states are tied to Android components, such as `Activity` or `Fragment`, and then how predefined components from the `Lifecycle` package can react to them. Then, we created and added a countdown timer component to the Repositories app.

Finally, we prevented users from cheating by making our timer component aware not only of the different lifecycle events and states of `Activity` components but also of the lifecycle of composables.

Further reading

In this chapter, we briefly covered how to create a lifecycle-aware component by making our `CustomCountdown` component aware of the lifecycle events that `MainActivity` exhibits. However, when needed, we can also tap into the lifecycle states of `LifecycleOwner`. To understand how you can do that, check out the official docs for an example: `https://developer.android.com/topic/libraries/architecture/lifecycle#lco`.

Index

A

B

C

D

E

F

G

H

L

M

N

O

P

R

U

V

Other Books You May Enjoy

If you enjoyed this book, you may be interested in these other books by Packt:

Android UI Development with Jetpack Compose

Thomas Künneth

ISBN: 978-1-80181-216-0

- Gain a solid understanding of the core concepts of Jetpack Compose
- Develop beautiful, neat, and immersive UI elements that are user friendly, reliable, and performant
- Build a complete app using Jetpack Compose
- Add Jetpack Compose to your existing Android applications
- Test and debug apps that use Jetpack Compose

Simplifying Application Development with Kotlin Multiplatform Mobile

Róbert Nagy

ISBN: 978-1-80181-258-0

- Get acquainted with the multiplatform approach and KMM's competitive edge
- Understand how Kotlin Multiplatform works under the hood
- Get up and running with the Kotlin language quickly in the context of Swift
- Find out how to share code between Android and iOS

Packt is searching for authors like you

If you're interested in becoming an author for Packt, please visit `authors.packtpub.com` and apply today. We have worked with thousands of developers and tech professionals, just like you, to help them share their insight with the global tech community. You can make a general application, apply for a specific hot topic that we are recruiting an author for, or submit your own idea.

Share Your Thoughts

Now you've finished *In-Memory Analytics with Apache Arrow*, we'd love to hear your thoughts! Scan the QR code below to go straight to the Amazon review page for this book and share your feedback or leave a review on the site that you purchased it from.

`https://packt.link/r/1-801-07103-9`

Your review is important to us and the tech community and will help us make sure we're delivering excellent quality content.

Printed in Great Britain
by Amazon